Making the Modern South
DAVID GOLDFIELD, EDITOR

Night parade on Royal Street, ca. 1963
Louisiana Photograph Collection, New Orleans Public Library

NEW ORLEANS ON PARADE

TOURISM AND THE
TRANSFORMATION OF THE
CRESCENT CITY

J. MARK SOUTHER

LOUISIANA STATE UNIVERSITY PRESS BATON ROUGE

Published by Louisiana State University Press
Copyright © 2006 by Louisiana State University Press
All rights reserved
Manufactured in the United States of America
First Printing

DESIGNER: *Amanda McDonald Scallan*
TYPEFACE: *text Whitman; display Alleycat ICG and Trajan*
PRINTER AND BINDER: *Edwards Brothers, Inc.*

Library of Congress Cataloging-in-Publication Data

Souther, Jonathan Mark, 1971–
  New Orleans on parade : tourism and the
transformation of the crescent city / J. Mark Souther.
      p. cm. — (Making the modern South)
  Includes bibliographical references and index.
  ISBN-13: 978-0-8071-3193-0 (cloth: alk. paper)
  ISBN-10: 0-8071-3193-8 (cloth : alk. paper)
  1. Tourism—Louisiana—New Orleans. I. Title. II.
Series.
G155.U6S639 2007
338.4'79176335—dc22
                              2006004711

For Stacey and my family

CONTENTS

Illustrations follow p. 72

ACKNOWLEDGMENTS

The publication of *New Orleans on Parade* not only represents the culmination of a book project but also reflects professional and personal relationships that sharpened my research and writing and sustained me in the process. I would like to thank Making the Modern South series editor David Goldfield, who in many ways has shaped my professional path since my first year as a doctoral student at Tulane University, when I first became acquainted with his scholarship on southern urban history. David progressed from model to mentor when he approached me about writing a book based on my doctoral research and has shaped my understanding of urban history and my own topic in innumerable ways. I am also grateful to Louisiana State University Press editors Rand Dotson and George Roupe for their wise guidance, as well as to the staff at LSU Press. I thank my dissertation advisor Lawrence N. Powell, who suggested that no historian had written satisfactorily on the topic of modern tourism development in New Orleans and that therein lay a rich story that needed to be told. Larry struck just the right balance in directing the dissertation stage of my project, allowing me to make my own discoveries and then challenging me to ask smarter questions, seek additional sources, and write more persuasively. He has been a true mentor and a valued colleague.

I am especially thankful for the friends and role models who prepared me for and sustained me through this project. My best friend Eric Light read portions of the manuscript and provided encouragement, criticism, and countless hours of comic relief. I was fortunate to have as teachers outstanding historians who served as scholarly models, especially T. Lloyd Benson, Edward Jones, Robert C. Kenzer, John Gordon, Hugh West, William E. Leuchtenburg, Clarence Mohr, Patrick J. Maney, L. Rosanne M. Adderley, Gertrude M. Yeager, Colin M. MacLachlan, and Ida Altman. In addition to Larry Powell, Arnold R. Hirsch and Randy J. Sparks shepherded my dissertation to completion and in no small way shaped the book that emerged.

Thanks to others who read and commented on various stages of my work, including Guillaume Aubert, Robin Bachin, Mary Wren Bivins, Nicholas Dagen Bloom, James Borchert, William F. Connell, Kent B. Germany, Edward F. Haas,

Allan Katz, Carolyn Kolb, Alan H. Lessoff, Raymond A. Mohl, Bruce Boyd Rae-burn, Judith Kelleher Schafer, Marguerite S. Shaffer, Julia Ridley Smith, Karen Sotiropoulos, and Anthony J. Stanonis. Kay Banning expertly prepared the book's index. I am particularly indebted to Richard D. Starnes, who served as a blind reader for my manuscript and helped me make a number of important improvements.

I owe tremendous gratitude to archivists and librarians who facilitated my research. Bruce Boyd Raeburn and the staff at the William Ransom Hogan Jazz Archive at Tulane University were very generous with their time. Bruce's assistance recharged me at a time when I needed direction, contributed significantly in coaxing me toward the current organization of the book, and was unflagging in his willingness to steer me to any sources that would be of interest. The sounds of New Orleans jazz that emanated from the back room of the archive, as well as conversation with the many jazz scholars and enthusiasts who streamed through the archive doors, enriched my experience. I thank Wayne Everard, Irene Wain-wright, and the staff at the City Archives at New Orleans Public Library, as well as the staffs of the special collections of Howard-Tilton Memorial Library at Tulane University, Amistad Research Center, the Earl K. Long Library at the University of New Orleans, and the Loyola University Library. Connie Cannon, Charlotte McCrary, and Gaile Thomas in the microforms and newspapers department at Howard-Tilton filed countless stacks of *Times-Picayune* microfilm cases and made my time in the library's dark basement as hospitable as they could.

I appreciated the intellectual environment of Tulane University and enjoyed scholarly interchange with commentators and audiences at conferences of the Urban History Association, the Society for American City and Regional Planning History, the Organization of American Historians, the Southern Historical Association, the National Council on Public History, the Rocky Mountain Council on Latin American Studies, and the Gulf South Historical Association, and at the University of Southern Mississippi and Georgia Institute of Technology.

Generous financial support made this project possible. Tulane University awarded me the John T. Monroe Dissertation Year Fellowship, and I received generous research funding from the Office of Graduate Studies and the College of Liberal Arts and Social Sciences at Cleveland State University. A course release from the History Department there facilitated the final stage of my revisions.

While *New Orleans on Parade* began in New Orleans, I completed it in Cleveland, Ohio. It was difficult to watch helplessly from afar as Hurricane Katrina sent floodwaters roiling through the low-lying streets even as I was putting the finishing touches on this manuscript. Instantly this book became in part a chronicle of a lost city, and yet watching the disaster from a distance, mediated as much by news reports as personal experience, I realized that my project might also point to future public debates and decisions as the ravaged city rebuilds. Not only did my distance from the Big Easy afford a new vantage point as I completed the book, it also proved beneficial in another respect. Cleveland State University provided a collegial and supportive atmosphere that saw this book to completion. I wish to thank my colleagues in the Department of History for their support and interest in my research.

William and Sandra Souther, my parents, nurtured my studies every step of the way. John and Virginia Souther and James and Lillian Gilmer, my grandparents, contributed immeasurably to my sense of the past and reverence for history. I learned more from them than words can express.

Above all, I want to thank Stacey, whose love, patience, companionship, and support have made all the difference.

NEW ORLEANS ON PARADE

INTRODUCTION

In the first decade of the twenty-first century, the "Big Easy" ranks among the most popular tourist destinations in the United States. Although its population has dwindled to less than 470,000, dropping it to thirty-fourth among the nation's cities, an estimated 11 million tourists visit New Orleans every year, often filling the city's more than 34,000 hotel rooms. Once confined to a few days during the city's Carnival celebration, the tourist influx flows throughout the year as tourism planners negotiate blocks of hotel rooms during Mardi Gras, Jazz Fest, Southern Decadence, and other public celebrations, filling in the gaps with mammoth national conventions and sporting events. Chartered tour buses and food-service trucks rumble through the streets much as steamboats once plied its river.

A tour of the city reveals the extent to which tourism has spatially reoriented New Orleans. Hotels dominate the downtown skyline. Huge convention, gaming, museum, shopping, and sports complexes contrast with the few remaining blocks of nineteenth-century commercial buildings. Brightly painted historic houses, for many years protected only in New Orleans's famed French Quarter and Garden District, now festoon large swaths of the city. In an arc from Carrollton to Bywater along the Mississippi River and extending up the Esplanade Ridge, more than a dozen historic districts draw tourists in an ever-widening circle from the historic center, even as gentrification displaces longtime tenants and increases racial segregation in a city once noted for its socially variegated residential landscape. A perusal of labor statistics indicates that some 67,000 New Orleanians work in the tourism industry. A trip on any bus or streetcar will likely acquaint the rider with a porter, waiter, cook, maid, tour guide, or entertainer commuting to or from the city's tourist spaces. A close reading of the daily *Times-Picayune* suggests how tourism has economically, politically, and socially recast New Orleans. Hardly a week passes without articles describing how the municipal government, private entrepreneurs, and concerned citizens engage in public debates about the role of tourism in a city beset by problems such as a failing public school system, crumbling infrastructure, blighted neighborhoods, chronic poverty, police inefficiency, violent crime, and an unskilled labor force.

This book assesses how New Orleans, once among the largest cities in the

United States, gradually embraced its cultural heritage as a hook for attracting tourists rather than competing head to head with more economically dynamic southern cities—especially Atlanta, Houston, Miami, Dallas, Nashville, Charlotte, and Tampa—that surpassed it in the second half of the twentieth century. Molding itself to meet tourist expectations reshaped the city's public policy and discourse, economy, social relations, distinctive culture, and the spatial relationships between people and places. Building a tourist's New Orleans necessitated exploiting public perceptions, preserving and marketing cultural distinctiveness, cultivating a sense of excitement in carefully controlled places and spaces, and building an infrastructure of attractions. Though the popular image of New Orleans predated the 1940s, only thereafter did the city's leaders, faced with intractable urban problems, begin to embrace tourism as an acceptable substitute for the commercial and industrial expansion they had yet to achieve.

New Orleans experienced a fundamental transformation in the six decades following the end of the Great Depression. In the 1940s, New Orleans—nicknamed the Crescent City for the way the Mississippi River cradles it—was still the fifteenth largest city in the United States and the largest in the South, with its population surpassing a half million. Its location astride the lower delta of the Mississippi near the Gulf of Mexico not only made New Orleans one of the world's busiest port cities but also attracted tremendous federal and private investment as a center for military mobilization and war production. Canal Street, touted as the world's widest retail thoroughfare, still brought throngs of shoppers to its grand department stores. Business and civic leaders envisioned a future in which New Orleans stood on a par with the nation's largest cities. Although tourists had long visited New Orleans, their presence only minimally shaped the contours of urban life, economic development, and the city's physical spaces until the 1940s. Even then, local boosters who called attention to New Orleans's tourist appeal did so by characterizing the city's famous French Quarter, or Vieux Carré, as a relict village surrounded by a thoroughly modern city. Indeed, New Orleans was seemingly becoming, on the whole, more and more like other American cities, with soaring skyscrapers and sprawling suburbs.

New Orleans's growing reliance on tourism is typical of a number of southern cities that, having failed to match national urban expansion following the Civil War, turned to tourism as a path to economic development in the twentieth century. Many of these cities' tourist trades relied at least in part on the preservation of historic architecture. After sporadic efforts by patriotic ancestral organizations to save notable buildings around the turn of the century, a group of civic leaders persuaded the municipal government in Charleston, South Carolina, to establish the Old and Historic Charleston District in 1931, projecting a national tourist image of a preserved colonial seaport city. Similarly, in the 1920s, tradition-minded women in San Antonio, Texas—worried about the modernization of their city's old Spanish-influenced heart—spearheaded an initiative that eventually led to the creation of the famed River Walk in the 1960s. In Savannah, Georgia, preservationists forged an extensive historic district in the 1950s which encompassed many blocks of colonial homes shaded by canopies of live oaks. Many other cities of the Old South, such as Annapolis, Maryland, and Wilmington, North Carolina, began to mold tourist attractions from the physical markers of their past. Likewise, New Orleans constructed a tourist image that showcased the heritage embodied in its architecture. Because New Orleans did not experience the same rapid growth that continually transformed New South cityscapes like Atlanta, Dallas, Houston, and Nashville, it retained more than a little of the appearance of a nineteenth-century city. When other means of economic development fell short, New Orleanians gradually recognized the value of cultivating the image of their Old South legacy, albeit one that erased slavery and cleaned up the messiness of the auction block.[1]

To understand New Orleans's transformation to a tourism-dependent city, it is helpful to discern the city's place in the larger context of southern history and regional identity. Situated to the south of Mississippi, New Orleans developed an unmistakably southern culture with its social and economic connections to the Delta region and racial attitudes, but it also retained a reputation as a place that defied easy categorization. Although its fortunes in the nineteenth century paralleled those of many other Deep South cities that relied on trading in cash crops such as cotton, sugar, rice, and tobacco, the Crescent City always stood somewhat apart. In a South comprised principally of white Anglo-Saxon and African American Protestants, New Orleans resembled a Caribbean city with large numbers of Roman Catholics of continental European and African descent. Indeed, the city was in the eyes of many observers a socially permissive Hellenic appendage dangling from the Bible Belt South. Built on land wrested from a watery waste between the Mississippi River and Lake Pontchartrain—increasingly with the help of an elaborate system of levees, pumps, and canals—New Orleans was literally and figuratively a city on the edge. From its beginning as a remote outpost of empire in which a tiny European settlement lived outnumbered by Indians and African captives, surrounded by swamps, always fearful of slave insurrection, tropical disease, and flooding storms, New Orleans gradually developed a distinctive culture, one that American newcomers perennially discovered in the years following the Louisiana Purchase in 1803.

Like many other southern cities, New Orleans emerged from the Civil War and Reconstruction reeling from social, economic, and political upheaval, its people finding solace in fabricating notions of a mythical Old South. In the years thereafter, those cities in areas that had depended most heavily on plantation agriculture fell behind more aggressive inland southern cities, whose urban boosters seized upon the promise of an industrialized New South to close the gap with long-dominant coastal cities. While the nation developed a fondness for cultural vestiges of the Old South, it was primarily Deep South cities, including New Orleans, whose residents recalled a golden age and sought to perpetuate this memory as a balm for wounded pride and a hook for northern investment. Into the twentieth century, New Orleans's social order became more stereotypically southern as whites used Jim Crow segregation to restrict black rights. Yet the city projected to the rest of the nation an aura of urban distinctiveness, creating a tourist image that built upon the city's unusual social and cultural customs, imagined sexual permissiveness, and exotic cityscape.

Much of the story that follows centers on the French Quarter. Because the Vieux Carré became the part of New Orleans most developed by tourism operators and most recognized by tourists, it is important to understand how locals and outsiders shaped the neighborhood and how its image steered the city's fortunes. In the twentieth century the French Quarter emerged as the focal point for the New Orleans tourist image. Long before visitors judged its narrow balcony-lined streets, resplendent townhouses, gas lamps, lush courtyards, and glossy banana leaves quaint and picturesque and conflated the French Quarter with New Orleans, the French Quarter *was* New Orleans. Indeed, long before it became enshrined as a place to pay homage to a romanticized mélange of French Creole culture, African American jazz, and Mardi Gras revelry, the future French Quarter was "la Nouvelle-Orléans" and "la Nueva Orleans," colonial capital of French and then Spanish Louisiana.

Even as the first "American" settlers poured into their newly acquired territory following the Louisiana Purchase, they privileged the city's French origins, ignoring the unmistakable Spanish colonial architecture of iron-lace balconies and galleries and bricked courtyards tucked away behind narrow carriage ways. The city's leading newcomers, whose fortunes rested on cotton, sugar, shipping, and natural resource extraction, built New Orleans into the nation's third largest metropolis by 1840. But increasingly they frowned upon the city's old French section, finding themselves in agreement with one New Yorker who in the 1840s called the district the "St. Giles of New Orleans . . . where poverty and vice run races with want and passion."[2] Disparaging in their attitudes toward what later became known as the French Quarter, newcomers to New Orleans "Americanized" by building anew across Canal Street from the colonial city, erecting handsome townhouses in the present-day downtown district and elegant city estates in Lafayette, later dubbed the Garden District because of its luxuriant foliage and manicured grounds. The Vieux Carré, in turn, became what M. Christine Boyer has called a "condensation point" for "the remnants of a Creole culture that wanted to withdraw from the process of Americanization." If the city's new leaders turned their backs on the old Creole section in establishing new businesses and homes, however, they admired, appropriated the manner of, and intermarried with the Creoles, even as they criticized their perceived fondness for merriment and disregard for moral strictures.[3]

Under Union occupation from 1862 until the fall of the Reconstruction government fifteen years later, the city fell on hard times. Just as many southerners rejected the postwar order by enshrining the myth of the Old South, in the years after the Civil War, New Orleans's substantial citizens found solace in the Carnival organizations they had begun to create even as they extended an olive branch to potential northern investors. As in other cities, to the extent that New Orleans business leaders already looked to tourism as an economic development strategy, they used civic celebrations primarily to showcase their readiness to welcome outside capital and distinguish their city from others. By the 1880s city leaders used the Rex parade and staged the 1884 World's Cotton Centennial and Industrial Exposition to entice northern investment to New Orleans.[4]

Despite civic leaders' best efforts to steer tourists to the city's many points of interest, Americans more often viewed New Orleans as a place to indulge weaknesses for drinking, gaming, and whoring. Nationally recognized for its horse races long before the rise of Kentucky's Churchill Downs, New Orleans also attracted a mostly male clientele who patronized its numerous taverns and brothels, where one could easily arrange sexual encounters without regard for moral restrictions or even the Jim Crow color line. In an effort to contain and marginalize the city's thriving prostitution trade, in 1897 alderman Sidney Story provided for the creation of a designated vice district in twelve square blocks just off Canal Street, presumably hidden safely from the view of newcomers. Yet, "Storyville" quickly became the city's most notorious attraction, especially when the Southern Railway opened a terminal along Basin Street, directly across from pleasure palaces and dollar cribs. Despite growing outcry from reform-minded citizens who believed Storyville compromised New Orleans's chances for more tasteful development, the district remained in place until the U.S. Navy insisted it be closed down upon American entry into the First World War in 1917.[5]

If some visitors flocked to Storyville, others began to discover the French Quarter, which many locals still snubbed as "Frenchtown." Northern writers for national periodicals often remarked about the African influences found in the old district, even as they compared the Quarter's appearance to that of French cities. Although African Americans no longer comprised a majority of the city's population as they had earlier in the nineteenth century, New Orleans remained one of the few American cities with a substantial black community at a time when large-scale black migration to northern cities had scarcely begun. In 1873 a *Scribner's Monthly* article reported that the French Quarter "might be Toulouse, or Bordeaux, or Marseilles!" But it also focused on the district as, in Christine Boyer's words, "a melancholic symbol" of a lost Old South, an exotic and erotic departure from other American cities. The article called attention to "buxom girls . . . with gayly-colored [sic] handkerchiefs wound about an unpardonable luxuriance of wool, . . . their conversation resounding for half-a-dozen blocks, interspersed with laughter which ripples like wine, effervesces like champagne." The following month, *Scribner's* followed up with another article that featured several heavily stereotyped lithographs of African Americans in the French Quarter, including images of a man lying in a cart with the caption "Waiting for a Job," old women trading hens and selling gumbo in the French Market, and workers lounging atop bales of cotton on the nearby levee. The article romanticized the labor of the black river hands and conditioned the reader to associate them with the exotic foreignness of the French Quarter.[6] Even as commentators peopled this stylized urban landscape with colorful characters, African Americans were producing a distinctive new form of music which gradually became intertwined with public conceptions of New Orleans. Over the course of the twentieth century, particularly after World War II, tourism promoters would increasingly dissociate the products of black culture spatially from their black producers in an effort to appeal to mostly middle-class white visitors in a time characterized by segregation and suburban tastes.

Because New Orleans leaders wanted to modernize their city, attracting tourists necessitated appearing thoroughly progressive, with perhaps an aura of distinctiveness, rather than preserving an antebellum cityscape. Although in *Harper's* in 1887, Charles Dudley Warner had called the district "specially interesting in its picturesque decay," most New Orleans leaders saw only the decay. Increasingly ensconced in newer streetcar suburbs that traced the arc of the Mississippi River, the city's leading families in what became known as Uptown stayed away from the old Creole section, which swelled with the influx of thousands of immigrants. Civic boosters' attitude toward the Quarter, like Storyville, reflected their fear that outsiders would not take the city seriously as a commercial center. In the 1890s, the Young Men's Business League reported finding that New Orleans suffered a reputation as being quaint but not conducive to business. Several years later the New Orleans Progressive Union, a precursor to the chamber of commerce, issued a pamphlet that cautioned: "A critical visitor disparages the look of shiftlessness without, no matter how busy the wheels may be within." The Progressive Union suggested that the only reason the Quarter would survive was that "the march of to-day is south and above Canal Street, where expansion is more easy and the opportunities more promising."[7] Such attitudes toward the Vieux Carré persisted into the middle decades of the twentieth century, when business leaders and preservationists clashed more and more over the neighborhood's worth to the city.

Significantly, although the Vieux Carré stirred the imagination of visitors even in the nineteenth century, it was not yet the clear focal point for tourists. "Doing the town" entailed visiting the French Market but also riding streetcars to outlying areas to behold Lake Pontchartrain, eat a fish dinner, tour the Jockey Club and the Metairie cemetery, visit the upriver town of Carrollton, and, in season, watch a Mardi Gras parade wend through the city streets. While perhaps most New Orleanians thought little of the French Quarter, Lafcadio Hearn, a Greek-born Irish folklorist who moved to New Orleans from Cincinnati, Ohio, and wrote for two local newspapers in the 1870s and 1880s, urged locals and tourists to view the Quarter as the city's cultural center.[8] If Hearn awakened some New Orleanians to the cultural wonders of the Vieux Carré, however, it was only many decades later that the process of place-making gave rise to a tourism industry that focused preponderantly on the French Quarter.

Before local leaders' attitudes toward the French Quarter began to converge with those of outsiders, it swelled with the influx of thousands of mostly Sicilian immigrants. The polyglot enclave, with its unpaved streets, bordellos, fruit vendors, peddlers, organ grinders, and pickpockets, seemed utterly distant from a French Creole past now relegated to fading memory. Although the immigrant population unsettled local politicos and civic and business leaders, who saw the French Quarter as an obstacle to rehabilitation and a reason for redevelopment, a few socially prominent New Orleanians attempted to appropriate French Creole heritage in the 1920s and 1930s. Accordingly, they restored a few buildings to house the Arts and Crafts Club, Le Petit Salon, Le Petit Théâtre du Vieux Carré, and the Quartier Club. As did architecturally significant urban districts in a number of American cities, the New Orleans French Quarter began a transition from civic embarrassment to cultural attraction in the 1920s, a time when Americans, increasingly mobile in the emerging automobile age, began to seek reminders of national and regional pasts.[9]

New Orleans might have cut its tourist image wholly from the cloth of its historic architecture and Old South legacy, as did cities like Charleston and Savannah, had it not already become such a notorious magnet for hedonists. Even before heritage seekers began to discover the French Quarter, the district had become a cauldron of intermingled images and realities that confounded efforts to create a singular cultural landscape. Indeed, within three decades following the closing of Storyville, the French Quarter had inherited much of the city's nightlife and—with its cheap apartments, exotic architecture, heterogeneous population, and proximity to the ships that daily and nightly deposited sailors on shore leave—it emerged as the place that visitors most readily associated with the city. Long captured in popular literature, notably in George Washington Cable's short stories, it reached further into the American consciousness through Hollywood, Broadway, and radio and television. In the tourist mind the Quarter connoted New Orleans not only because its buildings looked distinctive but because it promised worldly pleasures set against a backdrop suffused with the imagery of French and Spanish colonists, swashbuckling pirates, American and British officers, slaves and longshoremen, concubines and voodoo priestesses, and Carnival and jazz.

Notwithstanding the growing local attention to the French Quarter in the middle decades of the twentieth century, New Orleans municipal and business leaders remained focused on the city's port as its primary economic engine. The U.S. entry into World War II seemed to be the moment when New Orleans might finally shake off its languorous past and realize the long-elusive promise of the New South. As historian George Brown Tindall has observed, the war set southerners on the move as never before, to distant battlefields as well as to shipyards, war plants, and military reservations. The world conflict stirred the Crescent City, which emerged from the war determined to expand trade, improve urban infrastructure, court corporate investment, reform municipal politics, and clean up the city's freewheeling, corrupt, and dissipative reputation.[10]

For all the promise of modernization along the lines of other cities that contributed to the war effort, World War II did not stimulate New Orleans to become a leading national center of commerce and industry. As returning GI's and their families began to take vacations in the postwar years, they found New Orleans a place apart. Although some local elites contributed their energies to expanding economic development in the postwar years, most seem to have retreated further into the insular whirl of their exclusive clubs, leaving a new group of emerging leaders to decide the city's future. Some of these came from the city's nonelite, including middle-class whites, Jews, and, eventually, African Americans. Such leaders gradually saw the futility of trying to pattern New Orleans after Houston or Atlanta and slowly warmed to the idea that the small but vocal number of historic and cultural preservationists had been pushing for years—that exploiting the city's past, and particularly its French Quarter, might be the very best means of modernizing. Having fallen from the first order of American cities, New Orleans, like other coastal southern cities, began to embrace what historian David Goldfield argues "southerners are best at—remembering," or, at least, remembering what they want to remember.[11]

As historian Hal K. Rothman has noted, Las Vegas, Nevada, became the first major American city whose economy relied entirely on tourism. Although urban tourism developed in the nineteenth century, the tourism industry dominated no other major city before the mid-twentieth century. Urban boosters seldom viewed tourism as more than a supplement to traditional economic enterprises. Until the latter part of the nineteenth century, few Americans possessed the means or the inclination to take sightseeing trips. Well into the twentieth century, even those cities that began to advertise their points of interest in guidebooks usually did not need to steer public policy toward underwriting their tourist trade because they continued to expand in manufacturing, commerce, and finance. Even though many southern cities lagged behind the rapid rate of national urban expansion in the first half of the twentieth century, as historian Don Doyle has demonstrated, their leaders still courted investment in new business enterprises. Thus, despite the emergence of historic preservation, evocative cityscapes did not automatically result in a wholesale retreat from the usual development strategies in favor of marketing local culture to the touring public. While World War II launched much of the South on an upward trajectory of industrialization, diminishing its regional variation in the latter half of the twentieth century, New Orleans proved unable to maintain its position among southern cities and gradually embraced the romanticized image that outsiders expected of it. In failing to match Atlanta's corporate offices, Houston's oil and petrochemical industry, or Raleigh and Durham's Research Triangle Park, New Orleans managed to preserve the very qualities and appearance that formed the foundation of its tourist appeal.[12]

Considerable scholarly attention has focused on the development of tourism in the American Southwest in the late nineteenth and early twentieth centuries, generally arguing that the region's distinctive Hispanic and Indian cultures contrasted sharply with the emerging urban-industrial American society, thereby affording leisure-seeking travelers an almost foreign encounter with an exotic "other." More recently, historians have examined the rising national interest in southern culture, many of them suggesting that the region's antebellum period provided a highly marketable image conducive to tourism. Although historians have studied urban tourism, they have dwelt either on the turn of the twentieth century or on Las Vegas, a city that offers many suggestions about the future of American leisure, as Hal Rothman argues, but whose tourism industry did not arise in a well-established, diverse city in which tourism represented only one of several potential courses of development.[13] This book seeks to shift the study of tourism in a direction that fosters a deeper understanding of its role in southern and national urban development in the twentieth century. If nineteenth- and early twentieth-century tourism developed as a pastime offering respite from modern urban society, tourism in the second half of the twentieth century emerged as a key shaper of modern urban society. New Orleans provides an ideal subject in that it continues to excite the nation's imagination. More importantly, its tourist transformation yields insight into the ways tourism reshapes economic development plans, urban life and culture, and the cityscape itself, offering lessons for other cities that experienced urban decline after the 1940s and continue to search for a path to revitalization today.

This book examines the role of race and class in shaping the rise of urban tourism, as well as the role of tourism in shaping public responses to urban decline. In New Orleans, like in other southern cities, tourism built upon racialized images. Since the rise of tourism in the nineteenth century, attractions often appealed to a mostly white touring public by presenting stereotyped racial otherness for tourists' entertainment. At the hotels of Saratoga Springs and Atlantic City, African Americans amused white guests with cakewalks and minstrel shows, while at Gettysburg excursionists marveled at both Civil War statuary and black watermelon-eating contests. Coney Island's amusement parks and the midways of world expositions at Chicago, Cleveland, and other cities featured exhibits that brought "exotic" peoples from equatorial Africa to the Arctic Circle under the tourist gaze. Similarly, the Great Northern Railway's Blackfeet Indians at the Glacier Park Hotel, the Fred Harvey Company's Indian image-making along the Santa Fe Railway, Coppinger's staged Seminole Indian villages outside Miami, and tours of opium dens in San Francisco's Chinatown enthralled Americans hungry for safe, controlled encounters with the "other" in ways that preserved social distance.[14]

Likewise, New Orleans's tourist image owed much to "picturesque" blacks who loaded cotton on steamships, served Creole dinners in French Quarter restaurants, tap danced or sold praline candies outside the French Market, conjured voodoo spells in shadowy cemeteries, carried fiery torches in Carnival parades, or blew Dixieland tunes on Bourbon Street. Indeed, at the Courtyard Kitchen, according to a locally produced guidebook in 1945, the tourist could look forward to being "served an ambrosial meal by charming Negro girls with crimson tignons tied around their heads," while at another French Quarter restaurant "Negro girls . . . are taught to serve with the best manners" in the Old South tradition.[15] In the second half of the twentieth century, the close connection between race and tourism endured as white tourists continued to seek forms of black popular culture, including the Zulu parade, jazz funerals, Mardi Gras Indians, and brass bands. While New Orleans and other cities continued to exploit the labor and culture of nonwhites, in the postwar years they had to choose between adapting to new national standards of racial equality or becoming economically marginalized. In the 1950s and 1960s, events in New Orleans underscored the fragility of its carefully tended public image of racial harmony as a series of ugly racial incidents threatened to jeopardize Carnival, the revival of jazz, and the city's bid for conventions and professional football. Thus, an examination of modern New Orleans tourism reveals the tenacity of racism as a basis for tourist attractions and the important intersection between civil rights and the continued development of the southern tourism industry.

As with many tourist destinations, in New Orleans the rise of the tourism industry reflected the emergence of a more diverse class of urban leaders. Although the city's image revolved in part around the commodification of black culture for white consumption, the growth of tourism in New Orleans also paralleled the rising influence of African Americans and others long marginalized in a city dominated by an old elite. For older civic and business leaders, tradition meant seeking urban progress through the expansion of locally controlled businesses while keeping old social customs, especially racism, as intact as possible. For newer leaders, however, progress meant turning to tradition by enshrining the image of New Orleans's heritage while embracing social change. As a result, New Orleans retained much of the appearance and mystique that captivated generations of travelers even as it became further integrated into a new national marketplace that privileged consumption over production and required greater social cooperation.

Indeed, tourism played an increasingly important role in shaping cities' strategies to retain their relevance as the United States gravitated from an economy based on production toward what historian Lizabeth Cohen has termed the "Consumers' Republic."[16] Although New Orleans never industrialized to the same extent as many American cities in the nineteenth and twentieth centuries, its diminishing share of oceangoing trade and subsequent oil-industry collapse produced similar effects to that of deindustrialization in the so-called Rust Belt. When viewed in the context of protracted economic distress, the city's tourism boom offers lessons to other cities seeking a remedy for urban decline, notably, Baltimore, Cleveland, Milwaukee, Pittsburgh, and St. Louis. Much envied by cities with fewer readily identifiable tourist attractions, New Orleans became a model of success that seemingly justified the rewards of tourism. Because few American cities boasted such a distinctive culture, exciting nightlife, and evocative cityscape, those that did not set out to make the best use of decaying urban spaces in the interest of stimulating tourism. Atlanta transformed the desolate waste beneath its downtown viaducts into Underground Atlanta, originally a Confederate-themed entertainment complex. Memphis rejuvenated Beale Street, creating a nightlife district revolving around the theme of blues music. Tampa turned Ybor City, once a vibrant area of cigar factories peopled by Italian and Cuban immigrant workers, into a cultural and entertainment district.

In turn, the more other cities tried to emulate New Orleans's successes, the more New Orleans attempted to adopt features of other cities, such as pedestrian malls, festival marketplaces, waterfront parks and museums, convention centers, sports arenas, and even gambling casinos. Despite the preservative impact on New Orleans, the growing reliance on mass tourism eroded its distinctive cityscape by introducing nationally standardized, formulaic tourist venues. But for New Orleans, like most cities, tourism required more than simply building facilities to entice and serve outsiders. While Las Vegas and Orlando, Florida, could create tourist demand by amassing casino hotels or theme parks, New Orleans's appeal rested on preserving and packaging symbols of its distinctive cultural heritage. As in other cities that preserved urban districts to create a mood conducive to tourism, notably, Charleston and Savannah, New Orleans's success in raising local commitment to historic preservation carried the seeds of dissension. Preserved places and spaces such as the French Quarter, the riverfront, the St. Charles Avenue parade route, Congo Square, and the sites of jazz heritage reflected their social construction, in which race and class interests often stood at loggerheads. Whites and blacks struggled over the presentation of black culture in white venues and the preservation of sites of black memory. Developers, merchants, tourism operators, history-minded home renovators, tourists, and longtime residents clashed over the proper disposition of historic buildings and the public streets and parks that gave shape to the urban landscape, continually contesting each other's visions of whose neighborhood the French Quarter was and whose city New Orleans was. Tourism, then, offers a lens with which to view evolving interplay between social relations and urban change in the modern South and, by extension, the modern United States.

The New Orleans experience compels a reexamination of the common scholarly assumption that tourism is an undesirable or regrettable developmental path, one that Hal Rothman calls a "devil's bargain" for many communities that have embraced the industry. He suggests that many places that became dependent on tourism did so in ways that privileged outside capital and outside interests, reserving the role of place making for outsiders, or "neonatives," to borrow Rothman's terminology. In the process, local culture often became adulterated to the point that it was little more than a caricature of itself. The tourist transformation of New Orleans in some ways follows a similar pattern to the one Rothman describes. Indeed, it was often newcomers—developers, preservationists, and cultural enthusiasts—who found value in the Crescent City's peculiarities even when most locals stood ready to turn their backs on their city's heritage. As New Orleans became more and more dependent on tourism, increasingly it abdicated power to individuals outside the circle of traditional native civic leaders. The neonatives, in effect, reshaped local priorities in favor of their vision of a New Orleans that appealed to the national nostalgia for regional distinctiveness, offering a mélange of Old South and Hellenic culture. Yet in New Orleans this transformation was not simply a devil's bargain. As tourists began to arrive in droves after the Great Depression eased, outside expectations in some ways enshrined forms of cultural distinctiveness that otherwise might not have retained the same degree of influence in locals' eyes. Many of those who advanced the tourist trade embraced the city's culture and made New Orleans their adopted home. In some cases the growing reliance on mass tourism seemed to erode local distinctiveness, as Rothman finds in the American West. Indeed, as Calvin Trillin wrote in 1975, even the city's distinctive Mardi Gras celebration gradually morphed into "an event that could be held in Fort Lauderdale or Daytona Beach without serious dislocation." Yet sometimes the embrace of tourism bolstered local cultural practices, especially as outsiders coaxed local promoters to expand opportunities for tourist participation in Carnival and to breathe new life into the fading music traditions in "the Birthplace of Jazz."[17]

In New Orleans a complex response to tourist expectations developed, one that rested on creating the illusion of cultural anomaly and timelessness even as it exerted dynamic and far-reaching power over the city's political, economic, and social life. In short, New Orleans reveals a more complicated impact of tourism than has tended to emerge from existing scholarship. Tourism preserved cultural distinctiveness even as it simplified it into a more salable package. It provided immediate opportunities for the masses of unskilled, undereducated workers mired in poverty, even as it created mostly low-wage jobs that limited their prospects for significant betterment. It also offered leaders an attractive way to demonstrate that they could revive a city beset by endemic urban decay. The longer the city followed this path in the years after the Great Depression, the more it wrote off the possibility of an alternative path. Indeed, in the early twenty-first century the cultivation of a tourist image still prompts considerable ambivalence among locals, but few New Orleanians believe that the Big Easy can be anything besides a tourist city.

CHAPTER 1

A "NEW" NEW ORLEANS?

New Orleans today is a grand illusion: all America thinks of it as a gay, silly princess of a city. It may be, but it is also a stevedore, tough as a sledge hammer, raucous, busy, powerful and dynamic.

—WILLIAM A. EMERSON JR. (1952)

One sultry evening in 1953, Mario Bermudez escorted several Latin American visitors on a stroll down Bourbon Street, New Orleans's famous nightlife strip. The group paused beside a black iron gaslight standard at the corner of Bienville Street beneath a backlit sign that beckoned tourists to the weathered "Historical Old Absinthe House," reputedly once a favorite haunt of the legendary pirate Jean Lafitte. There Bermudez pointed toward a sidewalk vendor's cart advertising twenty-five-cent hot dogs and forty-cent tamales. Perhaps the sight reinforced in the visitors' minds the idea that New Orleans embraced the culture, in this case the food, of its neighbors to the south of the Gulf of Mexico. For Bermudez this would have been a point worth emphasizing, for he served as director of international relations for the city of New Orleans and International House, a private world trade organization based amid the skyscrapers just blocks away across Canal Street.[1]

In the early nineteenth century, when "Americans" poured into the Creole city steeped in French and Spanish colonial tradition, Canal Street emerged as the neutral ground between a newly settled "American Sector," later known as the Central Business District, and an old French section, later dubbed the French Quarter. Even in the mid-twentieth century, Canal Street remained something of a boundary between a city striving for modernity and a relict village still basking in the dimming glow of a bygone era. The Americanization of New Orleans lifted the city to the pinnacles of prosperity within a generation after the Louisiana Purchase. Although many of the tourists who shared the street with Bermudez and his guests surely enjoyed the city's carefully cultivated image as a place where the ghost of Lafitte might present itself around any corner, their counterparts in the early nineteenth century had beheld a bustling city on the make. In 1840, only New York and Baltimore counted larger populations than the Crescent City. In the years that followed the Civil War and Reconstruction, however, New Orleans sputtered economically as it lost ground to other American cities. Even as regional cities like Atlanta, Nashville, and Birmingham embraced the promise of the New South, New Orleans relied increasingly on the comfort and remuneration of its annual Mardi Gras festivities, Creole cooking, sexual libertinism, and other sensory pleasures.[2] By the twentieth century its reputation as the "City That Care Forgot," a place strangely aloof from the modernization of the rest of the United States, was widely recognized.

New Orleans's national image reflected not only its unusual culture but also its often unseemly politics. By the 1930s Americans had become well acquainted with Louisiana's unsavory politicians, thanks to the corruption and antics of Governor Huey P. Long and his political friends. If New York was America's nerve center, New Orleans was its moral escape hatch. Although Long died in 1935 and many of his cronies were serving prison sentences by the early 1940s, the Kingfish's ally Robert S. Maestri remained mayor of New Orleans. In his first term as mayor, Maestri had proven himself an able leader. He streamlined the city's budget, made improvements to the infrastructure, won millions of dollars in Works Progress Administration contracts for New Orleans, and helped underwrite the symphony, the ballet, tourism promotion, and even the restoration of Catholic convents.[3] By his second term, however, the mayor had to fend off charges of political favoritism and gradually trimmed back city services such as garbage collection and street maintenance. Under Maestri, the French Quarter became a tawdry mélange of brothels and gambling dens operating with impunity under lax law enforcement. Given such conditions, it is hardly surprising that the rest of the nation regarded New Orleans as an almost foreign city rather than as an urban beacon of the New South.[4]

New Orleans's failure to match the growth of other southern cities in the six decades after Reconstruction resulted in no small measure from the tight-knit, almost oligarchic control of its upper-class white civic leaders, who tolerated shady politics and believed in the inevitability of New Orleans's continuation as the South's leading city. To be sure, the city's white elite, who had built fortunes on the surrounding sugar and cotton plantations, disliked the corruption of Maestri and the long-entrenched Old Regular Democratic machine that had kept such mayors in office for many years since the late nineteenth century.[5] Yet upper-class whites felt little need to oppose Maestri because they rested comfortably in the center of New Orleans's social and business circles, dominating the city's port and its leading banks, as well as its Carnival organizations. The elite in New Orleans favored forms of economic development that enabled them to maintain their social standing. They belonged to prestigious organizations like the Boston, Louisiana, and Pickwick clubs, as well as secretive Mardi Gras organizations such as the Mistick Krewe of Comus and the Knights of Momus. The men annually rode on horseback or atop floats in mask and tossed trinkets to the multitude of locals and tourists who lined the streets. Their dominance of the Carnival celebration reinforced in a very public way the exclusivity of social status in the city.

In addition to spending their energies in prestigious social organizations, the upper class demonstrated their exclusivity in other ways. They tended to send their children to Tulane University or Sophie Newcomb College for Women, usually held membership in either Holy Name of Jesus Catholic Church or Trinity Episcopal Church, and occupied comfortable and sometimes palatial homes along the oak- and palm-lined boulevards in the city's Uptown section, which lay upriver from downtown New Orleans and included the famed Garden District. For most of the year they interacted with the most prominent civic leaders among the 1 to 2 percent Jewish population in New Orleans, yet during Carnival season they routinely turned their back on wealthy Jews and retreated into the Gentile preserves of their Mardi Gras "krewes." Commentators often observed that the old elite's obsession with Carnival planning siphoned time and resources away from other civic endeavors, leaving the Jewish community to lead "everything else in town— charities, the opera guild, the symphony, the museums, and organizations like the League of Women Voters." Jews exercised such influence in nonsocial aspects of New Orleans civic life, in fact, that they won the prestigious *Times-Picayune* Loving Cup, given by the leading daily for "unselfish service to New Orleans," more than one-third of the time. In a city with large numbers of African Americans and people of Sicilian ancestry, native-born whites and especially the old-line leaders among them seemed to hold the keys to the city's future.[6]

From their lofty perch, these men not only planned lavish social events but also exercised overwhelming influence on the city's economic direction and its politics. The elite continued to control freight forwarding, cotton brokering, warehousing, and shipping, and expanded into key positions in law and banking, working assiduously to expand the city's economy even as they sought to seal out new competitors. Through overlapping directorates on the boards of numerous businesses, banks, and governmental agencies, the old-line elite exercised a degree of economic and political influence far greater than their numbers might suggest. William B. Reily and Company, Westfeldt Brothers, and J. Aron and Company, all headed by old-line New Orleanians, controlled much of the city's lucrative coffee trade. Similarly, Robert Gibson Robinson, a Tulane and Princeton graduate, board director of Hibernia National Bank, and member of the Boston Club, owned one of the South's leading lumber companies and established himself as the dominant importer of Nicaraguan mahogany.[7] The Whitney and Hibernia national banks, reflective of their old-line control, studiously avoided making medium- and long-term loans, especially to those outside the social circle occupied by bank directors. As late as the early 1970s this "power establishment," as author John M. Barry has dubbed them, dominated the powerful Board of Liquidation of the City Debt, which had complete control over the issuance of bonds.[8] Only gradually did they lose faith in Maestri's mayoral administration and throw their support to a reform-minded politician who promised substantive change.

New Orleans struggled to appear progressive even as it nurtured longstanding allegiances to social rank, aristocratic tradition, and racial discrimination. Crescent City leaders still longed for the promise of the New South—industrialization—that might yet replace the world they had lost in the Civil War. With the onset of World War II, it appeared that the city might finally scrape away years of cultural accretions and refashion itself as a booming New South metropolis. New Orleans boosters dreamed of skyscrapers, plazas, and freeways, and usually showed little affection for physical reminders of their city's past. The rise of tourism, while not new to the postwar era, ultimately proved an attractive alternative to the elusive industrialization that urban boosters sought. In the 1940s, however, New Orleans appeared to be on the cusp of a future that turned its back on the past.

Although the French Quarter, with its exotic streetscapes, romantic restaurants, risqué nightlife, and vivid local color, undoubtedly worked its magic on visiting soldiers, sailors, and workers during World War II, it seemed that New Orleans was quickly becoming ripe for an economic, political, and social transformation that might diminish the city's image as a place rife with dissipation. The arrival of newcomers in the 1940s began to shake the solid foundation of the old elite and the Old Regulars. Widely celebrated for its exotic landscape of iron-lace galleries, narrow streets, and luxuriant gardens, New Orleans suddenly bore the unmistakable imprint of war. Military operations mushroomed on Lake Pontchartrain, a large tidal bay where locals swam, fished, and cast oyster nets. Army personnel practiced landing amphibious craft on the beaches in preparation for European maneuvers. The Southern Yacht Club, long a bastion of old-line New Orleanians, became a U.S. Coast Guard reservation, while bombers and Navy seaplanes lent a martial atmosphere to the city's lakefront Shushan Airport, named for one of Huey Long's political appointees.[9]

Shipyards and military equipment factories, especially those of Higgins Industries, dotted the Crescent City. On the Industrial Canal, a channel dug through swampy tangles between the lake and the Mississippi River, Higgins operated a large shipyard, as did several other companies. Closer to the fabled French Quarter, Higgins employed workers in its equipment facilities on St. Charles, Felicity, and Polymnia Streets. Bayou St. John, a placid waterway lined by several plantation houses and emptying into Lake Pontchartrain, became a Higgins testing canal. Seven hundred miles of bus routes brought white and black workers from the rural hinterlands of Louisiana and Mississippi to work in the Higgins factories. Thousands of them built airplanes in Higgins' City Park Avenue plant, just four miles from the bordellos and burlesque clubs of Bourbon Street.[10]

The wartime boom quickened the pace of life in the Crescent City, which grew from about 495,000 residents on the eve of the war to more than 570,000 by 1950. Between 1939 and the peak of the war, the city's industrial workforce soared from about 25,000 to about 85,000.[11] One observer remarked that "the city is now full of uniforms, Army, Navy, Marine, Coast Guard, and Merchant Marine. . . . There is seldom room available in a hotel without a week's reservation and the restaurants are crowded to the doors at mealtimes."[12] When one journalist for the *New Republic* stopped in New Orleans in 1944, he observed conflicting responses to the impact of the war. Waiting in a long line for lunch at Antoine's, billed as America's oldest restaurant, his host, the president of one of the "old, established banks," remarked, "I liked New Orleans better when it was a city of 200,000. It was quiet and you could live comfortably." The following day the writer found himself at Antoine's again, this time with shipbuilding tycoon Andrew Higgins, himself a relative newcomer to New Orleans. Judging the queue outside the venerable French restaurant, the industrialist commented, "This is wonderful. Crowds everywhere. New Orleans and the South are really breaking through. This will be the great metropolis of the future."[13]

Throughout the South, as historian Numan V. Bartley has argued, World War II marked more of a break with the southern past than the Civil War, pointing the way to the first significant, sustained modernization of the South's agriculture-centered economy.[14] At least in the initial postwar years, it appeared that New

Orleans, too, would take its place among Sunbelt cities, and only gradually and with much ambivalence did it stray from that path. The hindrance of wartime defense measures to East and West Coast port traffic gave New Orleans a golden opportunity to seize a large share of foreign trade in the early 1940s. In addition, federal expenditures in war production and nearby military bases bolstered the local economy. Even before the war ended, a group of concerned business leaders drawn mostly from outside the ranks of the old elite began to strategize ways of building upon the fortuitous conditions wrought by the war. With the city's Dock Board wrested from the political control of Huey Long's embattled political machine in 1940 and rival New York's shipping crippled during the war, these leaders decided to press New Orleans's southern hospitality into the service of stimulating foreign trade through the Mississippi River port. It was not the first effort to harness the city's distinctiveness to court economic investment, for in 1884 New Orleans had tried, unsuccessfully, to woo northern industrialists with the World's Cotton Centennial and Industrial Exposition on the site of a former sugar plantation. Whereas that venture tried to lift New Orleans out of the doldrums of the Civil War and Reconstruction, the effort six decades later focused on building upon a wartime boom.

During the war several civic leaders, including Mississippi Shipping Company chairman and Bavarian native Rudolf Hecht, cotton broker and port manager E. O. Jewell, Associated Press veteran correspondent Charles Nutter, and local 7-Up bottler William Zetzmann, decided to organize a meeting place where visiting business leaders could learn about trade opportunities, display their wares, research other markets, and seek various services while in New Orleans. Though sharing with old-line elites an interest in expanding trade, these men generally stood outside the power establishment. They hoped to translate the city's famous hospitality into an important business service called International House, which would serve their growing effort to capture the benefits of trade between the Mississippi Valley and Latin America. The venture suited a city that for most of its history had shown greater aptitude for hosting, handling, and facilitating than producing. At first the leading social and business elite showed little interest in the idea.[15] Undeterred, the organizers pitched their case broadly and ultimately won support from the Cotton Exchange, Association of Commerce, Young Men's Business Club, Board of Trade, and several prominent women's clubs, raising half a million dollars to renovate a ten-story bank building on Camp Street.[16]

If the South continued in the postwar years to rely on land, labor, and natural resources as pillars of economic development, as historians David Goldfield and James C. Cobb have argued, New Orleans found yet another way of harnessing its reputation for hospitality to its own natural resources, most notably its location astride a nexus of continental and world trade.[17] *Fortune* magazine likened International House, which opened in June 1945, to "the bayou resort the brothers Lafitte used to operate for their customers."[18] It offered private offices staffed with bilingual secretaries, maintained a staffed reference library, and, in typical New Orleans fashion, provided dance partners, dinner companions, and a meeting place apart from the insular halls of the elitist Boston, Pickwick, and Louisiana clubs where the city's businessmen "could meet over a planter's punch or a jambalaya."[19]

International House was hardly the only example of forging an image of a city eager to appeal to outsiders. Tours of the French Quarter, such as the ones Mario Bermudez guided, may have enthralled Latin American visitors, but some local leaders recognized the need to convince them that New Orleans was a suitable home away from home. Just as International House attempted to extend a warm welcome to visiting Latin American officials and shipping executives, other New Orleans establishments worked to make the Crescent City as Latin-friendly as possible. The city's Maison Blanche department store had since the 1920s operated small shops on board Mississippi Shipping Company passenger vessels, but in 1953, under Maison Blanche president Isidore Newman II, the Canal Street retailer opened *Centro de las Américas*, a department catering to Latin Americans. Staffed with Spanish-speaking clerks and filled with Latin American fashions and even Spanish-language city guidebooks, *Centro de las Américas* quickly grew to serve more than seven hundred Latin American customers, including prominent national leaders like Nicaragua's Anastasio Somoza. By 1959, six major New Orleans retailers offered full-scale Latin American divisions with salesmen savvy enough to understand intraregional variations in taste, like the differences between women's fashions on Honduras's northern coast and its capital of Tegucigalpa. Likewise, the Ochsner Clinic and Hospital, opened in 1941 by Dr. Alton Ochsner, a noted surgeon and non–New Orleans native who found his way into the city's power establishment, began attracting Latin American patients in the postwar years by staffing his hospital with interpreters from numerous Central and South American countries.[20]

In the fifteen years after World War II, growing numbers of Latin Americans visited New Orleans, attesting to the efforts of those who pushed the city's trade movement. As one observer noted, "You can not walk past the shops of Canal Street without hearing Spanish. The night clubs of the French Quarter fill up with Latin American businessmen vying with Texas oilmen in a race to spend money."[21] While some Latinos traveled to New Orleans to conduct business, seek medical care, or do seasonal shopping, others chose to make the Crescent City their home. Doubtless their decision to some extent reflected New Orleans's similarities with Latin America. Indeed, with its palms and tropical foliage, French Quarter balconies and patios, Roman Catholicism, and Carnival tradition, New Orleans was hardly alien to those hailing from below the Rio Grande. Yet the conscious efforts on the part of city and business leaders strengthened the ties between New Orleans and Latin America.

The use of hospitality to reshape national conceptions of New Orleans was only one part of a larger effort to reenergize the city. A considerable public-private partnership for trade promotion and economic development appeared during these years, thanks to thirty-four-year-old ex-colonel deLesseps Story "Chep" Morrison's victory over the incumbent Maestri in the 1946 mayoral race. A scion of an old-line Creole family with social ties to the New Orleans Carnival elite, Morrison counted among his ancestors a Louisiana cotton planter, a prominent New Orleans judge, the creator of the Storyville red-light district, and even the builder of the Suez Canal in Egypt. He was able to push policies to modernize the city while enjoying the support of the old-line elite, who were by the 1940s sufficiently dissatisfied with Maestri to get rid of the Old Regulars' machine-style politics, which had controlled New Orleans for more than half a century.

Morrison entered office determined to overcome the inertia of New Orleans's reputation as a freewheeling city for pleasure seekers. There had been earlier efforts to shed the city's image as the "City That Care Forgot," notably in the bid to entice northern investment with the 1884 World's Cotton Centennial and Industrial Exposition and again with the slogan "The Gateway to Panama Canal" during the construction of the isthmian waterway, but Americans continued to view New Orleans primarily as a place to have fun. Morrison supported tourist events such as Mardi Gras, the Sugar Bowl football game, and Spring Fiesta, with its Natchez Pilgrimage–inspired antebellum pageantry, but he hardly saw them as the primary basis for the city's future prosperity. The energetic mayor relied much more on the newly opened Moisant International Airport, the stimulus of the war years, and redoubled efforts to increase port business to provide a foundation for his vision of a new New Orleans. In the decades that followed, "America's Most

Interesting City" struggled to give meaning to a new booster slogan: "Gateway to the Americas."

Morrison worked tirelessly to promote modernization. He allocated funds to pave hundreds of miles of dirt streets; constructed the city's first unified passenger terminal, its first expressway, and several new civic buildings and plazas; and appointed a panel headed by the influential New York planner Robert Moses to devise an arterial freeway blueprint for the city.[22] While the improvements during the earlier national Good Roads movement had already connected New Orleans by causeway to the mainland across Lake Pontchartrain, ending the city's more than two centuries of relative isolation save by boat, the coalescence of postwar infrastructure improvements with economic prosperity and explosive growth in automotive and air travel seemed to place New Orleans squarely within the phenomenon of Sunbelt growth.

While Morrison's infrastructure improvements ultimately did more to facilitate the tourist trade than to industrialize the city, his efforts to court Latin American trade appeared capable of remaking New Orleans. Morrison set the tone for his administration's economic development efforts even before he assumed office, inviting about one hundred Latin American dignitaries and more than seventy-five mayors from the Mississippi Valley to attend his inauguration. International House heartily endorsed the new mayor, noting that he had "in effect established a State Department for Latin America in the City Hall."[23] At the advice of Rudolf Hecht, he soon formed a municipal International Relations Office and built such a name for the city abroad that *Fortune* likened Morrison's New Orleans to Renaissance Venice. In his unprecedented four terms as mayor, Chep Morrison made more than two dozen trade missions to Latin America, where he often peppered his speeches with Spanish phrases. Wherever he went, the mayor, who once averred that "spiritually, I consider myself a Latin," told audiences of the warm welcome they would find in his city. In a public address at the Inter-American Investment Conference in 1955, he boasted that New Orleans was "one place in this entire nation where you can really and truly feel completely at home. You have here a beachhead for your culture, your customs and your traditions. And when we say . . . '*esta es su casa,*' we sincerely mean it."[24]

Under Morrison's supportive administration and with the financial backing of the New Orleans–based Pan-American Life Insurance Company, the trade boosters behind International House opened the city's International Trade Mart in 1948. The city's great strides in fostering international commerce through the port paid handsomely. In 1945, before Morrison took office, the port of New Orleans handled $683.8 million of imports and exports. By 1951, thanks to the new business climate fostered by Morrison and segments of the business community, as well as the discovery of massive oil, gas, and sulfur reserves along the Gulf coast, the figure soared to nearly $1.7 billion.[25] The trade boom, according to historian Arthur Carpenter, led national observers to describe New Orleans as "a vibrant city shedding its legacy of business lassitude and political corruption."[26]

In the 1950s New Orleans's dream of using its port to leverage economic development began to unravel. The city's effort to attract new Latin American air routes was only one example of the difficulties. After opening Moisant International Airport in 1946, the mayor had set out to get the Civil Aeronautics Board (CAB) to approve new routes into Mexico and Central and South America. While Miami already boasted thirty-four daily Latin American flights, the Crescent City counted only two. Unfortunately, the CAB approved new flights for Houston and Dallas while inexplicably dragging its feet on New Orleans's application. Finally, in 1957, eleven years later, New Orleans obtained nonstop flights to Mexico City and Mérida, but only after its Texan rivals had taken their places alongside Miami in cornering Latin American air travel.[27]

The failure to expand air connections to Latin America joined a host of other setbacks. The campaign to parlay foreign trade expansion into a transformation of New Orleans began to reveal the strains of operating in a city hampered by social exclusivity, insularity, and conservatism. It appeared that the city's leaders did not wholeheartedly subscribe to efforts to woo Latin Americans. Notwithstanding the mayor's claim that New Orleanians shared similar cultural inclinations as their Latin neighbors across the Gulf of Mexico, the city's businessmen failed to follow through on plans to host the Inter-American music and art festival in 1957, ostensibly because they were unable to complete "an exotic outdoor concert stage." In the view of a writer for the *American Mercury,* "The truth is Latin culture did not seem like a worthwhile investment to New Orleanians." This claim, whether well founded or not, paralleled earlier public complaints that the Morrison administration was spending an inordinate amount of time and money courting foreigners while much-needed urban improvements proceeded at a snail's pace. In response, the mayor closed the city's International Relations Office and reassigned its responsibilities to the privately run International House. The leading newspaper, the *Times-Picayune,* owned by the old-line Ashton Phelps family, systematically neglected to report on the trade movement and even refused to ship its paper to

Latin American cities, unlike leading dailies in Miami and elsewhere. In fact, only one of the three local dailies, the *Item,* consistently carried each week a whole page "crammed with some dribblings of Latin news."[28]

Worse, as Carpenter argues, the city's leading banks, the Whitney and the Hibernia, were nationally insignificant and thus ill situated to finance a sustained trade expansion. In 1940 they ranked only 58th and 125th in the United States, respectively, in total assets. Twenty-five years later Whitney National Bank had sagged to 74th largest in the nation, while the Hibernia had tumbled to 172nd. While other banks assumed risks and built the capital necessary to fuel the spread of multinational corporations, New Orleans banks shied away from risky ventures and confined most of their lending to short-term investments. Perhaps most damning, according to Carpenter, was the loss of a common vision among trade promoters. In typical New Orleans fashion, too many different agencies handled Latin American trade relations, which ultimately led to disarray. While the International House and the International Trade Mart sparred over who was responsible for what, the city's trade declined.[29]

These local troubles appeared in the context of larger international developments that made trade more difficult. First, growing Latin American nationalism in the 1950s and 1960s emboldened Latinos to insist on processing raw materials at home rather than shipping them to handlers in the United States. Second, the rise of multinational corporations based in large American cities with ample financial strength threatened to eclipse insular, conservative New Orleans. Third, shippers complained that New Orleans dock workers demanded too much pay relative to their counterparts in many other port cities. Finally, as changing technologies produced a shift toward the use of container cargo ships, the city suddenly found its port woefully inadequate to meet new standards. Gone were the days when New Orleans could reap the rewards of foreign trade simply by relying on its location near the mouth of the Mississippi River and counting on its southern hospitality to win new business. The city's dependence on its river port illustrated a pattern of local faith in extracting the wealth from natural resources, a pattern that eventually reappeared with oil and tourism.[30]

If the 1940s and 1950s found New Orleans leaders working to restore their city's economic fortunes after several disappointing decades by making it the "Gateway to the Americas," these years also marked a growing awareness of the economic benefits of maintaining the city's distinctive image and promoting tourism. Most leaders viewed tourism as a way of attracting outside investment and encouraging visitors to return and settle in New Orleans. Indeed, the modern tourism industry was still relatively underdeveloped when compared to what followed in later decades. As the city's primary strategy of enticing trade and industrial development began to decline after the late 1950s, local leaders gradually showed greater interest in promoting tourism and conventions as ends in themselves. By the end of the 1960s, with the city's port clearly struggling, it appeared that tourism would gravitate toward the center of public policy and local discourse.

While Mayor Morrison seldom showed nostalgia for the bygone era depicted in the fanciful reenactments of antebellum life in Spring Fiesta, he understood well the role that heritage could play in giving New Orleans an advantage over regional competitors like Houston, Dallas, and Atlanta. Indeed, in spite of the disinterest shown by Uptown social elites and downtown merchants, Morrison understood that the French Quarter, if not his desired focus, remained an important enticement to the type of outside investment that could modernize his city. Like Mario Bermudez, the mayor himself often took visiting dignitaries on nighttime tours of the old French district.[31] He espoused the same rhetoric often heard in the middle years of the twentieth century—that New Orleanians had set aside an ancient, historic preserve around which they were building the city of tomorrow. At his inaugural address in May 1946, the mayor called attention to the commonly held opinion of the city's exceptional character: "In this city, as nowhere else in America or in the world, there is the most perfect blend of the culture and grace of the old world with the ambition and energy of the new."[32]

Morrison and many New Orleanians believed that tourism, like the verdant vegetation that engulfed its French Quarter courtyards, was an organic part of the city which could grow on its own. Indeed, the City That Care Forgot had attracted outsiders searching for leisure and entertainment since the antebellum period. As early as the late nineteenth century, some businesses and individuals—notably, railroads, hotels, and downtown merchants—promoted New Orleans as a tourist destination. Yet well into the twentieth century they spent relatively little money on such efforts. New Orleans, they assumed, needed little marketing because of its national notoriety. Tourism operators such as hoteliers and restaurateurs could count on handsome profits without substantial tourism promotion. For decades the profits of the tourist trade, like those in shipping, were a treasure closely guarded, a prize for a small and influential group of businessmen, some of whom rarely looked beyond their own ledger sheets. Indeed, tourism benefited primarily the proprietors of French Quarter restaurants, taverns, and night clubs, and the operators of the city's few first-class hotels, as well as the downtown merchants whose stores tourists often visited. In fact, New Orleans's business establishment concentrated its attention on shipping, warehousing, banking, insurance, and planning Carnival activities months in advance. It turned its back on tourism, which most New Orleanians took for granted, and essentially left it to nonelite entrepreneurs, including a number of Jewish and Italian businessmen who saw in the French Quarter an opportunity for profit.

New Orleans's tourist trade, like its wholesale and retail trade, reflected the involvement of a diverse population. Old-line New Orleanians, having made their fortunes handling the cash crops that aggrandized a southern aristocracy in the previous century, generally avoided involvement in what they certainly saw as crass commerce. Italian Americans, almost all of them from Sicily, ran many of the businesses in the French Quarter in the 1940s and 1950s. Many of the 24,000 Italians who had settled in New Orleans by 1910 lived in the Quarter. A number of them opened corner groceries and produce stands in and around the French Market. Even as the Sicilian population fanned out across the city by the 1940s as a result of suburbanization, many Italian American entrepreneurs remained in the Quarter to operate longtime businesses.[33] Others started restaurants, inns, nightclubs, and services that catered to the emerging tourist trade. A. V. LaNasa, who ran a hardware store in the vestigial Italian enclave on Decatur Street near the old French Market, took advantage of the city's tourist appeal, forming Royal Tours, a company that whisked visitors into the French Quarter from outlying tourist courts such as his own Hollywood Motel. Likewise, Steve Valenti's Paddock Lounge and Sid Davilla's Mardi Gras Lounge were among the few French Quarter establishments specializing in traditional New Orleans jazz. James "Diamond Jim Moran" Brocato purchased La Louisiane Restaurant just off Bourbon Street on Iberville Street in 1954, proclaiming that his eatery offered the "Food of Kings." Some Italian Americans rose to greater prominence, including the Vaccaro family, whose shipping fortune extended to the operation of the Grunewald Hotel, later the Roosevelt, and William Monteleone, a cobbler who opened the dominant hotel in the French Quarter.

Jews, who never comprised much more than 1 percent of the city's population, enjoyed a considerable role in retail and leisure establishments. A trip down Canal Street revealed the prominence of Jewish retailing: Freidberg's, Godchaux's, Gus Mayer, Kreeger's, Rubenstein's. Seymour Weiss, a Jewish barber from Abbeville, Louisiana, and crony of Governor Huey Long, rose to become the president of the city's leading hotel, the Roosevelt, and headed the city's hotel association. Like retailing, tourism, aside from events surrounding Carnival and Spring Fiesta, was a business that upper-class New Orleanians usually abdicated to those they saw as social inferiors.

If tourist dollars enriched businessmen who could profit from the popularity of the French Quarter, only low wages went to most of the many African Americans who worked in such establishments. New Orleans had long appealed to the white traveler in search of the romance of the South. Shaded by moss-draped live oaks, laced with black iron galleries, and lighted by flickering gas lamps, the Crescent City's historic homes conjured in tourists' minds vivid pictures of the Old South's greatest city. The pageantry of Mardi Gras and profligacy of Bourbon Street, combined with the strains of jazz and the aroma of simmering Creole food wafting through the languid air, completed the city's romantic but gritty image. African American cultural contributions underlay most aspects of the tourist experience in New Orleans, but in the French Quarter, white promoters cast blacks merely as supporting actors who furnished service and amusement in a tourist-oriented tableau. Blacks cooked famed Creole delicacies in French Quarter restaurants, sold pralines in the French Market, carried flambeaux or threw coconuts in Carnival parades, played jazz music for second-line processions, and drove mule-drawn tour buggies around Jackson Square. Although much of the city's peculiar charm sprang from Afro-Caribbean roots, blacks were seldom beneficiaries of their own contributions. On the eve of World War II, even the recognition of jazz had largely abandoned the art form's originators. Tourism development, as becomes clear in subsequent chapters, rested to a great extent on white exploitation of African Americans.

As was true with shipping, the greatest profits from tourism found their way into rather few hands. When Morrison took office, the leading taxicab company, Toye Brothers, was the official airport shuttle service and held the local franchise for Gray Line Tours, the nation's most recognized tour bus operator. In concert with the city's leading hotels, Toye Brothers' Gray Line and Royal Tours funneled business to a few Bourbon Street night clubs and the dominant tourist-oriented French Quarter restaurants and bars such as Antoine's, Arnaud's, Broussard's, Court of Two Sisters, and Pat O'Brien's. As was true before World War II, in the postwar years New Orleans had only about four thousand first-class rooms in nine hotels. Of these, four hotels—the Roosevelt, the St. Charles, the Monteleone, and the Jung—dominated the local market, with the Roosevelt enjoying the unwritten privilege of first refusal of any major convention being held in the Crescent City. After a stint in the state penitentiary for his unscrupulous dealings with Long, Weiss parlayed his hotel business into de facto control over the city's tourist trade. Heavily influenced by Weiss, the New Orleans Hotel Association discouraged the building of additional hotels. The city's dominant downtown hotels so effectively attracted guests that their owners even refused to let travel agents book rooms for clients because they did not want to pay a commission to agents for rooms they could easily fill on their own. Likewise, they snubbed offers from airlines to promote the city through special tour packages.[34]

With limited accommodations and convention space, it was difficult for New Orleans to expand its tourist trade. The situation became particularly acute during the Sugar Bowl and Carnival season, when many visitors could not find hotel rooms. In a city where hoteliers resisted attracting new competitors, in 1949 the New Orleans Association of Commerce resorted to running an ad in its weekly newsletter asking, "If you haven't, have you a friend with room to rent for [the] Sugar Bowl?"[35] This situation troubled some business and government leaders, especially Mayor Morrison. In 1948 he wrote letters to dozens of airline, railroad, shipping, and oil industry executives explaining the city's dire need for new accommodations and asking them to contribute funds for a new hotel, to no avail.[36]

Six years later a plan surfaced that promised to remedy the city's inadequate accommodations. In 1954 Whitney Realty Company, a local syndicate, approached the mayor about acquiring the Civil District Courts Building in exchange for $750,000 worth of real estate it owned. The company hoped to replace the building with a new French Quarter hotel. The imposing, white marble court building, which had replaced an entire block of late eighteenth- and early nineteenth-century buildings in the middle of the Vieux Carré in the early 1900s, reflected progressive business and civic leaders' disdain for the old district, which they viewed as an obstacle to the natural expansion of the downtown business district. A half century after the court building's construction, city leaders remained at best ambivalent toward the French Quarter. When plans surfaced to build a new court building elsewhere, the municipal government hoped to redevelop the property once more. While some citizens proposed that the building be turned into a new opera house to replace the beloved French Opera House, which had burned down in 1919, the Whitney Realty syndicate's desire to replace it with a hotel caught the city's attention. James N. Harsh, who headed the syndicate, told the mayor that the hotel would help rectify the city's problem of having to turn down about three hundred of the approximately six hundred annual applications to hold a convention in New Orleans each year and would please downtown merchants.[37]

As was true across the United States, in the 1950s downtown merchants and business interests in New Orleans were anxious to see continued development. Even as they reached their zenith, central cities faced a troubling future in competition with burgeoning suburbs.[38] J. Parham Werlein of Philip Werlein, Ltd., the South's largest music store, told city officials that the lack of hotel rooms made it exceedingly difficult "to make reservations for customers and travelling salesmen," adding that a new hotel would bolster the Canal Street retail district. Likewise, B. Manheim Galleries on Royal Street, which billed itself the "Antique Treasure House of the South," welcomed a hotel that would ease its difficulty in obtaining reservations for prospective clients. Sam Friedberg of Friedberg's Men's Wear at 521 Canal Street echoed the sentiments of downtown boosters at midcentury: "Here's for a bigger and better New Orleans with more hotels."[39]

Some of the leading tourism operators in the French Quarter heartily approved of the plan to replace the Civil Courts Building with a hotel, for they understood the likely benefits to their own businesses. Owen P. Brennan, French Quarter businessman, third-generation Irish American, and son of the late restaurateur Owen E. Brennan, told Morrison that the city's hoteliers could only benefit from the construction of a new hotel. He noted what his father had told the mayor in 1950 about the example of Miami Beach, which had several times the number of hotel rooms found in New Orleans. The elder Brennan had reasoned that "if sand and sun alone can support such accommodations, what could we expect our city's attractions to support once the tourist is properly accommodated[?]"[40] One of the operators of Pat O'Brien's Bar reminded the mayor that increased tourist traffic resulting from a new hotel would enable Pat O'Brien's to pay even more than the average of ten thousand dollars in annual amusement taxes to the city.[41]

To the ears of Mayor Morrison, however, the pleas from shipping interests probably spoke most loudly, for he was a staunch advocate of building up the city's port business. A local representative of the New York–based Holland-America Line complained that not only importers and exporters contemplating using their line but also the company's own executives "who visit us with a view of promoting new business via New Orleans" had trouble securing a place to stay downtown. The Isbrandtsen Venezuelan Line related similar difficulties: "We must not only call every leading hotel in town to secure accommodations but usually find that the final answer is 'no.'" A company official, understanding Morrison's commitment to the port, concluded that the mayor's support of a new hotel "can not but be a continued reflection of the progressiveness of your [Morrison's] endeavours on behalf of a greater New Orleans."[42]

While Morrison wanted a new downtown hotel, it remained low on his mayoral agenda. In any event, Whitney Realty's proposal proved unacceptable. First, its offer of $750,000 fell far short of the $1 million that city hall had determined the court building property was worth. Second, and more critically, the syndicate's offer to swap $750,000 of its own real estate for the court building would have left the city with the burden of trying to get its price for another piece of property, effectively placing it no closer to its goal of building a new facility.[43] Although the hotel scheme foundered, a young attorney from Brooklyn would succeed in bringing to fruition another hotel project in a way that underscored changing local sentiments toward the city's French Quarter, stimulated a boom in hotel construction that continued almost unabated for the next twenty-five years, and foreshadowed a sea change in the city's business community. In the meantime, New Orleans leaders remained uncommitted to expanding the city's tourist trade.

Just as hoteliers were satisfied with the status quo, business leaders were content to spend little to promote the city to tourists, relying on the free publicity from national coverage of Mardi Gras and the Sugar Bowl. The city's business establishment, like Morrison, considered tourism little more than an adjunct to an economy based on waterborne commerce and the harvest and extraction of nearby natural resources such as sugar, cotton, seafood, oil, and natural gas. They continued to believe that the city's location between the Gulf of Mexico and the fertile Mississippi Delta assured New Orleans's future prosperity. Lloyd S. Cobb, president of International House, boasted to the Young Men's Business Club in 1951 that New Orleans was "a village compared to what it will be 30, 40, or 50 years from now. There are many today," he continued, "who will live to see this New Orleans of ours one of the three or four greatest cities of this nation—a city of three to five million or greater population, a mighty emporium foreseen by the founding fathers before 1800 when they spotted this geographical location as one of the greatest on earth."[44] With such a future supposedly at hand, these leaders hardly cared to spend much to promote New Orleans's past.

To be sure, the New Orleans Association of Commerce maintained a convention and visitors bureau. The bureau, however, represented only a tiny fraction of the organization's budget, most of which it directed toward commercial and industrial inducements. The failure to appropriate greater funds for tourism promotion reflected the business establishment's view that the city sold itself. In the early 1940s, the Association of Commerce had concluded that it made little sense to raise funds for advertising tourism because of inexpensive promotional efforts done in collaboration with the Illinois Central Railroad. The presence of so many military personnel in the area, as well as the free news publicity generated by Mardi Gras, which "splendidly advertise[d] the City," only reinforced the association's lack of interest in tourism promotion. After World War II, the association continued to hold a laissez-faire view of tourism promotion, allocating a paltry $32,000 to its convention and visitors bureau in 1946. The association's weekly *News Bulletin* boasted that Mardi Gras needed little help to attract visitors, enjoying publicity from the five major news reels in the United States. The organization, along with the Dock Board and International House, jointly operated a headquarters for visiting members of the press to encourage this otherwise free promotion.[45]

The bureau's lackadaisical approach toward promoting the city concerned Mayor Morrison, who believed that the association, renamed the Chamber of Commerce of the New Orleans Area by the early 1950s, should use the city's distinctiveness as a hook for economic development. In 1952, the mayor discussed his idea for a new, independent tourist bureau with Owen P. Brennan. Since World War II Brennan had emerged as a leading advocate for expanding the city's tourist trade, which probably explains why Morrison viewed him as a likely ally. Brennan agreed to approach Whitaker F. Riggs Jr., one of the approximately 1,500 men listed in that year's local *Social Register* and husband of Eleanor Riggs, a founding member of the New Orleans Spring Fiesta. Riggs snubbed the idea. Roosevelt Hotel operator Seymour Weiss agreed, arguing that the chamber of commerce was already doing a fine job with a limited budget. Weiss feared that hotel operators might see no need to continue supporting the chamber if a separate tourist agency were created.[46]

Although leading convention hotel owners and the city's prominent business leaders placed little faith in expanding tourism as a boost to their own profits, motel and tourist court owners on the outskirts of the city thought otherwise. Unlike convention hotels, whose peak season ran from October to April, New Orleans's motor courts, situated mostly along the Old Spanish Trail (Airline Highway to the west and Chef Menteur Highway to the east), relied on summer tourists who could not afford to stay downtown. Motel operators charged that the chamber's convention and visitors bureau, which worked closely with the dominant downtown hotels, focused too heavily on conventions and did not do enough to entice leisure travelers. The motel owners wanted to increase the tourist trade to the city but were naturally hesitant about contributing additional funds to the chamber.[47] They were correct to distrust the chamber, whose public relations committee, headed by Ray Samuel, had never bothered to report the findings of its 1956 study of tourism promotion in other cities to the full chamber. The report, dubbed Project X, found that New Orleans spent only a fraction of what many other cities did, and that a number of cities used the taxation of tourists to fund much larger promotion efforts. Only in 1959, when it was leaked to the press, did Project X enter public discourse.[48]

Meanwhile, Mayor Morrison finally persuaded the chamber of commerce to take up public debate on the issue of a new tourist commission. Just days after the chamber's report appeared, Seymour Weiss told fellow chamber members on March 16 that the convention and visitors bureau needed a more substantial budget than the existing $37,600, suggesting that $60,000 would enable the chamber to compete more effectively for conventions. For Weiss, conventions were critical to high hotel occupancy. He contended that discretionary tourists, or leisure travelers, could not fill a single hotel in the city. Morrison, who was present at the meeting, replied that New Orleans needed to join the eight out of eleven cities with populations over 500,000 which operated a separate tourist commission. Thus, while the chamber was willing to expand the tourist trade only if it could exercise control over it, Morrison believed that tourism was capable of generating revenues that could be spread more widely.[49]

Two days later, Morrison convinced the chamber of commerce to hold a special meeting with city officials, the press, and representatives of the hospitality, oil, and shipping industries to debate whether to start a separate tourist commission. After everyone had offered suggestions and observations, Morrison's call for a show of hands revealed that thirty-two of forty-five favored creating an independent tourist commission. Eight preferred forming a tourist commission within the chamber, and only five favored increasing the chamber's budget. The overwhelming support for a new tourist agency led the chamber to support Morrison and set up a planning group to investigate setting up such an organization.[50]

The mayor's appointed Tourism Planning Committee, headed by Harry M. England, the president of the local 7-Up bottling company, spent the next year devising a plan to make New Orleans competitive with other major cities. In a study of twenty-six convention and visitors bureaus, the committee found that ten of the top fifteen were independently operated and that the average budget for all twenty-six was almost $125,000, more than triple that of New Orleans's bureau within the chamber of commerce. The committee recommended establishing an agency with an initial $156,000 budget, which would place New Orleans among the top ten cities in the nation.[51]

In April 1960 the Greater New Orleans Tourist and Convention Commission (GNOTCC) began operations with a $156,000 budget. Glen Douthit, Mayor Morrison's public relations director, became the executive director of the commission in the first year, with Harry England serving as the agency's leader for the remainder of the decade. The composition of the GNOTCC's officers and board of directors reflected the disinterest of most old-line elites in tourism promotion. The power establishment found serving the boards of the port authority, shipping firms, and old-line banks, and planning the activities of elite luncheon clubs and Carnival krewes far more respectable than pandering to tourists. Only three of the forty-two GNOTCC officers and directors, George Dinwiddie, Darwin Fenner, and Richard Freeman, enjoyed inclusion in the *Social Register*. The principals of hotels, restaurants, media companies, railroad and steamship lines, and tourist services—notably, longtime tourism operators Seymour Weiss, Arthur Jung, and George Toye—commanded leadership roles in the new organization. There were also newer leaders associated with neither the old elite nor established tourism moguls.[52]

Throughout the 1960s, the GNOTCC carried out the functions previously handled by the chamber of commerce, albeit with a quadrupled budget. With the promise of new hotels in the first half of the 1960s, the commission's funding enabled it to boost New Orleans's booking of conventions from nineteenth to fourth nationally in only three years. The commission found it much more cost effective to market the city to a list of organizations known to hold annual meetings for hundreds or even thousands of delegates than to spend its money courting individuals and families as prospective vacationers. By the late 1960s, the GNOTCC could sell prospective meeting planners on holding their conventions in the newly opened Rivergate, an exhibition facility operated by the New Orleans Dock Board adjacent to the towering International Trade Mart, which replaced the original mart from the 1940s. Wooing the discretionary leisure traveler remained a low priority in the commission's budget for many more years. Such marketing was limited mostly to one-time articles in newspapers and magazines around the country. While Harry England defended this practice as equaling an additional half-million dollars in the budget, such publicity did not create the sustained presence that direct advertising might have produced.[53]

The GNOTCC's fixation on conventions rather than vacationers reflected the limitations of its initially impressive budget increase. The municipal government granted $25,000 toward the tourist commission's budget in its first year (a number that remained fixed through the 1960s).[54] By the late 1960s, the city's fixed $25,000 subsidy to the agency ranked far behind that of many other municipal governments. Miami Beach, for instance, directly funded $1,750,000 for convention marketing alone, and San Francisco spent $665,000. The city of New Orleans allocated even less than Cleveland, Ohio, and Grand Rapids, Michigan.[55] Although tourism gradually assumed a more prominent position in the city's economic development strategy, through the 1960s it still did not enjoy the degree of support accorded to the port.

For all the attention directed toward augmenting the city's promotion of its convention business in the 1950s and 1960s, a coherent leadership policy that unequivocally privileged tourism over other economic pursuits had yet to emerge. The 1960s proved a tumultuous decade for New Orleans as for the nation itself. Deindustrialization and an accompanying decline in production became evident, but most cities were not yet ready to embrace entertainment and heritage tourism as a replacement for jobs lost in industry and trade. In 1961 the ebullient Chep Morrison left office after four terms as mayor to become a congressman in Washington. His political protégé city councilman Victor H. Schiro won the mayoralty that year. Unlike Morrison, Schiro had no familial ties to the city's power establishment. As a Sicilian American, he faced discrimination from the leading Carnival organizations, which continued to snub most Jews and ethnic whites, not to mention African Americans. As a result, Schiro's tenure as mayor was marked by growing disengagement from the business elite. Worse, Schiro did not maintain the warm relationship with foreign leaders that Morrison had built in the interest of stimulating trade. Under Schiro's watch, New Orleans began to suffer difficulties associated with racial desegregation, white flight, an eroding tax base, laborsaving strategies in port facilities, and the continued perception among outsiders that the city was a better place to visit than to conduct business.

In the 1960s the city's tourist trade continued to expand, but New Orleanians remained just as likely to look toward the elusive promise of industrialization as toward the historic French Quarter. Indeed, something of the zeal for escaping its past which had characterized the city during World War II remained twenty years later. Schiro shared with his constituents the hope that New Orleans would become once again a leading American city. In the early 1960s the National Aeronautics and Space Administration (NASA), working with Martin Marietta, retooled the old Higgins Industries shipbuilding facility in eastern New Orleans for use in building Saturn V rocket boosters for its Apollo lunar program. The NASA contract for the Apollo missions funneled millions of dollars of investment into New Orleans and sent more than ten thousand newcomers to the Crescent City by mid-decade. At the peak of production in 1965, New Orleans boosters produced a promotional book that dubbed the city "The Heart of the Space Crescent," an imaginary arc that spanned the Gulf Coast from Houston to Cape Canaveral, Florida. For a short time local discourse reflected an optimism that, once again, New Orleans's natural advantages were going to enable it to escape its own past and the unfolding urban crisis that troubled Detroit and other production-oriented metropolises.[56]

By the late 1960s, however, it was becoming clear that neither NASA nor any other manufacturing enterprise was going to be an economic panacea for a declining river port. While NASA slashed its local payroll, Crescent City shipping firms also trimmed their sails. Even as Miami and other rival port cities modernized their dockland facilities to meet the growing need for containerized cargo-handling capabilities, New Orleans's maritime community lay inert in the face of internal feuding and larger difficulties it could not control. The completion of the St. Lawrence Seaway in the late 1950s made Chicago a port for oceangoing ships, gradually shrinking New Orleans's share of exports from the Midwest, while the transition from trains to trucks for land transportation to and from ports further undermined New Orleans's grip on shipping. Growing Latin American nationalism, coupled with the rise of multinational corporations elsewhere in the United States, also combined to deny New Orleans the raw materials and capitalization crucial to the city's plans for a manufacturing boom. By 1967 the Vaccaro family's Standard Fruit Company, one of the nation's leading banana importers, was in the midst of a merger with the Honolulu-based multinational Castle and Cooke, which announced its plans to move its banana unloading operation to Gulfport, Mississippi. As control passed from local hands, Mayor Schiro and Governor John J. McKeithen Jr. chastised the Dock Board for making no effort to inform them so that they might have interceded on New Orleans's behalf. In less than a decade, the rest of the city's banana trade ceased when the United Fruit Company also pulled up stakes for Gulfport. Even New Orleans–based Mississippi Shipping, by that time renamed Delta Steamship Line, fell prey to a corporate takeover by a Dallas-based corporation that in turn sold out to Memphis-based Holiday Inns of America, which one New Orleans company official complained "didn't give a damn about New Orleans or trade or shipping." New Orleans's reliance on shipping meant that tens of thousands of workers, including many African Americans, would lose their jobs in the 1960s and 1970s, leaving a void that, seemingly, only tourism could fill in short order.[57]

Reflecting on the situation a few years later, one journalist likened New Orleans to Scarlett O'Hara in Margaret Mitchell's *Gone With The Wind*—"too poor to paint and too proud to whitewash" and watching helplessly as "her shipping commerce sails off to Houston where the oil barons already are entrenched."[58] A century after the Civil War, New Orleanians might not be able to envision a bright future, but they still could find solace in a storied past. It was this tendency to reflect on an imagined golden age, coupled with New Orleans's difficulty in capturing Sunbelt growth and prosperity in the postwar years, that primed the Crescent City for a long ascent of local and outside interest in its culture. During World War II it had seemed that a new breed of leaders in New Orleans might wrest the city from dwelling in its own past, and yet in the years that followed the Crescent City did not forsake but rather embraced its heritage.

CHAPTER 2

PRESERVATION AND PROFIT IN THE FRENCH QUARTER

> In the mind of the preservationist, there is a sign on every French Quarter building: Do Not Touch.
>
> Orleanians will not be skyscrapered, monorailed or rocketed into the twenty-first century while there's still some good living left in the twentieth.
>
> — CHARLES SUHOR (1970)

"New Orleanians have not saved the French Quarter . . . It's the out-of-towners who did it." At least that was how Mary Morrison remembered it. In 1939 she and her husband Jacob, an attorney and half-brother of future New Orleans mayor Chep Morrison, moved from Mississippi to a nineteenth-century cottage on Governor Nicholls Street. The Morrisons, along with other "expatriates of the United States," found in the French Quarter a quaint community with affordable, charming houses that evoked the romantic images of French Creole families popularized by George Washington Cable, Grace King, Lyle Saxon, and other southern writers. "Everyone down here was from somewhere else," she recalled. She remembered a colony of Chinese restaurateurs and laundry operators on Bourbon Street, many Italian immigrants, and residents from around the country. "None of us had any money, we were Depression people. You could buy any property in the French Quarter back then for about $4,000." Like Paris's Montmartre and New York's Greenwich Village, the French Quarter's exotic mystique and low cost of living attracted a Bohemian element of artists, writers, and other sojourners who stood on the cusp of neighborhood transformation.[1] Despite the initial wave of preservationists who joined them in the 1920s and 1930s, however, the French Quarter remained a blot on the city in the eyes of many New Orleanians.

The Morrisons and the few preservation-minded French Quarter pioneers they joined were at odds with the broader public view of the old district into the 1940s and even 1950s, a time when most civic leaders still zealously eyed developments that might return New Orleans to the forefront of American cities. Despite the colorful history and architectural treasures of the Vieux Carré, as late as 1952 only about two dozen of the approximately fifteen hundred householders listed in the city's *Social Register* resided in the old French section. Some civic leaders wished, privately and even publicly, that the French Quarter might be consumed by fire or leveled to build new structures. Preservationist Lou Wylie, who had served as publicity hostess for Pan American Airways at International House, later recalled that at a party for Mayor Chep Morrison's first inauguration in 1946, she heard downtown merchant Leon Godchaux, bottler William Zetzmann, and Louisiana governor Sam Houston Jones remark that "the Vieux Carre needed a good fire so the business section wouldn't have to grow out Canal Street." Even Mary Morrison's brother-in-law, once he became mayor, confided to a visiting journalist that he would gladly trade "all of the glamour in the French Quarter for a few blocks of really modern apartments."[2] For many longtime New Orleans business and civic leaders, preservation seemed antithetical to the progress they sought.

The French Quarter of the 1940s merely marked time. Preservationists renovated some buildings as others crumbled or even toppled into the narrow streets below. Reflective of the transitory state of the Vieux Carré, whose warehouses, breweries, hotels, and other commercial buildings punctuated the mosaic of Mediterranean rooflines, four French Quarter lumber companies and wrecking yards serviced the gradual demolition of structures old enough to have greeted General Benjamin Butler's Union occupiers in the Civil War. Preservation pioneers mined these wrecking yards for period architectural adornments to refurbish their houses. Mary Morrison described the swapping of hardware by "beachcombers" who paced the buckled sidewalks with heads lowered so as not to miss discarded artifacts. While the attention of artists, writers, and civically active socialites contributed to the transformation of the neighborhood from ethnic ghetto to cultural preserve, the arrival of bourgeois residents like the Morrisons ensured that the Vieux Carré would assume a mythical presence in the city's development. The shared experience of architectural salvage and the act of restoring an urban neighborhood to an imagined heyday bonded Mary Morrison and her neighbors together as cultural guardians of the city's past and united them in one common purpose—to resist alternative visions for the French Quarter's future which compromised their own.[3]

Although the French Quarter had attracted outside comment in the popular press as an exotic tourist destination even in the nineteenth century, only much later did it emerge as a major force in redirecting civic attention toward prioritizing the city's tourist image. To be sure, members of Le Petit Salon and the American Architects Association had successfully petitioned Mayor Martin Behrman to shepherd the adoption of an ordinance creating the Vieux Carré Commission

(VCC) in 1925. The state charter given the VCC in 1936, which bolstered its reg-
ulatory powers over the exteriors of French Quarter buildings, and the advent
a year later of the New Orleans Spring Fiesta, the city's answer to the Natchez
Pilgrimage, reinforced the efforts of writers and heritage tourism advocates like
Harnett Kane and Lyle Saxon to call both local and national attention to the romantic French Quarter.[4] Prior to World War II, the French Quarter was already
becoming an important contributor to the city's economy, leading some old-line
leaders to see it as an ideal hook to lure the well-heeled tourist. Despite growing
interest in historic districts, however, the war years stimulated urban boosters to
modernize their cities and made them ambivalent toward the merits of saving
such tarnished relics. As late as the 1940s it remained anything but clear that the
French Quarter would sustain its role as a magnet for history-minded renovators
and nostalgic tourists.

In addition to the pressures of downtown modernization, the wartime influx
encouraged some property owners to exploit the city's ribald, risqué image by
opening adult-oriented nightclubs that threatened the French Quarter's old-world
ambience. As Bourbon Street filled with rowdy nightspots in the 1940s, preservationists began a gradual transition from redeeming the district from further
decay to safeguarding it from those who would exploit its appeal. In the war years
the Quarter became indelibly etched in the American mind not only as a living
museum where one could imbibe—if not relive—an imagined past but also as a
raucous twenty-four-hour entertainment destination where one could escape the
moral strictures of Dallas, Dayton, or Des Moines. If Storyville, especially Basin
Street, epitomized the early twentieth-century libidinous allure of what historian
Alecia Long calls the "Great Southern Babylon,"[5] the French Quarter's Bourbon
Street replaced the infamous red-light district as the focus for an ongoing civic
struggle.

Along with an influx of visitors during and after World War II came new questions about what role the French Quarter should serve in the city, questions that
often placed residential property owners at odds with tourism operators as the
two groups struggled to impose their will on the Vieux Carré. Preservationists and
pleasure seekers shaped the actions of politicians and profiteers and the contours
of public debate over what, in the half-century after the Great Depression, became
the engine of the New Orleans economy, a tourist site that dominated the city
much as steel mills built Pittsburgh and automobile factories drove Detroit. The
transformation of the French Quarter illustrates the limits of the modernization

ethos and the growing influence of cultural tourism as a thinkable alternative path of urban growth. This path in some ways resembled the fortunes of other southern and southwestern cities—Charleston, Savannah, San Antonio, and Santa Fe—whose distinctive cityscapes reinforced and refracted regional historical and cultural patterns, and lay on the margins of the tremendous economic expansion that characterized much of the southern tier of the United States in the century following the Civil War. New Orleans, however, largely as a result of the tourism-oriented preservation of the French Quarter, emerged after World War II as an influential model that other cities ultimately adopted as they grappled with the severe economic and social dislocation wrought by deindustrialization and urban decay in the 1970s and 1980s. Indeed, in predating the national metamorphosis from a manufacturing to a service economy, tourism and the preservation movement in the Vieux Carré offered glimpses not only of one distinctive variant of the antebellum southern urban past but also of the postindustrial American urban landscape.

In the 1940s New Orleans, like Cleveland, Detroit, Los Angeles, and Seattle, swelled with the influx of wartime workers. In addition to being home to growing war factories, New Orleans also lay in the middle of a region flush with military installations. Army bases and naval air stations sprang up across the Deep South and regularly sent thousands of young men on leave to the Crescent City. These wartime sojourners and the transient men and women who hoped to profit from the heightened activity helped transform the Vieux Carré in the minds of New Orleanians from a decaying relict enclave that many believed detracted from the city's modernizing strides to the vibrant heart of a postwar effort to preserve a nineteenth-century urban fabric that could propel a tourism-based economy. Their activities in the French Quarter also contributed to the emerging struggle between preservation and profit in the years that followed. World War II often undermined cities' local distinctiveness as transients wrought physical and social transformations. Although the French Quarter had survived incremental commercial and industrial encroachment and a drift toward an overcrowded immigrant enclave, the wartime boom seemingly heightened preservationists' sense of urgency even as it excited eager tourism operators.

For the duration of the war, the Vieux Carré reflected the presence of nearby military bases and training camps. In Jackson Square, once a colonial French and Spanish plaza and military drill ground, one could see servicemen on leave "lounging around contentedly on the fresh-cut grass."[6] In the surrounding blocks, a number of "gypsy women," reputedly the wives of men engaged in local defense plants, set up fortune-telling operations along Decatur and Chartres Streets, gazing into tourists' futures through crystal balls or reading palms or cards.[7] About 175 soldiers from Camp Shelby in Hattiesburg, Mississippi, visited the French Quarter in late April 1945, according to one newspaper. The USO arranged for a floor-show breakfast, blind dates for hotel dinners, and a walking tour of the Quarter for the guests.[8] Such excursions kept New Orleans hotels and tourist establishments busy despite tire and gasoline rations and the resulting sharp downturn in civilian leisure travel.

The French Quarter's popularity resulted in part from the considerable media coverage it enjoyed during the war. The *Army-Navy Screen Magazine,* a series of twenty-minute film reels shown periodically in military installations in the United States and abroad, featured New Orleans in the spring of 1945.[9] In the Crescent City, Higgins Industries' company magazine featured numerous articles prepared in conjunction with the New Orleans Association of Commerce that focused workers' attention on French Quarter attractions such as the Cabildo and St. Louis Cathedral. The *Old French Quarter News,* the official organ of the Old French Quarter Civic Association, began publishing weekly in 1941 and regularly featured articles calculated to enchant visitors. The paper promoted romantic notions, including assertions that exotic voodoo charms were still widely available throughout the city and that they differed little from those supposedly concocted by the legendary Afro-Creole voodoo priestess, Marie Laveau. The paper also pointed out that one could on certain nights witness voodoo adherents scratching crosses on Laveau's tomb in St. Louis Cemetery No. 1 as they "mumble their petitions and leave again in the darkness." One might also still see the residue of charm powders on the front stoops of Creole cottages in the French Quarter. Such depictions of New Orleans rendered the city a collage of familiar images, all of which invited the visitor to experience a sense of exoticism and timelessness.[10]

Unlike Atlanta, Chattanooga, Richmond, and Vicksburg, where the tourist image usually fixated on the Old South as it related to the Civil War experience, the New Orleans brand of southern mythology tended toward melding antebellum imagery with a dose of foreign flair, resulting in a tourist image that effortlessly melded disparate themes and time periods. The old-line Association of Commerce, which viewed tourism as an important vehicle for enticing new residents and investment to the Crescent City, compared New Orleans to the Old South and Europe as a way of courting more affluent visitors. It attempted to steer wartime visitors to the Spring Fiesta, where "the spirit of the old South" was "brought back to life again," and to the sixty-five-mile "floral trail," which business leaders had promoted for several years. Reminiscent of language widely used during World War I as part of the "See America First" movement, the Association of Commerce placed ads in national magazines. One such ad captured the white leadership class's sense of the French Quarter as a bit of Europe close to home: "You Can't Go Abroad But . . . You Can Come To New Orleans . . . where you will get glimpses of Europe. The atmosphere of old France, old Spain has been preserved in New Orleans." Using this backdrop of foreign allure, French Quarter businesses looked forward to a bonanza even as war ripped apart the real Europe.[11]

Vieux Carré businesses scrambled to capitalize on the presence of so many free spenders. Owen E. Brennan, who later started the popular "Breakfast at Brennan's" tradition at his Royal Street restaurant, bought the Old Absinthe House at 240 Bourbon Street in 1943. The tavern, reputedly the site where General Andrew Jackson and pirate Jean Lafitte plotted against the British in the War of 1812, had, at least since the early 1900s, appeared in the occasional tourist guidebook, but Brennan boosted its popularity by adding wax figures of Jackson and Lafitte.[12] Like restaurants, hotels flourished. By 1944 Anthony Spatafore, manager of the Monteleone Hotel on Royal Street, observed that the majority of the patrons at the hotel's club were men in uniform.[13] Tourist establishments took full advantage of the wartime boom. One visitor complained that the same two-dollar hotel room and thirty-cent breakfast he had enjoyed in 1942 cost him five dollars and seventy-five cents three years later. He added that, despite wartime rationing, the French Quarter's Creole restaurants were "crowded with people more interested in being able to say they ate at Antoine's or Arnaud's than in getting something to eat."[14]

The military presence was perhaps most palpable at night. Nightclub operators explicitly targeted their advertising to attract soldiers and sailors, as well as other tourists. Some built upon the city's reputation as a place where sexuality lurked just beneath the surface. An advertisement for the Fern Ballroom on Iberville Street, practically in sight of the former Storyville red-light district, promised "60 dancing girls as partners." Others enticed young military men with the opportunity to engage in some preliminary war games. A local columnist noted that a coastguardsman and a marine could be found nightly in Tugy's Famous Bar at 201 Bourbon Street taking shots, presumably with darts, at a target of Adolf Hitler's face.[15]

Servicemen passing through New Orleans on their way overseas created memories of a raucous, fun-filled city that did not soon fade. Private Joseph Lasker, who was stationed at Camp Van Dorn, Mississippi, wrote that the Quarter conjured images of Greenwich Village and Maurice Utrillo's paintings of Montmartre. Recalling that New Orleans afforded "the best time I ever had on a pass," Lasker remembered his hotel room as resembling "a burlesque skit" and vividly recounted Lafitte's Blacksmith Shop, a famed tavern, as "a mellow, old, crumbling place, lit by candles, muskets on the wall, bare bricks showing a fire in the old forge, [and] a pianist playing classic French folk tunes and Debussy."[16] Another serviceman noted that the Crescent City was a "gay, brightly lighted, carefree capital of fun—a welcome contrast to the smoke infested . . . munition[s] dump in which I work."[17] James D. Holland of Oakland, California, visiting New Orleans during the Labor Day weekend in 1946, recalled having seen the French Quarter for the first time three years earlier after a long, hot train ride and being so impressed that he vowed to visit again with his wife as soon as his tour of duty ended.[18] These servicemen's impressions of the French Quarter doubtless mirrored those of many other wartime sojourners who, in the postwar years, would plan vacations to New Orleans and in turn contribute to reshaping the city as a tourist fantasyland.

The influx of transients during the war presented a new challenge to preservation-minded Vieux Carré residents. "We had no problems with Bourbon Street before the Second World War," Mary Morrison recalled decades later. The war "just about created Bourbon Street as we know it now. . . . There were maybe one or two clubs on Bourbon Street, but they were just incidental." City leaders, she added, tried to make people think the Bourbon Street nightlife strip was a "traditional" part of the French Quarter, but it was no such thing.[19] Jacob Morrison recalled that "during the war bars crowded into every empty building to get in on the high spending and easy money."[20] Bourbon Street emerged during World War II as a new menace to those who, like the Morrisons, had come to live the past in weathered, iron-laced cottages and townhouses arrayed around lush courtyards of patterned brick and verdant foliage. Unlike the waves of immigrants, drifters, and Bohemians who had washed into the Quarter before them, these preservationists were self-conscious urban pioneers who sought antiquity at a time when upwardly mobile Americans were increasingly flooding into new suburbs in an effort to sate their hunger for a more pastoral lifestyle. In short, the choice of place for primarily aesthetic reasons made the preservationist community very protective of "their" neighborhood and quick to criticize its commercialization and people who in their view could not possibly appreciate the French Quarter the way they did.

To the self-styled cultural guardians who had begun even in the 1920s to colonize the careworn, immigrant-filled Vieux Carré as a relict French Creole enclave, the influx of wartime visitors presented new worries. New Orleans, already the South's most populous city, ballooned with newcomers who soon outnumbered available housing. The United Seamen's Service (USS) converted two hotels, one on St. Charles Avenue and another in the French Quarter, into barracks for merchant seamen. The presence of so many transients in the Vieux Carré made the neighborhood's new bourgeois guardians uneasy that their efforts to resurrect the district and stanch racial and ethnic diversity might fail. When the USS announced its intention to welcome African American seamen in the Senator Hotel at Dauphine and Iberville Streets, the Young Men's Business Club, the VCC, the Vieux Carré Property Owners and Associates (VCPOA), and U.S. congressman F. Edward Hebert protested the decision, prompting the USS to admit only white occupants.[21] The racist undertone of lily-white preservation efforts in the Quarter revealed itself again and again as the neighborhood's new guardians frowned upon the black presence.

The self-appointed cultural stewards of the Vieux Carré also feared that the wartime boom might encourage a rampant spread of night clubs and taverns that might render the historic district undesirable to genteel tourists and heritage-minded residents. In 1945 the VCPOA, formed in 1938 as a preservation watchdog group, called on the city to issue a moratorium on new liquor licenses in the French Quarter for any establishment that failed to obtain the signed consent of at least 70 percent of the property owners within a three-hundred-foot radius of the proposed tavern or club.[22] This action was spearheaded by Elizabeth Werlein, transplanted midwesterner, preservationist, and wife of Canal Street musical instrument purveyor Philip Werlein III, and grew out of her frustration that bar operators seemed uncontrollable. Werlein had moved to New Orleans from Michigan in 1908. Over the ensuing two decades she developed a love for the architecture of the French Quarter and moved into a house on St. Ann Street. Despite her effort, bars and nightclubs spread unchecked in the years that followed, increasing from fourteen to thirty-nine on Bourbon Street alone between 1945 and 1971.[23]

If the Quarter evoked a colorful past, it also emerged by World War II as the heir apparent to Storyville as New Orleans's "Sin City." Bourbon Street nightclubs became "notorious for clipping suckers from the hinterlands," perpetuating a long-standing tradition of criminal exploitation of unsuspecting nightspot patrons. One soldier remarked that in the war years the city attracted "the greatest crop of suckers in history," adding that "every day and every night is like the height of Mardi

Gras as far as the possibilities of extracting money from fools are concerned."[24] The specter of lawlessness and licentious conduct in a carefully tended heritage shrine highlighted the growing fissure between those who sought preservation or profit in the French Quarter.

Elected in 1946, Mayor Chep Morrison roared into office vowing to rid the French Quarter and the city of gambling and other forms of vice, but he was careful to make the distinction that he wanted to clean up, not close up New Orleans. Unfortunately for advocates of French Quarter preservation, Morrison promised a cleanup of the worst excesses of vice on Bourbon Street but otherwise showed little concern for finding a way to reconcile the growing rift that was developing over control of this Sodom of the South. French Quarter preservation and tourism interests, catering to travelers with more refined tastes, squared off against nightclub and taxicab operators serving tourists hunting for sybaritic pleasures.[25]

With the war over and the Morrison administration in office, hordes of visitors poured into the French Quarter to spend their evenings in the growing strip of neon-signed nightclubs. Burlesque clubs and cocktail lounges, staffed mostly by young transients from all corners of the continent, enticed crowds of gawking tourists with a variety of flamboyant acts that shocked the sensibilities of society women who were never too busy planning garden tours and costume parties to tender their disapproval of the scandalous turn the French Quarter had taken. By the late 1940s, Bourbon Street was known for its floor shows. Nightly at the Sho-Bar, Mississippi-born dancer Kitty West, better known as "Evangeline, the Oyster Girl," emerged scantily clad from a giant fluorescent-painted oyster shell to the strains of jazz. Within a few blocks one could see the Cat Girl, a native of upstate New York, the Cupid Doll, the daughter of a poor sharecropper from Winnsboro, Louisiana, and dozens of other exotic acts.[26]

Bourgeois newcomers had replaced the Italian families who gradually abandoned the Quarter by the 1940s and 1950s, and they stood at loggerheads with nightclub operators, who were preponderantly of Italian descent and did not always share preservationists' notion of the Vieux Carré as a fragile historic district. Indeed, Bourbon Street became an adult playground where club owners employed young women from across the nation to tempt patrons with sexually suggestive choreography and spare costumes. These establishments, whose windows sometimes displayed photos of women in various states of undress, often hired "barkers" whose hard-sell tactics made a Coney Island Bowery out of Bourbon Street. The clubs served well-watered drinks with the help of flirtatious barmaids, often running afoul of law enforcers caught between conflicting pressures from those who were either pleased or outraged by the nocturnal spectacle of striptease artists and B-girls.

Mayor Morrison wanted to clean up New Orleans's image as a wide-open city where gamblers, prostitutes, and racketeers had operated in the French Quarter with impunity under his political predecessors; yet he did not wish to quash racy nightlife because he understood the necessity of maintaining an atmosphere that outsiders found alluring. In response to growing public outrage, however, particularly among French Quarter residents, the mayor could not ignore vice in the neighborhood. In 1948 the mayor confided to an associate that he was enduring "considerable criticism on the spicy shows in the French Quarter and general immorality in that section of the city." As a result, the city passed an ordinance the following year to strengthen bans on lewd and obscene entertainment. The 1940s and 1950s saw sporadic eruptions of enforcement driven by sensational crimes and local press exposés.[27]

If Morrison's 1946 election bid brought a swift and highly visible citywide clampdown on gambling and alleged mob dealings in slot machines and bookmaking operations, within a few years public attention shifted to the immoral image of the French Quarter. With Bourbon Street establishments facing growing competition for the tourist dollar, they strove to offer the most risqué entertainment that law enforcers would tolerate. Indicative of the clash between preservation-minded French Quarter watchdogs and profit-minded nightclub operators were disputes over obscenity and nudity on Bourbon Street. In 1948 the Old Barn Bar at 200 Bourbon Street shocked and repulsed French Quarter residents when it commissioned an artist to paint a mural of bare-breasted women holding a sign proclaiming "Girls, Girls, Girls!!! Anything Can Happen" on the plate-glass window along the street. While the display of titillating photos in nightclub windows was nothing new, this case illustrates particularly well the growing defiance of tourism operators toward Vieux Carré preservationist regulations. When the VCC demanded that the club owner remove the sign, he retorted that it was not a "sign" but rather a work of art. Furthermore, the mural was executed by applying each layer of paint in reverse order from inside the nightclub in a clever, mocking attempt to thwart the VCC's authority, which did not extend to the interior of French Quarter buildings.[28]

As in the struggle to cleanse the street of potentially offensive signs and images, preservation advocates pressured city and state officials to investigate displays of obscene behavior inside Bourbon Street nightclubs, which they believed contributed to the freewheeling atmosphere that encouraged lewd conduct, B-drinking, prostitution, and more serious crimes that could tarnish the quaint atmosphere conducive to preservation and cultural tourism.[29] While the Morrison administration seldom heeded preservationists' calls for decisive and sustained action against nightclubs that proved important to the city's longtime image as a southern Sodom, the city could not ignore open violence. On New Year's Day in 1950 a wealthy tourist from Nashville fell dead in a French Quarter nightclub. The subsequent investigation revealed that a Mickey Finn, or knock-out drops, had killed the man, who was in town for the Sugar Bowl football game.

French Quarter advocates, the local press, and many tourism interests demanded that police address the rampant use of B-girls to exploit and sometimes rob bar and club patrons from out of town, warning that failure to do so would ruin the city's tourist image. At a meeting of the Independent Women's Organization in March 1950, Mary Morrison charged that the Quarter was in the worst shape she had ever seen, claiming that many of its 165 bars were fronts for prostitution and openly practiced various forms of racketeering. One cartoon in the *New Orleans States* depicted the French Quarter as a chess board whose pieces were liquor bottles and jars labeled with skulls and crossbones, while another showed the outstretched legs of a prostrate tourist beneath the swinging saloon doors of a Bourbon Street tavern. Both implied that lawlessness in the French Quarter could destroy the city's tourism industry.[30]

Following the Mickey Finn incident, Bourbon Street nightclubs became lightning rods in a civic drive against conditions believed to have contributed to the crime. In 1950, after a stint on Broadway, Lilly Christine, the "Cat Girl," returned to Leon Prima's 500 Club on Bourbon Street with a new act called "The Pillow of Love." She appeared on stage in only a G-string and transparent black negligee trimmed in grey mink, carrying several pillows. After tossing some of the pillows to men who sat ringside, Christine rested her head on a large pillow as she sang, "Would you like to put your head upon my pillow?" The Cat Girl's double entendre attracted long lines of eager collegians, servicemen, and conventioneers outside the 500 Club night after night, leading the state Alcoholic Beverage Control (ABC) board to investigate the tavern. After watching Christine's sultry performance, three inspectors concluded that the routine was "positively beyond the bounds of decency," consisting only of "writhing and panting" and "little movement of the feet." The ABC board threatened to close the club if the Cat Girl did not cover herself more and make some effort to dance. Cooperating for a few nights, soon Christine resumed her usual act with impunity, demonstrating that in the Morrison years the image of reform was often more important than substantive action. Though the Mickey Finn controversy prompted a flurry of public debate and threats to Bourbon Street nightspots, in the end the city settled back into old ways, leaving preservationists frustrated and alienated. Even when police arrested the Cat Girl and some thirty other exotic dancers in 1958 as part of the first major nightclub vice raid in eight years, all defendants escaped prosecution, leading VCPOA president Lawrence J. Dumestre to charge that the Morrison administration was not serious about rooting out "illegal activities."[31]

The struggle against questionable forms of entertainment on Bourbon Street climaxed with the newly elected district attorney Jim Garrison's early 1960s war on French Quarter vice. In 1962 Garrison, with strong support from reform-minded uptown New Orleanians and French Quarter preservationists alike, ordered several Bourbon Street clubs padlocked following late-night raids. In one raid, plainclothes agents outwitted a club barker by boarding a city bus at the corner of Canal and Bourbon, ordering the driver to stop in front of the club, and then dashing inside to arrest a B-girl. Although the Garrison raids demonstrated officials' understanding that the French Quarter's image was important to the city's economy, their closure of burlesque houses ultimately produced an unintended result—the spread of tawdrier adult nightspots. In the short term, however, Garrison and city officials could boast of having rid the Vieux Carré of activities unbecoming a first-order tourist destination.[32]

Despite sporadic attempts to clean up the French Quarter to appease affronted preservationists and tourists, the city government was torn between tight enforcement and the imperative of satisfying the devil-may-care attitude of tourists who expected a little naughtiness. In the wake of the Garrison raids, some New Orleanians worried that Bourbon Street might become no different from any other American commercial street. Jerome Conforto, president of the Bourbon Street Association of Nightclubs, even threatened to close all nightclubs during major conventions to "avoid subjection of conventioneers to embarrassment and humiliation at the hands" of the D.A., adding that letting "Mr. Garrison's 'Angels of Light' choose the time to make a spectacle of themselves" would only "advertise New Orleans as an unfit location for future conventions." But the word seemed to spread anyway. The *New York Times* noted that Bourbon Street was becoming "a street where tourists are less likely to get clipped but more likely to get bored." Striptease artists kept their distance from patrons, and some of the street's racier burlesque dens closed and reopened as more subdued establishments. The rollicking Old Opera House at 601 Bourbon Street, where "in 1950 one of the roughest sets of strippers could be found on the runway," became the Ivanhoe Piano Bar, "a Sunday school frolic compared to its predecessor."[33]

The rancor surrounding adult entertainment illustrates the extent to which the Vieux Carré in the postwar years had descended; in the eyes of preservation-minded New Orleanians such immoral depths had been unmatched since the closure of Storyville. Walt Disney, according to an apocryphal tale, once remarked of Bourbon and Royal Streets, "Where else can you find iniquity and antiquity so close together?" Disney's observation bespoke the public image that had attached itself to the French Quarter. Indeed, the close juxtaposition of two streets catering chiefly to opposite genders symbolized the city's gendered tourist attractions by midcentury. Although preservationists, with women leading the way, sought to make the Vieux Carré reflect the values of antique- and curio-shop-lined Royal Street, they found themselves unable to diminish the influence of naughty Bourbon Street.[34]

Bourbon Street epitomized the gendered spaces of tourism that catered to not only soldiers and sailors but also male conventioneers. Historians have often pointed to making urban spaces commodious to women as a necessary prerequisite for the emergence of a mass commercial culture as well as urban tourism in the late nineteenth and early twentieth centuries.[35] Others have called attention to the important role that reform-minded middle- and upper-income women played in carving out urban districts acceptable to respectable women.[36] If Bourbon and Royal Streets managed to create distinct gendered spaces, the commercialized portions of the French Quarter generally resembled a checkerboard of spaces catering primarily to either men or women. The Quarter's preservationist defenders had hoped to extend Royal Street's atmosphere to create a wholesome setting for women and families, one befitting refined public events such as Spring Fiesta. By the 1940s and 1950s it was becoming clear that their efforts ran counter to a resurgence of tourist interest in forms of entertainment that threatened their notions of propriety.[37] They fumed at the thought of young women who had seemingly left their morality behind in their hometowns to cavort barely dressed before eager throngs of depraved outlanders. Mary Morrison found gratification and a sense of community in her interactions with women who shared her love for an imagined Creole past and revulsion toward Bourbon Street.

If portions of the Vieux Carré might be considered male-oriented, they also proved a powerful magnet for women. While Mary Morrison and other preservationists felt responsible for perpetuating the French Quarter's imagined dignified legacy through the control of this tourist space, Suzanne Robbins, like other young women, quit her hometown for the bright neon lights, handsome pay, and noto-riety that few southern places besides the French Quarter could afford. Robbins recalled a sense of personal validation and camaraderie when she spoke about her time as burlesque personalities Wild Cat Frenchie, Jezebel ("The Girl with 1,000 Movements"), and Galatea ("The Statue Brought to Life by Love"): "Every girl had her own act, with music and wardrobe. When we weren't dancing, we were back-stage, beading costumes. . . . People would even ask for our autographs." Robbins and others blamed the city's brief encounter with Garrison for turning an urban space whose exotic acts, if an affront to some, were often sufficiently tasteful to attract well-mannered men and women, into a tawdry strip of establishments such as the Unisex Club, with its "World Famous Love Scenes" by women and female impersonators, and the Ellwest Studio Theatre, with its nineteen screens of twenty-five-cent peep shows. Thus, Garrison's crackdown did not produce a fam-ily-friendly French Quarter; it privileged one vision of tourism over another.[38]

Although some city leaders saw the need to maintain a degree of control over French Quarter nightlife to prevent its worst excesses, they did not always agree that the Vieux Carré should be preserved, especially when preservation might trample upon property owners' rights. Many city and business leaders viewed French Quarter protection as an obstacle to the logical redevelopment of a place that had so many decaying buildings. Nonetheless, preservationists sprang into action whenever Quarter buildings appeared threatened. Prior to the 1950s, when the pressures of commercialization began driving up property values and forcing many owners to turn to tourism-oriented business endeavors, preservationists' main fear was the continued decay of historic buildings. With the French Quarter becoming a noted tourist destination, many property owners hoped they might allow their buildings to decay to an advanced state, seek permission to bring in the wrecking ball, and sell out to a developer. When the cornices of two Royal Street buildings collapsed in April 1948, preservationists inveighed against the deleteri-ous effect of vibrations caused by the rumbling of heavy trucks through the French Quarter.[39] Nevertheless, the VCC, its budget a meager $8,255 in 1950, was virtually powerless to enforce its provisions.[40] Symptomatic of officials' lack of appreciation for the French Quarter, Charles S. Spies, assistant chief building inspector, argued that about 60 percent of French Quarter buildings should be dismantled and their salvageable materials used to build replicas.[41]

Reacting to growing preservationist outcry in the late 1940s and early 1950s as property owners bombarded the VCC with numerous requests to demolish unsound buildings, the commission finally adopted a new policy on March 15, 1955. It promised "to discourage or deny all applications for demolition, unless such demolition can be shown to be part of a work of restoration or rebuilding."[42] Unfortunately, the policy left plenty of latitude for approving the destruction of architectural gems, for its phrasing enabled developers to argue that their planned projects would enhance the Quarter's historic appeal even if it meant replacing genuinely historic structures with modern imitations.

The "demolition by neglect" problem aroused public notice at the same time that business-friendly politicians were whittling away at the edges of the Quarter. In one of his last acts as mayor before the inauguration of Chep Morrison in 1946, Mayor Robert Maestri had secured VCC approval to de-annex from its purview properties between the river and Decatur Street, along North Rampart Street, and in the square bounded by Royal, Chartres, Iberville, and Bienville Streets, in the latter instance to enable an unchecked expansion of the Monteleone, the French Quarter's only large tourist hotel. The move represented the first outright assault on one of the most fundamental provisions of the VCC's 1936 charter.[43] Thereafter, preservation advocates urged the municipal government to revisit the issue in hopes of restoring the original boundaries of the historic district.

Reflecting the ongoing neglect that compromised the French Quarter, a tourist from Wisconsin wrote Mayor Morrison about his impression of the historic section on a visit in 1959: "Here is a great tourist attraction—one that could be exploited the world over . . . and it has become almost a slum in many sections . . . and in others junk shops catering to the tourists. I do hope that someday the people of your community will realize what they have in [sic] their doorstep and do something to preserve it."[44] Although the mayor still looked on the Vieux Carré with considerable ambivalence, it became difficult to ignore the growing importance of the district to the city's economic health, particularly in light of New Orleans's failure to attract major industrial investment in the postwar years.

In fact, the exploitation of profits from tourism was spreading well beyond Bourbon Street by 1959. That year the Central Area Committee of the chamber of commerce released the results of a Chicago consulting firm's study, which concluded that the Quarter boasted the "single largest day-in and day-out concentration of out-of-town visitors" of any U.S. center of urban tourism. The report found that most tourists who traveled to New Orleans visited the French Quarter.[45] The study merely underscored what a growing number of New Orleanians already knew. The French Quarter was becoming a cash cow, a "gold mine," as preservationist and architect Mark Lowrey noted, "with thousands of visitors and natives invading it by day and night, each eager to leave behind some payment for physical or visual experiences."[46] Preservationists learned to use tourism as a basis for their efforts to save endangered Quarter buildings from "demolition by neglect" and deliberate attempts to replace existing historic structures with modern replicas.

In the next decade, as Tulane University, the Bureau of Governmental Research (a local civic organization), and the U.S. Department of Housing and Urban Development released their own studies demonstrating the French Quarter's fragility and singular importance to the city's future, city hall began to evince a greater willingness at least to pay lip service to Quarter preservation. While Mayor Morrison had ignored calls for the restoration of the French Quarter's old boundaries in the 1950s, his successor Victor Schiro raised preservationists' hopes. Shortly after taking office in 1961, he wrote preservationist and author Harnett Kane, "I regard the threat of suit and the petition of the City Council by the Louisiana Council for the Vieux Carré to remove the controversial 1946 Vieux Carré exemption ordinance as friendly acts in the best interests of the city."[47]

Preservationists, however, soon began to question the mayor's commitment to boundary restoration. William J. Long, by that time editor of the *Vieux Carré Courier*, a recently formed, preservation-oriented weekly, told Schiro that it was inexcusable to allow the demolition of two structurally deficient 1790 buildings on Royal Street adjacent to the Monteleone Hotel to make way for the hotel's extension of its Queen Anne Room: "While there will be arches and iron work on the proposed substitute buildings, they will be dishonest replicas, not honest antiques." He added that it was only natural that such old buildings were in bad condition and charged that the owner "has let his property go, milked it, and now when penalty [of citation for demolition by neglect] is imminent he asks for permission to demolish, and the Commission swallows his snow job and agrees to grant a permit. How," he demanded, "can the Commission tell an ordinary property owner to build this way or that and let the owner of a rare antique destroy a monument of such value . . . ?" Long threatened to withhold future political support from the mayor in the *Courier* and warned that his inaction would "denude the Quarter and the city of the reason for tourist attraction."[48] In 1963 Long and two other French Quarter advocates, Lawrence J. Dumestre and Evelyn Gladney Witherspoon, filed suit against the VCC, Mayor Schiro, and other public officials and called on the city to nullify the boundary ordinance. A civil district court judge found the 1946 ordinance unconstitutional and, despite an appeal by the city under pressure from the Monteleone, Jackson Brewery, and other affected business interests, the Louisiana Supreme Court upheld the restoration of the French Quarter's original boundaries in 1964.[49] The struggle against the erosion of the neighborhood's 1936 boundaries suggests the degree to which the Vieux Carré was a sharply contested historic district by the 1960s. In contrast, in 1966 the Historic Charleston Foundation successfully tripled the area of the Old and Historic Charleston District, which had been written into a 1931 ordinance.[50]

Even as the Monteleone struggled to remain exempt from architectural oversight, the sudden development of new hotels and inns, either within or in place of dozens of historic structures, emerged after the late 1950s as an issue that often pitted preservationists against tourism interests. As activists protested urban renewal projects to replace historic buildings in New York's West Village and Philadelphia's Society Hill, preservationists in New Orleans sought to limit private-sector efforts to build hotels that mimicked the distinctive architecture tourists expected in the French Quarter.[51]

Jefferson Parish developer Vernon Dupepe opened the pink pastel Provincial Motel in a dressed-up French Quarter ice warehouse in 1959, but it was not until one year later that the Royal Orleans became the first major hotel built in the Quarter since the Monteleones opened their hostelry on Royal Street in 1907. In the intervening years, demand for first-class downtown hotels had leveled off as a result of the Great Depression, World War II, and the growing popularity of small tourist courts on the federal highways that fanned outward into the surrounding swamplands. The resumption and meteoric increase of vacationing after the war, by automobile and commercial airliner, severely taxed the prewar stock of hotel rooms. The opening of the Royal Orleans Hotel in 1960 pointed the way, for nearly a decade, of encroaching hostelries built to resemble the delicate façades of the historic buildings they replaced. Although in a sense the hotel, with its nods to traditional nineteenth-century Quarter designs, set a positive precedent for future Vieux Carré Commission permits for replacement architecture, preservationists rightly worried about its sheer size and its tendency to legitimize the practice of adding cast-iron ornamentation to new structures that replaced "real" Vieux Carré buildings.

The Royal Orleans grew from the determination of cotton broker, civic luminary, and philanthropist Edgar B. Stern Jr. and his wife Edith Rosenwald Stern, heiress to the Sears, Roebuck fortune. According to the hotel's historian John DeMers, the Sterns, who claimed to have derived the idea from Pontchartrain Hotel proprietor E. Lysle Aschaffenburg, envisioned the Royal Orleans as a civic effort to restore the St. Louis Hotel, once a center for social functions and even a slave market before suffering irreparable damage in a 1915 hurricane and being demolished. By the 1950s, a lone praline shop and a lumberyard consumed by a tangle of glossy banana trees occupied the site.[52] Though not of the social establishment, which routinely snubbed Jewish civic and social leaders in its Carnival organizations and sealed them out of the city's *Social Register*, the Sterns nevertheless enjoyed the respect of their mostly Roman Catholic and Episcopalian counterparts. Their wealth and influence were too great to ignore—the Sterns dominated the financing of schools, museums, the symphony orchestra, auditoriums, housing developments, and even the city's first television station, WDSU. Some in the power establishment were even willing to contribute to Stern's effort to rebuild the ill-fated hotel.

The endeavor to build the Royal Orleans epitomized the growing assertiveness of civic leaders outside the circle of the city's traditional social and business elite in the years after World War II. It also helped burst the bubble of Seymour Weiss's dominance in what had for years been a lucrative but closely guarded tourism industry in New Orleans. Rather than challenge Weiss directly, the Stern family turned to a newcomer to the city, Lester E. Kabacoff. The son of Russian Jewish immigrant parents in Brooklyn, Kabacoff left a promising early career in a Wall Street law firm to enter military service during World War II. While stationed in New Orleans in 1942, Kabacoff met and cultivated the family during spirited tennis matches at Longue Vue, the Sterns' in-town estate. He quickly became Edgar Stern's business protégé and, despite his inability to partake of New Orleans's insular elite social activities, ultimately rose to the forefront of the city's next generation of leaders. Taking up Mayor Morrison's unsuccessful bid to attract a national hotel chain to the French Quarter, Kabacoff tried to persuade Hilton, Sheraton, and other leading hotel corporations to underwrite and manage the hotel. When these companies expressed hesitation about financing anything more than an ordinary modern hotel, Edgar Stern decided to put up the necessary money to acquire the property through a holding company he called Royal St. Louis.[53]

In 1954, at Stern's suggestion, Kabacoff approached several of New Orleans's most influential civic leaders. Over a round of golf at the New Orleans Country Club, Darwin S. Fenner, the New Orleans vice president of Merrill, Lynch, Pierce, Fenner, and Smith of New York and a prominent figure in the local Carnival establishment, promised Kabacoff $50,000. Kabacoff then obtained an additional

$100,000 from Richard W. Freeman of the local Coca-Cola Bottling Company, who was chairman of Delta Airlines and among the most civically active of the city's old elite families, and $200,000 from Boston Club member and oil magnate William G. Helis Jr. In all, Kabacoff raised approximately $1.5 million from some of the city's most powerful figures, only $200,000 of which came from Stern. Once it became clear that Kabacoff had raised sufficient capital, the New York–based Hotel Corporation of America agreed to operate the hotel.[54]

The 365-room Royal Orleans was only the most prominent of dozens of architecturally evocative French Quarter hostelries that opened in the decade after 1959. Within ten years, the number of hotel rooms in the Quarter soared from 740, of which nearly 600 were in the expanded Monteleone, to 2,655.[55] While the power brokers who stood behind the Royal Orleans characterized their effort as a civic project and hoped to bring "people of substance and importance" to New Orleans, the hotels that followed clearly did more to reinforce New Orleans as a tourist Mecca rather than enhance it as a national seat of commerce and industry.[56]

Unlike the hotels built primarily with the financial support of local investors and old-line banks such as the Whitney and Hibernia, those constructed in the 1960s reflected a rapid shift toward outside financing that pointed the way to the eventual demise of the old elite's economic clout in the city. Indeed, when local institutions proved unwilling to finance French Quarter development, investors from Texas, Arkansas, Tennessee, and other states often provided capital. Preservationists bristled at the thought that outsiders were chipping away at their control over the direction of French Quarter restoration. For example, unlike the locally directed project to replace the destroyed St. Louis Hotel, when Le Downtowner du Vieux Carré replaced the vacant Bourbon Street lot where the old French Opera House had burned forty-five years earlier, its financing came from outside the city.[57] Even more damning was the effort by Texas developers to redevelop a site dear to the city's self-styled cultural guardians. As one preservationist lamented, "At the rate things are going and being taken over by people from Texas we will soon have to change the slogan—New Orleans: America's Most Interesting City, to 'New Orleans: America's Most Texasized City.'"[58]

Like the Royal Orleans, most of the new hotels in the French Quarter evoked the neighborhood's traditional character through details such as cast-iron galleries and Palladian windows, but the discerning eye could readily distinguish these newer, crisper additions as Disney-like encroachments in the historic neighborhood. Although some preservationists decried these interlopers as architectural frauds, this argument actually reflected deeper concerns about whose neighborhood the French Quarter might be in the years to come. As white preservation advocates made impassioned pleas to save historic Vieux Carré structures, first from "demolition by neglect" and then from replacement by architectural facsimiles, the city's African American community evinced a very different sense of the French Quarter, one that reflected a lack of nostalgia for a place where blacks were welcomed only as service workers and entertainers catering to tourists. The racial contours of the preservation debate were particularly pronounced in the controversy over whether to allow the development of the Bourbon Orleans Hotel in the 1960s, which saw blacks favoring redevelopment rather than preservation.

Developers Wilson Abraham, a Baton Rouge–based builder, and Sam Recile, son of a Louisiana truck farmer, fixed their attention on the poorly maintained Convent of the Holy Family at the corner of Bourbon and Orleans Streets. Since the 1890s the convent sisters had operated St. Mary's Academy for black children in the building. Unlike the Royal Orleans, which drew little criticism because the VCC had provided for the restoration of an important historic site rather than allowing a nonconforming modern structure on an empty plot of land, the Bourbon Orleans ignited a firestorm of antipathy between preservationists and developers.[59] Preservationists felt a sense of ownership of the district because they had found a decaying village and lavished their attention and resources on it. Now they watched as tourism, which they had warily encouraged as a bulwark against the expansion of downtown New Orleans into the Quarter, seemed to portend that very transformation, albeit one wrapped in a veneer of iron lace and gas lamps.

For many whites, the importance of the convent centered on the Orleans Ballroom, widely believed to have been used prior to the opening of the convent as a rendezvous where white planters, brokers, and merchants chose Afro-Creole, or light-skinned, women as mistresses in a social practice known as *plaçage*.[60] They naturally recoiled at Recile and Abraham's idea of demolishing the convent for a hotel and using the Orleans Ballroom (also known as the "Quadroon Ballroom") as a wax museum to house recreated scenes from the city's past. Ironically, the most vocal and active spokesperson for opponents of the hotel was a woman who, unlike her preservationist friends who lived in the Quarter, was a high-born New Orleans native with close ties to a plantation past and an unlikely affection for an arcane social institution that encouraged male infidelity and interracial sexuality.

Martha Gilmore Robinson, who counted among her ancestors a West Baton Rouge Parish sugar planter, grew up in the silk-stocking Uptown section and was educated at the city's prestigious Academy of the Sacred Heart and Sophie New-comb College.[61] Although married to Robert Gibson Robinson, an old-line New Orleanian whose pine and mahogany lumber trade marked him as supporting economic expansion, she demonstrated an unusual attachment to New Orleans's history and culture as she understood them. Martha Robinson inherited the tru-isms common to wealthy southerners who cherished the memory of antebellum times. Robinson grew up with the notion that New Orleans had been a vibrant, cultured city of gentleman planters and southern belles who lived in harmony with their contented slaves until the onus of Reconstruction wrecked their way of life and that of the old Creole families who had lovingly maintained the Vieux Carré. Even though she was not a descendant of the Creoles, young Martha de-veloped a love for the romance of the imagined Creole past and a disdain for the district's subsequent transformation into an immigrant slum. She later recalled that even in the venerable Jackson Square apartment blocks erected in 1850 by the Baroness de Pontalba of France, Italian immigrants often "moved in four families to one apartment, strung their washing along lines on the porches and even took pigs and chickens up and kept them on the balconies." Such people, she believed, could not possibly comprehend the French Quarter's storied past.[62]

The small but increasingly vocal segment of New Orleans women who spear-headed many of the city's preservationist causes in the middle years of the twen-tieth century clearly sought to shape public memory and heritage tourism by imposing a high-born white order on the Vieux Carré. Reflecting efforts since the 1920s to make the French Quarter a heritage tourism destination, Robinson and other preservationist women in New Orleans argued that the proposed hotel would ruin an important Old South attraction. Robinson explained that the Qua-droon Ballroom was once "the scene of some of the most glorious social events in the history of the city."[63] The local chapter of the Louisiana Colonials, situated in the French Quarter, adopted a resolution in January 1963 that, as part of its ongo-ing commitment to "aid and assist in the preservation of historical buildings," it condemned the municipal rezoning of the convent necessary for the construction of the hotel.[64] The Christian Woman's Exchange, a French Quarter–based organi-zation founded in the Progressive era to assist disadvantaged young women, also assured Robinson of its opposition to the hotel plans.[65] Robinson's sister, Edith Gilmore Huguley, a preservationist in Atlanta, wrote Mayor Schiro a letter that underscored the prominent white women's vision for the French Quarter: "The beauty and integrity of the old," she argued, "should be preserved and protected in the cause of tradition."[66]

Preservationists hoped to maintain their position as an effective counterweight to the influence of Bourbon Street, which was in the 1960s slouching toward tawdrier forms of adult entertainment. Martha Robinson wrote chamber of commerce president James J. Coleman and city planning commission chairman August Perez Jr., imploring them to maintain the residential use of French Quarter buildings. She argued that perhaps the convent could be converted to luxury apartments for winter sojourners rather than a regular hotel. In doing so, she noted, New Orleans might "cater to the better class of tourists."[67]

At the height of the civil rights struggle, many African Americans viewed the Holy Family convent as a bitter reminder of white domination. They felt little connection to a white conception of the French Quarter's history, for they had never felt particularly welcome in a district that exploited their labor and culture for white consumption. Many felt less antipathy toward the developers, who would at least provide more tourism jobs. An editorial in New Orleans's leading black newspaper, *Louisiana Weekly*, urged that "Negroes . . . should view this matter from an unsentimental businesslike angle. . . . For when the issue is bared in the light of a cold and barren logic, the property in question has very little honorable heritage for Negroes." The editorial observed that the preservationists on a crusade to save the Orleans Ballroom were "holding fast to the monuments of the long-dead antebellum southern traditions." In fact, the editorial continued, the balls themselves were "nothing more than accepted supermarkets of vice in which well-to-do but lecherous white men could . . . make contact with their future concubines. . . ." Agreeing with attorney Ivor A. Trapolin's contention that the Holy Family sisters saw the building as "a part of our history for which we cannot be justly proud," the editorial recommended that the convent be demolished without further discussion.[68]

Amid the public debate over the convent's future, the New Orleans city council took up the matter of rezoning the property. Vieux Carré Commission chairman William I. Ricciuti, reflecting the sentiments of developers who dressed up modern buildings to avert denial of construction permits, defended the introduction of hotels by characterizing the new development as a positive response to a century of decay between 1830 and 1930. He argued that a "living community can't become just a museum. We must recognize that the Quarter can progress normally without turning into glass and steel."[69] Nevertheless, the commission ultimately recommended against approving the hotel. Accordingly, the city council voted six to one to retain the existing zoning of the convent on March 14, 1963. Martha Robinson expressed her relief that the council had finally heeded the VCC's recommendations and acted judiciously toward the French Quarter. "When Chep [Morrison] controlled the [City] Council," she noted, "you only had to see him. . . . Now, we have an independent Council."[70]

The developers now proposed building a French Quarter–style "apartment hotel" around an interior courtyard and swimming pool. The VCC approved the latest plan after Abraham promised to restore the Orleans Ballroom as the hotel's centerpiece. Mary Morrison, who by that time had assumed leadership of the VCPOA, noted that an apartment hotel, under existing law, could have two thousand guest rooms and only two apartment units and still be considered an apartment hotel, but she felt reassured when city councilman Joseph DiRosa proposed tightening the definition of apartment hotels.[71]

In 1966, with the apartment hotel nearing completion, city councilman Daniel Kelly, who had cast the lone dissenting vote in the 1963 decision against rezoning, succeeded in arranging a new zoning hearing, at which the developers' attorney argued to the council that the property should never have been zoned residential given its history as an educational institution. While he failed to acknowledge the distinction between a building used as a school and one that would house hundreds of tourists, the city council nevertheless reversed its 1963 decision and approved a full-fledged hotel. Thus, the Bourbon Orleans swallowed another entire square in the historic French Quarter.[72]

The triumph of the hotel developers provoked mixed feelings among preservationists. While they clearly understood that tourism provided an easy justification for their efforts to save antiquity, preservationists lamented that neighborhood restoration had come to include the practice of replacing existing buildings with newer ones that met VCC regulations and tourists' expectations of what the French Quarter should look like. Addressing a meeting of the local chapter of the Louisiana Colonials in Amite, a small town to the north of Lake Pontchartrain, Robinson told members that "diversity of architecture in the Vieux Carré makes for a lot of its charm. We are not anxious to have it all of one level and one kind."[73]

Some tourists seemed to agree. In fact, even as tourism undermined the residential desirability of the French Quarter, it also added to the ranks of those who sought to shame the city into preserving itself. One St. Louis woman wrote caustically that the hotels' "Miami Beach Renaissance" motifs were little more than a "horrible green fungus that's enveloped at least a third of the French Quarter and destroying the old—not renovating it—tearing it down and building new abortions out of the lovely old handmade bricks and mortar." A resident of Esplanade Avenue averred that he had moved to the Vieux Carré in the late 1950s because he "thought this city believed in preserving its heritage," adding "I am not sure now." Likewise, M. J. Davidson, who moved to Bourbon Street from "the North" in 1953, decried the "sugarcake imitation" of new French Quarter hotels and added that "all the towns up North look alike; they have no personality, no charm, but they do have lots of new motels and hotels." Others, such as one visitor from Memphis, emphasized that the destruction of historic buildings in the Quarter was a loss not just for the city but for all Americans.[74]

Even those who made their living catering to tourists in the French Quarter sometimes expressed similar sentiments as diehard preservationists. Robert Pinson, a black-bearded artist who moved to the Quarter in the mid-1950s with his wife and twelve-year-old stepson, spoke fondly of the aura of his adopted neighborhood, recalling how his stepson had been enthralled with the courtyards and his acquaintances with "writers, painters, soldiers of fortune." Although he spent his time talking with friends over beers in a Quarter dive while he waited for tourists to notice his paintings displayed on the tavern's outside wall, Pinson suggested that the French Quarter's historic charm and social diversity were the true sources of its value as a place to live and work.[75] Clearly, those who viewed the Quarter with an outsider's perspective often were among the most appreciative of its qualities.

Even so, some New Orleans leaders who longed to turn the French Quarter into something shinier looked to California for inspiration. In 1966 Walt Disney, long an admirer of the French Quarter, unveiled New Orleans Square, a three-quarter-scale replica of the Vieux Carré at Disneyland in Anaheim, California. Disney's creation, with its evocative architecture, lush courtyards, and even its own miniature Mississippi River, became one of the park's most popular attractions because it conjured a sense of place among American travelers who had either visited or hoped to visit the real French Quarter. New Orleans Square's Blue Bayou dining room hummed with swampy sound effects and electric fireflies. Disney even staged nightly Mardi Gras parades. To some New Orleanians, the theme-park attraction seemed a bellwether for what the real French Quarter might become. Disney's mockup molded tourists' image of the French Quarter and provided "the most impressive single piece of free tourist promotion the city could ever get." A *Vieux Carré Courier* reporter, disgruntled in the wake of years of shaping the French Quarter to meet tourist expectations, pointed out that "a large number of New Orleans civic and political leaders have visited New Orleans Square and apparently have decided they like it better than the original." A *Chicago Daily News* writer observed that it would be ironic if "the chief preservationist of beautiful New Orleans turns out to be the California film genius who created Donald Duck and Mickey Mouse."[76]

The French Quarter—or perhaps a hybrid of the French Quarter and Disneyland—fired the imaginations of urban planners nationally, influencing restorations of historic markets, rail terminals, warehouses, and factories in an era of urban industrial decline. In turn, recreated historic tourist venues exerted pressure on New Orleans leaders to make sure the Quarter could meet evolving public expectations of a festive, clean, safe, programmed setting where one might connect with the city's distinctive aura by consuming Creole food, listening to traditional jazz, and purchasing evocative souvenirs. Just as tourism interests encouraged the construction of new French Quarter hotels that responded to tourists' expectations of how Vieux Carré buildings should look, the city government sought to make the neighborhood attractive for the same middle-class, largely white suburban clientele that Walt Disney hoped to entice. As older cities across the United States faced the exodus of retailers to sparkling suburban shopping malls and white flight, particularly following the onset of efforts to desegregate public schools, municipal leaders took a variety of actions to try to make downtown districts more inviting.

Clearly, city officials already understood the lucrative possibilities that could result from shaping the French Quarter to please tourists rather than the middle-class newcomers who had colonized the Quarter as a residential preserve over the previous few decades. And yet city hall also recognized the tremendous pressure tourists exerted on the French Quarter. Even as the VCC continued to approve the construction of what William J. Long derided as hotels "of the Neo-Creole, crushed provincial design, by which five stories are built to the height of two or three normal Quarter stories," the VCPOA, the Crescent Council of Civic Associations, and other civic groups urged the city to consider an ordinance to prevent new hotels "posing as part of the antique setting."[77] Even the president of the French Quarter Hotel-Motel Association, doubtless concerned that only so many hotels could make a profit in so small an area, told Mayor Schiro in 1968 that a ban on additional hotels should be instituted to preserve "the Old World atmosphere of the French Quarter."[78] Presaging a flood of municipal legislation that reflected the need to tread gingerly the fine line between profit and preservation, in 1969 the city council passed a ban on any further hotel construction inside VCC boundaries beyond projects already underway.[79] The hotel moratorium added to longstanding efforts to fend off unwanted changes inside the French Quarter a new concern over the impact of what was built immediately outside it, as developers in the 1970s would simply erect skyscraper hotels behind the obligatory restorations of nineteenth-century Canal Street façades.

The public debate over hotel development in the Vieux Carré underscores the success of history-minded locals and tourists in transforming a once-neglected urban district into a heritage shrine that developers found lucrative. The excitement of wartime Bourbon Street may have ensured that ex-GIs would return to fill new hotels in the postwar years, but the preservation movement could claim credit for painstaking efforts to encase those hotels in a shell adorned with iron lace, stucco, and gas lamps. Yet their very success in mandating high standards for hotel construction forced preservationists to refocus on preventing the wholesale redevelopment of the French Quarter with ersatz replicas. Just as they steered public policy toward preservation, women who belonged to ancestral and patriotic organizations or lived in the Quarter, as well as tourists and newcomers, were often among the most vocal opponents of these "sugarcake imitations." For them the French Quarter's authenticity depended on holding the line against modern encroachments, a sentiment seldom shared by African Americans, who found little reason to view the city's past through rose-colored glasses. The Quarter had modernized incrementally without comment for more than a century. However, once it became invested with historical associations that appealed to preservationists, society women, and nostalgic tourists and newcomers, any new construction symbolized the opening salvo in a modernizing offensive. Perhaps nothing demonstrated this aversion to change more palpably than the concurrent struggle against a transportation plan conceived at the behest of the Morrison administration.

The French Quarter's international reputation as a heritage shrine and tourist destination was reinforced in the postwar years by preservationist advocacy, the rise of leisure time, personal incomes, and jet travel, as well as representations of the Quarter in popular culture such as Tennessee Williams's 1947 play *A Streetcar Named Desire* and Elvis Presley's 1950 silver-screen feature *King Creole*. This reputation played an integral role in defeating perhaps the greatest threat to the city's future as a tourist attraction—a proposed riverfront expressway. As political scientist Alexander J. Reichl contends, New Orleans's preoccupation in the 1960s with a controversial plan to construct an elevated freeway along the edge of the Mississippi River in the French Quarter deserves much of the credit for popularizing the preservationist position and making it a useful restraint on progrowth leaders who only belatedly came to view the Quarter as an essential ingredient in the urban economy.[80]

Prior to 1959 it appeared that the Interstate Highway Act, passed three years earlier, would reshape cityscapes nationwide, pleasing downtown interests who believed the most serious problem facing central business districts was inadequate automobile access. That year, however, San Francisco citizens balked when the new double-deck Embarcadero Freeway threatened to hide their view of the picturesque Ferry Terminal along the bay, pointing to a decade-long struggle that the press eventually dubbed the freeway revolt. In city after city, protesters either hampered or forced the abandonment of plans to build interstate highways through downtown areas, sometimes because they jeopardized poor neighborhoods but more often for aesthetic reasons.[81] In New Orleans the revolt bypassed a roadway slicing through a predominantly African American neighborhood and centered on the city's prized French Quarter.

As in other cities, downtown New Orleans merchants stood at the forefront of efforts to stimulate further business by encircling the central city with multi-lane freeways which, they argued, would speed suburbanites' access to downtown while relieving traffic congestion on city streets. With few broad streets and parking spaces, the nineteenth-century fabric of downtown New Orleans was hardly conducive to heavy traffic. In 1958, twelve years after Mayor Morrison had commissioned Robert Moses to sketch a plan for the city, the idea for a riverfront expressway through one side of the French Quarter resurfaced thanks to the recently formed Central Area Committee (CAC) of the city's chamber of commerce.[82] The CAC held that downtown New Orleans's survival depended on the public perception that it was convenient to reach by automobile. Representing powerful downtown business interests, including figures in the Carnival establishment and those outside its ranks, like Jewish merchants, the CAC enjoyed the support of old-guard allies such as the *Times-Picayune,* the New Orleans Dock Board, and New Orleans Public Service, Inc. (the public utility that supplied electricity and gas and ran streetcar and bus lines). With the exception of some elite women like Martha Robinson, New Orleans's power establishment, sequestered in their uptown neighborhoods, felt little affinity toward the French Quarter, which despite its ongoing restoration remained, like Storyville, a place they associated with transients, ne'er-do-wells, illicit activities, and immorality. As a result, they took no discernible stand on behalf of French Quarter preservation.

As in the earlier civic battle over San Francisco's Embarcadero Freeway, the effort to construct an elevated freeway alongside the French Quarter sparked a bitter, protracted public debate whose resolution would dictate the future of tourism in New Orleans. When the CAC unveiled the plan for the new road, which was to connect the Pontchartrain Expressway along the Mississippi River to the proposed Interstate Highway 10 by passing along the riverfront through downtown and the French Quarter, preservationists mounted a determined resistance campaign. The most visible opposition to the expressway arose from VCPOA president William J. Long's *Vieux Carré Courier*. In a 1962 editorial Long dubbed the road a "Chinese Wall" that would cast a dark shadow across historic Jackson Square.[83] Expressway opponents, including Long, contended that the CAC and project planners operated under a veil of secrecy. Although the CAC made a pretense of transparency by forming a Vieux Carré subcommittee, it seldom included its members in planning the project. In 1964 it circulated a report only to those sympathetic to the project and made the details of the report fully public a year thereafter.[84]

Worse, the prospect of an elevated expressway threatened preservationists' hopes for a riverfront public park to afford citizens and visitors a panoramic view of the great crescent of the Mississippi River on one side and, on the other, the geometrical central plaza flanked by the iron-galleried, red-brick Pontalba apartments and backed by the St. Louis Cathedral's slate-wrapped spires. Although in the 1960s most of the city's riverfront remained obscured from view by a solid rampart of steel sheds atop wharves, some preservationists had hoped for an extension of the sightline from Jackson Square to the river since the early postwar years. They had had reason for optimism when the Army Corps of Engineers had dug a sixty-mile ship channel from the Industrial Canal to Lake Borgne in the late 1940s and early 1950s to shorten the river route to the Gulf of Mexico. The city's Dock Board had promised that the new ship channel would prompt the transfer of port facilities away from the riverfront. Despite Martha Robinson's attempt to use her position within the old elite to appeal to the old-guard Dock Board to grant the use of the Dumaine Street Wharf for a public park, the board was not ready to abandon the old wharves for the time being.[85] When the board finally removed the dilapidated wharf in 1963, preservationists' hopes for a riverfront restoration resurfaced, only to face expressway backers who now argued that, after some seven decades without a view of the river, motorists could at last enjoy a bird's-eye view of the churning river and French Quarter rooftops.

Expressway foes invoked economic considerations to support their contention that the road would harm rather than benefit downtown New Orleans. One French Quarter advocate asserted that the city's leading businessmen had never appreciated the importance of the Vieux Carré to the vitality of the central business district. He noted that these leaders believed erroneously that the port sufficiently enriched the city's economy. "How many of the dollars that flow through the port remain in this community," he inquired, "and how many flow right on through to New York and Chicago?" He argued that the downtown district might become "a business graveyard" if not for the French Quarter's favorable tourist image, which he pegged as the sole reason for New Orleans's tourism industry. Harnett Kane concurred that the Quarter "means New Orleans to the outside world." Likewise, Martha Robinson wrote the *Times-Picayune* that it was "shortsighted for the governing powers of our city and our state not to try to resolve this controversy to prevent the harm that is being done to the image of New Orleans as one of the three most interesting cities in the United States."[86]

Indicative of the growing realization that the French Quarter could not be dismissed from public debate, expressway advocates peppered their rhetoric with platitudes about their concern for the protection of the Vieux Carré. The CAC insisted that the riverfront expressway would actually safeguard the French Quarter by rerouting heavy traffic around the periphery of the historic district. Despite evidence that local trips within the neighborhood accounted for most Vieux Carré traffic, Leon Godchaux II, who owned a prominent department store and served as chairman of the CAC, claimed that merchants were "fighting for the life of the French Quarter" and that "if this roadway is not built the Quarter will die."[87]

Expressway boosters even suggested that their road would prove a tourist attraction in its own right by affording a stunning view overlooking the river and the Quarter. George W. Healy Jr., editor of the city's two leading newspapers, told Martha Robinson, "I don't think that St. Louis Basilica looks nearly as well from the levee at Jackson Square as it would from an expressway," to which Robinson responded bitingly that unlike Healy, who was "not a native of New Orleans," "our people have lived and worked in New Orleans and made it what it is." Although Robinson belonged to an elite that generally did not openly oppose the expressway, she preferred to connect herself to the French Quarter's romanticized Creole past, which emboldened her to judge herself justified in speaking for the city's needs.[88] Similarly, Michigan syndicated columnist Russell Kirk decried the "progressive vandalism" of the Quarter in the fall of 1966, arguing, "Cities are places to live in, not speed through." Kirk's warning that in "a time when real urban renewal is so badly required, we are senselessly making our cities uninhabitable by projects like this" never made it onto New Orleanians' breakfast tables, for the pro-expressway *Times-Picayune* withheld his column.[89]

Amid the controversy, Mayor Schiro tried unsuccessfully to give French Quarter advocates a fair chance. While he did not approach the degree of commitment to city-sponsored protourism French Quarter initiatives that most of his successors would show, neither did Schiro share his predecessor Chep Morrison's disdain for the Vieux Carré. In the 1960s the French Quarter, whose preservation had for most of the twentieth century seemed an uphill battle, emerged as a hotly contested space that often set public officials, business leaders, and residents at odds. New Orleans had not yet embraced tourism as its economic development priority. If he did not always side with preservationists in disputes over VCC approval of construction projects, the mayor did evince a willingness to consider alternatives to the expressway route that was producing such rancor. At the first public hearing on the expressway in April 1965, Schiro, sensing the growing opposition to the project, urged further study to determine if an alternate route could be identified. As set forth in its charter, the Vieux Carré Commission had to review any construction within the area bounded by the river, Esplanade Avenue, Rampart Street, and Iberville Street (one block off Canal). Commission vice chairman Thomas C. Nicholls Jr. reminded those attending the hearing that the VCC had gone on record several times as being opposed to a riverfront expressway and favoring ongoing efforts to create an open vista between the cathedral and the river. The mayor's recommendation for another study irked the *Times-Picayune*, which editorialized that there had been "too much conversation and too little action." Two months later, another hastily conducted study funded by the city concluded once again that no alternative was feasible.[90] The following year a furor developed over whether to commission yet another study, leading the *Times-Picayune* to grouse that thirteen studies had all shown conclusively that a riverfront expressway was needed. Although Tulane School of Architecture dean John Lawrence complained that "we have had one study thirteen times," on June 16 the city council, in an eleven-hour meeting, finally voted against a restudy. Lawrence lamented that "New Orleans really has no notion of what it is becoming or what it is trying to be as a city."[91]

Even the highway backers' seemingly dominant position in the debate, however, began to erode. In 1965, Mary Morrison and Mark Lowrey met with Secretary of the Interior Stewart L. Udall and representatives from the National Park Service in hopes of persuading them to name Jackson Square a National Historic Landmark District. Within a few months Udall secured the federal designation for the entire Vieux Carré.[92] Ironically, two federal agencies were now supporting irreconcilable ends—preservation of a historic district on the one hand, and construction of a superhighway through it on the other. Business leaders greeted the news with much dismay, with CAC member Joseph W. Simon charging that the landmark status was a "mere gimmick" contrived expressly to cast the highway in a negative light. Foolishly, the city council voted to refuse the status, oblivious to the fact that the designation was never contingent on municipal acceptance. The city's refusal to accept the honor made national headlines and prompted Martha Robinson to write Louisiana congressional leaders in Washington as well as a number of individuals in whose cities similar landmark districts had been established. In nearly every case, she found that the designation prompted no takeover of the affected areas by the Department of the Interior.[93] Nonetheless, the CAC was right to fear the status, for in 1966 a new federal preservation statute held that, beginning in 1968, the government would delay final action on funding any highways when doing so conflicted with designated historic districts.[94]

Hoping to defuse the controversy over building a federal highway through a federally designated landmark district and win final approval for the expressway, the CAC informed President Johnson's wife "Lady Bird," a staunch supporter of highway beautification, of its concurrent efforts to enhance Canal Street. As part of the publicity stunt, the committee got delegates from a florists' convention to pose for pictures while walking on Canal Street and urging its beautification.[95] Not surprisingly, neither the CAC nor French Quarter preservationists nor the city's leading press flinched as chainsaws and backhoes were meanwhile leveling a stand of century-old live oaks just blocks away along North Claiborne Avenue to construct another elevated expressway to carry I-10 through the heart of the Faubourg Tremé, the symbolic center of the New Orleans African American community. Indeed, white New Orleans stood silent, ensuring that there would be no biracial coalition in the city's freeway revolt and demonstrating the power of white-centered tourism in shaping public discourse.

Although the freeway revolt gradually consumed the efforts of activists in affluent and working-class neighborhoods outside the Vieux Carré, the need to maintain the French Quarter's attractiveness to tourists provided the greatest weapon against the prodevelopment Goliath.[96] Failing to sway the local power structure, preservationists mounted a national campaign that relied on the French Quarter's tourist popularity to try to defeat the riverfront expressway. They hoped to raise indignation among history-minded individuals and organizations throughout the nation who found the Quarter an appealing travel destination. Martha Robinson persuaded friends and acquaintances in Louisiana, including sympathetic business leaders and members of women's historical, ancestral, and patriotic organizations, to write letters to Governor John J. McKeithen Jr. and President and Mrs. Johnson.[97] Among the letters to the governor was that of Bernard Trappey of B. F. Trappey's Sons pepper sauce company in New Iberia. Referring to the French Quarter's image as a historic shrine, Trappey warned that "anything that is done that will destroy this image will prove detrimental to the city as a tourist attraction." A. Wylie McDougall, who lived in the French Quarter and owned McDougall's Travel Service in the Monteleone Hotel, expressed similar concern for the neighborhood's character. She told McKeithen that Canal Street merchants and downtown real estate speculators were simply trying to shore up their own selfish interests in the wake of suburban decentralization.[98]

Robinson cast her net further as well. Through her interest in historic preservation, she had cultivated friends in other cities, whom she now wrote to ask support.[99] She also turned to Mrs. Simons Vanderhorst Waring, who descended from generations of Low-Country South Carolina planters and had fought for historic preservation in Charleston. Waring, who had served as a national officer of the National Society of Colonial Dames, had also elicited a national outcry in response to municipal efforts to lease ground-level space in the French Quarter's Upper Pontalba Building for tourist shops and eateries. Recalling Waring's efforts, Robinson told her that local and state appeals against the expressway had come to naught and pleaded that she use her influence to arouse a similar response among the Colonial Dames.[100]

From across the country and overseas, letters flooded into the Louisiana Council for the Vieux Carré, a preservation society headquartered in Robinson's mansion on palm-lined Audubon Place in uptown New Orleans. Many of these letters expressed fear that the expressway would speed the degradation of the French Quarter as a desirable tourist destination. Sending ten dollars to further the anti-expressway initiative, Elizabeth La Branche of Washington, D.C., whose ancestor built the iron-laced landmark La Branche House on Royal Street, wrote, "My ancestors lived in St. Charles Parish and one of them was responsible for an interesting building that I hope is still on the rue Royale in New Orleans. I have never had the good fortune to visit New Orleans. I confess I had assumed there was no particular hurry."[101]

The VCPOA, the Louisiana Council for the Vieux Carré, and other anti-expressway groups also found a powerful ally in Edgar Stern, whose interest in the French Quarter led him to commission his own study of the expressway plan. When the report, conducted by a Cambridge, Massachusetts, planning firm, found that all previous studies had merely attempted to validate Robert Moses's original plan, Stern took action. Just as he had enlisted Lester Kabacoff to spearhead his push for a new French Quarter hotel in the 1950s, in the next decade Stern threw his support behind two young attorneys, William E. Borah and Richard O. Baumbach Jr., who despite being part of the city's Carnival establishment were deeply disturbed about the expressway's implications for the Vieux Carré. Borah's father was a federal judge and served as Rex (King of Carnival) in 1946, a highly coveted civic honor, while Baumbach's father was director of the New Orleans Dock Board. Prior to Stern's proposition, Borah and Baumbach joined the preservationist campaign against the expressway, forming the organization Help Establish Logical Planning, or HELP, in 1966, which agitated against the project in local newspapers and distributed hundreds of thousands of flyers nationally and in the Vieux Carré. One flyer, entitled "A Connecticut Yankee in King Arthur's Cotton," urged tourists to protest the roadway: "If you don't, . . . [New Orleans] will look like any other town." Returning a favor to the elder Baumbach and sympathetic to an ailing Judge Borah, blueblood real estate broker Clifford Favrot asked CAC head Lou Brown to take the young men into the fold and impress upon them the importance of the riverfront expressway. Borah and Baumbach took advantage of this opening to gather facts damaging to the expressway initiative. The young lawyers determined that the primary goal of the CAC was not easing traffic, as was publicly claimed, but rather increasing property values in the vicinity of properties owned by key figures in the CAC. The men found themselves ostracized by the Carnival power establishment when it became clear that they were lobbying against the freeway.[102]

Ultimately, however, the young investigators concluded that the interests of preservationists and downtown businessmen need not be at odds. They discovered a forgotten study that showed that downtown accounted for a greater proportion of retail sales in metropolitan New Orleans than in any other large American city. The report asserted that one of the principal reasons for the vitality of the downtown area was "the lateness in the development of major expressway networks," precisely the opposite of what downtown leaders claimed. While Borah and Baumbach were unable to impress these findings upon business leaders, they enjoyed the support of Stern and Archbishop Philip Hannan, who as head of the city's Roman Catholic diocese was very influential and was concerned about a plan that could prove damaging to the St. Louis Cathedral.[103]

Even with the outcry of some vocal New Orleanians and people around the nation, the expressway plan proved remarkably resilient, forcing the issue into court, where the French Quarter's image again became a key point of discussion. In 1967 the VCPOA, the Louisiana Landmarks Society, and the Baron and Baroness de Pontalba, descendants of the French woman who built the nation's oldest apartment blocks on either side of Jackson Square more than a century earlier, became plaintiffs in a lawsuit directed against the Louisiana Department of Highways, the city of New Orleans, and Mayor Schiro. The suit charged that they were disregarding the mandate of the VCC to preserve and protect the portion of New Orleans that had become so important aesthetically and economically. The brief filed with the suit lambasted the expressway as a "Berlin Wall" giving people in the French Quarter "a super-modern kaleidoscopic view of a flying carpet . . . of varicolored vehicles by day and glaring headlights by night." The brief argued that if the state and city governments had the power to violate the Quarter's "quaint and distinctive character" by endorsing a freeway, they could hardly expect private property owners with speculative interests in the neighborhood to respect the authority of what would surely be a much weakened VCC.[104]

In 1969, after the case proceeded from civil district court to a federal court in Baton Rouge, the federal government was finally moved to act decisively. Following a meeting of the President's Advisory Council on Historic Preservation to inspect the route of the proposed expressway, the council determined that the road would damage the historic neighborhood and recommended withholding federal support, whereupon the VCC broke ranks with the city council to accept the Quarter's designation as a National Historic Landmark District.[105]

Despite a last-ditch effort by expressway boosters, the weight of public opinion now proved insurmountable. In July 1969 Secretary of Transportation John A. Volpe announced that the project was no longer under consideration.[106] The defeat of the riverfront expressway eased the most immediate threat to the French Quarter's tourism development. Preservationists had been so persuasive in their protourism rhetoric that they unwittingly played into the hands of commercial interests, fueling a feverish pace of new hotel construction in the 1960s and, as it would turn out, an unprecedented degree of municipal direction of tourism-oriented development projects beginning in the 1970s. While the long struggle to define the future of the riverfront produced a broad consensus that the French Quarter was crucial to downtown vitality, differences remained over the shape that development should assume. Public debate shifted from whether the French Quarter should be preserved as an important cultural and tourist icon to whether projects in and around the Vieux Carré were compatible with the public consensus favoring preservation of that icon.

By 1970, the French Quarter had fallen irrevocably under the sway of preservationists, tourism promoters, and commercial interests. No longer was the French Quarter neglected. Indeed, in the wake of the numerous clashes over its future in the 1960s, it had emerged by 1970 as a place of international fame and local preoccupation, a place where façades were lovingly maintained even as hordes of tourists coursed through the Quarter. As one observer noted, "We are faced with the ludicrous possibility of a French Quarter that is crammed with more and more appreciators who have less and less to appreciate. When creative artists can no longer afford to live in the Quarter, the highbrows will be chagrined to discover that they have nothing to look at but the old buildings and each other."[107] Mary Morrison had seen it coming for some time, lamenting several years earlier that perhaps, in its successful bid to persuade New Orleans municipal and business leaders of the value of a well-preserved French Quarter, the VCPOA had "saved the lamb and fatted it for the ultimate slaughter."[108] If preservationists managed by the 1960s to convince tourism interests that safeguarding the French Quarter was profitable, tourism interests realized by the 1960s that protecting the rights of all tourists to see the French Quarter could also bring dividends.

Despite a preservation movement that dated to the 1920s, much of the
French Quarter remained in a state of decay in the 1940s.
Walter Cook Keenan Collection, New Orleans Public Library

Bourbon Street solidified its role as New Orleans's best-known entertainment
strip by the 1950s. Owen Brennan's Old Absinthe House (left) and Vieux
Carré Restaurant (right) became mainstays for tourists in these years.
Louisiana Photograph Collection, New Orleans Public Library

Greater New Orleans Tourist and Convention Commission officials Glen Douthit, Harry M. England, and Charles W. Genella examine a promotional poster. The commission formed in 1960 and became the official mouthpiece of the local tourism industry.
Louisiana Photograph Collection, New Orleans Public Library

The Bourbon Orleans Hotel, which replaced a Catholic school for African Americans, was completed in 1966 following disagreements between white preservationists and blacks over whose history should be enshrined.
Louisiana Photograph Collection, New Orleans Public Library

Le Downtowner du Vieux Carré, a hotel meant to replicate antebellum French Quarter architecture, was among the "sugarcake imitations" that preservation-minded detractors feared would diminish the Quarter's authenticity.
Louisiana Photograph Collection, New Orleans Public Library

The proposed riverfront expressway, part of Robert Moses's blueprint for New Orleans freeways, aroused intense preservationist hostility in the 1960s. To defeat the project, local activists tapped public fears that the French Quarter's tourist appeal might be irreparably harmed.
Special Collections, Earl K. Long Library, University of New Orleans

New Orleans Square, which opened at Disneyland in 1966, recreated the French Quarter at a time when it was undergoing tremendous pressure from tourism-oriented redevelopment.
The Cleveland Press Collection, Cleveland State University Library

In the three decades after World War II, Bourbon Street's adult-oriented nightspots like the Gunga Den overshadowed other businesses.
Louisiana Photograph Collection, New Orleans Public Library

Southland Records' album covers evoked New Orleans's African American culture and rendered it picturesque and accessible for a mostly white audience of jazz enthusiasts and tourists.

GHB Jazz Foundation

Preservation Hall, which grew out of pass-the-hat sessions in the late 1950s, billed itself as a rare place where visitors could hear traditional jazz reportedly unchanged since the halcyon days of the art form.
Louisiana Photograph Collection, New Orleans Public Library

"Big Eye" Louis Nelson DeLisle plays Preservation Hall in the early 1960s.
Grauman Marks Collection, New Orleans Public Library

Crowds await the arrival of the Rex parade in downtown
New Orleans on Mardi Gras Day in 1946.
Alexander Allison Collection, New Orleans Public Library

Workers put finishing touches on floats in a Carnival krewe den. Mardi Gras
became increasingly tourist-oriented as float builders like Blaine Kern
supported the movement toward more crowd-pleasing parades.
Louisiana Photograph Collection, New Orleans Public Library

Mayor Moon Landrieu and his wife Verna walk to the dedication ceremony in
1975 for the redesigned French Market, which became a festival
marketplace catering to tourists.
Municipal Government Collection, New Orleans Public Library

By the 1970s, streets like Pirate's Alley, near Jackson Square, became spaces where artists, shoeshine boys, and other entrepreneurs vied for their share of the tourist dollars in a district once dismissed by most New Orleans civic leaders.

Louisiana Photograph Collection, New Orleans Public Library

The risqué image of Bourbon Street enhances New Orleans's reputation
as a round-the-clock entertainment district.
Photo by the author

Jazz clarinetist Doreen Ketchens entertains tourists on Royal Street as a tour
carriage passes. Since the 1970s, city officials have encouraged and regulated street
performers as the French Quarter transformed into a major tourist destination.
Photo by the author

CHAPTER 3

INTO THE BIG LEAGUE

> Although a Deep South City, we like to think that our horizons are broader, our
> tolerance greater, our hospitality more spontaneous than elsewhere. We are, we
> believe, a completely cosmopolitan city. We have no continuing history whatso-
> ever of serious disturbances between our white and Negro peoples.
>
> —MAYOR VICTOR H. SCHIRO (1965)

On the mild winter night of January 10, 1965, the Sugar Bowl stood empty, awaiting a torrent of fans for the American Football League (AFL) All-Star game, an exhibition that forty-year-old businessman David F. Dixon had lured to New Orleans
to benefit the Police Foundation. More importantly, the city sought to reinforce its
claim to the National Football League (NFL) that it had eliminated all racial barriers in its bid to land an expansion team. Dixon was among the new generation
of leaders who sought to expand the city's attractions. Across town, Clem Daniels,
an exceptional black player for the Oakland Raiders, stood with some teammates
outside Seymour Weiss's Roosevelt Hotel, waiting for a taxi to the French Quarter.
Although six cabs had lined up along University Place, which runs in front of the
hotel, the drivers had all left their cars to avoid serving the black players. After
much frustration, Daniels recalled, "Finally, we stood in the middle of the street
and a cab stopped rather than run us down."[1]

On Bourbon Street, Daniels and his friends were mocked, insulted, and turned
away by bouncers except at Al Hirt's and Pete Fountain's jazz clubs, which extended a warm welcome to the All-Star players. Unlike the seedy striptease clubs
that could rely on the steady patronage of locals, seamen, and men seeking escape
from the sexually repressed Alabama, Mississippi, and Louisiana hinterlands, Hirt
and Fountain sought to provide first-rate entertainment for more discriminating
tourists. The African American players had an even more difficult time hailing a
taxicab back to their hotel. Only one driver stopped, and he averred that he could
not risk arrest for transporting the men several blocks through the heart of the
city. The players ended up asking directions and walking back to the hotel. After
hearing the complaints of the twenty-one affected black athletes, the AFL shifted
the game to Houston.[2]

For decades the Crescent City had painstakingly tended its image as a genteel, cosmopolitan city while clinging tenaciously to segregation. For many years white New Orleanians could afford to engage in racial proscription without worrying about the loss of tourist dollars. With its balmy climate, rich cultural heritage, celebrated hedonism, and flamboyant French Quarter, New Orleans could bank on a steady influx of tourists with only scant inducement. Because its tourist trade continued to cater primarily to white southerners, New Orleans easily clung to old ways. After the mid-1950s, when many white northerners began to question Jim Crow, it gradually became essential for cities to drop such practices in order to maintain a progressive image. Conventions and professional sports teams, increasingly coveted by cities seeking to enter the "big league," could go wherever their leaders wished, and by the 1960s an increasing number of these leaders blacklisted cities that failed to integrate racially.

Black activism and federal legislation ultimately delivered U.S. cities from Jim Crow. Historian Lizabeth Cohen has demonstrated that the ideology of what she dubs the "Consumers' Republic" increasingly "bore the burden of making postwar America more egalitarian and democratic," so much so that by the 1960s even southern whites "were getting a clear message that the consumer marketplace could not easily be preserved as segregated space."[3] In New Orleans, the desire to develop the tourist and convention trade and host professional football played a similarly important role. Once it became clear that segregation was hurting the city's national image, white political and business leaders became more receptive to African American civil rights activists' demands for equal access to places of consumption.[4]

Unfortunately, efforts to ameliorate racial proscription revealed the reactionary tone of local political discourse, rooting white New Orleans leaders more firmly in the soil of southern racial values than in that of the progressive changes. Concern over national image and the black struggle for equal access to public spaces, schools, and jobs, however, gradually forced Crescent City decision makers to rethink their allegiance to discrimination.[5] Just as French Quarter preservationists learned to make economic arguments about the fragility of the tourist trade to defeat the riverfront expressway, civil rights activists employed a rhetoric of tourism to defeat segregation in public accommodations.

Whereas African Americans had comprised a majority in early-nineteenth-century New Orleans, their numbers diminished dramatically until World War II, which brought a surge in the city's black population. This change mirrored a national movement of African Americans from rural areas to urban centers. The pull of bustling war industries and the centripetal effects of agricultural mechanization in the rural Deep South raised the Crescent City's black population from less than one-third of the total in 1940 to nearly half by 1970. As had been the case for more than two centuries, New Orleans continued to have a three-tier racial order that resembled Kingston or Port-au-Prince more than Atlanta or Birmingham. Tracing its heritage to French and Spanish provisions for manumission, interracial sexual relations in slave society, and waves of immigration in the wake of the revolution in Saint-Domingue, the city's light-skinned Afro-Creoles rose to positions of social and economic prominence in the black community and occupied a social middle ground that blurred the color line.[6]

While in the antebellum years white society worried about the hopeful message that successful free people of color sent to the slave population, by the twentieth century New Orleans's white ruling class had become content to exploit the color rift within the black community because it often hindered the potential for racial solidarity against Jim Crow. After all, Jim Crow laws only saw black and white, not subtle shades in between. Nevertheless, Afro-Creoles and other blacks managed to challenge segregation. The rising black population also hastened the day of reckoning for the city's white elite, which had long controlled city hall. As the black population approached fifty percent in the wake of 1960s federal civil rights legislation, New Orleans's African Americans were well positioned to exercise the right of the ballot. The city's politicians, in turn, had to grapple with black voting power and could no longer deny demands for legal equality.

Prior to the 1960s, however, New Orleans's white leaders faced no political or economic imperatives for racial change, contenting themselves with reaping the benefits that arose naturally from the city's being both a well-situated seaport and a rich repository of history, food, music, and illicit pleasures. Jim Crow customs—mostly unwritten but widely understood—and the city's longstanding effort to attract white visitors dictated strict racial separation in tourist facilities and attractions. Mayor Morrison explained the city's segregated public accommodations to a prospective tourist in 1948: "These laws are an outgrowth of unfortunate experiences during and after the Reconstruction Era, and are deemed advisable by most Southerners in order to prevent conditions leading to racial intermarriage." Tourism operators could seemingly afford to turn away blacks because for many years promoters filled New Orleans's hotels and famous restaurants with white tourists and conventioneers with only minimal marketing efforts.[7]

Especially before southern cities began to open up racially and to a lesser extent for many years thereafter, black tourists experienced New Orleans very differently from whites. Prior to the 1960s many African Americans found it too expensive, unpleasant, and even dangerous to take vacations, particularly in the Deep South. Unless one could afford to take the train, it was necessary to drive through some of the most racially intolerant areas in the United States. One could reach "America's Most Interesting City," which lay amid swamps, bayous, and lakes, only by passing through the Delta or Piney Woods sections of Louisiana and Mississippi, where it was exceedingly difficult to find roadside services catering to blacks but all too easy to find mean-spirited whites. New Orleans jazz musician Danny Barker later remarked that "every stop on the train to Chicago was bad territory and to be avoided." Under such circumstances, most blacks who traveled to New Orleans did so to visit family and friends. The dearth of hotels open to them meant that sojourning African Americans generally stayed with family or friends or in rooming houses.[8]

While whites flocked to the world-famous French Quarter, most blacks either had no interest in visiting an urban space they viewed as a white attraction or did not wish to risk harassment by the New Orleans police. For the local black community, the Vieux Carré was a place where blacks worked as cooks, dishwashers, porters, bellhops, musicians, and domestics—not a place to spend leisure time. The epicenter of black entertainment and leisure lay beyond the periphery of the French Quarter in Faubourg Tremé, where Orleans and North Claiborne Avenues crossed in the city's rough-and-tumble Sixth Ward.[9]

The Crescent City's tourist spaces posed problems even for visiting African dignitaries, whose position barely won them any special dispensations in a city trained to view people as either white or black. In June 1954, just weeks after the U.S. Supreme Court's *Brown v. Board of Education* ruling forced school desegregation, the visit of Ethiopian emperor Haile Selassie and his all-black official delegation to New Orleans presented Mayor Morrison with a delicate situation. Under pressure from trade promoters, the Roosevelt Hotel, which billed itself "The Pride of the South," agreed to lodge Selassie but, as International House official Charles Nutter recalled, Seymour Weiss vowed to "burn all the bedding and the furniture when he leaves." Weiss vehemently refused to allow the black leader and his entourage to enter the hotel's bar, restaurant, or Blue Room supper club. City leaders kept the visitors occupied on a harbor cruise and at dinners and receptions so they would not have time to see the ugly face of the city's racial prejudice. Morrison's public relations director personally sat in the Roosevelt lobby one night until 3:00

A.M. to see whether the Selassie party would attempt to venture into the French Quarter, where they surely would have faced overt discrimination. Municipal leaders operated under extreme pressure, trying to invite leading local black citizens to meet the delegation but not so many that white leaders would be offended. In the end, both blacks and whites were offended. The Morrison administration emerged not with a realization that the city's public accommodations should be open to all but with greater reluctance to invite black luminaries in the future. The time had not yet arrived when concerns over the city's image could facilitate social change or the spatial reconfiguration of black access to New Orleans's tourist offerings.[10]

The controversy over school desegregation and the influx of rural blacks in the postwar years contributed to the hardening of Jim Crow customs in New Orleans, threatening the image of racial permissiveness that set the city apart from other southern metropolises. In the two years following the *Brown* decision, bitter southern politicians defiantly passed draconian statutes that further codified longstanding Jim Crow practices.[11] In a reactionary show of massive resistance to what they deemed federal meddling, Louisiana legislators ratified twenty-three new state constitutional amendments in December 1954. These included measures that made black voter registration more difficult and proscribed civil servants who associated with any organization that advocated racial equity, such as the Urban League or the National Association for the Advancement of Colored People (NAACP). The July 1956 statute, which barred interracial contact in any form of public accommodations, angered African Americans and portended far-reaching, ill consequences for New Orleans, a city with a cosmopolitan, open tourist image to uphold.[12]

The law gave police license to raid bars and clubs that welcomed a mixed clientele. While African Americans usually preferred not to venture into the French Quarter's nightspots, some intrepid white tourists journeyed to black clubs in dilapidated wards beyond the tidy precincts of the Vieux Carré. There they hoped to experience New Orleans entertainment in a less programmed setting. They flocked to the Dew Drop Inn and the Snowflake to catch jazz gigs, or to the Caldonia Club, where drag queens danced on the bar under purple lights.[13] By the latter half of the 1950s they risked arrest for straying across the color line, although the periodic raids in black neighborhoods still left more room for interracial contact than was possible under authorities' watchful eye in the Quarter. In one of the more notorious raids, police bagged Hollywood actor Zachary Scott and his party at the Dew Drop.[14]

The segregationist measure even forbade the longstanding practice of black and white musicians sharing the stage in bars and clubs. When enforcing the law against integrated bands, policemen concentrated on the French Quarter, the urban space most visible to white natives and tourists. In January 1957 they arrested black trumpeter Ernest "Punch" Miller and five other men, black and white, allegedly for disturbing the peace following a performance at a Quarter bar. When they appeared in court, the judge dismissed the case and warned the black jazzmen, "Don't mix your cream with your coffee."[15] African American trumpeter and New Orleans native Louis Armstrong, whose sextet included blacks, whites, and a Hawaiian of Filipino extraction, scorned the 1956 statute and vowed not to perform in his hometown until the law was repealed. The musician, who had boarded a northbound Illinois Central passenger train for a Chicago-based jazz career in 1922, lamented, "They treat me better all over the world than they do in my own hometown—that even includes Mississippi."[16]

More injurious to New Orleans promoters' hopes of expanding the tourist trade was the new state ban on all interracial contact at sporting events. Of particular concern was the Mid-Winter Sports Carnival, whose Sugar Bowl football game ranked among the nation's leading intercollegiate postseason matches and stood behind only Mardi Gras in the number of visitors it attracted to the city. A Georgia politician fired the opening salvo of racial contention surrounding the Sugar Bowl several months before the Louisiana legislature launched its legal barrage. In late 1955 the Mid-Winter Sports Association (MWSA) invited the University of Pittsburgh and Georgia Tech to square off in the New Year's gridiron battle. In the interest of economic gain, the organization prepared to accommodate Pittsburgh's one black player and even allowed the university to sell its share of tickets on a nonsegregated basis. When Georgia governor Marvin Griffin attempted to bar Georgia Tech from participating in the "integrated" game, the University System of Georgia's Board of Regents upheld Tech's Sugar Bowl bid but agreed to bar all future participation by state-supported schools in integrated sporting events.[17]

Conservative Sugar Bowl backers raised no organized outcry against the mixed sports ban until it was essentially too late. After both houses of the Louisiana legislature voted to bar interracial sporting events, however, the MWSA made a frenzied effort to persuade Governor Earl K. Long to veto the bill. Like his brother Huey, Earl relished any opportunity to stick it to the Crescent City. The bowl leaders noted that the stands had always been segregated according to custom and needed no help from the state. They urged Long to give "serious consideration" to the bill's effect on the state economy, but the governor signed the measure.[18] Beset by internal disagreement, the chamber of commerce also failed to provide any unified, official voice of moderation which might have countered the racist maneuvering of Baton Rouge politicians. After affirming his belief in segregation, New Orleans Hotel Association president E. Lysle Aschaffenburg told fellow chamber members that New Orleans should show some respect for how the rest of the nation saw the race issue, if only to salvage the city's tourist economy. Reminding his colleagues that the United States Naval Academy had already cancelled its football game against Tulane, Aschaffenburg urged them to write Governor Long in lieu of an apparently unlikely unified chamber response.[19] In the wake of the statute's passage, the Sugar Bowl allocated a paltry seventy-five seats to African Americans in the 82,000-seat Tulane Stadium.

The MWSA's sluggish response to the quickening of racial proscription in Louisiana reflected the longstanding social and economic conservatism not only of the city's complacent, self-satisfied bluebloods but also of many southern businessmen who, according to historian Carl Abbott, acted as "a rearguard rather than as pioneers."[20] In New Orleans, as elsewhere in the South, Numan Bartley argues, "tradition, respect for old wealth, concern for the style of social life, and an elitist outlook acted as barriers to changes in social and ideological outlook."[21] With the exception of a handful of civic-minded and progressive individuals such as Darwin S. Fenner and Richard W. Freeman, most of the old elite quietly supported the conservation of their own static, privileged position in New Orleans society.

Into the leadership void rushed those New Orleanians who had little stake in integrating their city more thoroughly into the national economy. Such men often belonged to the Citizens' Council of Greater New Orleans, an outspoken branch of the segregationist Jackson, Mississippi–based Citizens' Councils of America, which exerted considerable pressure against racial progress as late as the early 1960s. This umbrella organization had sprung from the original Citizens' Council, formed in 1955 in Sunflower County, Mississippi, as a vehicle of massive resistance to the *Brown* decision. In New Orleans, the Citizens' Council strongholds lay in the city's newer middle-class districts, such as Lakeview and Gentilly, which arose in the mid-twentieth century from the drained swampland abutting Lake Pontchartrain. The Citizens' Council strove to influence municipal government officials, who were torn between maintaining racial customs and opening the city to national influences.[22] While more moderate civic leaders, including middle-class black civil rights leaders and white business leaders outside the power establishment, already understood that New Orleans could not retain a nineteenth-century racial order and still fulfill its aspirations to expand commercial activity and the tourist trade, only gradually did they begin to invoke a protourism, probusiness rhetoric in opposition to the more rabid white supremacy manifested by the Citizens' Council. A series of events in the 1960s slowly galvanized an unlikely coalition of black civil rights leaders, city officials, tourism interests, exceptional members of the old elite, and a rising, restless business class drawn from outside the old Carnival establishment.[23]

On November 14, 1960, as little Ruby Bridges walked to the William Frantz School, one of the two initial New Orleans schools chosen for token integration, angry white women, some holding small children, spewed invectives and hurled rotten eggs. The white crowd, whom Harnett Kane seemingly hoped came from rural Mississippi rather than his beloved New Orleans, shouted, "Two, four, six, eight, we don't want to integrate!" and "Glory, glory, segregation" to the tune of the "Battle Hymn of the Republic." Although New Orleans police arrived by midmorning, they made no concerted effort to disperse the hate-filled mob.[24] The jeering and occasional violence continued day after day.

Amid growing racial unrest, the city's old elite, including its unofficial mouthpiece, the *Times-Picayune,* provided little direction. As corporate attorney, civic leader, and former King of Carnival Harry B. Kelleher later recalled, the uptown New Orleans establishment remained mostly silent as a segregationist governor and legislature in Baton Rouge and a recalcitrant local Citizens' Council dominated white discourse.[25] If the city's old-line leaders avoided engagement with the race issue, Leander Perez, the ruthless political *caudillo* who in effect ruled neighboring Plaquemines and St. Bernard parishes as kingdoms of white supremacy, provided a stark contrast to New Orleans's carefully cultivated image as a permissive, tolerant, fun-loving, European-minded city. While more responsible leaders kept silent, Perez struck fear into a dutiful, prosegregation crowd, estimated between 6,500 and 8,000, that assembled in the city-owned Municipal Auditorium on November 15. Following a skit in which several white children—some in blackface—kissed and hugged each other to suggest the interracial trysts that were sure to follow integration, Perez raised the crowd to a fever pitch when he bellowed, "Don't wait for your daughter to be raped by these Congolese. Don't wait until the burr-heads are forced into your schools. Do something now!" The next day a mob of some two thousand white youths roamed the downtown streets, attacking blacks and throwing bottles, forcing the fire department to turn fire hoses on them and leading to about two hundred arrests.[26]

Those New Orleanians with interests inextricably tied to the city's favorable national image, including Mayor Morrison, tourism leaders, and some other business leaders, began to see the maintenance of law and order as more critical than upholding Perez's brand of racial apartheid. A few responsible voices made themselves heard over the strident chorus of intolerance. One hundred and five business and professional men signed a full-page advertisement in the December 14 Times-Picayune calling for a change in local attitudes toward integration. Tellingly, although Kelleher, Darwin Fenner, and lawyer and civic luminary Harry McCall placed the ad, very few others from the city's Carnival elite signed. A week later, the Greater New Orleans Tourist and Convention Commission (GNOTCC) issued a statement that urged restraint and care to safeguard the economic benefits of tourism. Many business and municipal leaders feared that the Crescent City would become another Little Rock in the national mind. Following the street violence, Morrison appeared on television and warned that rioting would kill New Orleans's reputation.[27]

Indeed, New Orleans received horrendous publicity in the two months following "D-Day." Time, Life, Newsweek, major television networks, wire services, and a host of other national media descended upon the city, which, one observer said, with a considerable dose of hyperbole, appeared ripe for something on the order of a "South American revolution."[28] Morrison called the national press outside agitators and even accused them of staging the ongoing standoff outside the Frantz School. The mayor made a personal appeal to a visiting New York Times correspondent to call for a moratorium on unfavorable press coverage because it created the "impression" that "New Orleans is a sea of turmoil and violence." He complained that the city was "suffering completely without fault on our part" and claimed to have received more than one thousand letters and telegrams about the situation, of which "no more than one dozen are unfavorable."[29]

Contrary to Morrison's claims, numerous angry letters from around the United States and Canada flooded the mayor's office in November and December 1960. A number of would-be tourists claimed they had reconsidered their plans to visit, some out of fear and others out of indignation. One Missouri physician wrote that never again would he vote that a medical convention be held in New Orleans.[30] Some letters called attention to the disparity between the city's gracious image and the reality of pervasive bigotry.[31] Others suggested that New Orleans's brutal excesses would become fodder for Soviet and Cuban propaganda mills.[32] In Morrison's form-letter response, he emphasized that fewer than 100 of the city's 627,525 residents had taken part in the hostility. Clearly, though, their actions reflected a much more widespread mentality.[33]

The ample publicity of the unrest produced direct negative consequences for New Orleans. The hotel and restaurant trade reflected the national backlash, with November sales tumbling more than 30 percent below those of the previous November. Maison Blanche department store on Canal Street reported a nearly 40 percent drop, and even Bourbon Street business and taxicab fares sagged. During the week preceding the Sugar Bowl game, French Quarter restaurants reported empty tables, and hotels still had vacancies.[34] One swamp-tour operator warned radio station WNOE that the tourism business was suffering and noted that he heard a national radio bulletin urging that Mardi Gras visitors exercise caution because a minor incident could trigger a "bloody race riot."[35] As Mardi Gras drew near, Morrison penned a letter to the editor of the *New York Herald Tribune* in which he promised that visitors would find New Orleans the same "traditionally hospitable, courteous and charming city," but the celebration that followed appeared muted in comparison with previous years.[36]

The ill effects of the school crisis lingered through 1961. Lysle Aschaffenburg told newly elected mayor Victor Schiro that during his extensive travels in the summer of 1961, he detected a sea change in attitudes toward the city. Whereas in the past the mere mention of New Orleans "worked like magic," he wrote, "now I find that everywhere I go I am on the defensive and the great image that New Orleans projected everywhere has certainly been badly hurt." He confided to the mayor that he had "always felt that New Orleans was just a little above the rest of the South in most aspects" but now saw Atlanta and Dallas as much more progressive in their handling of the race issue.[37]

After a tidal wave of negative publicity surrounding the school desegregation crisis, municipal leaders became very protective of the city's tarnished urbane image. Indeed, the bitter memory of the school crisis remained fresh for years. When NBC's *Today* show contacted the chamber of commerce in 1963 about its plans to film a week's worth of programs in New Orleans during the Mardi Gras celebration, local business leaders expressed mixed feelings. The editor of the *Times-Picayune* remarked to the chamber president, "You may remember that in 1960 NBC covered the 'demonstrations' when several schools were desegregated in a way which some of our citizens considered gave a distorted picture of the real situation in New Orleans and seriously damaged the good name of the city." He suggested that the chamber should think twice before offering any assistance to *Today*.[38]

The chamber understood, however, that the television program also had the potential to encourage would-be tourists to visit New Orleans. One month earlier, in the midst of the Cuban Missile Crisis, the Florida Keys appeared destined for one of its worst tourist seasons. After *Today* broadcast from Key West, with the close assistance of the chamber of commerce, municipal and state leaders, and the Florida Development Commission, the town enjoyed a sudden resurgence of tourist interest.[39] Accordingly, the New Orleans chamber embraced the show and implored NBC producers to focus on the city "from a business and tourist standpoint" and to avoid any mention of the racial situation. It allocated to NBC $30,000, raised from members, local utilities, downtown merchants, and tourist businesses eager to bolster consumption.[40]

The careful, behind-the-scenes negotiations between city leaders and NBC producers to portray New Orleans as the city of Carnival, food and music, French heritage, and gracious Old South homes did not sit well with African American civil rights activists, who began to employ a rhetoric of tourism in their efforts to end segregation in New Orleans. One wrote *Today* anchor Hugh Downs, deploring the show's neglect of the Crescent City's jazz tradition and reminding him that blacks could not join whites in the city's leading restaurants, hotels, movie theaters, and Carnival balls. "Are you aware," he inquired, "that the *Today* program is being used as part of the Great Whitewash of the South; that it is being used to propagandize the Great Myth of New Orleans as a Cosmopolitan City when actually it is a city with a wall separating freedom and liberty from tyranny and despotism which is thicker and higher than the Berlin Wall?"[41]

Amid the wrangling over the city's image in the three years after the school crisis, civil rights activists struggled to erase the color line in other types of public accommodations. Although much of this activism initially focused on downtown lunch counters, these early struggles fostered an atmosphere of impatience with the status quo that led to subsequent efforts to desegregate more tourist-oriented facilities. More immediately, they also led some white New Orleanians to claim that racial integration would damage the local tourist trade. Seven months after the pioneering student sit-in demonstration at the Woolworth's lunch counter in Greensboro, North Carolina, collegians staged the first New Orleans sit-in on September 9, 1960, at the Woolworth's at the corner of Canal and Rampart Streets on the edge of the French Quarter. Two of the seven protesters were white, all were members of the Congress of Racial Equality (CORE), and all either were or had been students at Dillard University, Louisiana State University of New Orleans, Southern University, or Tulane University. After police arrested the students for criminal mischief, another contingent of four expanded the sit-ins to McCrory's five-and-dime store the following day.[42] The sit-ins continued intermittently, and by the end of the following year, store managers had grown confrontational. At McCrory's, employees dumped mustard, grease, ammonia, and chocolate all over the counter where the students sat quietly awaiting service. Store-hired thugs even poured unknown solvents over the heads of some demonstrators and burned a CORE cap that one was wearing, while the manager waved a pistol and shouted obscenities.[43]

The Citizens' Council, predictably, provided the shrillest cries against the sit-ins. Its members vowed to boycott any business that integrated its eating facilities and to increase patronage of those that upheld Jim Crow. One of the organization's leaders announced that its members would stage a "paper-bag brigade" by bringing sack lunches in lieu of ordering food at the lunch counters.[44] The Greater New Orleans Citizens' Council even initiated what became known as the "Freedom Rides North" movement, a perverse imitation of CORE's "freedom rides," in which Citizens' Councils in several southern cities offered to buy one-way bus tickets to any northern city for African Americans who felt unwanted in the South. Although the project probably transported fewer than 250 blacks out of the region, it symbolized the complete disregard by a considerable segment of the city's white population for black economic power and the benefits to be gained by aligning New Orleans's practices with national ways. And, in the national eye, the project affixed the ugly emblem of bigotry on New Orleans.[45] WDSU-TV, owned by the liberal-minded Edgar B. Stern and a rare voice of responsibility in the local media, berated the idea of "a small band of extremists who are attempting to drag Louisiana back to the 19th century."[46]

Another weapon in the Citizens' Council's arsenal was issuing dire warnings that racial mixing would harm the Crescent City's tourist trade. In the midst of the lunch-counter sit-ins, Shelby Gillis, a board member of the New Orleans branch of the Citizens' Council, warned that desegregation would create a "great big monster." He told fellow council members that he fully expected blacks to target the city's famed restaurants as soon as they had forced their way into downtown lunch counters. As soon as that happened, he predicted, tourism would decline.[47] The idea that segregation threatened tourism had not yet taken root among the city's municipal and business establishment, making them willing to listen to Citizens' Council extremists. While the fall 1960 school crisis had pointed to the impact that Jim Crow could have on tourism, the fear of repelling prospective visitors centered not upon segregation itself but instead on the prospect of civil disorder. The same mentality continued during the sit-in movement, as chamber of commerce officials bemoaned the bad publicity the city received while thousands of tourists were in town for the Sugar Bowl and considered developing some modus operandi for coaxing the press toward stories that depicted the city's "progress."[48] Until city leaders began to view segregation as an impediment to the city's nationalization, white supremacists continued to find an audience for the message that southern indignation made integration bad business.

At the request of the NAACP, dominated locally by the city's influential but hardly militant Afro-Creoles, CORE reluctantly agreed to suspend sit-ins in favor of negotiations with white merchants beginning in March 1962.[49] After exactly two years of hard-fought campaigns against Canal Street merchants, the New Orleans branch of the NAACP successfully negotiated a settlement with the store owners. On September 11, 1962, two years after the sit-ins began, some forty stores, including Katz and Besthoff (K&B) drugstores, D. H. Holmes and Maison Blanche department stores, and Woolworth's and McCrory's five-and-dime stores, opened their lunch counters to African Americans.[50]

With the city's leading downtown lunch counters desegregated, attention turned to hotels. As late as 1963, the small but powerful New Orleans downtown hotel oligarchy dominated by Seymour Weiss exercised no leadership in helping the Crescent City adapt to evolving national standards. Unwilling to modify his prosegregation attitude, Weiss told the chamber of commerce that because New Orleans was losing considerable convention business as a result of racial discrimination, it was essential that the business community concentrate on attracting more all-white convention groups to the city. In a press interview, he added, "I'm not advocating any change. I'm merely stating the facts as a realist."[51]

Although New Orleans boosters could choose to host conventions with no black delegates, they could not keep out African American athletes who played on a number of professional teams by the 1960s. The effort to attract an NFL expansion team required that the city demonstrate not only that black athletes were welcome but also that it could handle press, staff, and spectators without regard to race. Although no blacks played in the NFL from 1933 to 1946, the formation in 1944 of two leagues that accepted blacks—the United States Football League (USFL) and the All-America Football Conference (AAFC)—exerted great pressure on the NFL to drop its racial barrier. Miami, once said to be the most "nazified of all the cities in the world on matters of racial equality," proved it could handle biracial sports when it started the Seahawks, an AAFC franchise, in 1946.[52] Because the South had few professional sports teams prior to the 1960s, Miami was exceptional among southern cities in having to confront the color line so early. In 1958, several years before New Orleans sought a football franchise, Houston began pursuing a major league baseball team and found that the demands of professional sports necessitated easing Jim Crow restrictions. In order to win the support of black voters, whose backing was crucial to pass a second bond issue for a state-of-the-art domed stadium plagued by cost overruns, Houston's mayor Roy Hofheinz and oil and real estate magnate R. E. Smith negotiated a deal with black leaders to open the facility on an integrated basis in return for their assistance in drumming up black support. The dome integration opened the way for the desegregation of other accommodations, for it quickly became apparent that downtown hotels needed to accept black athletes as guests. Mayor Hofheinz worked with John T. Jones, whose syndicate owned four of Houston's leading convention hotels. Jones agreed to desegregate and pressured other hoteliers, who also integrated in April 1962 in time for the first Colt .45s (later the Astros) game.[53]

The promise of professional sports did not work the same magic in the Crescent City, where the realization of open access to tourist spaces proved much more gradual and contentious. The domination of the hotel market by a few old establishments, especially the Roosevelt, whose restaurants, parlors, and cocktail lounges had built a stable, loyal clientele of white southerners and local uptown luminaries, made it exceedingly difficult to persuade hoteliers of the potential for future losses if they did not open their properties to all people.[54] One city official warned Mayor Morrison in 1959 that New Orleans needed "more tourist spectator attractions—the road to which is narrowed, if not blocked by the racial law." He added,

We have champion fighters that have to either fight out of their class here or go out of town. We can't have Major League baseball games, because every Major League baseball club has Negro players. . . . I have just come back from a baseball excursion to Florida where I saw three good games. . . .

I saw jai-alai in the Miami Fronton and passed up three dog tracks[,] all of which are doing good business. . . . So, at the moment, I question that it is timely for New Orleans to spend a lot of money, trying to attract tourists in competition with places like Miami . . . until we have more to offer. We are getting the added hotel rooms—now we have to change a law, and then build additional attractions.[55]

In the Crescent City, even sporting events remained segregated one year after rival Houston had integrated its baseball stadium and its leading hotels.

David Dixon, who exemplified the emerging civic leadership that slowly eroded old-line dominance, decided that a professional sports team would confer big-league status on New Orleans, which was by that time sagging economically despite its Sunbelt ambitions. Dixon understood well the potential damage that segregation and bigotry could inflict on New Orleans's football hopes. In an effort to demonstrate to the NFL the city's readiness to embrace racial progress, Dixon coordinated several exhibition games, the first of which was held at City Park Stadium in 1962. Dixon's effort grew out of a 1962 AFL exhibition game organized by Jack DeFee and other business leaders and held in City Park Stadium. At that game, which featured the Houston Oilers and the New England Patriots, state regulations confined African American spectators to a small section. Despite the appearance of Billy Cannon, a Heisman winner from Louisiana State University who had signed with the Oilers, attendance proved lackluster.[56]

Undeterred, Dixon hired public relations guru David M. Kleck, who suggested that a fully integrated double-header exhibition game played in the prestigious Tulane Stadium would best enable New Orleans to curry favor with the NFL. Dixon understood that Tulane would be thwarting the state statute banning all interracial sporting venues. Fearing possible embarrassment to the university and to the city should an ugly racial incident result, Dixon decided to try to get the mixed-sports law repealed. After failing to impress upon white attorneys the need to overturn the statute, Dixon and Kleck met with seventy-five black leaders at Peter Claver Hall on Orleans Avenue, including thirty-four-year-old attorney Ernest N. "Dutch" Morial, an NAACP field secretary and one of the city's most prominent Afro-Creole leaders. The black leaders were sympathetic but told Dixon they had other priorities. Dixon recalled that he had eight thousand dollars cash with him that day, and when Morial indicated that he might speed up the process for a two-thousand-dollar fee, Dixon said he would have to think about it. Not wanting Morial to know he had been prepared to pay four times that amount, Dixon retired to a restroom, where he carefully separated two thousand dollars into another pocket of his suit. He returned a few minutes later and paid Morial, who filed suit in federal district court, resulting in the repeal of the mixed-seating ban within three months.[57]

Dixon next had to convince Tulane University's board of administrators to allow the game to take place in the school's stadium. He got William Ford, owner of the Detroit Lions, to write to the board, asking them to integrate their stadium and noting that the Ford Foundation—a major source of funding for institutions of higher learning—would look favorably on such an act. The board appeared unlikely to consent until Joseph Merrick Jones and Darwin Fenner suggested that New Orleans would be hopelessly mired in provincialism unless civic leaders took positive steps on the race issue, whereupon the board agreed to sell all tickets on a nonsegregated basis. As with other integration coups in public accommodations, no one announced the decision, but news traveled by word of mouth. The double-header, which pitted the Dallas Cowboys against the Detroit Lions and the Baltimore Colts against the Chicago Bears, was perhaps the most integrated professional football game ever held before or since in the South, with more than 30 percent black attendance. The only tense moments came when a sudden thunderstorm sent fans running for cover beneath the stands. Dixon later recalled, "I had a vision of blacks and whites hammering each other under that overhang, the media reports that would result, the end of my dreams of an NFL franchise. . . . I was so scared I was shaking and I rushed down from the press box to try and stop the carnage. But when I got there, everyone was laughing. They were brought together by their discomfort." With the city's primary sports venue integrated, the problem of hotels remained to be solved.[58]

The pressure of courting the NFL and the ongoing loss of national conventions to more open cities, coupled with increasingly insistent demands from the city's black activists and even Afro-Creole elites, began to effect a change in some of New Orleans's more farsighted leaders. By 1962, Houston, Dallas, and Miami had succeeded in opening their leading convention hotels to blacks, yet Atlanta and New Orleans establishments remained as wholly "unreconstructed" as their counterparts in small southern towns with no convention traffic. Three events in particular—two lawsuits and the loss of one of the nation's most coveted conventions—speeded the push for discrimination-free hotels in New Orleans.

In the early 1960s, a loose biracial coalition of leaders began urging the integration of downtown hotels. Afro-Creole leaders like Dutch Morial, podiatrist and travel agent Dr. Leonard L. Burns, NAACP official Arthur J. Chapital Sr., and Urban League officer Harry Kerns joined Pepsi-Cola bottling executive and tourist commission president Harry M. England in trying to negotiate an agreement with hoteliers. Burns later recalled speaking with Seymour Weiss, who growled that the Roosevelt would never integrate. Working closely with New Orleans black leaders, Atlanta civil rights activist Daisy Bates attempted in late 1962 to check into the Roosevelt and was told that the hotel could not honor the reservations of African Americans. Hiding behind a pillar in the lobby, Burns and Morial overheard the clerk's response, and Morial set out to draft a lawsuit.[59]

Heeding a directive from Washington, D.C., Burns and other leaders decided it might prove more fruitful to delay forcing Weiss's hand and instead exert pressure on New Orleans's few hotels affiliated with national chains, which they reasoned could not afford risking their good names.[60] Daisy Bates next tried to register at the Sheraton-Charles Hotel (formerly the St. Charles), which also refused her on racial grounds. Morial and other NAACP attorneys soon brought suit against the hotel's parent company, the Sheraton Corporation in New Jersey. Meanwhile, prominent CORE official James T. McCain of Sumter, South Carolina, failed to secure a room in the Royal Orleans Hotel in the French Quarter, leading to a separate lawsuit by CORE and the American Civil Liberties Union.[61] The conservative *Times-Picayune* remained silent on hotel segregation until May 1963, when federal judges John Minor Wisdom, Herbert W. Christenberry, and E. Gordon West, considering the cases together, ruled the Louisiana law unconstitutional in *McCain v. Davis*. At first glance the decision seemed to be a breakthrough; in fact, the courts had no jurisdiction over the hotels, leaving the decision whether to integrate up to hotel management.[62]

New Orleans anticipated the arrival of some sixty thousand visitors that September for the American Legion national convention. It was to be the city's first hosting of the convention since 1922. In the spring of 1963, convention planners announced they were considering moving the event elsewhere because of concerns that New Orleans hotels might not accommodate black delegates.[63] Arthur Chapital called on the local American Legion host committee to demand equal treatment of blacks in the city's hotels. Rather than pointing to the demoralizing effect of the bar against blacks, Chapital invoked a protourism rhetoric, declaring, "We believe that a sincere policy of democracy in action and true [C]hristian fellowship would not only enhance tourism and the image of New Orleans and the American Legion but would benefit the economy of this area."[64]

If New Orleans black leaders were learning to enlist the city's tourist image in their fight for racial equality, white business leaders remained of two minds on whether to sacrifice a generations-old social custom for the economic lift that would accompany the Legionnaires for one week in the "City That Care Forgot." Symptomatic of the city's indifferent white leadership, no one stepped forward to assure the Legionnaires that local hotels would welcome all of them uncondi- tionally. At a chamber of commerce meeting in late April, Joseph W. Simon Jr., president of the chamber, reported having had a telephone conversation concern- ing the possibility that the Legion might withdraw from the city, but apparently he did little or nothing in response.[65] The federal court ruling in *McCain v. Davis* destroyed whatever chances New Orleans had of retaining the convention. Al- though the court ruled that the 1956 statute forbidding integration of Louisiana hotels and motels was unconstitutional, it implied that it would not enforce hotel desegregation. Despite chamber of commerce discussion of the imperiled conven- tion as well as ample local press coverage, Mayor Schiro expressed surprise but demonstrated remarkably little concern. "Of course," he pointed out, "the man- agement of our hotels is still a matter of private enterprise and owners of these have their rights."[66]

By the spring of 1963, in the wake of "Bull" Connor's brutality against Bir- mingham civil rights demonstrators, the slow pace of change accompanying the negotiation strategy of more conservative black and Afro-Creole leaders incensed CORE members. Pointing to the ongoing problems with lunch counters, which were nominally integrated but often segregated in practice, New Orleans CORE chairman Oretha Castle expressed doubt that negotiations alone could bring true racial integration. In June she demanded the desegregation of all facilities in mu- nicipal buildings within ten days, as well as the lifting of the racial bar in hotels, restaurants, and theaters within thirty days, or "we will initiate mass demonstra- tions in the City of New Orleans."[67] Although the resumption of demonstrations in the summer focused once again on lunch counters and municipal facilities rather than hotels and other accommodations, perceptive hotel operators, if not city hall, could see that change needed to come quickly.[68]

The cumulative effect of numerous CORE threats, convention cancellations, the court's ruling against hotel segregation, and the crushing blow dealt by the American Legion persuaded the operators of three downtown hotels to announce they would integrate on September 10, 1963. The Sheraton Corporation and the Hotel Corporation of America, operators of the Sheraton-Charles and the Royal Orleans, respectively, ordered their New Orleans establishments to integrate.

Likewise, Arthur Jung broke ranks with the city's leading locally owned hotels and desegregated the Jung, then in the midst of an expansion that would make it the largest convention hotel in the Crescent City. Although the desegregation of three leading hotels represented a giant step forward in New Orleans, the hotels still had to abide by a city ordinance that forbade racial mixing in establishments that served alcohol unless the service area was divided by a partition. Thus, for the time being, a hungry African American guest had to venture outside the hotel or order room service. As with the federal court's ruling earlier that year, the *Times-Picayune* studiously avoided any commentary on the watershed event.[69]

Other leading downtown hotels, including the Roosevelt and the Monteleone, remained committed to segregation. The Roosevelt had built a loyal clientele, especially among southerners, while the Monteleone continued its position as the dominant tourist hotel in the French Quarter. Seymour Weiss did not flinch when the U.S. Department of Defense prohibited active-duty military personnel from participating in sessions of the Adjutants General Association of the United States at the Roosevelt in April 1964. Weiss's hotel had refused to accommodate Colonel Otho Van Exel, a black delegate from Brooklyn. New York governor Nelson D. Rockefeller ordered his state's delegation home from New Orleans. Scarcely two weeks later, CORE pressure persuaded the Mississippi Valley World Trade Conference to abandon the Roosevelt for the Jung. Weiss seemed indifferent: "There is a Civil Rights law pending in Washington now. Until it is passed and there is a law that says I must integrate my hotel, I will continue our policy."[70]

On July 4, 1964, the *Times-Picayune* reported near-total compliance with the Civil Rights Act passed the previous day. The famous Café du Monde coffee stand in the French Market, along with leading French Quarter restaurants, served its first black patrons.[71] African Americans doubtless approached their newly won freedoms with considerable circumspection. Old habits died hard, and few blacks ventured into the French Quarter, which they considered a white attraction. Bourbon Street establishments reported business as usual. A waitress at the Paddock Lounge said she knew of no blacks seeking service in the first week after the enactment of the measure.[72]

Although most establishments in the French Quarter and Central Business District complied with the Civil Rights Act of 1964, New Orleans faced embarrassing compliance problems elsewhere, revealing the extent to which the presence or absence of tourists had segmented racial practices in the city's consumer spaces. The local branch of the NAACP filed complaints against the Frostop drive-in hamburger stand chain and Lee's Hamburgers on Tulane Avenue in Mid-City, which continued to display a "This window for Colored Only" sign.[73] Likewise, Schwegmann Bros. Giant Supermarkets, the city's dominant (and locally owned) grocery chain, resisted change. CORE testers repeatedly were denied service at Schwegmann's lunch counters that summer. While John G. Schwegmann Jr. occasionally promoted the gigantic Gentilly Road store, billed the "World's Largest Supermarket," as a tourist attraction in the local press, he understood clearly that his suburban stores drew primarily local whites. In support of Schwegmann's dogged determination to resist integration, the Citizens' Council took out a large ad in the *New Orleans States-Item* that urged white patrons to shop the supermarkets and "show these Negroes who really runs the economy."[74]

As long as overt discrimination retreated to "back-of-town" neighborhood restaurants and bars, out of sight of visiting conventioneers and tourists, city leaders could claim that New Orleans was on a march to greatness. When prejudice appeared in the city's "front yard," however, officials began to fret. After the AFL opted to move its 1965 All-Star game to Houston following the regrettable mistreatment of African American football players in various French Quarter tourist establishments, Mayor Schiro rushed to his city's defense. Schiro deplored the walkout, which could not have come at a worse time. The New Orleans Pro Football Club was just then ardently courting one of two proposed NFL expansion teams. Dixon expressed dismay at the unfortunate incident and commented that a taxicab driver had given his friend, a San Diego sportswriter, a "filthy piece of literature discussing mixed marriages and sordid relations between the races." Dixon added, "You can imagine the impression that this would make on a visitor to our city."[75] Seemingly more concerned with stopping the bleeding than with remedying the underlying problems, the mayor argued that the black players "should have rolled with the punch. Almost all of them," he added, "are educated college men who must be aware that you cannot change human nature overnight." Schiro remarked that "they have done themselves and their race a disservice."[76] Convinced that the whole incident was the dirty work of outside agitators "on a mission," Schiro refused to admit publicly that even if laws could not guarantee equal treatment, they could go a long way toward dismantling a century of increasingly resolute bigotry among some southerners.[77]

Echoing Schiro, WWL-TV sports editor Hap Glaudi decried the breach of contract and questioned why the "mutinous Negro players" were going to Bourbon Street strip clubs in the first place. Losing sight of the fundamental issue of insidious racial barriers in one of the nation's most popular sporting events, Glaudi argued that the AFL had "made a binding contract to play a football game here on January 16th . . . not to conduct a social function." Furthermore, Glaudi ranted, the only reason the previous year's Sugar Bowl game had passed without incident was "because the Sugar Bowl people recognized it wasn't wise to permit the Syracuse Negro players to wander aimlessly around our town" and had taken them aside and explained where they would and would not be welcomed.[78]

Such comments seem incongruent with the popular image of New Orleans as a freewheeling city, one that Atlanta's mayor William Hartsfield might have called "The City Too Carefree to Hate."[79] Yet Schiro's proclamations become less perplexing when considered in the context of the prevalent southern racial climate of the 1960s, from which New Orleans never stood completely apart. The civil rights struggle was shifting toward greater militancy, reflected in the more strident rhetoric of the Student Nonviolent Coordinating Committee, race riots that set dozens of cities aflame, and southern expressions of resistance such as white flight and the obstruction of federally mandated school integration.

The AFL debacle and Schiro's feeble efforts to justify the glacial pace of New Orleans's desegregation elicited a flood of editorial reactions and correspondence from around the country. One Kansas City man noted that New Orleans's "image at one time was that of a city of warm-blooded, fun loving, joyous and happy people," but now "prejudice and bigotry have poisoned the place."[80] Another Kansas City visitor, an African American, went to the Crescent City around the time of the AFL walkout and reported facing racially motivated mistreatment. As he stood on Canal Street during a downpour, several taxicabs drove past him to collect white patrons just a few feet away. On another occasion a clerk refused to sell him a ticket for a Gray Line sightseeing bus tour. A porter advised him that tours for blacks needed to be "pre-arranged," but even then the company usually denied blacks tickets with a series of carefully worded excuses.[81]

Some would-be tourists, appalled by city hall's callous stance toward the players, vowed to stay away from New Orleans. An African American man from Schenectady, New York, wrote that he had been stationed at Jackson Barracks in New Orleans during World War II and had liked the city very much but had since had no desire to return because of the worsening racial climate. He suggested that the untold tourist losses should prompt the mayor to spearhead the education of citizens, who "will let a Negro mind [their] children and cook [their] food" yet would not dream of sharing public accommodations.[82] At least one major national convention, that of the American Chemical Society, expressed serious reservations about the advisability of holding a future meeting in the Crescent City.[83]

A *Boston Globe* columnist summed up the thoughts of many when he wrote that no one visiting New Orleans should be forced to "roll with the punches." He observed that Schiro might be correct in saying that human nature could not change overnight, but "in New Orleans, 'overnight' has extended about 100 years. . . . Why should [blacks] slink around town as second class citizens while their presence in the game's line-up brings profit to the cabbies and the other white promoters?" He concluded that New Orleans did not deserve to win a professional football team.[84]

White New Orleanians and other Louisianians exhibited a range of reactions to the cancellation. As in the aftermath of the school desegregation crisis four years earlier, local white opinion assumed a heavily segregationist slant. A number of letters to city hall echoed Schiro's allegation that the walkout was premeditated under pressure from national civil rights activists.[85] Others displayed a more virulent strain of racism. One New Orleanian charged that what "these negroes really wanted was a chance to ogle white strippers."[86] Another claimed that he and his friends had no intention of going to the game "to see those negroes play our white boys" and were "glad that those black apes walked out."[87]

Not surprisingly, those whose livelihoods relied primarily on local rather than national connections tended to be among the more outspoken critics of the AFL action. The editor of the *Citizens' Report*, the monthly publication of the prosegregation, Metairie-based South Louisiana Citizens' Council, saw no need to compromise racist principles to lure a professional football team to New Orleans. In a letter to the mayor, he wrote, "Don't you realize that every time these interracial Gladiators come to New Orleans they create a dangerous problem by insisting on sleeping in the same hotels, eating in the same restaurants, attending the same night spots, and riding in the same taxicabs as the white players?" Employing rhetoric that more squarely evoked Senator Joseph McCarthy's red-baiting in the 1950s, he contended that the city had been "harassed long enough by leftwing pressure groups, outside agitators, fifth columnists and assorted snoops." Calling on the mayor to return to the conservative, segregationist principles on which he ran his 1962 mayoral campaign, the Citizens' Council leader implied that the majority of white voters would forsake him in 1966 unless he mounted "a firm stand against any idea of a pro-football league."[88]

Reaction to the AFL incident even found its way into French Quarter entertainment. Almost immediately after the league moved the game to Houston, three young white actors staged a comic revue at the Original Old Absinthe House, a popular tourist attraction and local hangout on Bourbon Street. The show, a bitter parody of civil rights, took jabs at the Freedom Riders, Dr. Martin Luther King Jr., and President Johnson. The act starred a local comedian, Billy Holliday, whom one Los Angeles reporter thought was, "perhaps, more opportunistic than bigoted. He gives the people down there what they want, and he plays to packed houses every night." Holliday used the AFL incident in his routine: "When 'em ballplayers come to town, I tole the manager, if one wants to come in heah, let him come and charge him 25 dollahs a drink. If he come back with a friend, charge 'em 50 dollahs a drink. If 'at friend come back with a friend, we charge 'em 75 dollahs. And, if they pay it, we kick all the white people out."[89]

While the city's old-line white elite generally remained aloof from the controversy in the manner befitting those who fancied themselves aristocrats, a few white New Orleanians expressed sympathy for the black football players. One Broadmoor woman recalled a recent taxicab ride during which her driver snarled "Animal!" as a black driver passed him. When she asked him to repeat what he had just said, the cabbie bellowed, "They are all animals." The woman suggested to Schiro that even the alleged improvement in race relations at the 1965 Sugar Bowl game between Syracuse and LSU, the first integrated Sugar Bowl since 1956, fell far short of the mayor's glowing remarks. "Perhaps the Syracuse squad was well treated," she allowed, "but in the stands . . . L.S.U. rooters were hollering, 'Get those nigger-lovers.'"[90] Another New Orleanian considered it "not a matter of the AFL 'acting hastily' so much as New Orleans dragging its feet. . . . The AFL must compete for the best players—is New Orleans willing to compete for the 'big leagues?'"[91]

Fortunately for those who wanted to bring professional football to New Orleans, by 1965 the NFL was concerned principally with securing an exemption from federal antitrust laws. Louisiana's senior congressional delegation—Senator Russell B. Long and Representative Hale T. Boggs—promised the exemption in return for the NFL's commitment to New Orleans, and the New Orleans Saints were born. Racial considerations appeared to melt away after the NFL had observed several exhibition games playing to a full Tulane Stadium.[92]

Local civil rights activists seized the momentum generated by the AFL incident to press city hall to ameliorate racial separatism. Black civil rights attorney Nils R. Douglas deplored the lack of courage exhibited by city leaders and the press in the football scandal and noted that blacks did not share the prevailing white notion that New Orleans enjoyed "racial harmony."[93] Many African American leaders continued to employ a rhetoric of tourism to bolster their condemnation of the city's unfortunate drift. In a statement before the New Orleans city council, Rev. John Baringer, president of the Community Relations Council, a Metairie-based nonpolitical, biracial association of concerned citizens, urged quick attention to salvage the city's image. Calling for the creation of a municipal human-relations commission, Baringer reminded councilmen that "such events as Mardi Gras, the International Jazz Festival and numerous national conventions . . . will be jeopardized unless long overdue actions are taken."[94] F. Winter Trapolin, a white insurance broker and civil rights activist, reminded Schiro of a letter he had sent the mayor in 1963 warning that "our cures so far have been *temporary* each time the panic button was pushed." In the wake of the AFL fiasco, Trapolin urged the mayor to delay no longer in appointing a human-rights council, which "would go a long way in restoring our tarnished image . . . [and] would show prospective industries and tourists, and our own citizens, we know how to handle and to prevent such emergencies."[95] Only in 1967 did Schiro finally create the New Orleans Human Relations Committee (HRC).

In the midst of the city's effort to woo the NFL, New Orleans's tourist image continued to suffer one setback after another, belying Mayor Schiro's contention that the AFL incident was an aberration in what was usually a cosmopolitan, open city. Just days after the AFL players packed their bags for Houston, three African Americans, including a Houstonian, were refused service at Castillo's, a popular Mexican restaurant in the French Quarter. The next night, police arrested two New Orleans NAACP leaders, Llewellyn Soniat and Walter Winston, for trespassing at the Jazz Corner nightclub at 1218 Canal Street after the activists ignored the barmaid's demand that they leave.[96] Black delegates to an American Federation of Labor–Congress of Industrial Workers (AFL-CIO) fund-raising dinner at the Roosevelt Hotel in November 1965 found themselves inexplicably channeled to all-black tables.[97]

Planners of national conventions continued to take such incidents very seriously and sometimes pulled the plug on scheduled meetings. One month after the football fiasco, Weiss, a staunch segregationist until compelled by federal law to play by national rules, suddenly became an unlikely critic of taxicab segregation, a form of public accommodation not covered under the Civil Rights Act of 1964. Weiss complained to the mayor that the National Labor Relations Board had called to cancel its planned meeting at the Roosevelt after learning that a black delegate to the recent American Bar Association convention had not been able to find a taxi to convey him from the Fontainebleau Motor Hotel to the Roosevelt for the meetings.[98] In June a black delegate of a national Methodist church convention was refused taxi service in New Orleans on several occasions.[99] Other black tourists experienced difficulty finding a taxicab just to go from Moisant Field (New Orleans International Airport) to their hotel in the city, sometimes having to pay more than the standard metered fare.[100]

Racial discrimination in tourist businesses continued to hurt the city's image throughout the rest of the 1960s. To be sure, the more reputable businesses in the French Quarter generally served all customers without regard to race, but Bourbon Street's numerous nightclubs remained highly popular attractions despite their often cool reception toward African American patrons. Strip clubs such as the Circus Club, Silver Frolics, Chez Paree, Club Hotsy Totsy, and Guys and Dolls, among others, continued frequently to turn away blacks, which perhaps reflected lingering racist notions of African American men as sexual beasts apt to deflower white womanly virtue (even in the form of an exotic dancer). Some of the clubs were known to quote higher cover charges, prices, and drinking minimums to blacks than to whites.[101] One group of black tourists from Houston tried to order food at McConnell's King of Hamburgers on Bourbon Street and wound up arrested, allegedly for disturbing the peace.[102] Other establishments in or near the Quarter sometimes charged blacks double for food and drink unless they opted for take-out, or refused to serve them altogether.[103]

Just as the 1963 cancellation of the American Legion convention helped precipitate the first wave of hotel desegregation in New Orleans, pressure for a local public accommodations ordinance became more pronounced by 1969 following a string of convention incidents and cancellations. Delegates at the mostly black Frontiers International convention at the Roosevelt Hotel in July 1969 were informed they had entered a "private club" when they tried to order drinks at the Jazz Corner on Canal Street and two other bars on University Place across from the hotel. At the convention's closing session, the Frontiers delegates adopted a resolution calling for the city government to take immediate steps or face a convention boycott. Such a boycott would deny the city not only future Frontiers International meetings but also a host of other conventions, for among the Frontiers members were the heads of several other major organizations planning to hold conventions in New Orleans, each with between three thousand and six thousand delegates.[104]

The delegates to the Head Start and Child Development Conference in New

Orleans complained of the menial positions blacks filled in the Jung Hotel as well as incidents in which the city's tourism businesses denied service to black delegates. The group demanded the passage of a city ordinance by January 1, 1970, threatening to contact the NFL commissioner and the players of both teams planning to play in the city's first Super Bowl. It promised to urge all organizations planning conventions in the Crescent City to revisit that decision.[105] Local black organizations responded very frankly to requests for information from groups considering whether New Orleans could properly handle their conventions, admitting freely that the city had considerable problems. The conservative chamber of commerce, mindful of the city's image but oblivious to its racial problems, tried to reassure one such convention, echoing the familiar refrain from the early 1960s that "teams are repeatedly sent back to the same bar to build up a case."[106]

When some white and black delegates in town for the American Federation of Teachers (AFT) conference in August 1969 attempted to test the two bars on University Place that had refused to serve drinks to Frontiers delegates, they faced the same discriminatory treatment. One barmaid allegedly remarked, "The only thing worse than niggers is whites that bring niggers in here," while a police officer removed one black delegate for refusing to leave. In addition to passing a resolution recommending that the AFL-CIO and all of its affiliates blacklist New Orleans when considering future convention sites, the AFT picketed the two offending lounges. Thugs manning the entrance to the Topaz Bar repelled picketers by spraying an unknown foreign substance. The AFT filed a $1 million lawsuit in federal district court against the two bars and Mayor Schiro.[107]

Discrimination in the city's most tourist-frequented spaces of consumption finally proved untenable. By the latter half of 1969, a broad coalition of tourism interests, business and civic leadership groups, neighborhood associations, civil rights groups, and churches rallied for a public accommodations ordinance.[108] Local supporters of an ordinance marshaled evidence of lost tourist business and the prospect of continued problems in their campaign to convince the New Orleans city council to act. They cited the persistent pattern of businesses relaxing discrimination during major conventions, only to revert to Jim Crow when the delegates left town. Charles Keller Jr., president of the Metropolitan Area Committee, a prestigious civic organization formed in 1966 to address community problems, warned of the damage that could result if the kinds of racial incidents in taxicabs and French Quarter businesses reported over the previous two years continued when the National League of Cities convention arrived in December.[109] In addition to developing a pamphlet, the Human Relations Committee reminded the mayor and city councilmen of the urgent need to pass a law before the Super Bowl game to avoid potential embarrassment.[110]

As the city council considered a public accommodations ordinance in December 1969, councilman Maurice E. "Moon" Landrieu, like Schiro a protégé of Chep Morrison, provided strong support for the proposal. Landrieu, who grew up in a working-class New Orleans neighborhood, had developed an understanding and sympathy for the plight of blacks. His years as an undergraduate and law student at Loyola University, where he cultivated Catholic beliefs and interracial friendships, influenced his attitude toward race. Landrieu was one of the rare Louisiana politicians who refused to cower before the glare of traditional leaders.[111] He understood the political implications of the city's shifting racial demographics and the social and economic necessity of completing the arduous process of integrating the entire city. Indeed, by 1969 New Orleans, whose African American population had reached about 45 percent, saw the full effect of black political mobilization wrought by the federal Voting Rights Act of 1965. Powerful black organizations such as SOUL (Southern Organization for Unified Leadership) in the Ninth Ward and the Afro-Creole-dominated COUP (Community Organization for Urban Politics) in the Seventh Ward embraced race as a viable organizing principle for mobilizing the black electorate and inserted themselves into the city's longstanding tradition of patronage politics. Landrieu understood and exploited this new reality.[112]

Although Landrieu, the city council's leading proponent of a public accommodations ordinance, had the support of the HRC and a coalition of community and business leaders, he faced narrow-minded opponents who either opposed or sought to dilute the bill. When Landrieu and Councilman Henry Curtis introduced the bill on December 16, 1969, none of their colleagues was willing to endorse it. The lack of support for concrete policies to prevent racial discrimination in public accommodations may reflect the tense racial climate of the late 1960s, when growing black militancy and racial violence jeopardized nascent white acceptance of black rights. Fellow councilmen proposed an amendment that would limit the bill's coverage to the Central Business District and the French Quarter, thereby allowing business owners to do as they pleased elsewhere in the city. The amendment represented the views of many white New Orleanians who still resented the protourism argument for integration. One letter to Mayor Schiro epitomizes this persistent mindset: "From the way new hotels are springing up in and around New Orleans I had thought that more tourists and conventions were coming to New Orleans to escape fratinization [sic] with Negroes. . . . The most disheartening part of [the push for an ordinance] is to see spokesmen for the hotels and others not even bother to conceal their motives with high moral tones. They frankly put the dollar above public concern or public safety. New Orleans has existed very well without mixed drinking and without the Super Bowl and it is time the white majority made their feelings known."[113]

Human Relations Committee leaders hurried to counter the amendment at a public hearing on December 23, when the council planned to vote on the measure. The HRC instructed the representatives of the many organizations supporting the original ordinance to argue against the amendment on the grounds that limiting coverage would insult local citizens; would not protect tourists who sought food, drink, or entertainment in the vicinity of Tulane Stadium or the New Orleans Fair Grounds racetrack; and would work against the GNOTCC's efforts to encourage visitors to stay longer and see more of the city besides the French Quarter.[114] At least one black leader expressed disbelief that tourism could be the primary consideration in passing an ordinance that any progressive city would have adopted anyway for the benefit of its own citizens. However, tourism industry leaders also deplored efforts to weaken the ordinance.[115] On December 23, the city council unanimously passed the ordinance without amendments, and it took effect January 1, 1970. Finally, after a decade of agitation, New Orleans took its place among the nation's cities.

Metropolitan Area Committee chairman Sam Israel lauded the councilmen, noting that "the public accommodations ordinance takes on added significance . . . when you realize that the change resulted from the democratic process and not from court action." For the African American community, this victory rang hollow. By 1969 New Orleans had muddled through half a decade since the federal order to desegregate public accommodations. The Plain Truth, a black newspaper published by New Orleans's Free Southern Theatre, contended that the ordinance would do little to help the plight of black New Orleanians but would bring "real and substantial benefits to the white business community . . . as a 'guarantee' to large conventions and the Super Bowl." In its bitter conclusion, the editorial suggested that perhaps the ordinance had done one thing other than to give black people a right that should already have been theirs: "Also, as a result of our experiences with the ordinance, we should now know how to exert economic pressure through outside conventions and the Super Bowl."[116]

The overdue public accommodations ordinance underscores the very selective nature of white civic leadership that characterized New Orleans into the late 1960s. While city leaders fostered tourism development, attracted a professional football team, and sparred over the proposed riverfront expressway, they failed to remove ambiguity from their stance toward racial discrimination—even risking the tourist trade they hoped to cultivate. Although the law proved almost anticlimactic after the tumultuous preceding events, it heralded a "new" New Orleans in which a modern tourism industry could flourish. The ordinance is best seen in the context of the whirlwind of social, economic, political, and cultural change that enveloped the city in the late 1960s and early 1970s. In the span of only a few years, the Crescent City achieved meaningful black involvement in local politics, infused its blueblood business community with a new breed of leaders, and laid Jim Crow to rest once and for all. The city stood on the threshold of a phenomenal oil boom that would give its dreamers new visions of closing the gap with Atlanta, Dallas, Houston, and Miami. It also stood on the cusp of a spectacular ascendancy of the tourism and convention industry over the next three decades, one that would revive New Orleans jazz and Mardi Gras.

CHAPTER 4

MAKING "THE BIRTHPLACE OF JAZZ"

> Nowhere do you hear jazz, New Orleans Jazz. Nowhere do you see any prospects
> of jazz in the future. Jazz was born in New Orleans but it doesn't live there any
> more. —KEN HULSIZER (1944)

> The "Crescent City"—snuggled in a bend of the Mississippi River and bordered
> to the north by Lake Pontchartrain—is alive with the music it spawned.
> —PAULA CROUCH (1978)

Heading southward through pine forests and worn-out cotton fields aboard the
Southerner in 1942, Sterling Brown, an African American schoolteacher traveling in search of New Orleans jazz, envisioned jazzmen Kid Rena and "Big Eye"
Louis Nelson DeLisle holding court in some musty dive on Basin Street. A black
sergeant from New Orleans who boarded the train in Anniston, Alabama, assured
Brown he would find Rena at the Fern Dance Hall on Iberville Street in the French
Quarter and DeLisle in the vicinity of Derbigny and Kerlerec Streets in neighboring Faubourg Tremé. Upon arrival, the eager tourist did not find the musicians;
actually he found little jazz of any sort. Basin Street was now North Saratoga, and
the Lafitte Housing Project cast crisp, geometrical shadows that belied any image
Brown may have conjured of the steamy, tropical, jazz-filled nights of Storyville,
New Orleans's famous red-light district. In one Afro-Creole family's apartment
in the Lafitte project, Brown was treated to coconut cake and ginger ale as the
sounds of Jimmy Dorsey's orchestra wafted from the radio. The visitor later recalled, "There were a few good jazz combinations in town, . . . but most of them
were playing in white places where I could have gone only at the cost of problems."
The disillusioned Brown concluded "that in New Orleans the feeling for jazz was
nostalgic, commemorative, quite different from the force that sustained the young
Louis Armstrong. . . . New Orleans gave jazz to the world; the world parcelled [sic]
bits of it back over the turn-table and the air-waves."[1]

Indeed, the city's wartime modernization seemed to have crippled the advance
of New Orleans's most famous art form. New Orleans had long been known as the
birthplace of jazz. Widely held to have sprung from the more primitive sounds
accompanying African American dances in Congo Square in the nineteenth cen-

tury, in the first two decades of the twentieth, jazz matured in Storyville clubs and brothels. Attracting jazz musicians as well as gamblers and prostitutes, Storyville solidified in the tourist mind the ribald image of New Orleans. Jazz figured prominently in that image, and yet it became increasingly scarce in the intervening years between Storyville's demise and Sterling Brown's visit. Tourist interest played a significant role in shaping a revival of local interest in preserving and promoting New Orleans–style jazz in the four decades after the Great Depression. Newcomers brought an interest in jazz and incited the popularization of the "Dixieland" tradition through marketing, concerts, tours, festivals, and brass band parades, encouraging the use of the music by commercial promoters and tourism officials in shaping public memory and packaging it for tourist consumption. Many of these efforts bound jazz to the city's most tourist-oriented urban space, the French Quarter, although eventually the jazz revival propelled tourists to venues throughout the city, including neighborhood taverns and clubs and, annually, to the New Orleans Fair Grounds. As with the promotion of French Quarter architecture, which encouraged tourists to step back in time by strolling narrow, balcony-lined streets, the commodification of jazz enticed newcomers to participate in the music by following parades or even joining local bands.

Like the preservation of the French Quarter and the racial integration of public accommodations, the resurrection of Dixieland jazz reveals the advance in the postwar years of the notion that responding to tourists' expectations served New Orleans's economic interests. The effort to revive traditional jazz also shares with the campaign to preserve the French Quarter a tension between those who dismissed the city's unique heritage, especially influential local whites, and those history-minded tourists and locals who embraced it. Predictably, African Americans did not always rush to embrace cultural preservation initiatives that either ignored or exploited them, yet ultimately they began to reclaim a degree of control over the public presentation of jazz. In building commercial demand for the art form, tourism set jazz apart from its cultural and spatial moorings and laid the foundation for the biracial grassroots interest in brass bands, street processions, and the preservation of local sites of jazz history, in turn creating a sustainable cultural resource that enriched the community even as it furthered tourism development. Thus, the checkered effect of tourism on the revival of New Orleans jazz complicates the common scholarly assumption that tourism simply erodes local culture.[2]

Upon the closure of the Storyville cabaret where he performed, African American jazz drummer Paul Barbarin purchased a railroad pass to Chicago at the Illinois

Central office on New Orleans's South Rampart Street in 1917. In the Windy City, Barbarin worked in the stockyards by day and played drums by night. Like many other jazzmen in exile, he found little reason to move back to New Orleans in the 1920s and 1930s. The demise of Storyville during World War I and the concurrent exodus of many blacks seeking better employment and freedom from the harsher manifestations of racial prejudice set New Orleans jazz on a long decline. Prohibition and especially the Great Depression spelled the end of many of the remaining New Orleans clubs that maintained performing jazz bands, and by World War II the city's jazz appeared moribund.[3]

Prior to the 1960s, in fact, few musicians could find steady employment. Reflective of the departure of so much talent, few Crescent City musicians recorded their music in New Orleans in the Depression years. Only three of six musicians in the famed New Orleans Rhythm Kings actually called New Orleans home. With the exception of Baby Dodds, none of the city's biggest figures, including Louis Armstrong, Freddy Keppard, Jelly Roll Morton, Johnny Dodds, and Kid Ory, recorded there. Not one New Orleans recording session in the 1930s featured African Americans. Only two sides, recorded in 1936 by the white trumpeter Sharkey Bonano, constituted the entire repertoire of 1930s New Orleans jazz recording. In the absence of economic incentive, African Americans tended to view jazz as little more than a familiar form of music that pervaded their lives only to the extent that many black funerals had a brass band accompanying mourners to and from the burial site. Although black societies and fraternal orders sporadically gave balls and vied with each other in hiring jazz bands, for many of the city's best musicians, like Paul Barbarin, leaving New Orleans afforded the only hope of realizing their full potential.[4]

Just as most white New Orleanians snubbed the French Quarter, they frowned upon jazz. During the first half of the twentieth century, with Jim Crow well entrenched, many old-line whites disdained the music, for it did not fit into their conception of New Orleans as a New South city with Old South values. Far from recognizing jazz as a potential tourist attraction, prominent New Orleanians usually either dismissed it as inconsequential or took it for granted merely as a suitable dance music. Noted jazz scholar Charles Edward Smith remarked that "the people of New Orleans enjoyed and sustained the music without the music itself getting more than a passing nod from the local guardians of culture," whom he described as "bigwigs . . . who knew their operas but not their four-in-a-bar." Just as elite whites associated jazz with the Pendergast era in Kansas City, the Capone era in Chicago, and decadent Harlem in New York, upper-class New Orleanians linked jazz with the crime, vice, and libidinous carousing that had characterized Storyville. Indeed, early twentieth-century accounts of jazz in the elite-controlled New Orleans press usually appeared only in the context of reports of knifings and shootings, and one *Times-Picayune* editorial in 1918 denigrated the music as one of the "manifestations of a low streak in man's tastes that has not yet come out in civilization's wash."[5]

Important demographic changes wrought by World War II dealt a sharp blow to whatever vitality New Orleans jazz retained. During the war New Orleans had the smallest proportion of African Americans of any major southern city, paving the way for a dilution of the black cultural forms that were rooted in an earlier period when the Crescent City had a majority-black population. The war-induced transition from merchandising to manufacturing prompted a considerable influx of rural, Protestant southerners into a city long dominated by Roman Catholics. Such newcomers often favored hillbilly music and held little regard for jazz or the permissive atmosphere in which it had flourished. French Quarter bars and clubs increasingly catered to newcomers' preference for country music. The growing popularity of radio fostered the standardization of national popular music tastes, and French Quarter bars increasingly installed jukeboxes to save the expense of hiring local musicians. The lack of appreciation of jazz musicians usually necessitated their taking up other jobs to supplement meager earnings from performing. Club jobs typically demanded long hours and provided abysmal wages. In addition, increased attention to war and commerce lessened the city's traditional penchant for revelry. Mardi Gras parades, perennially a major source of income for the city's musicians, did not roll for the duration of the war. One of New Orleans's two steamboat lines ceased its moonlight excursions on the river, further undermining employment opportunities for jazzmen. Thus, a number of factors diminished the vitality of jazz by the 1940s.[6]

By World War II, jazz had practically disappeared from the urban spaces of New Orleans most frequented by tourists. Leading downtown hotels had once employed local talent in jazz concerts, vaudeville acts, or in programs such as "The Night in Dixie," a racist skit at the Grunewald Hotel's Cave and Lounge depicting to conventioneers "the life of the plantation darky." By the 1940s, national acts had almost thoroughly replaced local talent in New Orleans's primary hotels. Hotel owners claimed that patrons preferred nationally known bands and performers and added that local bands played too loudly. In the rare cases when a local jazzman did find steady work in a New Orleans hotel, he often found it less than desirable. Trumpeter Sharkey Bonano complained that the management of the Roosevelt Hotel made him use a mute in his performances in the hotel's Fountain Lounge. Insisting that he never played loudly enough to need a mute, Bonano added, "But if they say mute, I use a mute. They are paying the bills." To be sure, plenty of talented musicians continued to play jazz in New Orleans, but only with difficulty could tourists find them. "It might well be true," Charles Edward Smith concluded, "that on an ordinary week end New Orleans would offer no more music than any other city its size."[7]

Although jazz appreciation stood at a low ebb in the 1940s, the actions of eager jazz pilgrims from around the world and a few local enthusiasts triggered a chain of events that eventually rendered the art form practically synonymous with New Orleans. The transition came in the midst of a crisis in which the city almost allowed one of its most recognizable cultural exports to die. World War II provided a tremendous boost to the local tourism industry, uprooting thousands of young servicemen and their families and redistributing them around the nation. New Orleans's proximity to a number of military camps, airfields, and war production plants enabled many Americans to discover the city's distinctiveness. One army corporal observed that, while New Orleans's downtown differed little from that of other cities, the French Quarter "has history written all over it."[8] The arrival of outsiders during World War II not only bolstered tourism but also stimulated local appreciation of New Orleans's rich cultural heritage.

Outsiders began taking an interest in encountering New Orleans jazz on its own turf. In 1940, Heywood Hale Broun, editor of the New York–based Hot Record Society's newsletter *H.R.S. Society Rag,* traveled to New Orleans in hopes of recording the remaining vestiges of traditional jazz before the old musicians died. He recorded trumpeter Kid Rena and clarinetists Alphonse Picou and Big Eye Louie at radio station WWL, initiating a wave of recording.[9] Other jazz enthusiasts in the World War II years also made pilgrimages to the "Birthplace of Jazz." William Russell, a classically trained violinist, percussionist, and composer, was among the jazz scholars who went to the Crescent City beginning in the late 1930s to collect material for the pioneering book *Jazzmen,* which appeared first in England and later in the United States. Russell discovered trumpeter Bunk Johnson on a farm near New Iberia, Louisiana, approximately 150 miles west of New Orleans. After helping Johnson get a new set of teeth and a trumpet, Russell recorded him in 1942. Over the next ten years, Russell documented the work of many other elder jazzmen.[10]

The influx of servicemen during World War II also played an important role in stimulating interest in New Orleans jazz. Even as more than a million African Americans flocked northward in the 1940s, carrying their folkways with them, war-induced migrations put northern G.I.s in contact with a variety of regional music, including gospel, rhythm and blues, and jazz.[11] Many soldiers stationed on bases around Louisiana, Mississippi, and Alabama, and industrial workers employed by Higgins Industries spent their weekends exploring the Crescent City's elusive, vestigial jazz scene. Remembering the transformation, one native later wrote of the years preceding World War II: "It was one hell of a pleasant time. Boy, music was everywhere! We didn't even know it was jazz. Not until World War II brought all the soldiers and sailors, and the marine pilots on the lakefront, and people from other places to build Higgins PT boats. They talked about jazz like they talked about the people who, for a few months into 1943, still carried blackberries on their head to sell from door to door. They talked about jazz like it was unusual—good, but unusual. We found out that all music wasn't jazz, but all jazz was music people loved."[12] More often than not, these sojourners found less jazz than they expected, and some later returned to ameliorate the problem. Richard Binion Allen contributed immeasurably to the city's jazz renaissance. Allen, a native of Georgia, discovered New Orleans jazz during World War II while he served in the navy in nearby Gulfport, Mississippi. In his spare time, Allen went to New Orleans, where he befriended longtime drummer Arthur "Monk" Hazel, who introduced him to the ins and outs of the city's music scene. Four years after the war ended, Allen moved to New Orleans and worked tirelessly for the cultivation of the city's living jazz traditions, eventually serving as the first curator of the William Ransom Hogan Jazz Archive at Tulane University.[13]

The transformation of New Orleans jazz took about twenty-five years to accomplish and reflected a national trend in which white promoters popularized and to an extent controlled black popular music. While most of the city's bluebloods probably cared little for jazz, a few broke ranks and became prominent among local enthusiasts. Some became members of jazz clubs which, along with foundations, museums, archives, and concert halls, initially provided the most effective vehicles for the jazz revival. Dr. Robert Goffin, international lawyer and jazz reviewer for *Esquire* magazine, and several New Orleans enthusiasts formed the National Jazz Foundation (NJF), the first New Orleans–based jazz club, in May 1944 to promote the music.[14] The NJF attracted a variety of members, including a few from the old elite. Dr. Edmond Souchon was a prominent surgeon and board member of the Pan-American Life Insurance Company. Merlin "Scoop" Kennedy was a newspaperman for the *New Orleans Item,* while Myra Semmes Walmsley Menville's ancestral lineage included a Confederate senator, a Rex (King of Carnival), a Boston Club president, and a New Orleans mayor. The organization intended to stage concerts and band competitions as well as to open a jazz museum. It also assisted tourists who went to New Orleans in search of jazz music. At least one such pilgrim, with the aid of the NJF, attended a jazz funeral on South Claiborne Avenue in an uptown black neighborhood far from the beaten path most tourists followed.¹⁵ The organization, however, focused more heavily on national performers than local musicians. Recalling his difficulties in getting support from the NJF, Crescent City jazzman Johnny Wiggs later wrote, "I learned that this fine group had no use for local musicians. No, they had to have big names like Benny Goodman, Condon, Louie. They spent thousands of dollars on these bands while the New Orleans musicians stayed buried under rocks."¹⁶ Although the NJF failed to start a museum and disbanded in April 1947, it set in motion a determined effort on the part of some leading New Orleanians to resurrect jazz.

Less than a year later, on Mardi Gras Day, a small group of jazz enthusiasts gathered along the Zulu parade route and, during their wait, decided to establish the New Orleans Jazz Club (NOJC) to continue the agenda of the defunct NJF. The founders called upon many of the same elites who had belonged to the NJF. Like its predecessor, the NOJC served primarily as a social vehicle for an upperclass group sharing a passion for jazz music, but it also furthered the resurrection of the art form through publicity and the employment of languishing musicians for concerts, festivals, and recording sessions. The club held its meetings, during which jazz musicians performed, in the St. Charles Hotel. In the 1940s and 1950s the group failed to admit African Americans as members except as outof-town correspondents, for doing so might have tarnished the NOJC's image in elite circles and hampered the delicate task of reversing decades of neglect of the indigenous music.¹⁷

Just as jazz enthusiasts from around the world awakened well-positioned New Orleanians to the possibilities the music offered their city, the rise of tourism shaped the course of the jazz revival. What had started as a reinvigoration of a black music genre by jazz enthusiasts gradually became a cash cow for tourism promoters. The tourist trade fostered jazz in much the same haphazard fashion that the white business community had always treated the music, exploiting it with little regard for the musicians' welfare. Equestrian Steve Valenti's Paddock Lounge at 309 Bourbon Street stood apart in the French Quarter in the 1940s and

1950s as one of the very few places that featured jazz. Musicians such as Octave Crosby played old jazz but in a commercial style geared to tourists. To the delight of tourists, every hour on the hour at the Paddock, Valenti forced band members to play a double-time "When the Saints Go Marching In" while marching from the stage to the sidewalk outside and back. Probably echoing the sentiment of many tourists, Mrs. Steve Valenti boasted in 1961, "As you can see, this is the only authentic Dixieland jazz, and the people love it." The jazzmen hated this forced march and the restriction of their repertoire to crowd pleasers.[18]

Even after traditional jazz began its gradual postwar renaissance, it remained difficult for most musicians to find work more than a couple of nights a week unless they were fortunate enough to sign on at one of the few hotels or nightclubs that kept a house band or performer. Sweet Emma Barrett only managed to perform once a week, while DeDe and Billie Pierce, once in high demand, languished on relief and played only at the occasional request of their neighbors. Most Bourbon Street clubs succumbed to the shift toward striptease acts, which had begun in earnest during World War II and accelerated during the postwar years. Sid Davilla's Mardi Gras Lounge at 333 Bourbon Street, in financial straits by the 1950s, finally scrapped nightly jazz performances in 1956 in favor of girlie shows. Beneath the club's neon sign once hung a placard reading "Fred Kohlman and his New Orleans Jazz Band, playing the music that made New Orleans Famous!" After the change, a new sign called attention to an "All Star Show" and photos of scantily clad women adorned the windows. Davilla, a clarinetist, told NBC newsman David Brinkley in 1961 that jazz simply could not bring in tourists anymore.[19]

Although jazz had flourished through the constant replenishment of musicians with young talent, the tourist trade devoted inordinate attention to the oldest musicians. To be sure, for many years New Orleans jazzmen had left the Crescent City for cities such as Chicago and New York, where they built their reputations and signed record deals before returning to their home town in the twilight of their lives. Nevertheless, on Bourbon Street, which remained the city's most celebrated tourist space, nightclubs and bars sought old musicians because tourists "expect to hear an older black man, white shirt open at the collar, suspenders, simply cut trousers, plain black shoes, and legs crossed." In addition, jazz tended heavily toward New Orleans style, or Dixieland, because that fit tourists' conception of what the music should be.[20] Much as white audiences reinforced their stereotypes of African Americans by listening to the increasingly popular rhythm and blues artists of the 1950s and 1960s, tourists who went to New Orleans sought encounters with presentations of black jazz that enabled them to retain their pre-conceived notions.[21]

While the enthusiasm of outsiders and the formation of local clubs devoted to the furthering of jazz contributed heavily to the jazz revival by awakening native and tourist appreciation for the music, locally orchestrated dissemination of jazz music across the nation proved a similarly important catalyst for harnessing the art form to the city's tourist trade. For many years New Orleans passively exported jazz with the emigration of its most promising young musicians to cities like New York, Chicago, Kansas City, and Los Angeles. There the music adapted to progressive, ever-changing tastes while New Orleans remained more insular. With New Orleans musicians either unemployed or steered toward accommodating tourist expectations, the city's jazz music remained less changed than that played elsewhere. The city served as the cradle for music forms that evolved after they left.

The retention of a distinctive, traditional New Orleans style seemed an ideal springboard for cultural tourism. Yet New Orleanians had failed to assert themselves for decades, allowing New York record labels to dominate the marketing of jazz music and cities. In the 1950s, New Orleans watched as cities like Newport, Rhode Island, and Monterey, California, began staging jazz festivals that won international acclaim. Further, because few French Quarter clubs showcased jazz in the 1940s and 1950s, visitors seldom experienced New Orleans–style jazz. Before New Orleans could revive its reputation as the birthplace of jazz and become a Mecca for jazz pilgrims, it had to find a way of taking Mecca to the pilgrims.

A succession of local initiatives in the two decades after 1948 brought New Orleans jazz more squarely into the national mind. A combination of radio broadcasting, recording, and touring proved essential in stimulating the city's cultural tourism. Shortly after the New Orleans Jazz Club formed, the organization began sponsoring a weekly jazz show broadcast on radio station WWL, located in NOJC official Seymour Weiss's Roosevelt Hotel. WWL, a fifty-thousand-watt radio station, could be heard in all of the lower forty-eight states in the evenings. Jazzman Johnny DeDroit found when he toured the countryside in the Gulf South that many people had already heard him on their radios. WWL also made a deep impression on Bob Morris, an editor at the *Amarillo Daily News,* who then took a job with the *New Orleans Item,* where he promoted jazz more than ever before.[22] In 1950, radio station WDSU partnered with the United States Treasury and the American Broadcasting Corporation to feature a weekly jazz broadcast called *Dixieland Jambake* to help sell U.S. defense bonds during the Korean War. All ABC radio affiliates in the United States and Hawaii carried *Dixieland Jambake*, giving New Orleans jazz another major boost. Mayor Chep Morrison reported receiving many letters from all over the country as well as Canada and Hawaii in response to the program, a clear indication that radio programs propagated a tourist image of New Orleans as birthplace of jazz.[23]

Like radio broadcasts, commercially available recordings and national tour itineraries proved invaluable in solidifying jazz as a tourist expectation when visiting New Orleans. The establishment of traditional jazz as a major tourist attraction in the French Quarter has often been attributed to the founding of Preservation Hall, a jazz venue that opened in 1961 to reintroduce a number of old, long-forgotten jazzmen. Preservation Hall built its reputation not simply by providing an authentic atmosphere that appealed to Americans' growing nostalgia for an imagined past but also by recording albums and sending its musicians around the world on tours. Although its promoters truly saw themselves as breaking new ground, the Preservation Hall model actually found its antecedent in the efforts of Joe Mares Jr.

Along with his brother, trumpeter Paul Mares, Joe Mares operated Mares Brothers Furs, purveyors of furs, pelts, and alligator skins at 520 St. Louis in the French Quarter. In 1953, Mares started Southland Recording Studio and the Southland record label in the fur company building. While William Russell's seminal recordings in the 1940s had enlightened a local audience, Mares's Southland recordings found their way into national distribution, putting the first real dent in the "colonial" co-opting of local talent by New York and Chicago labels. Mares intended Southland to give New Orleans musicians, passed over by outside recording companies and unable or unwilling to leave the city, a chance to be heard. In addition to recording old jazz legends, Mares recorded many younger musicians who later achieved national fame, including Pete Fountain, Al Hirt, Jack Delaney, Johnny Wiggs, Sharkey Bonano, and Santo Pecora.[24]

As at Valenti's and Davilla's Bourbon Street clubs, Southland Records aimed squarely at white tourists and jazz enthusiasts. Its cover art often featured romanticized depictions of African Americans belting out jazz in a dimly lit club or serenading a dancing crowd from a Mississippi steamboat. Other covers presented stylized views of the Bourbon Street strip.[25] Cover notes suggested that the records would make excellent souvenirs of one's visit to the Crescent City. They underscored Mares's sense of having captured and resuscitated an endangered folk music purportedly unchanged since its formative years, an appeal to tourists' desire for authenticity. While disavowing any attempt "at recreating the sounds of yesteryear," Southland's recording of older musicians such as John "Papa" Joseph, who began playing in 1888, enabled it to deliver an "octogenarian echo." The recordings supposedly evoked the "humble negroe [sic] chanting his worksongs in the fields by day, moaning his troubles with blues in the night, and shouting his gratitude to God on Sundays," who had created the jazz that entertained businessmen, seamen, and tourists in Storyville.[26]

In addition to recording New Orleans musicians, Mares took them to perform on the West Coast, laying the groundwork for what eventually became a favored tool of the city's tourism officials for invoking interest in visiting the Crescent City. Mares's marketing ploy followed the lead of earlier promoters, notably those who exhibited ethnic peoples or recreated miniature resort lodges at international expositions. Mares negotiated with producers Frank Bull and Gene Normand to feature jazzman Johnny St. Cyr at the Dixieland Jubilee at Shrine Auditorium in Los Angeles in 1954. Two years after his first music-promoting trip, Mares took clarinetist Pete Fountain to California, where he got his big break when television personality Lawrence Welk discovered his talent. Trumpeter Al Hirt landed a job playing in Las Vegas shows after the same trip.[27]

By 1961, Mares's affiliation with the Dixieland Jubilee had led Walt Disney to take notice. That year Disney hired a six-piece New Orleans jazz band fronted by St. Cyr to play aboard the stern-wheeler *Mark Twain* as it plied the Disneyland River in the Magic Kingdom, replacing the rather lackluster sounds of wild animals and the crackling flames of a log cabin supposedly set afire by Indians. Beginning the following year, Mares and his musicians appeared in "Dixieland at Disneyland," which succeeded the annual concerts at Shrine Auditorium.[28] By 1964, Dixieland at Disneyland featured several Dixieland bands in a floating Mardi Gras parade on the Disneyland River. As each raft passed, a history of the nationwide dissemination of jazz unfolded from the narrator's script. Sharkey Bonano and His Kings of Dixieland belted out the "Bogalusa Strut" and other tunes aboard a raft decorated to represent Bourbon Street. For the finale, all the musicians congregated on Tom Sawyer Island as the riverboat *Mark Twain* sailed in with more than two hundred park guests holding sparklers. Roman candles and other fireworks exploded in the night sky above the island as Louis Armstrong blew "When the Saints Go Marching In."[29] After the show, the various bands scattered throughout the California theme park. Sweet Emma Barrett's band entertained at the Golden Horseshoe in Frontierland, while Sharkey's band jammed at the Tahitian Terrace in Adventureland. Kid Ory and the Young Men from New Orleans reminisced about their youth in "Storyville Memories," and Disney even staged a New Orleans fish fry.[30] The New Orleans Jazz Club of California, one of several such West Coast organizations dedicated to Crescent City music, observed, "To jazz fans, this is like Mecca coming to the pilgrim."[31] In 1966 Walt Disney opened New Orleans Square, his three-quarter-scale French Quarter replica, in his Magic Kingdom, affording a more evocative setting for jazz music.[32] The Disney shows in the 1960s reflected more than the personal tastes of Walt Disney; they reflected the growing popularity of New Orleans culture across the nation as the media made the city known in most every household. One newspaper noted in 1965 that several New Orleans–style restaurants and even an entire suburban subdivision with French Quarter–influenced architecture had recently sprung up in Los Angeles.[33]

If Joe Mares, assisted by Disney, supplied the prototype of going on the road to market New Orleans jazz to potential tourists, the founders of Preservation Hall brought the model to perfection and, in effect, created an evocative physical space that made the "Birthplace of Jazz" resonate with tourists. Outsiders' enthusiasm for New Orleans's musical legacy began to stir residents from their apathy, though it did not cure them completely. Just as the influx of servicemen and jazz devotees in the 1940s provided essential ingredients for the first wave of the jazz revival, newcomers determinedly provided an exception to the rule of strip shows and other cheap thrills in the French Quarter in the 1950s and 1960s. E. Lorenz "Larry" Borenstein, the son of Ukrainian Jewish immigrants to Milwaukee and grandnephew of Leon Trotsky, relocated to New Orleans in 1941 after an early career in circuses and sideshows in the Midwest. An avid art collector, Borenstein opened a succession of small shops in the French Quarter and eventually started the Associated Artists' Gallery in 1954 at 726 St. Peter, adjacent to Pat O'Brien's courtyard bar. Unable to leave his shop in the evenings to hear jazz shows, he enticed musicians to play informal sessions in the back of his gallery. Borenstein supplied beer and passed a kitty (a can for tips) to pay the jazzmen. Although he insisted he was simply a patron of the arts and expected no profit, Borenstein did use the concerts as an occasion to make business contacts.[34]

Borenstein's sessions evolved into Preservation Hall, essentially a jazz cooperative, which officially opened its doors to the general public on June 10, 1961. Prior to that, Borenstein called it Slow Drag's Hangout, after bassist Alcide "Slow Drag" Pavageau, and then Authenticity Hall.[35] Early audiences included mostly locals and Tulane University students, in contrast to the tourist traps on nearby Bourbon Street. Unlike the gaudy Bourbon Street clubs, Preservation Hall's interior was essentially unadorned except for a few Belgian paintings. The Hall served no drinks and provided only a few chairs for patrons. Advertisements billed the club as having "No Drinks—No Girls—No Gimmicks—Just Real Music!" Indeed, the music itself served as the focal point.[36]

Although Preservation Hall failed to turn a profit in its first two years, it soon soared in popularity as tourists became its main clientele. In 1962 Borenstein turned the Hall over to Allan and Sandra Jaffe, jazz enthusiasts who had come to New Orleans from Philadelphia the previous year. Allan Jaffe, the son of a mandolinist and music teacher and grandson of a Jewish musician in a Russian Imperial Army band, was born in Pottsville, Pennsylvania, in 1935. After studying cornet and piano as a child, Jaffe settled on the tuba, which he played in the marching band at Valley Forge Military Academy before enrolling in the University of Pennsylvania. He and his wife enjoyed listening to jazz phonographs and decided to move to New Orleans to pursue their interest. There, Allan worked as assistant controller for the D. H. Holmes department store on Canal Street, while Sandra took a job at a local market research firm. They searched for good jazz in the evenings and expressed dismay at the paucity of music they found. Jaffe later observed, "When we first came here, there was never a mention of jazz in the newspaper, or television." Disillusioned by the commercialized music catering to tourists on Bourbon Street, one night the Jaffes found themselves invited to Borenstein's gallery after a concert by the Eureka Brass Band outside the Cabildo, a couple of blocks away. They soon worked their way into Borenstein's circle and helped form the New Orleans Society for the Preservation of Traditional Jazz, which existed solely to promote Preservation Hall.[37]

Like Jacob and Mary Morrison, the Jaffes satisfied their nostalgia for the city's heritage by affixing their own imprint upon its most celebrated urban space. Immersing themselves in the timeless milieu of the French Quarter, the Jaffes moved into the former apartment of Pop Weitzel, a famed jazzman, on St. Peter Street near their jazz hall. Allan began sitting in on tuba, while Sandra passed the kitty. In the first year of official operation, the average donation amounted to a paltry thirteen cents. In the winter of 1962–63 the club finally broke even but again slipped into deficit when hot weather arrested the tourist traffic. Nevertheless, the club gradually caught on.[38]

The Jaffes observed that tourists believed erroneously that Preservation Hall had been in operation since the halcyon days of jazz and that the musical style remained unchanged since that time. Understanding that perception often was more important than reality when building a tourist attraction, the Jaffes studiously avoided making any changes to either the building or the performances. Further, the couple disliked the increasingly touristy feel of the French Quarter and wanted their jazz hall to provide an alternative to the many garish tourist traps then proliferating throughout the neighborhood. Indeed, the more commercialized the French Quarter became, the more authentic Preservation Hall seemed.[39]

Preservation Hall's popularity relied not only on its perceived authenticity but also on promotion through the news media and tours. Publications ranging from jazz journals to popular magazines and newspapers lavished praise on the venue. An appearance on the nationally televised *David Brinkley's Journal* on NBC perhaps gave Preservation Hall its most valuable billing. However, touring accomplished more than any news story, for it actually took the music to people across the country and around the world. Touring began in earnest in 1963 with a summer trip to Chicago by train. Shortly thereafter, the Jaffes took a Preservation Hall band on a three-month tour of Japan, playing ninety-two concerts for more than a quarter million people, including forty concerts in Osaka's three-thousand-seat Festival Hall. By the late 1960s, several different Preservation Hall bands were making regular tours. Through these tours, the Jaffes managed to plant Preservation Hall in people's minds as a must-see site on any future New Orleans itinerary.[40]

Preservation Hall's greatest contribution to the jazz revival lay in providing steady employment to forgotten, downtrodden New Orleans jazz players, many of whom lived in dire poverty in the sunset of their lives. The Hall also provided an after-hours meeting place for civil rights lawyers and activists, although police sometimes raided the place for allowing mixed-race sessions, often using the vague charge of "disturbing the peace."[41] Musician Harold Dejan later observed that the Jaffes did a great service not only to jazz enthusiasts, who as late as 1983 still paid only a one dollar admission, but also to musicians. "If you didn't have no horn, he'd [Jaffe] try to get you one. I don't know what would have happened to a lot of musicians without him."[42]

Preservation Hall might have had an even more dramatic impact on tourism in New Orleans had jazz promoters joined ranks more completely. Instead, factionalism within the ranks of jazz enthusiasts—including among the NOJC, Preservation Hall, the Jazz Archive at Tulane University, and others—precluded the kind of cooperation that might have led to a more comprehensive cultural tourism marketing campaign. When Brinkley visited New Orleans in 1962 to prepare his television digest on jazz, everyone with whom he spoke at the NOJC told him their organization was the city's one true guardian of traditional jazz. When Brinkley inquired about the role of the promoters of Preservation Hall, Dr. Edmond Souchon dismissed them as so many Communists.[43]

Even though jazz promoters did not always support its mission, Preservation Hall succeeded beyond the wildest imagination of its founders. It fed off the spectacular rise in tourism beginning in the 1960s, the ascendant American penchant for seeking the nation's cultural roots, and the increasing rarity of old jazzmen. For many visitors from around the world, Preservation Hall provided perhaps the most accessible means of encountering authentic New Orleans jazz. When 155 French youths visiting New Orleans told a representative of the NOJC that they wished to see one of the city's famed jazz funerals, in which brass bands accompanied African Americans to and from burial services, she first tried to explain that jazz funerals did not follow any set schedule and then recommended that they visit Preservation Hall instead.[44]

The Hall's success quickly led to spin-offs like Dixieland Hall and Southland Hall, although those clubs fizzled. Dixieland Hall, which opened in March 1962 on Bourbon Street, made a direct appeal to tourists by making its bands march around the club and by adding a clown and a singing dance trio. The Jaffes objected to such antics, preferring to let the music stand on its own.[45] Preservation Hall proved so successful, in fact, that in later years young musicians, who had come of age during the height of the civil rights struggle and associated Dixieland with segregation, hard times, and an Uncle Tom mentality, became inspired to take up the traditional style of playing. The Jaffes' establishment gave its owners a sense of stewardship of local culture and musicians a reason to cultivate their talents, and it also tapped a growing tourist appetite for transcending mass culture by seeking "authentic" experiences in evocative urban spaces. Preservation Hall was, perhaps, two decades ahead of its time, for only in and after the 1980s would New Orleans tourism promoters, like Civil War reenactors, planners of ethnic heritage festivals, and first-person interpreters at historic sites, fully tap the potential of authentic heritage experiences to stimulate discretionary or leisure tourism.[46]

The Jaffes operated under the assumption that they were helping traditional New Orleans jazz enjoy a dignified last stand before it sank into oblivion. In addition to his determination to provide a no-frills venue in which locals and tourists could enjoy Dixieland without being forced to observe an exorbitant drink minimum, Allan Jaffe supported another fading jazz tradition by sponsoring occasional Sunday afternoon French Quarter parades led by the Eureka Brass Band. In 1963

Jaffe confessed that he fully expected the revival to last only five to ten years because no younger musicians seemed to have an interest in the art form.

Jaffe was not alone in his belief that the revival of Dixieland jazz represented a golden opportunity for the world to experience New Orleans's unique cultural commodity before it died forever. Many others also sensed the passing of an era. Dr. Edmund Souchon of the NOJC observed, "The young Negroes don't want anything that smacks of Uncle Tom or minstrelsy."[47] With the death of Paul Barbarin, who had returned from Chicago to lead the Onward Brass Band, one Tulane student wrote that the city lost one more piece of its soul forever: "When the last New Orleans jazz musician blows the last dirge, a great era of American music will come to an end."[48] On the occasion of an Olympia Brass Band performance in Houston's Old Market Square in 1969, a Houston journalist put it even more starkly: "The hot winds of New Orleans jazz—the thumping, groaning, belching sounds of old Storyville—will be blowing cold in a few short years. The Dixieland greats, who took the Crescent City and the country by storm before World War II, are tottering one-by-one into their graves, replaced by a new cool syncopation and by the heady yowl of acid rock."[49] By the mid-1970s, however, the city was sprouting a new crop of enthusiastic musicians eager to learn traditional jazz, leading Jaffe to conclude that Preservation Hall might remain a New Orleans cultural icon for many years to come.[50]

While Preservation Hall gave New Orleans a highly visible, year-round, jazz-related tourist space, the establishment of an annual jazz festival assured an influx of tourists to the Crescent City in the late spring, traditionally a time when tourism slacked off. In a city noted for Mardi Gras and the Sugar Bowl, a jazz festival would lend cultural pastiche and inform the world that New Orleans had more to offer than fun and games. The staging of a festival would not only help reinforce the city's claim of being the birthplace of jazz but also draw wide attention to the art form's continuing vitality. What began as an unfulfilled part of the NOJC's mission in the 1950s turned into an event of international repute by the end of the next decade. However, the success of the undertaking, like that of attracting professional football and large-scale national conventions, awaited city leaders' realization of the necessity of working across racial lines. Whereas the NOJC, Southland Recording Studio, and Preservation Hall witnessed whites promoting segregated talent, the jazz festival ultimately involved both races not only on stage but in planning.

The idea of staging a jazz festival in New Orleans originated in the New Orleans Jazz Club, which held a small event with eight concerts in 1949 and 1950 in Congo Square, the site in Faubourg Tremé where African American slaves had met for evening leisure activities in antebellum New Orleans. By 1951 the format had evolved into one large concert with several bands playing in Municipal Auditorium. The NOJC reported that the event drew visitors from at least eleven states. Rather than building upon this promising start, however, the festival encountered difficulties for the rest of the decade. In 1953 the NOJC inadvertently scheduled the festival at the same time as a Nat King Cole concert. Unable to reschedule at the last minute, the NOJC canceled the festival. The following year the club partnered with the Crippled Children's Hospital and planned to give a portion of the proceeds to the New Orleans institution. When the festival cleared only $890, an editorial in the NOJC's newsletter *The Second Line* griped that the hospital's "infinitesimal cooperation . . . in no way helped ticket sales." Worse, the Dixieland Rhythm Kings, a band from Dayton, Ohio, playing at the festival, angered local bands when New Orleans newspapers gave them the lion's share of reviews. Band members also suffered physical assault in a seedy Bourbon Street bar and were threatened by police. The festival's ill fortunes continued in 1955. That year the NOJC entered a promotional agreement with the cosmetic firm Helena Rubenstein to help promote its "Hot and Cool Jazz" lipstick line. The cosmetics company asked the NOJC to represent traditional, or "hot," jazz at the festival in return for national publicity in magazines. To the dismay of NOJC officials, only one three-quarter-page advertisement ever appeared in print. Adding to the dashed hopes for national attention, the festival endured squabbles between NOJC and musicians and finally a tropical deluge that discouraged many people from venturing out on the day of the festival.[51]

Efforts to launch a jazz festival on sound footing languished into the 1960s largely because the NOJC tried to handle the event single handedly. Typical of the many isolated, insular efforts to stage tourist events in the city, broader civic cooperation was the missing essential ingredient. In 1958 a *Times-Picayune* editorial pointed to the Newport Jazz Festival, then in its fifth year, and charged that New Orleans was missing the boat. In 1959 the *Second Line* editorialized that the festival should be just as popular as the Sugar Bowl and Mardi Gras. The lack of an independent tourist commission before 1960 did not help matters. Instead, the New Orleans Board of Trade, the chamber of commerce, and the International Trade Mart—agencies whose charges extended far beyond simply promoting tourism—repeatedly held meetings trying to figure out ways of attracting tourists to

New Orleans during the slack season. Apparently they never contacted the NOJC to learn how they might cooperate in promoting the jazz festival, and the editorial suggested that perhaps the NOJC itself had not been sufficiently aggressive in making overtures to these organizations.[52]

By the 1960s the NOJC was coordinating its annual jazz festival with the New Orleans Spring Fiesta Association's two-week festival.[53] This marriage of upper-class promotion of colonial and antebellum houses and gardens with twentieth-century jazz marked the first organized effort on the part of the city's ruling class to infuse the imagined romance of New Orleans's halcyon days of elite white influence with the flowering of black musical artistry. Ironically, no sooner had this meshing of cultural imagery been accomplished than the blueblood conception of the city's proper packaging escaped their control. Indeed, the rising tide of jazz marketing coincided with the rampant profiteering of entrepreneurs opening any sort of tourist-oriented business that could in any way embody the increasingly heterogeneous mixture of tourist images—including strip clubs, jazz halls, rock 'n' roll and rhythm and blues clubs, Creole eateries, and Mardi Gras–themed souvenir and trinket shops. As jazz and Mardi Gras assumed a higher position in the hierarchy of marketable tourist images, the more genteel image of moonlight and magnolias gradually retreated to being a mere backdrop or stage set for tourists' sensory adventures.

In 1962 local 7-Up bottler and Greater New Orleans Tourist and Convention Commission president Harry England, Royal Orleans Hotel general manager Olaf Lambert, and Lester Kabacoff began discussing how to make the jazz festival reach its full potential. In December 1964 a number of prominent business and civic leaders met to discuss a festival to be held in late May 1965, and within a month they had secured the services of a producer, George Wein, a Jewish jazz enthusiast who had opened Storyville, a nationally known jazz club in Boston, as well as started the nation's first annual jazz festival in Newport. Just as Seymour Weiss, Edgar and Edith Stern, and Lester Kabacoff played an enormous role in the French Quarter and the hotel trade, Jews like Larry Borenstein, Allan Jaffe, and George Wein proved some of the most influential figures in stimulating jazz as a local tourist draw.

The first broad-based civic effort to stage a major jazz festival in New Orleans ran aground as a result of a tense racial situation. Less than a week after the leaders announced that Wein would produce the show, on January 14, 1965, backers suddenly postponed the event indefinitely, ostensibly because of the need for more thorough planning. However, extensive planning had been underway for three years, and the festival backers had raised $37,500 of the needed $50,000 in only two weeks. The real reason for the sudden reversal lay in the unfortunate racial incidents just days earlier that had forced the cancellation of New Orleans's AFL All-Star Game. The disorder in the city's most popular tourist space gave the promoters of a jazz festival second thoughts about the advisability of hosting an event that might be marred by a similar display of racism.[54]

Despite the damage caused by the AFL discrimination scandal, Mayor Schiro remained determined that the city should host a jazz festival. Answering Schiro's call, Jefferson Parish assistant district attorney Dean A. Andrews Jr. hastily organized the Annual International Jazz Festival of New Orleans, Inc., in preparation for "the greatest array of traditional jazz musicians ever assembled under one roof." Operating on a shoestring in a rent-free hall, Andrews staged the festival with no input from the city's jazz establishment, claiming that jazz leaders "hate my guts." Harry V. Souchon said Andrews had never invited the NOJC to participate. Drawing few known jazzmen, the 1965 festival barely registered with aficionados.[55]

The same civic and business who had led the abortive effort to host a festival that year began planning for the 1968 New Orleans International Jazz Fest, which would coincide with the two-hundred-fiftieth anniversary of the founding of New Orleans. By the second half of the 1960s, New Orleans's public accommodations generally complied with the Civil Rights Act of 1964. Leaders became more aware of the value of cultural heritage events like jazz festivals in promoting economic development, and festival backers finally acknowledged the need to involve the black community in planning the event. The festival promoters asked Larry McKinley, manager of radio station WYLD, and George "Tex" Stephens, a writer for Louisiana Weekly, to serve on their planning committee.[56]

In keeping with the festival's new name and broader goal of stimulating tourism, the event's promoters recruited internationally known musicians to augment local talent and set out to market the event worldwide. Festival backers differed over whether to emphasize national acts, and they vacillated when considering two candidates to produce the event, both of whom felt that only a mixture of national and local musicians could ensure the festival's success. Considering George Wein too interested in making a personal profit off Jazz Fest, promoters finally chose Tommy Walker instead. Walker, a Wisconsin native who had moved with his family to southern California in the 1930s and worked as a minor Hollywood actor, was building a bigger name for himself as a producer of football halftime shows and Walt Disney's *Wonderful World of Color*. In addition to advertising Jazz Fest in European cities, promoters emphasized the French influence on New Orleans music and worked with European travel agents to bring in foreign tour groups. In cooperation with International House, the festival devoted exhibits to several countries.[57]

After the inaugural Jazz Fest attracted about twenty thousand people to its events and netted just over $3,000, the 1969 Jazz Fest lost nearly $24,000. Not only did the event prove unsuccessful on the balance sheet, but it also did not satisfy critics, who noted the tremendous wage disparities between outside and local bands as well as the lack of recognition accorded the local jazzmen. While most national acts received between $2,500 and $5,000 for their performances, New Orleans acts usually got only $50 to $500. Although a number of local musicians took part in the Jackson Square and Canal Street pageantry preceding the opening of the festival, "these men were being used to advertise the music of others coming in from far corners of the jazz world." Jazz critic Charles Suhor lamented that New Orleans musicians "have a way of turning up in the national media. And when their talents are adequately fossilized, their instruments museum pieces, and the musical forms they are creating safely a part of jazz history, they probably will show up on the cover of the [*Times-*]*Picayune* Sunday supplement." Clearly, token black involvement proved insufficient to safeguard the interests of local musicians, even once Louis Cottrell, president of the local black musicians' union, joined the festival's board of directors in 1969. More balanced control of Jazz Fest awaited the liberal leadership of a racially inclusive city administration and the formation of the New Orleans Jazz and Heritage Foundation in 1970. Like most tourist-oriented events in the Crescent City up to 1970, the jazz festival relied essentially on white entrepreneurs' exploitation of black talent to entertain white visitors.[58]

In addition to stimulating a revival of recordings, concerts, tours, and festivals featuring traditional New Orleans jazz, the rise of tourism helped resurrect the city's brass band tradition. Like efforts to preserve the French Quarter, those who worked to revive jazz often served white nostalgia and economic interests as a primary goal. Just as racial desegregation of public accommodations fused with a rhetoric of tourism, white actions on behalf of blacks often said more about their own needs than those of the people they assisted. Yet the impact of tourism on the resurgence of New Orleans jazz produced perhaps the earliest signs that African Americans might ultimately begin to reclaim some of the dividends from their contributions to the city's tourist image. As with other manifestations of the tourist transformation of New Orleans, the jazz revival, especially the resurgence of street processions, reflected the ability of cultural preservation and promotion to empower those long marginalized. If the preservation of the French Quarter and Dixieland jazz gave voice to "neonatives" and the handful of local whites who sought to preserve what most old-line leaders disdained, the growing popularity of parading brass bands provided both a source of revenue and a foundation for black cultural resistance to white projects detrimental to the black community.

New Orleans brass bands date to the antebellum period, when the German military band tradition, brought to the city during a wave of German immigration, fused with African musical traditions. For a number of years bands played from sheet music, only gradually shedding this formality. In the 1880s bands such as the Excelsior, Onward, and Reliance Brass Bands developed a recognizable repertoire, appearance, and manner. The bands typically played dirges, marches, and hymns while marching through the city's streets. Gradually, by the early twentieth century, they became an important part of African American culture in the Crescent City.[59]

In predominately black neighborhoods such as Faubourg Tremé on the fringe of the French Quarter, a number of social aid and pleasure clubs formed after the Civil War as an indigenous form of mutual benefit society, in which a member paid dues to a fund used to assist any member who faced financial straits and to provide him a funeral with brass band accompaniment. Whenever a brass band played, a crowd customarily gathered around and danced as the band wended through the streets. This contingent, often carrying brightly festooned umbrellas and waving handkerchiefs, became known as the *second line,* a term that gradually became conflated with the whole spectacle. Although brass bands might be heard at most any time, the primary second-line season occurred from August to December when many social aid and pleasure clubs held their own parades. In addition to funerals, bands often played for picnics, family reunions, cornerstone layings, and dedications, and occasionally for Mardi Gras parades. Prior to World War II the custom remained largely unknown outside New Orleans, for it tended to occur beyond the French Quarter, out of the view of tourists.[60]

Jazz funerals became increasingly anachronistic in the postwar years as greater burial coverage by insurance policies rendered social aid and pleasure clubs less crucial.[61] Such organizations often continued their charitable work but focused more heavily on the component of revelry, often in conjunction with the growing popularity and proliferation of Mardi Gras parades. In addition, fewer black families buried their dead in the city's old above-ground "cities of the dead," opting instead for far-flung suburban cemeteries such as Mount Olivet Cemetery in Gentilly and Providence Park in Jefferson Parish. The tradition of brass band accompaniment could not bridge distances that required automobile processions.[62]

The dwindling number of existing brass bands geared their activities more toward the outside world as mass tourism and mass media built their reputation. Even as the custom receded, records, television, and especially films spread the second-line tradition to potential tourists. In 1951, two Harvard students, Alden Ashforth and David Wyckoff, made the first sound recordings of a parading band, the Eureka Brass Band. Within several years, Atlantic became the first major recording company to record a brass band when it issued an LP of the Young Tuxedo Brass Band. In addition to recordings, New Orleans brass bands found their way onto television and the silver screen. In 1953 the Cinerama Film Corporation staged a mock funeral featuring John Casimir and Young Tuxedo for a segment in its travelogue *Cinerama Holiday*. Three years later, Frederick Ramsey Jr. who had coedited the influential book *Jazzmen* a dozen years earlier, filmed Eureka in New Orleans for the CBS television documentary *Odyssey*. By 1965 Eureka enjoyed its first appearance in a full-length feature film, *The Cincinnati Kid*. Countless Americans gained access to the peculiar second-line tradition through such media, much as concurrent efforts to showcase other forms of New Orleans jazz added to the image of the "Birthplace of Jazz."[63]

By the 1960s, with their role in the black community in decay, most brass bands represented self-conscious attempts by nostalgic black and white musicians to revive a fading tradition for show. Of all the new brass bands that formed concurrently with the rise of tourism, Olympia Brass Band became the most famous. Assembled in 1960 by Harold Dejan, an African American and New Orleans native who in his earlier years had played aboard Mississippi riverboats, the integrated but mostly black marching unit took its name from a series of earlier bands, beginning with cornetist Freddy Keppard's Olympia Orchestra in the first decade of the twentieth century.[64] Like many New Orleans jazz bands, Olympia counted natives and newcomers among its members. In contrast to the typical scenario, in which black musicians left the plantation South for a new life in New Orleans, Olympia took in outsiders drawn to the city purely to soak up its musical legacy. For instance, Olympia trombonist Paul Crawford, born in Atmore, Alabama, in 1925, moved to New Orleans at age twenty-six and joined the band after graduating from the prestigious Eastman School of Music in Rochester, New York. Likewise, by the mid-1960s, Allan Jaffe could be seen playing his helicon as Olympia strutted through the narrow streets of the Vieux Carré.[65]

While Keppard's band and subsequent Olympia bands had played primarily for community functions, the new Olympia eagerly courted a tourist audience as well.[66] As the jazz funeral slowly lost its traditional function, Olympia became a cultural icon, a totem of yesteryear that joined other New Orleans curiosities as marketable commodities. Like Joe Mares's musicians and the Preservation Hall Jazz Band, the Olympia Brass Band gained widespread attention through its touring. In the second half of the 1960s, tourism officials began using jazz bands to promote New Orleans as a distinctive tourist destination. In the summers of 1966 and 1967, Olympia played in Washington, D.C., on the terrace of the Museum of History and Technology as part of the Smithsonian Institution's celebrations featuring American folk customs. In 1967, the 250th Anniversary of the Founding of New Orleans Committee, a group of city leaders promoting a year-long celebration in 1968, sponsored Olympia's appearance in Washington.[67] The Louisiana Tourist Development Commission, in conjunction with the Southern Travel Directors Council and the United States Travel Service, sponsored performances by the Olympia Brass Band as part of the Travel South U.S.A. mission to Europe in 1967 and 1968 and also sent the band to the annual convention of the National Association of Travel Organizations in Detroit in 1968.[68]

In addition to appearances in Brussels, Copenhagen, London, Madrid, Paris, Rome, and a host of other leading European cities, in West Berlin the Travel South U.S.A. delegation participated in the German-American *Volksfest* amid a makeshift recreation of the Vieux Carré. The festival, sponsored by the New Orleans chamber of commerce, the tourist commission, the Board of Trade, and International House, featured New Orleans exhibits and films, a Creole restaurant, amusement park attractions, a Mardi Gras–style parade, and daily performances by Olympia.[69] Paul A. Fabry, managing director of the International House, exclaimed at the *Volksfest*, "Everyone who has heard the Olympia Brass Band play here wants to come to New Orleans."[70] The 250th Anniversary Committee again underwrote the performances, demonstrating that tourism leaders in the Crescent City increasingly viewed jazz as a marketable commodity.

Given the lingering racial discrimination incidents that continued to plague New Orleans and the rest of the South into the late 1960s, some Europeans wondered to what extent southerners had corrected past mistakes. Noting the irony in the South's attempt to use African American culture as the centerpiece of its ploy to attract foreign travelers to a region still struggling with racial divisiveness, a London writer described how the Olympia Brass Band was "trouping all over Europe with a home-grown delegation of white chamber-of-commerce types who were trying to sell places like Mississippi, Alabama, and nine other Confederate states as tourist paradises, presumably on the assumption that Europeans don't read newspapers. . . . It makes a wonderful, horrendously funny, pitiable, sad contrast—these well-fed, pink-and-paunchy white folks showing off their six li'l darkies. Only this week it's not 'Hey, BOY! Shine mah shoes,' but rather, 'Yes suh, Herr so-and-so, these FINE gentlemen are typical of the rich cultural heritage of our southern states. . . .'"[71] Clearly, New Orleans's efforts to cultivate an air of cosmopolitanism left room for doubt.

Between foreign missions to promote New Orleans and the South, the cultural ambassadors of Olympia also fulfilled promotional needs at home. In 1967 the band marched into the Tulane Stadium (Sugar Bowl) to play in the "Sights and Sounds of New Orleans" halftime show devised by Tommy Walker for the inaugural New Orleans Saints football game against the Los Angeles Rams. The spectacle of strutting, umbrella-toting second-liners and brass musicians drew "amused laughter and applause, [and] some comment that this was really Mardi Gras." The NAACP frowned upon the "carnival skit" after its leaders saw the televised halftime show.[72] Less than three years later, millions of Americans saw "one of the greatest ads ever seen on television for New Orleans"—New Orleans's first Super Bowl. CBS televised the game's "Way Down Yonder" halftime show, again produced by Walker. This time trumpeter Al Hirt played "Streets of Dreams," the Southern University Marching Band from Baton Rouge performed a rendition of "South Rampart Street Parade," and "adopted natives" Lionel Hampton and Doc Severinson entertained. Following a mock Battle of New Orleans replete with cannon and cavalry, Walker trotted out the Olympia Brass Band in another staged jazz funeral.[73] Olympia even appeared in the 1973 James Bond film *Live and Let Die*, accompanying a jazz funeral through a suspiciously empty French Quarter street alongside Jackson Square.

On one level white promoters prostituted the black second-line tradition by harnessing it to television, film, professional sports, and tourism, stripping it of all meaning and forcing it into the service of the perpetual carnival that outsiders expected in the Mardi Gras city. It is, nonetheless, important to recognize the complicity of Olympia's musicians in this process. Like the musicians who followed Joe Mares to Disneyland or filled the dark recesses of Preservation Hall with song, Olympia found a way to make a living in a city that offered fewer and fewer job prospects beyond tourism. The bandsmen also understood and, on some level, accepted their role as cultural ambassadors for their city. Much as the Jaffes viewed themselves as preservers of a dying custom, the musicians of Olympia proudly billed themselves as one of the last two authentic Dixieland marching bands (along with Eureka).[74]

While most tourists surely learned of the city's brass band tradition through highly orchestrated appearances such as television and Hollywood depictions, promotional tours, and football halftime extravaganzas, not a few visitors to New Orleans sought to experience the second line in its indigenous context. From time to time, more adventuresome tourists reconnoitered the vestigial jazz funerals that still occasionally filled the streets. These funerals, which tended to serve as jazzmen's memorials to fallen brethren, appealed particularly to white jazz enthusiasts as well as other tourists who happened to catch wind of funerary itineraries. Sometimes the local media turned funerals into very public spectacles, especially if the memorialized was a famed jazz player. In 1961, for example, WDSU-TV filmed the Olympia Brass Band at jazzman Alphonse Picou's funeral, one of the station's first outdoor broadcasts.[75]

Heightened public attention often rubbed jazz enthusiasts the wrong way because it seemingly threatened to profane the sacred use of the brass band. Just as newcomers to the city often joined jazz ensembles in an attempt to insert themselves into local folkways, tourists often sought to experience jazz by joining the "second line" in jazz funerals outside the traditional tourist spaces of the city. Tulane jazz archivist Dick Allen observed that the 1966 jazz funeral for Avery "Kid" Howard in Tremé drew even more onlookers (four densely packed blocks) than Alphonse Picou's funeral, which had attracted many tourists in town for Mardi Gras.[76] Tulane jazz archive staffer Eleanor D. Ellis watched another funeral in the following year that drew a racially mixed crowd that appeared to her to include many tourists. She discerned an extra "put on" for the cameramen, indicating the ability of tourist expectations to alter native behavior.[77] Ellis also witnessed a jazz funeral in the Carrollton section of uptown New Orleans that had been advertised on a broadsheet in Preservation Hall. "A large and mostly tourist-looking" second line congregated in the cold outside the Zion Traveler's First Baptist Church or across the street in a corner grocery. She was appalled by the "many, many people with cameras, some of them . . . rolling around on the ground to get a good angle and other such antics."[78] Allen, who attended jazzman and friend Paul Barbarin's funeral during the Carnival season of 1969, echoed Ellis's sentiments: "I marched along with the family. But because he was so well-known, the funeral was publicized to the extent that it became like a Mardi Gras parade. It wasn't quite right."[79] Clearly, as anthropologist Helen A. Regis has argued, the injection of a tourist second line subtly altered the character and mood of the jazz funeral from an inward expression of reverence, mourning, and jubilation, to an outward, self-conscious spectacle for consumption by an audience who could never fully comprehend the milieu from which the spectacle sprang.[80]

The renewed brass band tradition did not always march in lockstep with tourists' desires and tourism leaders' plans. As was true with the Bourbon Orleans Hotel controversy, the black community did not always view cultural heritage through the same lens as whites. If brass bands increasingly found themselves putting on a show for growing hordes of tourists, occasionally they snubbed them in a demonstration that the music was not simply for outsiders' pleasure. The Olympia Brass Band did not forget the community from which its tradition issued. Accompanying the Tremé Sports Social Aid and Pleasure Club's annual parade in 1967, Olympia was supposed to take a detour to Jackson Square to pick up a second line of waiting tourists. From Jackson Square they were to lead them to the Royal Orleans Hotel for a concert to benefit the Cultural Attractions Fund, a fledgling agency intended to underwrite several performing arts groups in the city. Marching through the Quarter, the band never made it to Jackson Square, veering instead to the Caldonia Club in the predominantly African American neighborhood of Tremé, where it played to a mostly local black audience.[81]

Despite its reputation as a leading cultural exponent of the city's tourism industry, on at least one occasion the Olympia bandsmen also used the jazz funeral idiom as a vehicle for social protest. After several blocks of the Faubourg Tremé were razed for the city government's Cultural Center, part of a locally funded urban renewal scheme designed to rid the inner city of impoverished neighborhoods, the Olympia Brass Band staged a mock jazz funeral to symbolize Tremé's untimely death. Recounting the experience later in the day, Dick Allen wrote, "The crowd was immense and unruly, making it dangerous, or at least unwise, to get too close." The band accompanied a crowd huddled around a casket containing a clearly visible dummy that apparently represented the Cultural Center. When the crowd reached the old Caldonia Club on St. Philip Street, the pallbearers shoved the coffin through a high window of the club, from which a terrific ruckus could be heard as a crowd inside set upon the "body," beating it mercilessly. Soon children began hurling stones and bottles at the building, one of those slated for demolition. Finally, Allen fled the scene, for he "couldn't hear the music, and was afraid."[82]

The brass band spectacle, like the city's famed above-ground cemeteries, fascinated tourists despite its unpredictability. Some tourists' inclination to forgo the more scripted experience of the French Quarter prompted considerable trepidation on the part of hotel concierges, convention planners, and the tourist commission, who feared that unsuspecting visitors might stray into reputedly unsafe black neighborhoods in their search for local color. As some tourists found out, whether from the concierge or personal experience, venturing beyond the confines of the French Quarter to experience the second-line tradition did not come without certain risks. Tempers often flared in the crowds that gathered around the brass bands. The New Orleans Police Department (NOPD), then a predominantly white force, sometimes practiced a draconian manner of crowd control, adding to blacks' distrust of them.

On one occasion, a visiting reporter covering the Jolly Bunch Social Aid and Pleasure Club's parade in Tremé observed a number of white NOPD officers on horseback, "grim, unbending, clearly not enjoying the outing." Periodically, they rode their horses into the crowd with no regard for the people they trampled. When one child screamed after a horse stepped on her foot, the mounted officer hit her, and a second policeman roughed up another youth from atop his horse. Suddenly, on the fringe of the Lafitte Housing Project, a cop on horseback and brandishing a pistol chased a black youth through the street until he disappeared into the crowd. One witness told the reporter, "Ought to kill all the —— cops." Shortly thereafter, a rumor circulated that a cop on nearby Tulane Avenue had killed a boy. A stone throwing match ensued that only subsided when the sounds of the Olympia band swept up the crowd once again.[83] In another incident, a spectator shot a woman in the leg. An observer noted, "The white second line was small to begin with, and became even smaller after this."[84] The racial tension in 1960s New Orleans, always festering just beneath the surface, could easily erupt whenever white policemen became overzealous about crowd control in black neighborhoods.

Typical of New Orleans's attempts to tame its wild side and package it as a commodity for tourist consumption, at least one show attempted to distill the ambience of second-line jazz from the rough streets of Tremé in a lively, safe setting. In the spring of 1980, the Olympia Brass Band starred in the musical comedy *Back-a-Town,* coproduced by community activist Edgar F. Poree Jr. and Olympia trumpeter Milton Batiste.[85] Locals often referred to the neighborhoods of Tremé, Central City, and portions of Mid-City as "Back-of-Town." This term may have reflected the lingering black notion of the areas toward the Mississippi River as white lands and the areas away from it as black lands, for the land situated in the great crescent of the river that gave New Orleans its nickname was once comprised of slender, pie-slice-shaped sugar plantations stretching far back into cypress swamps. In antebellum days, slaves often occupied these rear portions, occasionally fleeing into the swamp as maroons. Even in the latter half of the twentieth century, much of New Orleans remained a racial checkerboard in which whites often clustered along and near broad, palm- and oak-lined boulevards while blacks congregated in dilapidated shotgun houses and cottages on side streets in what geographer Peirce F. Lewis calls "backswamp ghettos."[86] The musical promised tourists a glimpse into this "Back-of-Town" neighborhood that hoteliers and tourism officials warned against visiting. In the play, the character Elijah Conners sits on his front stoop and regales passing tourists with outlandish tales of old Tremé laden with racial stereotypes. In eight scenes, the play careens spatially and temporally among depictions of black life in "an African village deep in the Mother Country," a river plantation, a voodoo ritual, a parade by the "Boogie-Bunch Social Aid and Pleasure Club," and a jazz funeral for Madam Fast Sally, at which time the Olympia Brass Band fires up its second-line sounds.[87] The play's producers apparently hoped to evoke a sense of exotic New Orleans in a safe, tourist-friendly setting.

In the years that followed, black street culture drew tourists in spite of official efforts to channel this culture into more regulated scenarios. Yet brass bands did not simply follow the tourist script with appearances in the French Market, the New Orleans Jazz and Heritage Festival, and mock funerals for conventioneers. Instead, they took advantage of the economic benefits of grafting themselves onto the local tourist trade while refocusing their sights on community-oriented appearances. In the decades that followed, their actions revealed a paradox. The commodification of the second-line culture coexisted with the renewal of black interest in brass bands as a vehicle for rebuilding a sense of community in the aftermath of official efforts to expropriate a broad swath of Tremé under the auspices of a local urban renewal plan. While the Dirty Dozen Brass Band, which began as a neighborhood party band inspired by Olympia, became popularized following a gig at the Hyatt Regency Hotel, the brass band revival reflected much more than an adjunct to the tourist trade, despite the remuneration such performances promised. Tremé-based organizations like the Tambourine and Fan Club encouraged the resurgent brass band tradition as a means of building community pride among the neighborhood's youth. Similarly, Milton Batiste's efforts to stimulate youth interest in local jazz and Danny Barker's forming of the Fairview Baptist Church Band as an incubator for budding jazz musicians represented a response to the tourism-fueled jazz revival and an assurance that new generations of jazzmen might replace aging ones.[88] Thus, the city's focus on tourism brought monetary rewards for continuing old traditions that, like other aspects of New Orleans jazz, had seemed increasingly out of step with the self-image of younger African Americans until a cultural reawakening ensued. As was true of the effect of tourism on the local culture of countless communities, in New Orleans tourism both adulterated and enriched traditions that might not otherwise have remained important to locals.

The tourism-stoked jazz revival of the 1940s and subsequent decades, originally viewed by many enthusiasts as the final flowering of a soon-to-be bygone era, achieved something more remarkable. Rather than merely arresting the demise of the music and enshrining only a stereotypical Dixieland sound, it fertilized the soil in which a new crop of innovative jazz eventually flowered by the late 1980s and 1990s. Had Sterling Brown been able to return to the "Birthplace of Jazz," he would have experienced no difficulty in finding the city's leading jazz bands playing in venues catering to blacks and whites, locals and tourists. Following the lead of the Dirty Dozen Brass Band in the 1970s, in the 1980s and 1990s groups such as Re-Birth, New Birth, L'il Rascals, and Soul Rebels brass bands combined traditional Dixieland styles inspired by Olympia and other older bands, and fused them with hip-hop, rhythm and blues, funk, and Caribbean sounds to produce something new.[89] Black brass bands not only entertained tourists at Jazz Fest or in the clubs and streets of the French Quarter but also played for community-oriented events, including funerals, family reunions, and neighborhood gatherings, celebrations, and street processions, many of them distant from tourist spaces. Young brass players, many drawn from the burgeoning ranks of the city's public high school marching bands, accompanied old-line parades during Carnival season and groups of tourists and conventioneers, and also found their way into bands that played to enthusiastic crowds in African American community nightspots. When they plugged into the tourist economy, they did so on their own terms.

In short, if the tourist transformation of the French Quarter relied on the white exploitation of a heritage that ignored or trivialized African Americans' contributions, the effect of tourism on local black attitudes toward jazz produced a decidedly more positive outcome.

The tourist transformation of New Orleans required the presence of cultural conditions that outsiders might view as distinctive in an increasingly standardized national culture. This requisite had for many years, until changing national standards dictated otherwise, placed another arrow in the quiver of local whites who sought to romanticize racial injustice as a window into the Old South. The tourist trade also worked a profound change in local attitudes toward the city's heritage. Even as decision makers continued to focus on trade development and industrialization as tools for building New Orleans as a Sunbelt metropolis, the importance of tourism to the local economy often prompted them to take positions in concert with cultural preservationists rather than in opposition to them. Just as local promoters learned to use the French Quarter, once derided as a hopeless ethnic ghetto, as a stage set for the presentation of cultural distinctiveness, they also learned to treat traditional jazz, once dismissed as a "low streak in man's tastes," as one of the voices for the expression of that distinctiveness.

CHAPTER 5

SELLING "THE GREATEST FREE SHOW ON EARTH"

It's a myth made of tinsel, yet a real way of life to those proud of French lineage
whether existent or not.   —SID MOODY (1972)

On the eve of the 1967 Mardi Gras celebration that plunged the Crescent City
into another fit of pre-Lenten revelry, a feature written by *New Orleans States-Item*
columnist Charles L. "Pie" Dufour appeared in *Southern Living*, the South's leading
travel-oriented publication. Dufour described the crowds that filled the streets:
"Lyndon Johnson walking down the street arm in arm with Joe Stalin or Khrush-
chev, threading his way through hordes of clowns and cannibals, astronauts and
alligators, bunnies and bunny girls, Batman, Superman, and little green men fresh
from their flying saucers, devils, Indians, pirates, Rebel generals, colonial dames,
and hundreds of others. . . . This is Mardi Gras in New Orleans. This is 'The Greatest Free Show on Earth.'" The *Southern Living* contributor went on to assure read-
ers that "there is nothing else on the North American continent like Mardi Gras
in New Orleans." Dufour was careful to emphasize that Carnival was authentic
because it was "financed exclusively" by private "krewes" without "a penny of subsidy from city, civic, or business interests," and without any coordinating efforts or
organization whatsoever. In a mere two pages, Dufour outlined the New Orleans
white elite perspective of Carnival by conjuring images of streets that filled with
maskers, parades that magically materialized on their own, and a celebration that
existed for New Orleanians themselves, and, of course, any tourists who wished
to join the party.[1]

Indeed, this characterization proved persuasive, for the French Quarter swelled
each winter with thousands of eager tourists in town for Carnival. Just as tourists
considered Macy's Thanksgiving Day Parade and the dropping crystal ball at Times
Square's New Year's Eve celebration to be New York traditions, they readily associated Mardi Gras with New Orleans. For the throngs of revelers perched on the
rickety iron-clad galleries, the narrow streets below presented a colorful mosaic
of humanity, often in drunken abandon. Hordes of onlookers joined the spectacle
of maskers, college students, hot dog and corn-on-the-cob vendors, and camera-
toting tourists outside neon-decked taverns and nightclubs as the wail of sirens
grew closer. Soon the first glimpse of the flashing blue lights of squad cars and the

flicker of flambeaux, the kerosene-fired torches used to illuminate parades, would announce the arrival of Comus, the last of several nightly processions through the Vieux Carré. For the next hour, thousands of outstretched arms would jostle for the colorful beads and baubles tossed by the city's self-styled aristocrats as they proceeded to their private ball.

Tourists probably seldom considered that the entire spectacle, despite its social meaning for many locals, was becoming not just intertwined with but gradually dominated by tourism interests. In order to understand the tourist transformation of Mardi Gras, it is essential to make a distinction between the pre–World War II celebration, which already featured some parades aimed especially at tourists, and that of the postwar years, which by the 1970s began to reflect the eclipse of the Carnival establishment's control over the shape and public image of the spectacle. Although many city leaders yearned to build upon the modernizing impetus of World War II to steer New Orleans away from the languor that the holiday epitomized, old-line Carnival organizations resumed their festivities with similar verve in 1946, little expecting that, in the ensuing decades of social, political, and economic change, they might lose their ability to dominate the most visible presentations of the city's social order to a national audience.

In the postwar years, the New Orleans Carnival celebration took up more time each winter as new parade organizations comprised of the middle class, black and white, took to the streets. Just as the city's jazz revival gradually drew upon a broader, biracial civic base, the expansion of the Mardi Gras festivities reflected the city's changing dynamics of race and class. Growing numbers of Americans, including many ex-GIs who had enjoyed their first taste of New Orleans revelry during the war, took advantage of improved highway, rail, and air travel that made the once-isolated city more accessible. For years the old elite continued to present the most popular parades and hold balls to which frustrated tourists could not gain access, but the postwar decades saw the emergence of new Carnival organizations and events that offered mostly middle-class locals and tourists more participatory experiences than old-line krewes provided. These became the new standards by which visitors (and even many New Orleanians) began to measure Mardi Gras festivities.

Despite Dufour's claim that Mardi Gras required no city expenditures or coordination, the annual celebration was anything but free and spontaneous. As historian David Glassberg argues, urban business leaders had since the late nineteenth century sought to appropriate civic celebrations such as Mardi Gras and harness them to the creation of a salable city image, yet they usually offered "representations of and for the collective but not necessarily by the collective."[2] Understanding the potential of Carnival to enrich the New Orleans economy, municipal and business leaders began in the twentieth century to search for ways to maximize tourist participation in a spectacle that still revolved around the classical and mythological names of a handful of upper-class parades and balls. The 1930s saw the formation of nonelite Carnival organizations like Hermes, with its dazzling, neon-lighted parade and tourist ball. Hermes contributed to the process of diminishing the dominance of Carnival rituals that excluded those whose social pedigree did not afford admission. However, the postwar demands of an increasingly tourism-dependent economy led to the development of new Mardi Gras organizations and events that finally eclipsed the centrality of the venerable parades of the elite by offering a more overtly tourist-oriented Mardi Gras celebration. As a result, Carnival, like the French Quarter and traditional jazz, offered visitors an opportunity to participate in New Orleans's continuing cultural legacy.

The changes in Mardi Gras reflected not only the emergence of dynamic new civic leaders and the concurrent slippage of old families but also the impact of the civil rights struggle. While civil rights victories did not lead to a truly integrated Carnival, they shook the foundations of white promoters' interpretation of black culture for tourists. They also increased white visitors' curiosity about black forms of street spectacle. Perhaps more importantly, they pointed to landmark changes in local notions of the proper use of public space which privileged newer, racially inclusive, tourist-oriented parade clubs over the blueblood krewes that had long appropriated St. Charles Avenue and Canal Street during Mardi Gras.

In the midst of these changes, city officials struggled to balance careful organization and control of Mardi Gras's distinctiveness with preserving the illusion of unchecked revelry and hedonism that tourists had come to expect from the city's promotional slogan "The Greatest Free Show on Earth." In fact, by the time Dufour's article appeared, the tradition of masking was drowning in a sea of unmasked revelers who were much more likely to conflate the event with annual bashes on Florida beaches. This chapter demonstrates the intersection of tourist expectations and local social and economic developments at a time when it was becoming increasingly difficult to safeguard the image of a spontaneous, exotic celebration from the debauchery of revelers and the standardizing effects of commercialized American culture. The Mardi Gras celebrations of the late twentieth century retained the patina of venerated traditions yet aimed at pleasing tourists increasingly accustomed to dazzling pageantry in theme parks and on television and the silver screen. In the years after 1970 New Orleanians wrestled with the place of Carnival in their civic life and with the problems wrought by its explosive growth. Among the results of growing efforts to please tourists was a reorientation of a black parade to cater to white expectations.

The parades of old-line Carnival krewes such as Rex, Comus, Momus, and Proteus and newer parades that mimicked their aristocratic air arguably impressed tourists because they appeared in such stark contrast to the menial or burlesque roles of the African Americans who shared the streets with them. In 1956, as the civil rights struggle was intensifying, Tulane University anthropologist Munro S. Edmonson rightly suggested that "Carnival royalty expresses symbolically what New Orleans used to be," especially "reflecting the old plantation society."[3] As had been true before World War II, racialized representations of social hierarchy lay at the heart of the public celebration of New Orleans's Carnival in the years following the war. Tourists to the Crescent City not only imbibed mint juleps, gin fizzes, and plantation punch in the taverns of the French Quarter, they also soaked up images of blackness filtered through the lens of the Old South myth, Jim Crow, and colonialism. Much of the city's tourist appeal rested on promoters' ability to situate New Orleans firmly within an Old South cultural tradition and to set it apart almost as a foreign realm in which the tourist could glimpse the juxtaposed images of European sophistication and Afro-Caribbean primitivism, all without leaving the comforts of a thoroughly modern American city. African Americans served tourists as cooks, waiters, musicians, porters, and hack drivers, and they also formed a cast of characters that enthralled visitors taking in the theatrics of Carnival. Just as tourists in New Orleans came to expect Dixieland jazz to be played by gray-headed black men, they also expected blacks to appear in stereotypical roles during Carnival.

Although African American participation in public Carnival consisted primarily of neighborhood processions that few whites saw, white tourists' primary contact with black Carnival was the Krewe of Zulu's parade, which snaked unpredictably through a variety of neighborhoods and business districts, black and white. Developing out of a Fat Tuesday procession in 1909 in which a "king" wore a lard-can crown and wielded a banana-stalk scepter in parody of Rex, Zulu began annual parades in 1915 and was incorporated as the Zulu Social Aid and Pleasure Club the next year.[4] Although Zulu served every day of the year as a fraternal and mutual benefit organization bringing together longshoremen, day laborers, vegetable peddlers, and other working-class African Americans, the organization became widely known for its zany depictions of African jungle life on just one day each year. Appropriating and parodying the tradition of minstrelsy, Zulu members appeared in blackface with jungle costumes, usually grass skirts and black tights. Float riders tossed hand-painted coconuts as souvenirs, while "warriors" waved spears. In addition to King Zulu, the parade's stars included Queen Zulu, the Big Shot from Africa, and the Royal Prognosticator. For members, Zulu was an outlet for satirizing the elitist assumption of aristocratic manners in the white community's staging of Carnival. While its members apparently had no qualms about producing a spectacle that painted a stereotyped picture of blacks, many New Orleans blacks began to frown on Zulu after World War II and increasingly during the civil rights struggle of the 1950s and 1960s.

If Zulu's conscious parody of Rex stirred mixed feelings among the city's African Americans, it also clearly sparked enthusiastic approval from elites who wished to safeguard segregation and tourism promoters who saw profit in upholding an image of racial disparity. Although not staged by the tourism industry, Zulu mimicked a receding entertainment tradition of comical routines performed by blacks or whites in blackface in Atlantic City, Saratoga Springs, Virginia Beach, Wildwood, and other U.S. resorts earlier in the century.[5] In 1940 New Orleans preservationist and author Harnett Kane described the Zulu spectacle in one local newspaper as a "theme out of Tarzan and Weissmuller, with or without credit to MGM," tying the parade firmly into prevalent American notions of Africa as the dark continent. Illustrated with cartoons depicting blacks with exaggerated features such as bulbous eyes, thick lips, round noses, and jet-black skin, Kane's article romanticized the racialized exoticism of Zulu for a white audience, even referencing cannibalism. Aware of its utility to white business leaders, in 1941 the krewe advertised its "Zulu Carnival Pageant and Voodoo Ritual" as a rare opportunity for the white public to glimpse Zulu's king, queen, warriors, and attendants, and their mock tribal customs. Billed as "Weird—Exotic—Primitive," the tourist show, like the sideshows that mushroomed alongside amusement parks and expositions, fed the insatiable white tourist appetite for social anomalies in an increasingly modernized society.[6]

While to an extent, Zulu, like the Olympia Brass Band, came to embrace its emerging role as a cultural icon for tourists in New Orleans, many African Americans began to question the efficacy of blacks' willingness to fulfill tourist expectations. The postwar period, as historian Reid Mitchell argues, saw deep divisions within the black community over the degree to which black involvement in Carnival should remain tied to pleasing whites, a development that also had important ramifications for the metamorphosis of one of the nation's most illustrious tourist attractions.[7]

As elsewhere in America, the experience of World War II had created growing black dissatisfaction and impatience with racial discrimination in New Orleans. Emblematic of this emerging trend, during Mardi Gras in 1946 Zulu boldly appeared for the first time on Canal Street, the center of the city's white commercial district. Not only did some blacks test the rigidity of the color line in downtown New Orleans, they also limited their support of white elite parades. For years African Americans had thrilled parade goers by twirling flaming torches attached to long poles. Originally intended to illuminate parades in the days before electric street lights cast a perpetual glow, flambeaux remained an important tradition that set Mardi Gras apart. Most blacks who carried flambeaux struck for better pay in 1946, leaving the Knights of Momus parade virtually dark. With economic conditions improving after more than a decade of depression and understanding that krewe captains valued the spectacle they offered the crowds, these black workers had no intention of accepting the same wage they had received prior to the war. Fearing the loss of the popular sight of black torchbearers marching in the shadows of the city's leading luminaries, prominent white krewe captains met the following day and decided to raise the hourly wage from $2.00 to $2.50, still far below the $5.00 that the carriers had demanded. The next night, the Hermes parade, a favorite of tourists, endured a similar absence of flambeaux.[8]

Fearful that the strike might inflict great damage on the city's Mardi Gras image, krewe captains, as Mitchell explains, arranged with the city's daily newspapers to run propaganda pieces that "urged that Negro ex-servicemen come forward as volunteers in order that the resumption of the Carnival festivities after a lapse of five years not be marred and that the thousands of visitors and service men and women here to enjoy the gai[e]ties not be disappointed." The suggestion that veterans resort to carrying flambeaux angered many African Americans. One war veteran fumed, "Of all the nerve, appealing to veterans. There's not a place along the parade route where vets' wives or children can find seats to see parades. All seats made available are for whites." Another added, "Who in the h[ell] wants to put on those monkey gowns and clown for people?" Another black New Orleanian complained that Carnival parades were not for blacks, who were able to attend only "because nobody has found out how to control a mob of people by roping off the streets and hanging out 'white and colored' signs." In 1947, the year that Zulu was prohibited from parading on the traditional elite white parade route under the pretense of municipal regulation of routes, blacks showed up in sufficient numbers to carry flambeaux for $3.50 an hour. However, the following year a new strike against Momus forced that krewe to accede to demands for at least $4.00 an hour.[9] To whites, flambeau carriers did more than simply light the way. They also reinforced popular notions of the "contented Negro" who enjoyed entertaining whites. One observer noted that "the antics of these fun-loving comedians gives [sic] a big percentage of the color to our ever magnificent parades."[10] If African Americans after the war would not participate in the white-dominated public spectacle without proper pay, the white Carnival elite decided that it had to maintain the illusion of white supremacy no matter the cost.

If flambeau carriers' blackness shed as much light on the dominance of white krewes as did their fiery torches, Zulu offered whites a parade that emphasized white refinement by juxtaposing a savage motif. Expressing the sentiments of many influential whites, leading newspapers publicized Zulu as a spectacle not be missed. A professor at New Orleans's Dillard University likened Zulu's role in Mardi Gras to that of a clown in a circus: "A man going up on a high wire is more effective if two clowns fall off first, and Rex is more beautiful because Zulu is ridiculous. The clown doesn't have to be a Negro . . . but in this area, where we think in terms of black and white, it's logical that it should be a Negro. . . . There's nothing in the South as important as being white or Negro, and you can't have an all-white Carnival or the whiteness wouldn't show."[11] The local press also encouraged the wild spectacle in articles with titles like "Head-Hunters on the Loose." One Zulu official remarked that "the merchants want this parade on the street. The Carnival would go on if there was no Zulu, but the life would be took out of Carnival." Hotelier Seymour Weiss admitted that the New Orleans Hotel Association gave money to Zulu every year. Echoing the commonly held paternalistic white view of Zulu and its role in the tourist trade, Weiss remarked, "It's an interesting, funny adjunct to Carnival, and the colored people don't have much money." Indeed, the Zulu parade featured all of the buffoonery that many whites ascribed to African Americans.[12]

As the civil rights struggle heated up, divisions along color, religious, and class lines once again opened wide in the city's black community. As Reid Mitchell demonstrates, this social rift set the stage for a dispute between the middle- and upper-middle-class Afro-Creole leaders within the movement and the black rank-

and-file who saw little wrong with staging a parade that was merely intended to appear as exaggerated in its own way as Rex did.[13] Afro-Creole leaders protested segregation by urging a black boycott of Carnival in 1957. United Clubs, Inc., an umbrella organization headed by Dr. Leonard L. Burns which encompassed black social clubs and the local black musicians' union, urged its members to cancel their Carnival balls to demonstrate solidarity with the Montgomery and Tallahassee bus boycotts. They admonished, "It is immoral for Negroes in New Orleans to dance while Negroes in Montgomery walk." Many well-established black Carnival clubs, including the Bon Temps and the Plantation Revelers, canceled their balls and refrained from costuming in the streets.[14]

When these leaders pressed Zulu to cancel its parade out of respect for black struggles throughout the South, Zulu and white business and civic leaders bristled. Four years later in 1961, black activists persuaded Zulu to vote to cancel its parade. In the *Louisiana Weekly* and even the *States-Item*, a notice of a petition against Zulu appeared. Signed by 27,041 people, including many students at Dillard and Xavier universities, the petition decried the spectacle of "Negroes . . . paid by white merchants to wander through the city drinking to excess, dressed as uncivilized savages and throwing coconuts like monkeys," adding that if "we want respect from others, we must first demand it of ourselves."[15]

Upon learning of the Zulu cancellation, Mayor Morrison and police superintendent Joseph Giarusso showed up at a krewe meeting and reminded Zulu leaders that their parade was vital to the city's tourism interests. The city's school desegregation crisis was eliciting international indignation that withered New Orleans's reputation as a hospitable city, and the mayor worried that news of Zulu's withdrawal from Carnival might confirm in tourists' minds that racial turmoil was a distinct possibility. The city officials promised to beef up police security for the parade if Zulu would reconsider. Zulu rescinded its initial cancellation vote but not before the mayor had sent letters to newspaper editors around the country promising that Carnival would be the "best and biggest ever" in 1961. Though Zulu did in fact roll on Fat Tuesday morning, the crowd surely sensed tension in the air. Accompanied by guard dogs and squad cars, the parade hurried along its route, in stark contrast to its usual ambling pace. Burns recalled, "I mean zoom, zoom, zoom, and it was over."[16]

As the 1960s progressed, blacks argued over the proper role of Zulu while city officials and affluent whites fretted over the implications of efforts to tone down Zulu's spectacle or get rid of it altogether. The controversy brought Calvin Trillin to town to observe the embattled Zulus for the *New Yorker* in 1964. By the late 1960s, city leaders, fearing that the weakened Zulu organization might disband, urged the krewe to abandon its more educational depictions of African culture and return to its familiar dark-continent imagery, and they also helped integrate Zulu more firmly into the tourist spaces of the city. Just as white nostalgia helped enshrine Old South iconography by preserving and presenting French Quarter architecture and reviving and staging Dixieland jazz, it came to the rescue of what many considered the highlight of Carnival's public component. Led by Durel Black, a charter member of the New Orleans Jazz Club, a number of affluent New Orleans whites formed the Zulu Social Aid and Pleasure Club Honorary Organization in February 1967. Alarmed by the prospect of Zulu's collapse, the organization issued an invitation to join "a selective group of prominent people who have demonstrated that they take great interest in our city's history and progress." Membership would, according to one advertisement, foster wider appreciation of Zulu, improve race relations, and provide new social opportunities "with other Honorary Members." As Mitchell suggests, no mention was made of making friendships across racial lines. The honorary club, like the old-line krewes that had dominated Carnival for a century or more, played to wealthy whites' sense of paternalism and even offered a special Zulu doubloon and coconut as souvenirs. That year the new club raised the vast majority of the $9,000 cost of staging the Zulu parade, which resumed its old style. The renegade *Vieux Carré Courier* lambasted the effort, noting that Zulu "has decided to return to the Uncle-Tomism of mock Africa; everyone knows they are financed by white business leaders."[17]

White interest grew in the years that followed Zulu's acquiescence to prevailing expectations, but the establishment lost its control over black participation as the implications of the booming tourism industry and civil rights victories began to manifest themselves. As the 1969 Carnival season approached, two white businessmen formed Creative Enterprises, Inc., and set out to publish an "Official King Zulu Mardi Gras Souvenir Magazine" for tourists. Even though the Zulu parade had in the past enjoyed warm support from a number of black businesses, as late as December 1968 only one black business had taken an ad in what many blacks apparently viewed as an "Uncle Tom" publication, reflecting "a great deal of animosity in the Negro community to Zulu," according to one advertising representative.[18]

City hall, too, worked to bolster Zulu's tourist potential. To the dismay of old-line Carnival captains, in 1969 Mayor Schiro granted Zulu a permit to use the standard St. Charles-to-Canal parade route previously reserved for white krewes. Although Zulu had appeared on Canal Street in the immediate postwar years, the hardening of Jim Crow subsequently had relegated the parade mostly to black neighborhoods. Thus, many white tourists had never seen the parade prior to 1969 unless they watched from certain areas on the periphery of the downtown business district, generally several blocks away from the municipal viewing stands erected for out-of-towners. Instead of ending the Zulu parade at the Geddes Funeral Home in the black neighborhood of Central City, about a mile north of the tourist activity on St. Charles Avenue, the parade now disbanded adjacent to the French Quarter at the Municipal Auditorium, long a white preserve during Carnival season. By harnessing a once unpredictable, erratic parade to a set route, the city government, with the support of the krewe's increasingly Afro-Creole membership, effectively pruned Zulu from its black working-class roots and grafted it onto the branches of the tourism industry as an essential sight one must see to have truly "done" Mardi Gras. Some New Orleanians, not surprisingly, were less than thrilled with the change. One woman residing on LaSalle Street in Central City complained that the new route was inconvenient for many blacks and added that "most of us probably won't be watching anymore." With the blessing of city leaders once determined to segregate Carnival festivities, Zulu brought its stereotyped interpretation of African culture fully into the tourist realm.[19]

During the black power phase of the civil rights era, "Negro militants . . . threw handbills attacking the Zulu philosophy" as float riders "handed carved coconuts down to the crowds." But white acclaim for Zulu drowned out the vestiges of a two-decade struggle. Indeed, Zulu became more and more absorbed into the standard tourist experience by the early 1970s. The krewe retained Blaine Kern, who designed and built elaborate floats for Rex and other leading white parades, to create a new look for Zulu that melded the jungle motif with his more mainstream, flamboyant designs. In 1971 the krewe's coronation ball moved to the Royal Sonesta Hotel (another "sugarcake imitation" French Quarter inn developed by Lester Kabacoff after his success with the Royal Orleans), underscoring the krewe's growing incorporation into mainstream Mardi Gras.[20]

If Zulu was becoming more and more a high-profile rival to Rex and other old elite parades by 1970, old-line krewes also faced continuing challenges from the blacks they hired to facilitate their parades. Black flambeau carriers for Comus, Momus, and Proteus developed the habit of abandoning the floats they were assigned to illuminate. Without warning, the men sometimes rushed with their oil-fired torches to the spaces between floats and put on a show of their own. Comus himself, accustomed to a grand finale before throngs of revelers on Canal Street, watched as his flambeaux departed. Pie Dufour, who often echoed the sentiments of old-line New Orleanians, groused that krewes paid for this service and suggested that carriers be forced by New Orleans Police Department (NOPD) officers to remain in their place and be required to don placards around their necks reading, for example, "Assigned to Float No. 5." While the carriers surely understood that staging their own street performances, rather than marching single file alongside floats, offered greater potential for earning coins tossed by spectators, they probably also viewed their actions as a means of resistance to the ruling class.[21]

Although the core of the public Carnival celebration in the postwar years and through the 1960s remained the parades staged by the city's old elite, the municipal government and astute business leaders outside the Carnival establishment worked to improve the tourist experience of a celebration that nevertheless had become synonymous with New Orleans itself and important to its economy decades earlier. With so many visitors clamoring to experience New Orleans's Mardi Gras, the city's hotels could not accommodate the influx. Many visitors took advantage of special tour deals offered by Illinois Central and Southern Pacific railroads and spent their nights in "Pullman Cities" with thousands of other travelers aboard hundreds of passenger cars stationed in five rail yards outside the French Quarter. In addition to his efforts to attract new hotel development, Mayor Morrison took stopgap measures, such as arranging to house visiting journalists who might otherwise be unable to publicize the event. The Morrison administration set up cots in city hall and in its Department of Latin American Affairs and placed other visitors in extra bunks in the city's forty fire stations. In addition, the New Orleans Association of Commerce continued its prewar program of directing tourists to private homes whose owners had agreed to house Mardi Gras guests.[22]

Despite the commonplace that Mardi Gras existed without municipal subsidy or interference, the city government did much more than assist in locating accommodations for overnight visitors. For many years the city had decorated street light standards with Carnival banners; planted royal palm trees on Canal Street despite repeated freezes; issued parade permits; provided police protection; erected steel viewing stands on St. Charles, Canal, Rampart, and other downtown streets; and swept and washed the streets clean after each parade. As tourism became more important to the city's economy, municipal officers spent considerable time making sure Mardi Gras won favorable impressions. Amid the 1960–61 school desegregation crisis, the mayor's office and the tourist commission became increasingly defensive amid unflattering national news coverage.

Maintaining a favorable national image required managing media coverage of prominent civic events like Carnival. Even as the number of parades soared, the municipal government worked to uphold the appearance of Carnival as a distinctive attraction. When wire-service reports characterized Mardi Gras as getting off to a "dismal" start, tourist commission official Glen Douthit complained that reporters had insisted on covering the tiny Gemini parade as the kickoff of Carnival rather than later, splashier processions by larger krewes.[23] Mayor Morrison called upon the *Dave Garroway Show* in New York to correct the unfavorable impression its coverage had given, to no avail. Unable to control outside newsmen, city officials and leading captains of Carnival met after Mardi Gras in 1961 to seek ways of safeguarding Carnival's image. Krewe of Mid-City captain Charles A. Bourgeois told of hoteliers' complaints that the proliferation of smaller parades had damaged tourist interest by making it possible for a visitor to get his fill of festivities in four or five days rather than eight to ten. The krewe captains urged the city council to adopt an ordinance that would restrict the official Carnival parade season to nine days, require a $2,500 cash deposit for each parade, disallow the renting to more than one parade of any float that entered the downtown area, and establish a minimum number of floats in order to receive a parade permit. Several months later the city council passed an ordinance adopting most of the captains' suggestions and banning the use of parades for any overtly commercial or political ends.[24] The proliferation of Carnival parades, then, forced those concerned with maintaining tourist interest to take decisive steps to safeguard the illusion of a grassroots celebration.

Apart from the city's efforts to accommodate and impress growing numbers of visitors during Mardi Gras, local entrepreneurs worked to create a more participatory celebration by taking advantage of television to reach local, regional, and national audiences of prospective tourists. In collaboration with the district manager of the General Electric Corporation, WDSU founder Edgar Stern offered the first telecast of the New Orleans Carnival in 1949, clearly appealing to the upper-middle-class whites who were beginning to purchase television sets and who fit the description of the typical guest of the Royal Orleans Hotel. From the steps of city hall and the front of the Boston Club, WDSU cameramen filmed nine parades, including some of the newer, nonelite krewes that now shared the streets with Comus, Momus, Proteus, and Rex. Aired up to one hundred miles into the flat hinterland surrounding New Orleans, Stern's broadcast likely inspired many day-trippers who would not need hotel accommodations during their short stays.[25] Another major boost was the "Greatest Bands in Dixie," sponsored by Optimist Clubs of New Orleans as part of the Mid-City parade, which brought more than three thousand high school marching-band members from across the South in the 1950s and 1960s and stimulated national television publicity.[26] In addition, several national programs, including the *Colgate Comedy Hour* on NBC and the *Arthur Godfrey Time* on CBS, filmed segments during Mardi Gras, bringing into suburban living rooms images once experienced only in motion picture news-reels.[27]

Although tourists could attend any of the city's parades, they frequently expressed dismay at their inability to view the storied spectacle of a Carnival ball, with its colorful "royalty." While the Krewe of Hermes had since 1937 promoted itself as an organization catering to tourists, each year it issued only a limited number of invitations for its ball to the city's leading hotels. In 1949, restaurateur Owen E. Brennan formed the Krewe of Bacchus and persuaded Dr. Henry A. LaRocca to reenact his Krewe of Alla ball specifically for tourists the following year. Working closely with Brennan, hotels and travel agents distributed more than three thousand invitations inside yellow souvenir folders with an illustration of Cinderella's pumpkin coach on the outside. The allusion to Disney's fairy tale was appropriate, for in effect Brennan cast himself in the role of the fairy godmother, satisfying tourists who for years had been barred from most Carnival balls. More than merely a reenactment of the Alla ball, the Bacchus event also promised that tourists would be actively involved in the festivities. Bacchus promised some eight hundred "call-out dances" that enabled female tourists to dance with Alla members and receive a krewe favor as a souvenir. Three years later, Hermes markedly increased its efforts to invite more tourists to its ball. Nevertheless, it remained difficult for tourists to peer behind the mask separating private and public Carnival. Indeed, the mayor's office continued to receive a flood of letters from around the country asking assistance in procuring ball tickets.[28]

As New Orleans became more dependent on tourism for its economic vitality, local public discourse focused with increasing sharpness on the state of Carnival. By the late 1960s many New Orleanians believed that the swelling hordes of unruly revelers that descended upon the city during the Carnival season were degrading Mardi Gras as a traditional family diversion and as a major tourist attraction. In the midst of these debates, local leaders drawn from outside the Carnival establishment worked to renew the celebration's capacity to drive the city's tourism industry, striving to contain disorder and preserve the image of a spontaneous, indigenous festival while managing the regulation and commercialization that promised to wring greater economic benefits from it. Their actions further undermined old-line Carnival leaders.

Meeting in Adelaide Brennan's Garden District home one day in 1968, her son Owen "Pip" Brennan Jr., float builder Blaine Kern, costume designer Larry Youngblood, and ten other young business leaders discussed their belief that New Orleans Carnival had grown increasingly inhospitable to tourists and dull for local citizens. Despite the crowds that choked New Orleans during the festivities, the city's hotels were scarcely more than half filled at the height of Carnival by the mid to late 1960s, and the weekend before Fat Tuesday offered no major parades. Understanding the potential to transform the final weekend of Carnival into a much more profitable tourist event, the group brainstormed about how to enliven the celebration. These men, who also included restaurateur Dick Brennan, two media executives, French Quarter businessmen, and the president of the Royal Orleans Hotel, exemplified an emerging new breed of tourism-oriented New Orleans civic leaders who found themselves excluded from the city's traditional Carnival social activities. Unlike the captains of Rex, who as early as the 1870s had understood their krewe's role as a cultural ambassador to those who traveled by passenger train to view the Carnival spectacle, these men did not simply try to increase the numbers of out-of-towners who went to see a moving tableau presented by those at the apex of the city's social hierarchy. Rather, Brennan and his friends sought to carve out a space where influential but socially marginalized New Orleanians could graft a more inclusive and visually captivating parade onto the calcified traditions shaped by earlier generations. Like the partisans of French Quarter architecture and Dixieland jazz, they were, in a sense, cultural preservationists who, in the process of imposing their interpretation of Carnival, helped transform it into a more consciously tourist-focused reconstruction of New Orleans's heritage.[29]

Their meeting led to a second gathering that attracted several hundred attendees, 270 of whom agreed to form a new Krewe of Bacchus. Unlike its namesake, which had lapsed by the mid-1950s following the elder Owen Brennan's death, the new Bacchus promised to stage a Mardi Gras parade on a scale never before seen. Since Rex, Comus, and other old-line krewes would not have them, these businessmen were determined to set a new standard for Carnival parades. Earlier parades, including new truck-pulled float processions by the Elks and Shriners and the krewes of Hermes, Babylon, NOR, and Mid-City in the 1930s and 1940s, had already begun to dilute old-line domination of Mardi Gras. But the important week before Fat Tuesday remained the preserve of the old elite until Bacchus appeared the Sunday night before Mardi Gras, intruding on their calendar space and their traditional parade route.[30]

The founding of Bacchus elicited upper-class reactions ranging from indifference to outright hostility. As columnist James Gill has observed, even the choice of "Bacchus," the Greek god of wine, as the krewe's name suggested its founders' sense of superseding old-line traditions, for in Greek mythology Bacchus was Comus's father. When Bacchus applied for a parade permit, Darwin Fenner urged Mayor Schiro to deny it, arguing that these young upstarts would detract from Carnival tradition. Schiro contended that Bacchus had a right to parade, whereupon the Rex captain became belligerent, ranting, "You can't do that!" When Schiro reminded the investment broker that he was the mayor and could approve any parade permits he chose, Fenner retorted, "*We* are Mardi Gras!"[31]

Notwithstanding the rancor surrounding Bacchus's debut, the new parade proved an instant hit. Bacchus parades were flashy extravaganzas with colorful themes such as "Chamber of Horrors" and "Bacchus Goes to the Circus." Unlike old-line krewes, who chose their royalty secretly within blueblood confines, krewe leaders selected a television or Hollywood film star to play King Bacchus. The high-profile organization's first parade in 1969 rolled into the Rivergate, where some sixteen hundred people attended a lavish party called the Bacchus Rendezvous—a radical departure from the tableaux, royal protocol, and call-out dances in the elite-controlled Municipal Auditorium. Unlike old-line krewes, Bacchus admitted as members businessmen from Houston, Dallas, Los Angeles, and other cities, as well as Jews and members of ethnic groups ostracized by the likes of Comus.[32] The Bacchus parade passed a Boston Club darkened in protest for four consecutive years until Bob Hope reigned as Bacchus V in 1973. The parade underscored the transformation of Mardi Gras from a dutiful elitist exhibition for the public to an event that focused on show business. Sam Scandaliato, captain of the eastern New Orleans–based Krewe of Pontchartrain, explained the chartering of suburban krewes by noting that "the quality of some of the downtown parades had left a lot to be desired, and people lost interest. But the emergence of Bacchus rekindled the Mardi Gras spirit."[33]

Not only did Bacchus wed carefully choreographed show business with a public event that many locals worried was at risk of rendering New Orleans a Fort

Lauderdale or Haight-Ashbury, it also seemed to offer hope of lessening the phenomenon that *New Yorker* correspondent Calvin Trillin recounted for a national audience. Jews perennially fled the city prior to Mardi Gras to escape a social season from which they felt excluded. Alluding to Sinclair Lewis's novel about the prejudicial suburban conformism of George Babbitt, Trillin suggested that Jews' inability to enter the circle of old-line elites lent credence to the idea "that underneath that gay Carnival costume beats the heart of Zenith, Ohio." Indeed, the pervasive atmosphere of anti-Semitism began in adolescence, when the bluebloods began grooming their children to be future Carnival royalty, planning social dances for eighth- and ninth-graders ("Eight O'Clocks" and "Nine O'Clocks") and supporting a "junior country club for overprivileged children" called Valencia. The sons and daughters of the city's elite learned early that Jews occupied a lower rung on the social ladder. Bacchus promised to draw attention away from the pretension that attached to the old-line Carnival krewes. Just as the economic imperative of image maintenance played a key role in building consensus for ending racial exclusion in public accommodations by the late 1960s, efforts to revitalize Carnival for tourists reduced the taint of anti-Semitism by introducing first-order Mardi Gras events that provided a viable alternative for prominent Jews to participate in the most visible expression of the city's civic life. In a symbolic departure from old-line krewes' practice of naming native Gentiles royalty, Bacchus named Danny Kaye, a Jewish actor from Beverly Hills, as the first King Bacchus.[34]

New Orleans Carnival luminaries had long ago transformed Mardi Gras from a spontaneous, grassroots celebration rooted in an Atlantic-world diaspora of pre-Lenten rituals into a carefully planned, elite-controlled civic enactment with the semblance of a broad participation. The arrival of Bacchus introduced a new chapter in the national image of Mardi Gras. By 1974 Bacchus had inspired another krewe, Endymion, to revamp its parade. Ed Muniz, a local radio salesman, got the idea for Endymion in 1965 when he observed that the New Orleans Central Business District no longer had a Saturday night parade on the weekend before Fat Tuesday. "All of the tourists usually come to New Orleans by Saturday for the four-day Mardi Gras weekend," he later recalled, "and not having a parade that night left a big void in the season." The following year, having assembled forty-two members, Muniz and his cohorts went door to door in their Gentilly neighborhood and managed to increase membership to 160.[35] Beginning with its first parade in 1967, Endymion used recycled floats from the Krewe of Carrollton, another neighborhood-based parade. Like Bacchus, Endymion chose a Jew as its first grand marshal, suggesting once again the break with old-line tradition. After several years of expanding, in 1973 Muniz accepted Blaine Kern's invitation to the Bacchus Rendezvous. He later recalled that when he stepped into the Las Vegas–style party, he "saw the Carnival of the future." Kern granted Muniz the exclusive right to rent rather than buy his floats at a great discount to enable Muniz to introduce a new Bacchuslike parade on Canal Street. When the new Endymion rolled out of City Park on its way to its own dinner-dance in the Rivergate in 1974, it featured Kern-designed superfloats and *Tonight Show* bandleader Doc Severinsen as its first celebrity grand marshal, thereby adding to the nationalization of Mardi Gras.[36]

Bacchus and Endymion contributed significantly to the emerging effort to re-cast Carnival as a series of discrete, well-planned attractions appearing in quick succession, with the object of wedding Carnival more firmly to the tourism industry. Like Pasadena's Tournament of Roses Parade and Rose Bowl, Las Vegas's Strip, and Orlando's Disney parks, New Orleans's Mardi Gras by the 1970s clearly offered tourists a glitzy extravaganza that travel promoters could neatly bundle in a three- or four-day package deal. The superkrewes also reconfigured the spatial practices of Carnival. About a century after the city's leaders had institutionalized Mardi Gras by forming parade krewes that followed set routes through top-drawer residential and commercial spaces, Bacchus and Endymion eroded the lines of race and class which separated float riders from sidewalk spectators. By parading to the Rivergate rather than the Municipal Auditorium, they symbolically solidified ties between the local festival and the global tourism industry.[37]

As Mardi Gras increasingly catered to tourists, some New Orleanians began to worry about what one observer called the vulgarization of Carnival. For another critic, the block-long double-decker floats popularized by Bacchus and Endymion were unseemly "Greyhound Scenicruisers in drag."[38] The 1960s and 1970s saw the reorientation of public Carnival from the exclusive affairs sponsored by Comus, Momus, and Proteus to the crowd-pleasing experiences offered by Zulu, Bacchus, and Endymion, and New Orleanians raised new debates about how to control the massive influxes of college students on spring break and youthful drifters drawn to one of the counterculture shrines of the Age of Aquarius. The city also began to grapple with the commercialization of a celebration whose popularity depended on its aura of uniqueness.

By the second half of the 1960s some city officials and business leaders became concerned that Mardi Gras was losing its distinctiveness, especially its masking tradition, and was transforming into just another spring break destination. The emphasis on the economic impact of Carnival seemed to eclipse the notion of a local celebration in the 1960s, with the daily newspapers annually reporting how many hundreds of tons of trash city sanitation workers removed from the streets as a barometer of how successful a tourist draw the event had proved.[39] As masking became rarer, Associated Press writer Jim Mangan suggested that police block off a portion of Canal Street and permit only maskers to enter. The captain of Rex also called for a return to the tradition but frowned on such coercive measures. With masking slowly disappearing from downtown and French Quarter streets, city leaders pondered ways of reviving it. At the suggestion of city traffic engineer John Exnicios, Mayor Schiro urged civic and business organizations to promote masking. Accordingly, the city's daily newspapers led a promotional campaign to urge more locals to appear in mask, leading to a short-lived revival by 1970. Nonetheless, it appeared that the trend toward an outdoor drinking party remained dominant.[40]

Mardi Gras did not suddenly make New Orleans a fleshpot in the 1960s and 1970s, for that reputation had adhered to the city more than a century earlier. But there was a growing sense that Carnival was degenerating into little more than a bacchanalia. One national magazine even blamed Mardi Gras for compromising national security, suggesting in 1951 that "pictures of drunken revelry in the streets appear in anti-American newspapers and magazines" and warning that "descriptions of the worst side of the carnival are circulated widely in Russia, make dramatic propaganda, [and] feed the frigid fires of the Cold War." Rev. Billy Graham echoed the sentiments of many when in 1954 he remarked of his visit to Bourbon Street during Carnival, "I thought I was in the middle of hell."[41]

In the 1960s Mardi Gras stretched the resources and patience of city leaders. Adding to the already unmistakable presence of sailors between assignments, the city's French Quarter swelled with the influx of youthful pleasure seekers. Beer flowed freely from sidewalk stands with little regard for law enforcement. Larry LaMarca, who owned the Gunga Den strip club and Bayou Room tavern on Bourbon Street, complained to Mayor Schiro in 1967 that "these stands crop up at the Carnival season, some without alcoholic permits, while we, as licensed operators are restricted as to who we might sell to." A block away on Burgundy Street, Buster Holmes's restaurant dispensed thirty-five-cent meals of red beans and rice with French bread, and a handful of rooming houses and soup kitchens catered to the needs of transients. One New Orleans columnist lamented, "I share with many people a sense of alarm and the growing, almost pathetic feeling that carnival is becoming an overgrown, often amateurish experience in self-indulgence." In 1969 police superintendent Joseph Giarrusso warned city councilman Moon Landrieu about the problem of local vendors dispensing cheap bottled alcoholic drinks to "boys and girls of college age who come from universities throughout the country."[42]

The popularity of the 1969 film *Easy Rider,* in which two nonconformists (Peter Fonda and Dennis Hopper) set out on a cross-country motorcycle odyssey that culminates in a drug-laced, alcohol-soaked Mardi Gras scene in the French Quarter, was in the minds of many locals to blame for the young mobs who descended upon the city during Carnival. Indeed, by the early 1970s, New Orleans became a crash pad for drifters and hippies, especially at Mardi Gras. Like Fonda and Hopper, the hippies who went to New Orleans for Carnival often set out in search of cheap living, exploration, and companionship. A *Vieux Carré Courier* feature in 1973 presented the observations of a number of young people in the city for Mardi Gras, illuminating its allure for the counterculture. Harlan and Debbie, two drifters from Daytona Beach, Florida, spent their days panhandling, people-watching, and lounging under the palm trees in Jackson Square as the sounds of guitars and flutes filled the air. Harlan, who called himself "Freedom," made the trip because he hoped to test the images he had of Carnival. "I've never seen it before," he exclaimed, "but I heard all kind of rumors and stuff about it. Supposed to be a big party, man, supposed to be one big party. I heard there's all kinds of beer and all kinds of good stuff floatin' around. . . ." Unlike the atmosphere of indulgence and permissiveness that Tennessee Williams conjured in *A Streetcar Named Desire,* however, hippies discovered during Mardi Gras a French Quarter fraught with tension as New Orleanians pondered the future of their famous celebration.[43]

Events in the winter of 1970 outraged many residents and worried tourism officials. On the Sunday before Fat Tuesday, police arrested eighty-eight youths on vagrancy charges for sleeping along the shore of Lake Pontchartrain. Six miles south in the French Quarter, the NOPD apprehended 103 "hippie types" for camping in Jackson Square and then proceeded to close the public park. Those who averted arrest spent the night in boxcars or on the dead end of St. Peter Street next to the river. The next morning a paddy wagon arrived to haul them to central lockup. A few blocks away a mob hurled glass bottles at policemen who beseeched one youth to climb down from his perch atop a lamp standard. Meanwhile, as the colorful floats of Bacchus creaked and groaned past Trinity Church and the Garden District bastions of the old elite and rounded the corner of Jackson and St. Charles, a brick hurled from the crowd struck jazz trumpeter and French Quarter club owner Al Hirt in the face. Police even arrested members of the Grateful Dead, an experience recounted in their song "Truckin.'" It seemed that a city known for its ability to handle massive crowds had lost control of its most important tourist attraction. Superintendent Giarrusso fumed that "thousands [are] coming down here with one thought in mind—an orgy." National news reports bred uneasiness in some would-be tourists. One Minnesota man wrote the mayor to ascertain whether the city could promise law and order at Carnival before he made arrangements for the next year's Mardi Gras.[44]

With tourists "besieged by flower children begging for a nickel" or hawking copies of the underground paper *Nola Express* in the French Quarter, some New Orleans business interests complained that Carnival was out of control. Philip Hannan, archbishop of the Roman Catholic Diocese of New Orleans, which was based in St. Louis Cathedral, castigated tourism leaders for suggesting that Mardi Gras in the French Quarter "is a gigantic, no-holds-barred celebration that borders on a bacchanalia."[45] Even some tourism leaders expressed dissatisfaction. Jung Hotel general manager Leon Prestia blamed hippie panhandling and drunkenness for a slump in tourist spending during the 1972 Carnival season and implored the city council to ban drinking in city streets.[46]

In response to several years of enduring hordes of unruly youths during Carnival season, the Greater New Orleans Tourist and Convention Commission (GNOTCC) gathered a blue-ribbon panel in 1972 to consider the problem of "undesirables" at Mardi Gras. Among the panel's recommendations was an initiative to reshape Mardi Gras as a community event. Following the panel's report, in 1973 the tourist commission officially abandoned its slogan "The Greatest Free Show on Earth." In its place the commission published a new pamphlet, "The Real Mardi Gras," which informed would-be revelers: "Mardi Gras has been called 'the greatest free show on earth.' It is the greatest, but it's not free. It's paid for by private organizations. Come and enjoy our fine restaurants, our entertainment, our shops, and our Mardi Gras. But please come as a paying guest as you would to any other great city or event. . . . The whole Carnival season is actually a rollicking family party given by the people of New Orleans for themselves."[47] In fact, the pamphlet's plea reflected the city's sense of having lost control over its own party, even if Mardi Gras had never been as inwardly focused as the power establishment might have wished.

If tourism leaders, municipal officials, and many New Orleanians detested the presence of collegians and the counterculture during Carnival, other locals blamed the city's tourist commission for creating expectations among those who went to New Orleans. Clarinetist Pete Fountain, who had since the days of Joe Mares's promotional tours gone on to operate his own Bourbon Street jazz club, sympathized with the youthful visitors, remarking, "Hell, if I were their age I'd be out there too. . . . We're going to have these problems as long as we allow liquor on the streets." New Orleans Human Relations Committee director John Pecoul, a member of the city's French Quarter Task Force, urged city officials to open up an island in City Park as a campsite for transients, who might otherwise sleep on French Quarter streets, in Jackson Square, or in rail yards along the river, where they were often arrested for vagrancy.[48]

The early 1970s brought a number of efforts to balance the competing interests of those who expected the "greatest free show" and the tourists, tourism promoters, city leaders, and residents who regarded them warily. Dialogue between young aides in city hall and counterculture leaders like *Vieux Carré Courier* managing editor Bill Rushton, restraint on the part of New Orleans police officers, and the efforts of concerned citizens kept a lid on Carnival disorder and helped safeguard the favorable reputation of Mardi Gras among tourists.[49]

Drawing support from business and church leaders, former Baptist minister Mike Stark founded the Health Emergency Aid Dispensary Clinic and the Mardi Gras Coalition to address the needs of the youthful pleasure seekers who crowded into the city each year. Stark refuted business owners' claims that hippies were ruining their business, reasoning that Bourbon Street proprietors had done little to keep up with changing public taste in entertainment, adding, "Why should anyone pay $2.50 per drink to watch a strip show?" Stark's coalition placed more than three hundred "peace keepers" on the streets to discourage clashes between police and visiting youths, directed visitors to housing, food, and temporary employment opportunities, and operated a hotline to assist those who were enduring a bad LSD trip.[50] A number of local churches cooperated by allowing young out-of-towners to sleep in their buildings or park their vans or campers outside. In 1970, working with the Community Action Council of Tulane University Students (CACTUS), the Mardi Gras Coalition persuaded university officials to open the school's football stadium to any visiting college student. The following year, slightly more than three thousand visitors stayed on campus, either in the stadium or in dormitories. Tulane offered five red beans and rice dinners to the youths during the days leading up to Fat Tuesday.[51]

Some of the counterculture's efforts answered concerns that hippies might ruin the French Quarter's tourist appeal. When business leaders complained that hippies were littering the Vieux Carré, Stark launched a broom brigade to clean up the neighborhood. To quell concerns over the hippie presence, Stark formed the Help Around the Neighborhood Directory, an employment agency that sought to dispel the idea that hippies did nothing but loaf and create a public nuisance. The ex-preacher also set up several co-ops and even organized Hire-A-Hippie, a guide service offering tours of the French Quarter "underground," a small-scale adaptation of the more commercialized Gray Line counterculture tours of San Francisco's Haight-Ashbury district in the late 1960s. For Stark and Rushton, the counterculture was not a source of crime and disorder so much as a force for revitalizing a neighborhood in serious danger of losing its Bohemian aura in its march toward crass commercialism. Just as he advocated for historic preservation, Rushton maintained that hippies, both resident and tourist, augmented rather than diminished the "magic" of Mardi Gras and the French Quarter, adding that Carnival "has the tacky, colorful wild exuberance that hip people are already into."[52]

Although public attention to the counterculture faded toward mid-decade, New Orleans continued to struggle to accommodate the crush of young sojourners who did not frequent the leading tourism-oriented establishments such as hotels and restaurants. By 1975, the Mardi Gras Coalition teetered on the brink of collapse. With Tulane Stadium closing in conjunction with the opening of a new downtown arena, no large-scale shelter could serve the visitors. Its staff complained that the city government continued to allow the tourism industry to promote Mardi Gras while shirking responsibility for hosting the multitudes who came without the means to support themselves during their stay. Coalition coordinator Todd Ochs complained that city leaders seemed to believe that "if they provide nothing, the kids will just stay away." In the years that followed, the city's emphasis shifted from accommodating young visitors to bolstering police presence on the streets of the French Quarter and along parade routes. Police Superintendent Giarrusso warned that "if those SOBs come in here like locusts, we're going to do what's necessary." The Mardi Gras Coalition, increasingly operated by area university students, no longer focused on securing shelter for visitors; after 1975 it concentrated on disseminating visitor information and legal and medical assistance.[53]

The local effort to mitigate the effects of promoting the "greatest free show on earth" underscores the impact of a growing tourist trade on New Orleans, which by the 1970s was billing itself as the "Big Easy," in suggestive mimicry of New York's "Big Apple" moniker.[54] As the French Quarter, jazz, and Carnival became more firmly affixed to the city's promotional efforts, each began to take on a larger role in redirecting local attitudes and priorities. Tourism reshaped the city's culture in ways that preservationists and promoters did not always foresee. By the 1970s New Orleans, whose unique celebration had spawned many imitations such as Tampa's Gasparilla, continued to propel its own Carnival traditions more completely into the world of commercialized national tourist attractions.

In a decade that saw many American cities pursuing plans to make their downtowns more accessible to suburbanites seeking comfort, convenience, and security, some New Orleans city and business leaders began to consider ways of directly packaging Mardi Gras as a controllable tourist commodity on a much larger scale than Brennan's earlier Alla ball reenactment. Although the city regulated Mardi Gras to an extent by holding krewes to officially designated parade routes, the spectacle was among the few modern tourist attractions in which visitors could conceivably partake without contributing much to the local economy.

The relatively unbranded nature of Mardi Gras festivities doubtless struck many tourists who visited New Orleans each winter. Following a visit in 1962, one of them, Hollywood public relations executive Don Gettings, wrote GNOTCC president Harry England that he had eagerly anticipated "the gala activities in store for me," only to be "disappointed in that the much publicized Mardi Gras parade lacked the magnitude it deserves." Gettings' disappointment was probably a common reaction among visitors who had read, seen, or heard the puffery that annually announced the coming of Carnival season in New Orleans. Gettings proposed that Mardi Gras be transformed into a more coordinated event of national and international interest by incorporating floats representing major U.S. cities, foreign countries, and popular musical acts, televising the Rex ball nationally, and even arranging an invasion of the port by "Spanish galleons in full regalia." But the Hollywood promoter misunderstood New Orleans's leaders' sense of their celebration. Although Mardi Gras was increasingly packaged with tourists in mind, local leaders always controlled how it was done.[55]

In 1967, amid efforts to build a domed stadium for the city's new NFL franchise, whose games would fill the arena fewer than a dozen times per year, promoters seized upon the idea of hosting conventions, trade shows, and extravaganzas to fill the facility more often.[56] Mayor Schiro and football promoter David Dixon met with Rex captain Darwin S. Fenner to ask his support for a plan that would route Mardi Gras parades through the mammoth dome, which they hoped to call "Mardi Gras Stadium." Dixon tried to sweeten the proposal by including plans for a Mardi Gras museum dedicated to the four original parading krewes—Rex, Comus, Momus, and Proteus. After securing Fenner's support, Dixon observed

that a dome-based Carnival "could make Mardi Gras into just about our most famous national celebration. It would mean substantially increased revenues from
tourism . . . [and] would almost certainly open up our Mardi Gras for heavy national television coverage."[57] Fenner reported general support from other krewe
captains, with the exception of Momus. The leaders doubtless liked the idea of
being able to bolster upper-class stewardship of Mardi Gras, which enabled them
to preserve and project cultural power at a time when nonelites were creating
their own Carnival traditions.[58]

The city government's stadium plan, much like Disneyland's New Orleans
Square, reflects what historian David Lowenthal suggests is a common preference for replicated experiences, even though parades continued to wend their way
through oak-canopied streets. The plan anticipated later efforts to harness Carnival's commercial potential. Officials envisioned parades rolling into the dome
through a tunnel "lined with magnificent Roman fountains with water sprays of
green, gold, and purple." They insisted that the dome was actually preferable to
streets for parades because the floats would not get hung on low live-oak branches.
Beyond Carnival itself, the plan called for the dome to serve as a year-round in-
door theme park called "Mardi Gras Land." Outside, tricolor lighting would bathe
the dome in Carnival colors. When tourists entered, they would encounter jazz, a
minstrel show, pirates, Mardi Gras parades, and giant illuminated decorations and
animated figures suspended from the ceiling to create an effect similar to Disneyland's Tiki Room. "Disneyland," stated one of the planners, ". . . has magnificently
capsuled the world of fantasy and make believe. Similarly, we must capsule New
Orleans." Although the dome plan never reached fruition, it pointed to a later use
of the arena for Mardi Gras festivities and suggests the growing linkage between
culture and economic development that characterized post-1945 urban strategies
in cities that suffered capital flight.[59]

In 1972 the Times-Picayune Publishing Corporation, whose Times-Picayune and
States-Item dominated the local print media, refused to publish a very unfavorable
article on Mardi Gras by the chief of the Associated Press's news features bureau.
In the article, which appeared in hundreds of newspapers around the nation, the
author observed that New Orleans leaders constantly fretted "about being Fort
Lauderdalized by scruffy kids on the one hand and Houstonized by crass commercialism on the other."[60] Despite the persistent myth that New Orleans Carnival
was a native celebration untarnished by outside money, the event became more
and more commercialized in the 1970s. Local entrepreneurs and national companies alike hoped to tap into Mardi Gras profits.

To be sure, Mardi Gras already required the massive, coordinated provision of municipal services, often at a loss to the city. Its returns flowed to restaurants, hotels, taverns, nightclubs, stores, transportation providers, tour operators, and thousands of small-scale entrepreneurs. Yet the festivities remained largely free of direct revenue-producing efforts. Parades remained the responsibility of thousands of individual New Orleanians who chose to support the tradition with their own funds. In the 1970s, however, the older idea of capturing some of the Carnival excitement in a controlled, profit-generating venue finally became a reality. In 1976 Bacchus began its parade in the central business district at Lee Circle and rolled through the Superdome. Underscoring the degree to which the krewe had devoted itself to city and state efforts to boost tourism, Bacchus's captain noted that "We've been part of a state-operated facility—the Rivergate—for those seven years and we want to be part of another state facility, the Superdome." Along with the parade, Blaine Kern Productions presented Ike and Tina Turner, the Southern University Marching Band, and several other well-known musical acts.[61]

The success of the Bacchus experiment prompted more elaborate efforts to stage Carnival. At the urging of the Young Men's Business Club, beginning in 1978, Kern and Richard Lazes produced "Popeye's Mardi Gras in the Superdome," a two-night televised extravaganza that featured Bacchus floats, Carnival royalty, and numerous national and local music groups. By the following year, the event attracted more than forty thousand paying customers, and in 1980 it featured Willie Nelson, Jimmy Buffett, Crystal Gayle, the Nitty Gritty Dirt Band, and the Rossington-Collins Band (formerly Lynyrd Skynyrd). New Orleans's Popeye's fried chicken magnate Al Copeland also took advantage of Carnival by starting an annual Popeye's doubloon promotion in 1976. Six years later the fast-food chain reported it would sell more than 250 tons of fried chicken and dispense some one hundred thousand purple "throws" to Mardi Gras revelers, as well as sponsor a sweepstakes to bring fifteen couples from around the country to Carnival. Similarly, Zapp's, a local food manufacturer, produced Mardi Gras–colored bags of potato chips for throws, and Anheuser-Busch sent the Budweiser Clydesdale horses annually after 1964.[62]

Although Mardi Gras in the Superdome proved the exception to traditional street parades, the commercialization of Carnival paralleled the growing tourist presence made possible by an expanding tourist infrastructure in the postwar years. Yet this commercialization remained surprisingly indigenous to the city. If national and multinational corporations searched for ways to appropriate New Orleans's Mardi Gras, they proved unable to brand the celebration itself, which remained closely guarded by locals. Indeed, even though Carnival was more than simply a "party given by the people of New Orleans for themselves," few residents felt any urge to turn to national sponsors. Aside from the national and international hotel chains that profited from Carnival, most of the benefit accrued to the local businesses that serviced the celebration. Indicative of the enduring localness of Mardi Gras even in events staged expressly for tourists, in 1980 the Knights of Sparta began a new tradition of restaging its tableau ball for tourists in various hotels. At the first ball, Sparta's captain landed from a smoke- and flame-filled "sky" on a golden chariot carried by a hydraulic lift. Carnival Productions, a local company owned by tourism promoter Stuart Barash, booked the event nationally for individuals and travel agencies. Featuring dinner, Sparta tableaux, dancing, and a purple-printed, gold-stamped proclamation from the king of Sparta wishing "joyous greetings to all loyal subjects within the realm," the Sparta extravaganza illustrated the extent to which Mardi Gras promoters sought to boost tourism to New Orleans.[63]

By the 1970s Carnival supported a year-round industry of manufacturing or importing supplies and accessories such as costumes, masks, beads, cups, doubloons, and floats. Float building alone ballooned into a multimillion-dollar enterprise. In the early twentieth century, Blaine Kern's father Roy, a local artist, had created marquees for New Orleans vaudeville houses and helped build floats for one parade in 1932. In 1947, at the age of twenty, Blaine Kern started Blaine Kern Artists, Inc., shortly after leaving active duty in the Army. Within two years, his colorful float designs caught the eye of Rex captain Darwin Fenner, who paid to send Kern on a tour of Valencia, Viareggio, Nice, Frankfurt, and Cologne, where he studied how to make Rex parades more flamboyant. Ironically, thanks to the support of Rex, particularly Fenner, Kern took advantage of old-line patrons to parlay his talents into an important symbol of the transformation of Carnival into a more standardized, democratized, tourist-oriented celebration. Kern developed a virtual monopoly on building floats for the city's leading krewes into the 1970s, and by 1981 his floats appeared in thirty of the fifty-one parades in the New Orleans metropolitan area.[64] Indeed, Carnival was no longer simply a special event that enriched the city through tourist spending for one week each year. Nor did it simply anchor the reputation for revelry that enticed curious travelers to spend their money in the city's hotels, restaurants, bars, and souvenir shops throughout the year.

New Orleans's Mardi Gras celebration, like its French Quarter and Dixieland jazz, experienced a tourist transformation in the decades after the Great Depression.

The upsurge in mass tourism that marked the postwar era not only reinforced tourist conceptions of New Orleans as a place apart, it also made city boosters see the benefits of ensuring that such conceptions continued to reflect a carefully maintained illusion of reality. Astute city and business leaders worked to increase tourists' sense of participation in Carnival, preserve Zulu's jungle theme, fill Mardi Gras weekend with star-studded parades and parties, and stimulate tourism without allowing public disorder and commercialization to eclipse Carnival's carefully tended image. Just as nonelite leaders dominated the campaigns to resurrect a crumbling French Quarter and to end the silence of aging musicians' horns, they worked to broaden the appeal and heighten the spectacle of Mardi Gras as a unique, living expression of the city's rich cultural legacy rooted in its Atlantic-world connections, ultimately forging a year-round industry to support Carnival. In the years that followed, Mardi Gras remained closely intertwined with the city's tourist trade. Indeed, in the 1970s and after, the tourism industry swelled unprecedentedly, buoyed by the city's success in preserving the French Quarter, expelling Jim Crow from public accommodations, reviving New Orleans jazz, and broadening and updating the appeal of Mardi Gras festivities.

CHAPTER 6

"CREOLE DISNEYLAND"

> But no one need worry. In spite of all the time and efforts expended by preserva-
> tionists, the Vieux Carré will ultimately wind up a Disneyland with only a histori-
> cal backdrop to distinguish it from the present California and Florida originals.
>
> —MARY M. MORRISON (1989)

On October 30, 1971, New Orleans Police Department (NOPD) motorcycles led a
procession of horse-drawn carriages, hoopskirted southern belles, and a Dixieland
brass band departing from the statue of New Orleans's founder Jean Baptiste Le-
Moyne, Sieur de Bienville. One of the carriages conveyed Marcel Robidas, mayor
of Longueuil, Québec, Bienville's onetime home. The mayor, along with the French
and Canadian consuls, several New Orleans dignitaries, and New Orleans mayor
Moon Landrieu, rolled through the narrow streets of the French Quarter, ending their circuitous route at Bienville and Dauphine Streets outside the Chateau
LeMoyne, the last of the "sugarcake imitations" completed under a grandfather
clause in the city's hotel moratorium, passed two years earlier. A syndicate of New
Orleans investors backed by a major Houston development firm built the hotel,
which replaced a modern French Quarter–style parking garage that the Vieux
Carré Commission (VCC) had approved only a decade earlier.[1] In their attempt to
paper over the public outcry against French Quarter hotels by fabricating a connection to the city's founding and its French heritage, the officials at the dedication reflected a budding relationship between city hall and the expanding tourism
industry that manifested itself more than ever in the 1970s. This relationship contributed to the transformation of New Orleans, especially the French Quarter and
the downtown riverfront, into a place that responded to white tourist expectations
of what New Orleans should be, leading one observer to characterize the Vieux
Carré as a "Creole Disneyland."[2]

Mayor Landrieu entered office in 1970 with a keen conviction that New Orleans needed to capitalize more aggressively on its tourist image. Economists'
warnings that the city could not realize its potential while remaining dependent
on tourism, shipbuilding, and the port went unheeded. Landrieu's ebullient, energetic persona, along with the gleaming skyscrapers that now soared above a

skyline little changed since the Great Depression, created an atmosphere of optimism about the city's future.[3] City hall had long been involved in tourism through its management of the French Market and Upper Pontalba Building, regulation of French Quarter façades, and law enforcement, crowd control, and sanitation during Carnival. But the Landrieu administration marked the arrival of unprecedented efforts to shape the tourist experience through redeveloping and enhancing the cityscape, marketing the city's distinctive image, and balancing competing interests in the public spaces impacted by tourism. This heightened municipal involvement continued into Dutch Morial's mayoralty, when the city also joined the state and federal governments to build a mammoth convention center and host a world's fair. This chapter demonstrates the broadening municipal influence over New Orleans tourism between 1970 and 1984, which set the stage for the elevation of tourism as the city's only remaining hope for progress in the troubling years that followed.

The tourism boom of the 1970s and early 1980s cannot be understood apart from a series of profound changes that swept New Orleans in the wake of the civil rights revolution—the election of a prodevelopment and socially progressive mayor who offered hope to an increasingly impoverished populace; expanding exploration of offshore petroleum reserves; and the growing strength of new business leaders who eclipsed the political, economic, and, to a lesser extent, social supremacy of the city's power establishment. The transformation of the city's political and economic order which became apparent in the 1970s overturned many of the conditions that had helped preserve New Orleans as an anomaly in the modern South; it also hastened the city's modernization and the expansion of tourism to become its leading industry. It did not, however, lift the city's poor out of their miserable lot. As historian Arnold Hirsch argues, one of the most critical factors in bringing fundamental change to New Orleans was the Voting Rights Act of 1965, which slowly enfranchised African Americans who had been largely shut out of municipal politics since the 1890s. The election of Moon Landrieu in 1970 owed much to the black vote, which had risen to nearly three-tenths of the city's electorate on the eve of his campaign. When Landrieu faced Jimmy Fitzmorris, the old guard's preferred candidate, in the second Democratic primary in 1969 (which was more important than the general election in a region that seldom elected Republicans to local office), he won on the strength of his appeal to up-and-coming nonelite business leaders and black voters mobilized by ward-based political action groups such as the Community Organization for Urban Politics (COUP) and the Southern Organization for Unified Leadership (SOUL). In his campaign, as Hirsch demonstrates, Landrieu castigated the old elite for holding back the city's development and promised to cultivate ties to emerging leaders and outside investment.[4] Reflecting his intolerance for the conservative establishment, the young mayor warned the Krewe of Rex that if it did not invite at least a token number of African Americans to its ball, he would not exchange the customary toast with the king from the steps of Gallier Hall, once New Orleans's city hall.[5] Likewise, at a 1973 chamber of commerce dinner for visiting Japanese dignitaries, Landrieu chastized several local businessmen for what he saw as their smug attitude, warning them that the city would remain a backwater as long as they persisted in their air of superiority.[6] Landrieu's political victory, then, promised at least a partial deliverance from the economic disappointments of the past.

Landrieu courted economic development in the form of major construction projects directed by nonelite developers, in many cases using outside capital. In a time of worsening urban poverty, the mayor hoped that these projects might provide jobs for his constituents. As was true in many cities, New Orleans suffered an appalling poverty rate. On the eve of the new mayor's inauguration, 47 percent of New Orleanians earned less than $7,000 annually, compared to roughly one-quarter of the populations of Atlanta, Dallas, and Houston.[7] Landrieu believed that the fastest way to deal with the crippling effects of a large, poorly educated, unskilled, and impoverished workforce was to encourage the rapid expansion of tourism, which seemingly offered boundless opportunities without the drawbacks of smokestack chasing.

As in New York, Chicago, Atlanta, and other cities, New Orleans leaders courted national hotel chains in the 1970s as a major part of their effort to promote downtown development. Between 1960 and 1982, developers built 319 downtown hotels in the nation's thirty-eight largest metropolitan areas.[8] The Crescent City, whose hotel construction remained mostly confined to locally financed inns in the French Quarter in the 1960s, joined the national trend in the 1970s, thanks to the French Quarter hotel moratorium, growing demand for convention hotels, and racial integration of public accommodations. Breaking an unwritten but longstanding gentlemen's agreement between local hotelmen and city hall that kept most national hotel chains out of the city, Landrieu facilitated a deal in which his friend Clancy Dupepe, a Jefferson Parish investor and grandson of Irish immigrants, contracted with the Marriott Corporation to erect the South's tallest hotel on Canal Street, just beyond the area restricted by the moratorium on new French Quarter hotels. Dupepe was no stranger to hotel development; his father Vernon Dupepe had pioneered the development of evocative Creole-architecture hotels with his Provincial Motel in the French Quarter more than a decade earlier.[9] Touring the hotel, with its garish furnishings and ersatz representations of local culture, one unimpressed visitor said, "Get me out of this hotel and take me back to New Orleans." Maverick journalist Bill Rushton sneered that the hotel, which he derided as a "plastic riverboat," was the new leadership class's attempt to thumb its nose at the old elite, most glaringly in naming one of its conference rooms "Bacchus," after the Carnival organization of which Dupepe was a founding member, while not naming other rooms for the city's old-line krewes.[10]

Though snubbed by many French Quarter partisans, the Marriott stood as a monument to a new order in which black citizens and tourists enjoyed complete access to the city's accommodations. Indeed, only four years after the city had allowed the Krewe of Zulu to begin following the popular St. Charles–to–Canal Street parade route once reserved for elite white clubs, the 1973 Zulu coronation ball filled the Marriott's Grand Ballroom, with its huge mural of the celebrated Natchez mansion Dunleith.[11] While white tourists might still find mint juleps, plantation punch, mammy dolls, and antebellum motifs such as the Dunleith mural in the Crescent City, they consumed these drinks, souvenirs, and images in the more socially inclusive places and spaces that Landrieu's leadership fostered.

Landrieu's emerging public-private coalition for growth owed a debt to an accident of nature. Typical of the city's reliance on exploiting natural resources as the basis for its economic development, in the early 1970s a dramatic spike in offshore petroleum exploration in the Gulf of Mexico injected new capital into New Orleans, which attracted regional headquarters of numerous energy corporations in a time before computer networks made the proximity of offices to operations less critical. During the oil boom, which remained strong from 1973 to 1981 and wavered for three more years before collapsing, thousands of newcomers poured into the Crescent City. Many settled on the rapidly developing West Bank of the Mississippi River and in new suburbs on recently drained swampland in eastern New Orleans.

The additional capital to support oil-induced development presented a problem in New Orleans, whose conservative leading banks still refused to make long-term loans to anyone without a longstanding account.[12] Indeed, when developers approached the city's leading banks, particularly the Whitney and Hibernia national banks, they were unable to secure capital for their projects. The Whitney and the Hibernia, with approximately three-quarters of their directors drawn from old-line families, together accounted for close to half of the entire metropolitan area's bank assets as late as the early 1970s. As a result, when denied capital, developers of downtown projects turned to Texas banks or to more progressive local institutions such as First National Bank of Commerce, which under Arkansas native and former Dallas banker James H. Jones eclipsed the Hibernia and closed the gap with the Whitney by the early 1980s.[13]

With the staunch support of Mayor Landrieu, who sometimes assisted them in tapping public sources of funding, developers relied on more progressive-minded lenders to build office towers, hotels, and other complexes just blocks from the French Quarter, which earlier leaders had worried was a drag on modernization. While Boston Club members mapped out the next quarter century of Carnival queens and planned their parades and balls, Houston real estate developer Gerald D. Hines constructed One Shell Square, a fifty-one story sister of Houston's One Shell Plaza. Downtown developer Joseph C. Canizaro, a newcomer from Mississippi, built Canal Place, an office, hotel, and mall complex that, to the chagrin of preservationists, towered above one corner of the French Quarter near the foot of Canal Street. Rejected financing by the Whitney and other local banks, Canizaro turned to a Baton Rouge bank and even the Shah of Iran for funds to build Canal Place.[14]

As in most cities that built stadiums and arenas in the 1970s, New Orleans leaders justified spending public funds on large-scale developments, the revenues from which would supposedly trickle down to counter the soaring poverty rate.[15] When New York banks refused financing, First National Bank of Commerce president Jimmy Jones cobbled together a southern syndicate of banks, including Atlanta's Citizens and Southern National Bank, enabling developers to begin construction of the world's largest domed stadium. The Superdome was New Orleans's answer to Houston's Astrodome, completed in the previous decade. It was intended not only to provide a home for the city's NFL franchise, the Saints, but also to provide visible evidence of New Orleans's arrival as a big-league city and, for Landrieu, a patronage plum to reward political supporters in the black organization SOUL with contracts for dome management.[16] The soaring skyline and flying saucer–like sports arena, which even began to usurp part of the Mardi Gras celebration, prompted *New Yorker* contributor Calvin Trillin to muse that nothing less than the "Houstonization of New Orleans" was afoot.[17]

The political ascent of a mayor who refused to be owned and the emergence of new leadership and outside money that launched projects like the Marriott, the Superdome, and Canal Place rendered the New Orleans Carnival elite increasingly irrelevant in the city's development. To be sure, their influence was starting to fade even before 1970. Beginning in the 1960s the heirs to the old-elite mantle either contented themselves with the social prestige of belonging to the Boston, Pickwick, or Louisiana Clubs while retreating from active involvement in a political and economic realm they no could no longer master, or they shied away from joining the venerable clubs altogether. Old-line luminaries like Darwin Fenner and Richard Freeman simply were not being replaced. The creation of the new Mardi Gras "superkrewes" Bacchus and Endymion signaled the growing unwillingness on the part of nonelites, including Jews, nonnative New Orleanians, and blacks, to stand on the sidewalks as Carnival royalty rolled past. It was the new breed of businessmen—Lester Kabacoff, David Dixon, Joseph Canizaro, Pip Brennan, Clancy Dupepe, Blaine Kern, and others—who eclipsed the old elite and, in concert with city hall, charted a tourism-dominated course for the city.

To the extent that the power establishment dominated New Orleans's tourist image through its Carnival events and its attempt to woo the "better sort" of tourists to pageants like Spring Fiesta into the 1960s, by the 1970s the elite had little direct influence over the creation of a "Creole Disneyland." Their primary contribution to its rise lay in their maintenance of a highly exclusive social circle, whose clubs remained closed in what Hirsch calls "splendid isolation." The insularity of this elite discouraged corporate investment and the arrival of new executives which might have created economic conditions capable of undermining the civic consensus favoring preservation of the French Quarter.[18] Thus, one of the most important factors in the city's response to the tourism boom that began in the 1970s was the separation of local leadership into the old social elite and a new political and economic cabal. In the midst of that transformation, Mayor Landrieu set out to make the French Quarter even more appealing to tourists.

Prior to the 1970s, tourism development efforts revolved around the old elite's Carnival parades, preservationists' special events to showcase the French Quarter, local business leaders' opening of hotels, restaurants, and souvenir shops, and municipal encouragement of tourism as a way of spurring new investment. On the eve of Moon Landrieu's mayoralty, WWL-TV editorial writer Phil Johnson, reflecting emerging sentiments among newer leaders, warned that "with Disneyland, Six Flags, Astrodome and Astroworld packing people in, we must realize that the French Quarter and iron lace balconies aren't enough anymore. We need something new. And we hope our next City Administration does something about it."[19] Beginning in the Landrieu years, the municipal government, working in concert with local and outside investors without ties to the old elite, played an unprecedented role in tourism development and promotion, primarily with the goal of stimulating mass tourism as an alternative to more desirable yet elusive forms of economic development. While earlier administrations generally directed minimal attention to fostering tourism, Landrieu made tourism his priority, nowhere more so than in the French Quarter.

In the several years after District Attorney Jim Garrison shuttered many of Bourbon Street's famed nightclubs for lewd performances and violations of numerous state laws, the tourist heart of the French Quarter gradually devolved into a filthy stretch of X-rated peep shows, adult services, sidewalk beer stands, and seedy strip clubs featuring female impersonators. Among Landrieu's first efforts to stimulate a new image in the Quarter was creating part-time pedestrian malls on Bourbon and Royal Streets. Still, Bourbon Street, with its sidewalks and gutters "all soaked in . . . wet black filth," repulsed many tourists and locals alike. One resident of suburban Metairie remarked that a walk down Bourbon Street underscored why Fat City, a 1970s suburban replica of the French Quarter along I-10 in Jefferson Parish, was so popular. Following repeated complaints, Landrieu finally resorted in 1977 to appointing a task force to consider ways of restoring Bourbon Street to its postwar heyday. The task force accomplished little, quickly realizing that perhaps it made little sense to take away the racy atmosphere that connoted New Orleans for so many visitors. While efforts to clean up Bourbon Street continued sporadically thereafter, Landrieu's French Quarter policy proved much more influential in its attention to areas beyond the neon strip.[20]

In earlier years, preservationists had argued for the redevelopment of the riverfront and continually implored city hall to take a more active role in protecting the French Quarter as the centerpiece of the local tourist trade. In the 1970s, it quickly became clear that they had succeeded but in doing so had stimulated interest in major development projects whose scale now threatened the desirability of the French Quarter as a neighborhood. Through a variety of municipal initiatives, the Landrieu administration set out to make the Vieux Carré an even bigger tourist draw. While the mayor spearheaded a facelift of Exchange Alley near the Monteleone Hotel and opened pedestrian malls for Royal Street during the day and Bourbon Street at night, he focused primarily on Jackson Square and the riverfront.[21]

Mayor Landrieu, like Robert Maestri in the 1930s, hoped to restore buildings in the vicinity of Jackson Square. Unlike Maestri, who tapped federal Works Progress Administration money to renovate the Pontalba buildings and the French Market to make the Quarter more appealing for residents and tourists alike, Landrieu's revitalization efforts aimed primarily at tourists. In 1970, shortly after Landrieu took office, he announced a plan to turn three of the streets surrounding Jackson Square into a pedestrian mall. The city began by erecting bollards astride the intersections on all four sides of the square, leaving Decatur Street open on the river side. Landrieu wanted to study the impact of the street closures on traffic flow and public opinion before taking further action. Seeing no adverse effect or public opposition, the city began work to transform St. Peter, St. Ann, and Chartres Streets into flagstone-paved plazas where artists, performers, musicians, and street vendors could entertain tourists in a bazaarlike setting. Once they learned the full extent of the mayor's intentions, preservationists became irate, viewing the move as a scheme to escalate the transformation of a neighborhood into a tourist destination. Martha Robinson urged the Advisory Council on Historic Preservation, a federal agency whose consent was necessary in any matter impacting public land in a designated National Historic Landmark District, to reconsider its approval of the mall. If the council would reconsider, she hoped, the Department of Housing and Urban Development (HUD) might withhold the matching funds it had committed to "this sorry plan."[22]

Despite ardent protest, Robinson and other preservationists proved unable to stop the creation of a permanent pedestrian mall but managed to force a scaling down of Landrieu's planned observation deck, which they scorned as an "Aztec temple flanked by hanging gardens."[23] They also succeeded in blocking the planting of ornamental trees in the plaza in front of St. Louis Cathedral, which they argued would detract from the simple formality of what they believed to be the original design of the French colonial Place d'Armes, reputedly a replica of the Place des Vosges in Paris.[24] In their determination to remain true to an imagined past, preservationists conveniently ignored that the square had been modified several times to conform to changing tastes over the past two centuries, including during the time periods they romanticized. In the 1970s, however, Quarter advocates remained fixated on the same century-old styles that earlier preservationists had prized and which were themselves a product of a nineteenth-century fixation on an imagined eighteenth-century ideal.

City hall hoped the pedestrian mall would bring a more controlled, tourist-friendly atmosphere to Jackson Square, which by the early 1970s had devolved, in the eyes of some city leaders, into a meadow dotted with lounging hippies and panhandlers. As part of its plan, city officials encouraged sidewalk artists, who had plied their trade in the narrow Pirate's Alley alongside the cathedral, to relocate around the iron fence enclosing the square. While restricting street vendors in Jackson Square to one ice cream cart and one Lucky Dog frankfurter stand, it set no limits on the number of artists, street musicians, fortune tellers, and sideshows that could set up on the pedestrian mall. City hall made no effort to require that entrepreneurs using the public space obtain licenses or pay taxes. All transactions were in cash, and fortune tellers skirted a state statute against their trade by simply suggesting a donation. Thus, city leaders empowered virtually anyone to operate a business in Jackson Square, in effect turning a public space into a sanctioned carnival.[25]

The Landrieu administration went beyond remolding a public space, also proposing to offer nightly *son-et-lumière* (sound and light) shows in the square to recreate the "mood" of New Orleans. Such displays were popular in Europe, notably at the Invalides in Paris, the Forum in Rome, and the Acropolis in Athens. Without informing the VCC or citizens, the mayor signed a contract with a French firm in 1971 to produce the show. Reflecting the selective, dramatized portrayal of history typical of commercialized tourist attractions in the 1970s, the *son-et-lumière* program was to begin with "the buzz of the mosquitoes, and the mud and the Indians," and end with the music of the late jazz trumpeter Louis Armstrong. The spectacle, admitted Landrieu's appointed VCC director Wayne Collier, was "not designed to stimulate the imagination of a man who can look at the Pontalba Building and imagine what it was. It's more for people like me, who can't." The plan involved cutting down several old live oaks that would block the lighting and turning the square into a tropical garden. Landrieu also sought to use the pyramidal observation deck as a stadium for the anticipated spectators.[26]

Four months after the announcement of *son-et-lumière*, the French Quarter Residents Association, the Vieux Carré Property Owners and Associates (VCPOA), and several concerned individuals filed a lawsuit in civil district court to secure an injunction against the display because it lacked the necessary approval of the VCC and had deliberately circumvented the public bid process in an effort to keep the project under wraps. Although the commission eventually approved the display in early 1974 over the objection of some of its members, the controversy over the proposal and its implications for the future of the French Quarter as a residential or tourist district became increasingly strident by the middle of 1975. Preservationists contended that New Orleans needed no gimmicks to enhance its distinctive heritage and charged that the shows would bring a noisy, carnival-like atmosphere to a residential area. In July some one thousand New Orleanians, joining attorney and preservationist James G. Derbes's Coalition to Turn Off Sound and Light, took to the streets in protest. Undeterred by one of the thunderstorms that erupt almost daily in the semitropical heat of a New Orleans summer, they carried placards scrawled with the messages "Spare the Square" and "Deliver Us From Doom—No Sound, No Light, No Moon." Derbes collected more than nine thousand signatures on a petition to stop the show. Even the *Times-Picayune,* normally supportive of Landrieu's French Quarter initiatives, ran several editorials decrying *son-et-lumière.* Finally, under great pressure, Landrieu abandoned the proposal.[27]

Similarly controversial was Landrieu's plan to transform the city's historic French Market into a "festival marketplace" along the lines of San Francisco's Ghirardelli Square, a 1960s restoration of a former chocolate and spice factory, and the James Rouse Company's transformation of Boston's Quincy Market, then underway. Operated since the 1930s by the French Market Corporation, an appointed municipal board, the historic emporium stood on a narrow strip of land between the Mississippi River wharves and Decatur Street, a seedy stretch of seamen's bars, flophouses, and dilapidated flats. Although the WPA had thoroughly modernized the market in the 1930s, even tearing down and rebuilding portions of it, the city's semitropical climate had in the ensuing decades worked its magic, lending a "deteriorated quality" that one observer concluded was "a necessary ingredient for romance." Tourists, who in the 1960s gathered in increasing numbers to experience the presumed antiquity of one of the nation's few remaining public markets, transformed a fiscal liability into a profit machine. Reflective of the residential decline of the French Quarter, the number of meat, seafood, poultry, and produce vendors in and around the market fell by almost half in the two decades after World War II. With revenues again sagging by the 1970s, Landrieu viewed it as an eyesore that repelled tourists.[28] Landrieu appointed his friends and leading tourism developers Clancy Dupepe and Joseph Canizaro to lead the French Market transformation by securing private-sector funding for the renovation.[29]

Landrieu's pedestrian malls and the transformation of a public market into a festival marketplace spoke volumes about the favoritism now accorded to tourism operators in the French Quarter. As preservationists feared, the opening of the renovated French Market on April 1, 1975, led to the departure of neighborhood businesses such as the Morning Call coffee stand and Battistella's fresh seafood market. In their place appeared retailers offering New Orleans souvenirs and gifts. Associating the market with childhood memories, when she and her father took weekend strolls through the Quarter, Martha Robinson recalled that the market "was dingy and old and dirty, and it was wonderfully colorful with its . . . jabbering throngs of French and Spanish and Negroes, and above all, with its real Indians. . . . [Now it is] pink and has no character."[30] She wrote to the editor of the *Times-Picayune*, "April first—April Fool's Day—a fitting day for dedicating the New French Market, an ersatz historic landmark."[31]

The French Market Corporation's marketing campaign targeted both locals and tourists by sponsoring events such as King Cake Day during the Carnival season, an Easter egg hunt, a Bastille Day celebration, and the Great Pumpkin celebration in autumn. Despite such gestures toward community gatherings, however, the market now existed primarily for entertaining tourists. At Au Vieux Photographe, for example, tourists could get their tintypes made dressed in reproductions of 1860s costumes, while Cookery New Orleans Style offered local foods, seasonings, and kitchen products.[32]

Like the numerous French Quarter–style hotels and parking garages that the Vieux Carré Commission allowed to be built in the 1960s amid the eighteenth- and nineteenth-century structures they mimicked, the redevelopment projects initiated by the Landrieu administration in the 1970s created a tourist infrastructure that encouraged visitors to see the French Quarter almost as a theme park meant for their enjoyment. These projects underscored the shift from municipal approval of private development to government-initiated redevelopment. With the ongoing spread of tourism-oriented businesses in the French Quarter, they provided an enviable model for other cities seeking to attract tourists. But they also carried cautionary lessons for preservationists, notably in Charleston, South Carolina, where tourism threatened to tip the balance of preservation and development in favor of the latter.[33]

Ironically, even as the Landrieu administration worked tirelessly to facilitate building projects that brought modern urban amenities associated with rival cities like Houston and streetscapes reminiscent of theme parks and shopping malls, it also supported efforts to persuade the traveling public to continue viewing the Crescent City as a place apart from the mainstream, a place where one could still experience the gumbo of history, revelry, music, cuisine, and sex for which the city had long been known. For as long as the city had attracted tourists, New Orleans leaders had allocated paltry sums of money to promote a place that most agreed sold itself, but by the 1960s they began to sense the necessity of self-promotion as more and more American cities attuned themselves to competing for a share of the booming tourist trade.

In addition to fostering an infrastructure of tourism, Mayor Landrieu understood his city's need for allocating more funding to promoting New Orleans to prospective tourists. With Schiro's failure to win city council support for increasing the city's contribution to the tourist and convention commission, a coalition of concerned organizations, including the Greater New Orleans Tourist and Convention Commission (GNOTCC), the chamber of commerce, the Council for a Better Louisiana, Louisiana Tourist Development Commission (LTDC), Goals for Louisiana, and the Metropolitan Area Committee (MAC), sought to make tourism promotion a key issue for the new mayor. While attending a convention in the Houston Astrodome in 1970, Lester Kabacoff pondered how Houston, with its apparent dearth of tourist attractions, was able to attract so many large meetings. When he returned to New Orleans, Kabacoff was made chairman of a special subcommittee of MAC to investigate ways of stimulating tourism in the Crescent City. Kabacoff, Roosevelt Hotel general manager Dan Mikulak, and Maison Blanche department store president Robert I. Sonfield headed the group of nineteen civic leaders in researching the state of tourism in New Orleans.[34] Pointing to a 1969 Gallup poll that showed New Orleans's national tourist appeal slipping in relation to other American cities, the MAC subcommittee found that the GNOTCC's budget stood only thirty-first among the nation's convention and visitors bureaus and strongly recommended the adoption of a $900,000 budget that would place the Crescent City among the leading cities in promotional expenditures.[35]

Further evidence of the city's shortcomings came from hotelier Albert Aschaffenburg, who complained to Landrieu in 1970 that the convention trade was "sick." He observed that many of the events scheduled in the Rivergate were meetings of local organizations, even high school proms, and reflected no influx of "new" dollars into the local economy. Aschaffenburg also indicated that the Rivergate had simply taken trade from hotels such as the Roosevelt, Jung, and Royal Orleans, suggesting that the existing convention trade pie could only be divided so many ways and that the city needed to become more serious about luring visitors.[36]

The MAC plan anticipated an arrangement in which state matching funds from the LTDC would provide the city $250,000 of the recommended $900,000.

Heeding the committee's recommendation, Landrieu lobbied the state legislature vigorously. Despite the unusually cordial relations between Baton Rouge and New Orleans under the leadership of Governor John McKeithen, the legislature only allowed the LTDC to offer $200,000 toward statewide tourism marketing, of which the Crescent City could receive $50,000. Thus, the GNOTCC budget for the 1971–72 fiscal year was pegged at $700,000, still a threefold increase over the 1970–71 budget of $185,000, which had risen by less than $30,000 in the entire decade of the 1960s.[37] In addition to its matching funds, the LTDC shared with the commission the running of a new French Quarter tourist information center in the historic Bank of Louisiana building at 334 Royal Street. The city's tourist commission also relied on cooperative efforts with outside media, foreign tourism offices, and the United States Travel Service (USTS), a short-lived federal agency. The USTS provided $25,000 in matching funds in 1971 and again the next year, enabling the commission to market the city in Mexico, Canada, Great Britain, France, and Germany.[38]

The GNOTCC continued to market New Orleans in much the same way it and the chamber of commerce had done for years. Although the most blatant exploitation of a romanticized, white-dominated Old South image subsided with the waning popularity and promotion of the Spring Fiesta in the 1960s and 1970s, the tourist commission still emphasized images that relied on the city's reputation as a place apart. Under the new direction of Jimmie D. Fore, who moved from a similar post in Houston, the tourist commission's 1971 ad campaign, unmistakably drawing upon popular images of Storyville and Bourbon Street, told visitors, "You'll Love New Orleans, and She'll Love You Right Back."[39] As had been true in travel literature dating to the early twentieth century, this ad personified New Orleans as a temptress waiting to seduce the visitor with her charms. While cities had long been personified in various ways, the persistence of the metaphor of New Orleans as prostitute is striking.

Other ads called attention to the city as historic preserve. An advertisement in the early 1970s ran: "The rich, reverberant, nearly extinct clip clop of hoofs beats on cobblestone streets. Come. Experience New Orleans." Another ad several years later proclaimed New Orleans "A European Masterpiece."[40] While earlier strategies had emphasized that by stepping into the French Quarter one could, in effect, step into another time and place, this old-world-village-in-the-modern-city dichotomy yielded to the tendency to conflate the French Quarter's foreignness with the city as a whole. Arguably, this conflation was a natural result of tourists' tendency to spend all or most of their time in the French Quarter after decades of increasing concentration of the tourist infrastructure—hotels, restaurants, nightclubs, and attractions—in and near the Vieux Carré.

Although so much of the city's tourist image built upon the contributions of African Americans and Afro-Caribbean customs, as late as the 1970s the GNOTCC made no attempt to recognize most of these connections or to promote black tourism. Its tendency to sever black heritage from the salable products of that heritage, however, was hardly unique, for American popular culture in general continued to cast blacks in stereotypically comical or subservient roles rather than attempting to look beneath prejudicial imagery. Ingrained practices learned during Jim Crow kept many black tourists from embracing New Orleans's dominant tourist image. Although the desegregation of public accommodations had forced many black-owned tourist services to close for lack of business, for many African Americans a trip to New Orleans did not necessarily revolve around the white-dominated, racially exploitive attractions of the French Quarter which the GNOTCC emphasized in its appeal to mostly white and middle-class travelers.

Typical of the continuing bifurcation of black and white tourism in New Orleans was Mason's Las Vegas Strip, a black nightlife district created in the early 1970s by Louis C. Mason Jr., in a dingy block of South Claiborne Avenue less than two miles outside the French Quarter. Mason, an African American who had progressed from shining shoes to investing in motels, recalled, "I figured the French Quarter and Fat City were doing their things. It was time to do mine." Mason transformed the Americana, a preintegration motel for blacks, into the Flying Fox Club, the V.I.P. Lounge, the Mardi Gras Lounge, and the South Claiborne Streetcar bar, which charged the old streetcar fare of seven cents as a cover charge.[41] As had been true for years, in the 1970s most visiting blacks supported black-operated businesses offering black entertainment in predominantly black areas of New Orleans. In contrast, for whites the New Orleans touted by the GNOTCC in the 1970s was a historical and sensory outdoor theme park, a place where vacationers could pursue pleasure in a controlled, packaged setting that still felt more authentic and less programmed than California's Disneyland, Florida's Busch Gardens, Michigan's Greenfield Village, or Virginia's Colonial Williamsburg.

The tourist transformation of the French Quarter into a "Creole Disneyland" did not come without a price. As was true with the creation of tourist-oriented cityscapes elsewhere, in New Orleans the transition exerted tremendous pressure on buildings and the people who inhabited them. By the late 1960s and early 1970s, due to soaring rents, the residential composition of the Quarter had changed markedly from the days when Mary and Jacob Morrison first settled there. Between 1950 and 1965 alone, the proportion of French Quarter residents who were blue-collar workers declined from about 45 to 21 percent, while professionals increased from about 16 to 35 percent. In the same period, single occupants rose from 30 to 51 percent, and French Quarter residents became more likely to be white, middle- to upper-middle-class homeowners.[42] In 1973, a taxicab driver, one of the estimated eight hundred African Americans who remained of the thousands who once lived there, recalled that in the years before preservationists called attention to the neighborhood, he had shined shoes and sold picture postcards to the much smaller number of tourists. He lamented the lost sense of community, recounting a time when black tenants hung lanterns outside their houses to welcome neighbors to Friday night fish fries.[43] Even the relatively affluent white residents who had increasingly displaced blacks and ethnic whites now bristled as they were forced to cope with massage parlors, peep shows, and penny arcades, as well as transient musicians, panhandlers, fortune tellers, obnoxious barkers, tap-dancing children, and tourists motoring through the Quarter in rented miniature antique cars "with one hand on the wheel and the other holding a beer."[44] Although tourism was critical in building a civic consensus favoring the preservation of the Vieux Carré, the increase of tourists and the commercial enterprises and itinerants that sought their money threatened to spoil the district's fragile balance of preservation and profit.

If it did not care about the impact of tourism on the residential composition of the Vieux Carré, the city government did embrace preservationists' arguments against unrestricted commercialization as a detriment to the Quarter's tourist appeal. Following the moratorium on new hotel construction in the French Quarter, which was strengthened in a city ordinance in 1970, the city government responded to the impact of tourism on structural integrity and quality of life by passing numerous ordinances to curb the ill effects of the tourist trade before they damaged what many called New Orleans's greatest asset. While many central cities experienced a decline in vehicular traffic as population shifted to suburban shopping malls and office parks, the French Quarter's soaring popularity kept automobile traffic heavy in downtown New Orleans. Outcry against heavy traffic in the Vieux Carré, however, was nothing new. For years preservationists had complained that large trucks and buses rattled the old buildings as they roared past, occasionally even destroying iron galleries in their failure to negotiate turns in the narrow streets. After about a decade of periodic discussion, in 1973 New Orleans Public Service, Inc., heeded the city planning commission's recommendation to remove city buses from the Vieux Carré, replacing them with minibuses painted olive green and mahogany to match the city's famous St. Charles Avenue streetcar.[45]

The city bus ban was a hint of the larger struggle to stop the many sightseeing tour buses from crowding into the Quarter, where they collected passengers at thirty-seven different hotels. District C Councilman Mike Early became preservationists' leading ally in city hall in the 1970s and 1980s. "The real culprit down there is the constant weaving in and out of large tour buses," Early argued. "That's what's causing the damage to streets and buildings."[46] While one representative of the city's leading tour bus companies, which roundly opposed regulation, predicted "economic devastation" if Early proceeded with his proposal, some Quarter tourism interests disagreed. One businesswoman reminded city officials and business leaders that the great tourist city of Venice, Italy, did not have a single motor vehicle.[47]

After several years of grappling with the issue, in 1979 Early introduced an ordinance prohibiting all sightseeing tours in the French Quarter using buses with chassis longer than thirty-one feet and restricting all buses to five designated stops near the edges of the neighborhood.[48] When the city council, bowing to pressure from tourism interests, failed to approve the measure in a tie vote, a Times-Picayune editorial remarked, "Although the American tourist has obviously evolved into a creature with limited powers of locomotion, our compulsive pampering of visitors is already threatening the environment they come to enjoy and local residents enjoy year-round."[49] After Early agreed to a compromise in which buses would be banned from the predominantly residential section between St. Peter Street and Esplanade Avenue while having stops at three leading Quarter hotels, the ordinance passed in city council. Building on his success, Early went on to shepherd an additional ordinance that removed all through traffic by heavy trucks on Decatur and North Peters Streets, which he had likened to a "huge wrecking ball" slowly destroying the city's heritage. After a two-year delay the ordinance finally passed in 1983 but not before the daily average of 715 large trucks had contributed to the separation of the brick Decatur Street façade from the cracking wall of the Lower Pontalba Building, which housed about a dozen tourist shops and services on its ground floor facing Jackson Square.[50]

French Quarter residents also chafed under the growing burden that Carnival placed on the district. Since the early postwar years, more krewes followed the example of Hermes by altering their routes to pass through the Quarter for tourists' enjoyment. Quarter architect and preservationist Mark Lowrey, describing a scene of "bedlam," noted that between 1962 and 1971 alone the number of parades passing his Orleans Street residence rocketed from five to sixteen.[51] Following an incident in which several people were killed or injured in the crush of parade goers on Bourbon Street, French Quarter advocates charged that Mardi Gras had gotten out of hand. In 1972 the newly formed Coalition of Vieux Carré Organizations, comprised of the VCPOA, Louisiana Council for the Vieux Carré, French Quarter Residents Association, and other area advocacy groups, persuaded leading Carnival krewes not to parade in the Quarter. Against the protests of the Monteleone Hotel, some real estate interests, and apartment dwellers who profited from the Royal-to-Orleans route, the city council voted to ban Mardi Gras parades in the French Quarter beginning in 1973 because of crowd-control issues.[52] Although the city council revisited the issue in 1976 and 1977, preservationists quickly shot down the proposal to reinstate the parades. With or without parades, however, crowds grew larger by the year. The French Quarter and Mardi Gras were intertwined, and therein lay the difficulty in managing the implications of tourists' expectations.

Perhaps the greatest affront that the tourist transformation posed for many Quarter residents in the 1970s was the growing cadre of street musicians, performers, fortune tellers, and peddlers who flocked to the Crescent City, some with little more than the shirts on their backs, to exploit the presence of so many tourists. As noted, the city encouraged the daily spectacle by creating carnivallike pedestrian malls that watered the seeds of an informal economy of tourism, which in turn sprouted and grew between the cracks of more grounded tourist enterprises. As had been true with the 1960s boom in new hotels, the 1970s proliferation of street businesses confronted resistance from the slowly declining number of Quarter dwellers who clung to fading hopes of salvaging the district's residential desirability. Equally important, Royal Street shopkeepers and Bourbon Street club owners complained that itinerant performers attracted tourist crowds that blocked the entrances to their businesses.

The controversy over street entertainers boiled over in 1974 when Dr. Frank Minyard, the city coroner, was arrested on the Royal Street Promenade on charges of begging and disorderly conduct for playing his trumpet with the French Market Jazz Band. Minyard's arrest, which utilized the city's soliciting and disorderly conduct laws in the absence of prohibitions on music in the street, brought national television news coverage to New Orleans's dilemma of balancing interests in its most famous section. Earl Duffy of Key Biscayne, Florida, a former Jazz Fest official, expressed disbelief that a jazzman could be charged with "begging on the street."[53] However, one resident, in response to a Massachusetts visitor's contention that tourists expected to be able to see musicians in the streets, expressed the disdain that many locals felt: "Not only is this noise wished on us, but we are blocked off from our homes and businesses. I would like to ship the same group of noise-makers directly in front of his home for a couple of months. . . . He even has the gall to state that the city should back them financially. The French Quarter is not a cheap box of Crackerjacks with prizes to dole out to visitors."[54] After contemplating an ordinance requiring performers to compete for fifty at fifty dollars apiece, permits, the city council settled for a ninety-day moratorium on stationary bands and musicians on Royal Street, doubtless fearing more adverse publicity.[55]

Later in the decade the focus shifted to the estimated thirty black children and young men who tap danced for tourist donations outside nightclubs in the French Quarter, often working for elusive pimps. Business and club owners complained that the tap dancers, like street musicians, blocked the entrances to their establishments, often prompting multiple calls nightly to police. As with the policing of disorderly conduct, illicit sex, and other behavior deemed part of the Quarter's aura and yet potentially damaging to its attractiveness, the police, as one cop admitted, "give them leeway until it gets out of hand. We tell them to keep moving, don't block sidewalks or the street."[56] Nevertheless, the street performer controversy remained unresolved, extending even to the music blaring from Bourbon Street nightclubs. City officials variously tried negotiation, threats of new ordinances, and spotty enforcement of existing laws to keep the problems in check, gradually shifting their focus in the 1980s to engineering the types of businesses that could operate in the city's tourist hub.

Even as the contest for control of the city's most widely recognized spaces heated up in the French Quarter, the search for profit extended to the decaying docklands along the Mississippi River, whose unsightly neglect ensured for a time that preservation interests would not oppose large-scale developments. In training its sights on the riverfront, New Orleans developers followed other cities' lead, notably New York's Battery Park City and South Street Seaport, and Detroit's Renaissance Center. With the riverfront expressway no longer a threat, port officials more amenable to a leisure-oriented redevelopment of the riverfront, and a national trend toward adaptive reuse of declining industrial waterfronts, New

Orleans was at last in a position in the 1970s to reorient the French Quarter and the downtown business district, long focused on Bourbon Street, Royal Street, and Canal Street, toward the arc of the Mississippi River. In addition to its efforts to transform Jackson Square and the French Market, the Landrieu administration oversaw the first major redevelopment of the riverfront since the construction of the International Trade Mart and Rivergate exhibition hall in the 1960s. Unlike its French Quarter initiatives, in the push to revamp the riverfront, the administration looked to private investment and public-private partnerships, sometimes using federal grants and loans as matching funds.

Although the Dock Board had opened the Dumaine Street Wharf for tourist use in 1963, it remained hesitant about conceding more ground for leisure-oriented redevelopment. The port's efforts in the late 1960s to transplant the entire port to the Mississippi River Gulf Outlet as part of its ambitious $395 million Centroport U.S.A. plan looked increasingly unlikely to reach fruition as the 1970s unfolded. Following staunch opposition from affected residents in the Ninth Ward, a struggling downriver neighborhood to the east of the French Quarter, conservative Republican president Ronald Reagan took office in 1981 and slashed federal funds for projects such as Centroport. The dream of a modern container port in eastern New Orleans modeled after Rotterdam's *Europoort* dissolved, necessitating the continuing use of the Mississippi River wharves. Thus, the New Orleans riverfront was the locus of years of sparring between the old-guard Dock Board and mostly nonelite tourism developers for control.[57]

Despite the opening of the International Trade Mart and the Rivergate near the confluence of Canal and Poydras Streets in the 1960s, the streets between St. Charles Avenue and the river remained dark and forlorn through the next decade.[58] Some municipal and business leaders worried that New Orleans would regress unless they took decisive action to enliven the downtown district. Like the Superdome that anchored one end of Poydras Street, the tree-lined boulevard created to accommodate the city's office building boom, the "Houstonization" of downtown New Orleans also touched the river end of Poydras. There Lester Kabacoff managed to persuade the Dock Board to grant air rights atop its wharves for International Rivercenter, his planned riverfront complex anchored by a 1,200-room Hilton hotel. While Kabacoff entertained the idea of a new convention center atop the Poydras Street Wharf, the movement to increase the city's exhibition space ultimately gravitated slightly upriver to the site where he and others spearheaded a plan to host an international exposition of the kind that had reshaped downtown Seattle in the 1960s.

In 1974 Baton Rouge businessman Ed Stagg, who served as executive director of the Council for a Better Louisiana, made public his idea for an exposition to encourage industrial expansion in the state. When a number of business leaders associated with Landrieu's new growth coalition picked up on the idea of holding a world's fair, they did so not so much to entice industrial investment as to leverage state and federal money for a new convention center. They hoped to keep pace in a market that saw a threefold increase in exhibition space in the two decades after 1970.[59] They also hoped the exposition would help revive what two local journalists later recalled as a "desolate neighborhood of run-down sheds, creaky wharves, railroad tracks and cratered streets" only a few blocks upriver from the French Quarter. In the nearly quarter-century lull in American world expositions between the 1939 New York World's Fair and Seattle's Century 21 Exposition in 1962, such events shifted from primarily educational endeavors to showcase American progress to engines for urban redevelopment. Seattle's fair left the signature flying saucer–capped Space Needle, while San Antonio's 1968 HemisFair gave the Texas city a convention center, sports arena, hotels, and heightened tourist interest in its verdant River Walk.[60] By the 1970s and 1980s such expositions represented only one of many types of staged events—including street festivals, jazz festivals, winterfests and summerfests, film fairs, and marathons—that U.S. cities used to draw tourists and garner media attention.[61] New Orleans was no exception. What had begun with the city's persuading the Dock Board to build and maintain the Rivergate became by 1980 a public-private partnership to stage a world's fair that would stimulate tourism, "open" the riverfront, and replace a seedy stretch of warehouses with new public venues such as a massive convention center.

The effort to stage the fair, planned for 1984, began with the formation of Louisiana World Exposition, Inc. (LWE), in 1976. While LWE included bluebloods Richard Freeman and Darwin Fenner and won the support of the partially old-guard MAC, it tapped mostly the energies of men who stood outside the Carnival elite, such as public utility executives Floyd W. Lewis and Carl F. Bailey. The fair planners hired Petr Spurney, the impresario who had supervised the 1974 Spokane World's Fair and the 1980 Olympics in Lake Placid, New York. Having read of Spurney's deft handling of mega-events in an article in *Fortune,* LWE leaders believed he was ideally suited to the task.[62]

Without the world's fair, it might have taken longer for New Orleans to line up sufficient support to erect a first-class exhibition hall, which was sorely needed. In the 1960s a number of other U.S. cities had constructed convention centers because existing hotels and even recently built exhibition halls could not match the demand, and the 1970s saw the opening of many dozens of new facilities. New Orleans's convention trade, restricted by the dearth of hotel rooms into the 1960s, now lost meetings to other cities because its Rivergate hall, with only 137,000 square feet of exhibition space, was inadequate. Replacing Jimmie Fore, who moved to Dallas in 1973, Lester Kabacoff recruited San Franciscan Edward J. McNeill to assume direction of the GNOTCC. McNeill began to investigate how the city could expand its convention business. As with tourism promotion, New Orleans, despite its internationally famous attractions, again found itself struggling to muscle its way into a more competitive position within the exploding convention industry, which had become a favored means of offsetting downtown decay in a number of cities. Although the Superdome eased the situation somewhat, enabling New Orleans to become one of the top ten cities nationally in the number of visiting conventioneers, the city had to expand its meeting capacity in order to keep pace in a rapidly changing market. Just as the Rivergate had opened only after many large cities built a first-generation auditorium or arena for conventions, New Orleans's plan for a larger second-generation convention center came rather late.[63]

In 1978, before the separate ideas of a convention center and a world's fair merged, Kabacoff drafted a bill, introduced in the Louisiana Legislature, that created the New Orleans Exhibition Hall Authority (NOEHA), a quasi-public corporation. Dutch Morial, who became mayor that year, smoothed the way for the construction of a new convention center. As the city's first black mayor, the former civil rights attorney owed his election to the same coalition of business leaders and African Americans who had supported Landrieu, suggesting that by the late 1970s the desire for economic development outweighed racial discrimination in the minds of many white voters. Morial announced that the city would lease to the NOEHA, for one dollar a year, a ten-and-a-half-acre riverfront parcel. It had been acquired from Kabacoff in a 1972 land swap under Landrieu which had facilitated Kabacoff's International Rivercenter project. In 1979 Morial also applied to the federal government for an Urban Development Action Grant (UDAG), a popular means of funding urban revitalization projects in the 1970s. Twice denied, the convention center planners received the UDAG only after former mayor Landrieu became secretary of HUD. Even with the UDAG and a special one-cent hotel tax increase, the project required more funding, leading NOEHA representatives Owen "Pip" Brennan Jr., Frederick J. Forstall, and Dr. Mervin Trail to ask the state to assist. Over lunch at Brennan's Restaurant in the French Quarter the men assured key legislators that the center would be able to house the Louisiana Pavilion at the planned world's fair and told Governor David Treen that it would be an ideal venue for hosting a future Republican National Convention. The state followed through with $30 million.[64]

Assembling the necessary capital for the world's fair, like the effort to fund the convention center, meant looking to nontraditional sources. Federal approval for the fair demanded raising millions of dollars in seed money from the private sector, a daunting task in a city that still had a substantial number of affluent luminaries known for their disdain toward funding projects that promised to benefit anyone outside their tight circle. It hardly helped that the *Times-Picayune* ran an editorial noting that New Orleans was the only American city competing for the exposition, which it suggested might "no longer be a plum worth fighting for."[65] Meeting with fair backers and local and state politicians in the Plimsoll Club atop the International Trade Mart on April 3, 1981, Secretary of Commerce Malcolm Baldridge shocked New Orleans leaders by insisting that they raise $16 million in five days or face denial. Governor Treen and LWE officials Kabacoff, Lewis, and Freeman persuaded the state's large oil companies and utilities, national-chain hotels, Coca-Cola, and Delta Airlines to contribute. With a list of fair commitments in hand, Spurney raced to meet Baldridge in Washington, D.C., before the deadline. Missing his flight, Spurney boarded another plane to Baltimore-Washington International and reached the capital just fifteen minutes before the Department of Commerce offices closed for the evening. President Reagan reluctantly approved the fair but told Baldridge to limit federal assistance to $10 million, far below the $200 million allocated by his predecessor Jimmy Carter for the 1982 world's fair, held in Knoxville, Tennessee.[66]

Mayor Morial approached the idea of a world's fair with considerable hesitation. Like Landrieu, Morial inherited a city beset by chronic socioeconomic troubles—problems that the oil-driven prosperity had at best masked. As an Afro-Creole and the city's first black mayor, Morial understood the challenges he faced, especially the difficulty of convincing African Americans of his sincerity in wanting to help them. Morial favored industrial development, noting that he was "not for New Orleans being a tourist city and nothing else."[67] His pet project, the Almonaster-Michoud Industrial District, an eight-thousand acre tract in eastern New Orleans that he hoped would bring fifty thousand high-paying manufacturing jobs to ease unemployment and poverty, suffered as federal funds for improvements dried up in the 1980s, pushing the mayor to grudgingly support the world's fair initiative. Morial worried that the fair might force the financially strapped city to provide expensive services for the six-month event. He also feared that his black constituents would not accept giving so much public money to a project so physically and emotionally distant from their community. Nevertheless, Morial decided that he had no choice but to take a leading role in planning the event so he could ensure the best possible outcome for the city. Accordingly, he lobbied the state legislature for a $15 million loan for infrastructure improvements and coaxed LWE officials into promising $12–15 million in additional tax receipts to cover the loan.[68]

In addition to allocating funds for heightened application of city services and police protection during the world's fair, in 1983 Morial undertook the most extensive public works project in the French Quarter since the 1930s, allocating $6 million to repave most of its streets, add brick crosswalks, and replace ordinary concrete sidewalks with brick or blue flagstone pavers.[69] When it appeared that the disruption of months of street improvements was hurting local business, Morial worked with promoters to launch the French Quarter Festival in March 1984 as a gesture to persuade New Orleanians, especially suburbanites, to rediscover the Vieux Carré.

From the outset, planners sold the idea that the 1984 world's fair would "give" the Mississippi River back to the people of New Orleans by offsetting the nearly one hundred years in which the port's wall of steel sheds atop the river wharves had prevented riverfront recreation. The exposition would, they argued, speed the process of reacquainting citizens with the legendary river. Ironically, the fair simply substituted one industrial monopoly of the riverfront for another. After removing the wharf buildings to reveal what one planner called the "theater of the river," LWE constructed the Louisiana Pavilion, which, after three expansions as the new convention center, gradually created a four-thousand-foot-long glass and concrete fortress that completely hid the river from view at street level. Giving the river back, then, ultimately meant giving it to visiting conventioneers, who flitted about the complex replenishing drained city coffers. The Louisiana Pavilion, combined with Kabacoff's Hilton, itself a concrete monstrosity, and the connecting International Pavilion that would become a new festival marketplace, delivered to the tourism industry more than a mile of prime downtown riverfront.

Fair promoters packaged the 1984 fair to appeal to the mostly white and middle-class traveling public that formed the backbone of mass tourism in the second half of the twentieth century. Throughout the United States in the years after World War II, middle-class Americans increasingly sought tourist experiences that provided a sense of escape in a clean, secure, family-friendly environment. Since the early 1970s New Orleans tourism leaders had worked to wrest the city's tourist image away from the tawdry, adult-centered Bourbon Street in favor of family-centered attractions that might fill hotels in a slow summer months. Increasingly by the 1970s, family attractions in suburbia had begun to compete with older leisure sites in the American city. Building upon a tradition that dates to late nineteenth-century attractions such as Chicago's 1893 Columbian exposition and Coney Island's Luna Park, opened in 1903, theme parks such as Disneyland and Knotts Berry Farm in southern California, or Busch Gardens in Tampa, recreated historical and naturalistic places to provide a sense of escape in a controlled setting. Urban versions of this mostly suburban landscape provided a way for flagging cities to recapture revenues lost in the national flight to suburbs in the postwar years.[70] If New Orleans leaders had worked for decades to tame the French Quarter into a "Creole Disneyland," providing a model for other cities' tourism efforts, the 1984 world's fair promised to further the effort to make the central city appear inviting to an increasingly suburban people.

Ironically, in New Orleans, the world's fair tried to create a place of escape from one of the world's most popular tourist destinations. To be sure, the fair sought to bottle the elixir of revelry, romance, and profligacy which professed to capture Storyville and, later, the Vieux Carré, and which had long set New Orleans apart from the dry Bible-Belt South to its north. Like the Mardi Gras extravaganzas held in the Superdome in the late 1970s, the world's fair tried to encapsulate the same atmosphere of Carnival, jazz, and titillation available for free across Canal Street and telescope it into a six-month spectacle aimed at families able to spend fifteen dollars per ticket. But the fair also strove to present a mythical fantasyland of lagoons, fountains, gardens, pavilions, and other whimsical attractions. One of the fair's planners promised "a fairytale land reminiscent of Oz, Jack and the Beanstalk, and Disney World on the banks of the Mississippi. . . . We want mom and pop and the kids to feel like they're following the yellow brick road."[71]

If only for six months, the fair would demonstrate the kind of family attraction tourism promoters hoped would broaden New Orleans's appeal as more than simply a "sin city." In preparation for the fair, city officials tried to tame and confine New Orleans's seamier side, particularly in the French Quarter, where fair visitors would surely wander after they tired of the plastic fantasyland. Orleans Parish district attorney Harry Connick waged war on prostitution in the Quarter, with the NOPD conducting fifty-seven raids that netted some five hundred arrests in the two years preceding the fair's opening. The city council agreed to convert Bourbon Street into an around-the-clock pedestrian mall, much as Moon Landrieu had done to Jackson Square a decade earlier. In addition, Lafayette Street, known as a haunt for the city's homeless, became a pedestrian mall to provide safe passage for tourists strolling between the Superdome and the world's fair. Conceived in part as a means of luring suburbanites back to the city, the 1984 exposition ended up contributing, in effect, to the suburbanization—and "Houstonization"—of downtown New Orleans.[72]

If Walt Disney had copied New Orleans in the 1960s, New Orleans copied Walt Disney in the 1980s. Covering eighty-four acres sandwiched between the Mississippi River and the central business district, the Louisiana World Exposition, like Disneyland, was divided into several sections with different themes—Bayou Plaza, Festival Park, Centennial Plaza, Cajun Walk, and International Riverfront. Flanking the side of the exposition opposite the river was the Wonderwall, a 2,400-foot-long Greco-Roman postmodern fantasy of towers, columns, cupolas, domes, and mythical statues intended to hide high-tension power lines on the edge of the site. Other attractions included the Aquacade water ballet theater, a Ferris wheel second in size only to the one in Vienna's Prater Park, and a 1.4-mile monorail. An aerial tramway with cable-suspended, Plexiglas-encased pods ferried fairgoers high above the river from the West Bank to downtown New Orleans. One journalist remarked on the strange juxtaposition of a serious, educational theme—"Rivers of the World: Fresh Water as a Source of Life"—with the frivolity associated with Carnival. Not surprisingly, in the age of television, satellites, and computers, most fairgoers opted for the daily Mardi Gras parade reenactments that meandered through the grounds rather than the series of lectures on topics such as water conservation and hydroelectric power.[73]

The honor of hosting a world's fair seemed to New Orleans leaders proof that their city was at last back on track in its rivalry with other regional cities. Just as earlier tourist literature had pointed to the unusual contrast of a quaint village amid the bustle of a progressive city, New Orleans leaders in the 1970s and 1980s could call attention to their ability to make the Crescent City prosper without selling its soul, as Houston had implicitly done. Even if Mayor Morial's dream of a dynamic industrial corridor in the swampy wastes to the east of downtown remained unfulfilled, civic leaders could pride themselves on having made the most of the resources at hand—vast petroleum reserves and distinctive culture. Not even a national recession diminished their optimism. No longer did progrowth leaders find themselves hamstrung by a conservative elite. Instead, a growing number of development-minded business leaders stepped into the power vacuum that in the late 1960s and early 1970s prompted more than one observer to conclude that the city stood at a fateful crossroads. Mayors Landrieu and Morial led administrations that seemed capable of enhancing the tourist experience, although detractors worried that the volume of tourism might upset the delicate balance between preservation and profit. The 1970s and early 1980s saw a strengthening of the consensus favoring the protection of historically and architecturally significant neighborhoods throughout New Orleans, and yet growing tourist demand emboldened developers to curry municipal favor for projects that preservationists worried would ruin their own investment and labor of love in the inner city at a time when most middle-income Americans were heading for leafy suburbs. Indeed, municipal involvement in staging tourism contributed, in effect, to the suburbanization of the central city and the French Quarter's inexorable drift toward a "Creole Disneyland," a situation which, in turn, forced New Orleans to manage the often unpleasant implications of becoming a city dependent on tourism. As events in the wake of the world's fair unfolded, it became far more difficult for New Orleans to stray from its well-defined role as a tourist city.

CHAPTER 7

A CITY ON PARADE

. . . we are so desperate for money that the gradual sacrifice of a heritage will not strike many as too high a price to pay. —JAMES GILL (1986)

What we've known and loved has been turned into a theme park to amuse visitors. —HENRI SCHINDLER (1998)

In 1986 Sidney J. Barthelemy, an Afro-Creole and soon to be New Orleans's second black mayor, began corresponding with the development division of Walt Disney. "As I sit here virtually on the eve of my inauguration as this great city's next Mayor," he wrote, "I cannot help but think of what awesome responsibilities I face in turning things around for our most deserving citizens and how much a Disney project here would accomplish precisely that." The mayor-elect hinted at the severity of the conditions that befell New Orleans in the mid-1980s. For Barthelemy, snaring a Disney theme park for the city's downtown riverfront seemed the perfect way to shore up New Orleans's sinking economic foundation. "We simply have to have you," he told a Disney representative.[1]

Although his overtures to Disney failed, Barthelemy further strengthened city hall's close relationship with a cadre of tourism-oriented developers and promoters who had begun to reshape New Orleans. If Mayor Moon Landrieu had seen tourism as an industry his administration could stimulate to ease the burden of the shipping and oil industries in steering economic development, Barthelemy was the first New Orleans mayor to view tourism as the city's only hope of fighting urban decay. In the 1970s and early 1980s, ballooning oil and natural gas prices had yielded a bonanza in tax revenues for the state treasury in Louisiana. Coupled with generous federal grants to cities, oil money enabled the city government and the private developers with whom it partnered to portray New Orleans as a veritable boom town. In the early 1980s, *Times-Picayune* articles carried headlines such as "Boom isn't coming to N.O.—it's here" and "Are we overtaking Atlanta?"[2] But beneath the veneer of prosperity lay intractable problems, including a poorly educated, low-skilled workforce, decaying neighborhoods and schools, rising poverty and unemployment rates, white flight to the suburbs, and a shrinking tax base worsened by a state-approved homestead exemption that freed nearly all New Orleanians from paying property taxes. In addition, assurances of economic expansion ignored the reality of a modernizing port that required fewer workers, an oil industry that despite billions of dollars' investment employed few New Orleanians, and a burgeoning tourism industry that generally replaced losses in the transportation and manufacturing sectors with low-paying service jobs.

Then, in the span of a few months in 1984 and 1985, the Louisiana World Exposition went bankrupt, leaving thousands of new hotel rooms empty. The price of oil plummeted, casting a pall over the city's seemingly bright future. In the next few years, the city lost about sixty thousand jobs and as many residents. Dutch Morial, already seeing federal support for cities drying up, had warned of the dangers of counting on oil, shipping, and tourism as substitutes for manufacturing jobs, but his successor Sidney Barthelemy felt compelled to embrace tourism. So did many newer business leaders, who by the 1980s had relegated the Carnival elite to little more than coordinators of parades and debutante balls.

In the midst of the oil bust and the tourism-led recovery that followed, the impact of tourism on the city's public policies, its landscape, and its culture only grew. In the 1940s New Orleans's leading newspapers rarely referred to tourism. A half-century later it seldom lay far from the center of any discussion of New Orleans in the local and national media. The increasingly impoverished city staked its hopes on the tourist trade, forgoing tackling the difficult problems that could not be resolved in the short span of one or two mayoral administrations, and its landscape and culture revealed the extent to which tourism reshaped local priorities to match outsiders' expectations. The French Quarter became commercialized to the point that the preservation-minded residents who had played such an important role in resurrecting the village often found themselves unable to endure what they could no longer control. While the Quarter and adjacent downtown area became more intertwined as a single tourist district, blurring the long-important Canal Street boundary that had historically separated them, the impact of tourism began to spill over into the rest of the city. Likewise, tourism continued to reshape Mardi Gras into an event that revolved more and more around drinking, carousing, and licentiousness, as well as parades that resembled moving Las Vegas floor shows. Despite its tendency to favor what tourists expected to find in New Orleans, however, tourism-stoked changes sometimes helped locals rediscover neglected traditions. The jazz revival, for all its emphasis on the Dixieland style, provided inspiration and financial support for budding generations of young musicians.

Although it certainly trapped the city's poor in low-paying service-sector jobs, in a sense tourism in New Orleans was not simply a "devil's bargain." Arguably it was the city's very failure to play Houston's and Atlanta's game of modernization throughout the twentieth century that ultimately preserved a cityscape and culture that retain the illusion of uniqueness. This chapter explores the conditions that led to the reorientation of New Orleans toward the needs of the tourism industry and the resulting impact on the French Quarter, jazz, and Carnival, as well as on the city itself. In its effort to recoup economic stature by exploiting its heritage, New Orleans became a place that existed to satisfy the nostalgic and sensory desires of outsiders, a place obsessed with maintaining a façade that mirrored what tourists expected to find—in essence, a city on parade.

The 1984 world's fair was supposed to be New Orleans's moment in the sun. Like the immediate post–World War II years, it was to be a time to display its readiness to recapture its former position as one of the nation's leading cities. But the timing was all wrong. Previous world's fairs had enjoyed considerable federal support, but the conservative Republican administration of President Ronald Reagan proved miserly toward the exposition. The national recession of 1982–83 hit just as fair promoters needed to make their push for corporate sponsors. With corporate support lagging, the conservative Whitney National Bank, the largest bank in Louisiana and still an old-line bastion of financial retrenchment, refused to lend to the exposition. Louisiana World Exposition (LWE) funds proved insufficient to pay construction bills as they came due, and the fair fell deeply into debt even before it opened. The exposition also had to compete for corporate support with the 1984 Summer Olympic Games in Los Angeles and Walt Disney World's highly popular EPCOT Center, opened two years earlier and itself an adaptation of the world's fair concept. Such major attractions on both coasts doubtless diminished New Orleans's ability to market its fair as *the* event of the summer. In spite of the warning signs, LWE president Petr Spurney remained resolute in his belief that the fair's success rested on creating a dynamic show, in his words, on giving guests "the sizzle with the steak."[3]

The exposition's problems became apparent even before it opened to the public. One day before opening day, some two thousand invited news reporters examined the fair, finding construction equipment, mud and litter, and unfinished attractions. Forklifts roared about as Orleans Parish Prison inmates scurried to clean up the muddy site. In newspapers throughout the nation, articles pointed to the fair's unpromising start. Awash in red ink by opening day, the fair needed to attract 12 million visitors in six months just to avert bankruptcy. Although an earlier projection of 11 million had steered planning, skyrocketing construction costs, lackluster federal and corporate support, and dismal advance ticket sales persuaded fair officials to fudge the numbers. They remained convinced that the allure of New Orleans and their efforts to create an exciting venue would fulfill attendance forecasts.[4]

For all the fair's promise, it proved a costly debacle. Despite drawing an opening day crowd of more than 83,000, attendance figures seldom topped half that number for the rest of the exposition's six-month run. Baffled fair officials struggled to explain the poor attendance, even suggesting that perhaps the turnstiles were not counting properly. More likely, the fair suffered because New Orleans lay far from major population centers and had to compete with other major attractions. Still more tellingly, the fair priced itself out of reach of many local residents. In a city in which one-fifth of the population and half of African Americans suffered in poverty, the fair charged fifteen dollars per guest, considerably higher than the ten-dollar admission on which planners based their rosy attendance projections. The fact that fewer than half of the city's blacks, who comprised more than half of New Orleans's population, attended the exposition underscored that for tourism interests the city's attractions still focused their appeal on middle-class white travelers.[5]

Despite hosting only 7 million of the projected 12 million patrons and becoming insolvent, the 1984 exposition transformed downtown New Orleans. Just as world's fairs had spurred downtown revitalization in other American cities, notably, Seattle and San Antonio in the 1960s, the LWE contributed to the reorientation of New Orleans's central business district toward the riverfront. A year after the fair the Louisiana Pavilion reopened as the New Orleans Convention Center (later renamed the Ernest N. Morial Convention Center), catapulting the city into the first order of convention destinations. Likewise, its International Pavilion, which ran on the river side of the Louisiana Pavilion atop wharves secured through an air rights agreement with the Dock Board, reopened as the Riverwalk, a festival marketplace designed by the Maryland-based James Rouse Company. Not only did the fair leave the tourism industry two mammoth venues, it also stimulated developments calculated to take advantage of the anticipated windfall from the fair. Lester Kabacoff opened a riverfront annex to his Hilton and International Rivercenter development. Several developers, including Kabacoff's son Pres, refurbished old buildings near the edge of the fair to create a "warehouse district" of loft apartments, art galleries, and restaurants. Local developers Darryl Berger, David Burrus, and Wayne Ducote navigated the labyrinth of Vieux Carré Commission (VCC) regulations and won approval to transform the old Jax Brewery, a multistory plant constructed in the late nineteenth century along the French Quarter riverfront and closed in 1974, into a festival marketplace that opened in time for the fair. The effect of the fair, like that of tourism promoters and developers over the previous three decades, only reinforced the centralization of tourism in and around the French Quarter itself.[6]

Unfortunately, the larger tourism infrastructure proved difficult to sustain. In addition to Kabacoff's 454-room hotel expansion, other developers opened several first-class convention hotels within a year of the fair's opening in hopes of cashing in on the bonanza. One tourism industry official recalled that everyone was "predicting sugarplums and lollipops" for the local hotel business. Concentrated within a few blocks of the exposition and the French Quarter, these hotels added close to six thousand new rooms to downtown New Orleans. The largest of them, the 1,200-room Sheraton, soared more than forty stories above the rooflines of nineteenth-century Canal Street storefronts. When the fair fell short of expectations, these new hotels suffered. In the resulting hotel glut, occupancy rates fell from 76 percent in 1981 to only 52 percent in 1985, with the July 1984 rate an abysmal 40 percent. By the summer following the exposition, seven downtown hotels had filed bankruptcy, and lenders had foreclosed on two others. The slump in New Orleans's hotel business coincided with the steep decline of oil prices in the closing months of 1984, removing any doubt that New Orleans's decade-long economic boom had ended.[7]

In this respect New Orleans was certainly not unique. Developers in the South and elsewhere overbuilt their downtown areas in the early to mid-1980s, taking advantage of favorable federal tax incentives, overeager lenders, rosy economic predictions, and a growing belief that conventions and large-scale events could sustain a year-round tourist trade capable of overcoming the troubles of central cities. Notably, in the early 1980s, Knoxville, which had seen only one new hotel constructed in four decades, built several large hotels in anticipation of hosting the 1982 Energy Expo. Intending to use the world's fair to leverage downtown redevelopment, Knoxville, like New Orleans two years later, created a formidable tourism infrastructure in the hope that it would emerge as a leading tourist destination. As in New Orleans, the fair in Knoxville proved very popular yet costly, giving way to several years of economic recession that challenged local leaders to make good on lofty promises for the exposition site. Although the fair itself suffered mismanagement and left behind struggling new hotels and restaurants, not to mention a $12 million U.S. Pavilion that the federal government ultimately had to resell for one dollar, eventually it offered a foundation for a new downtown entertainment district. With far more tourist attractions than the Tennessee city, New Orleans proved abler in converting a short-term exposition into a long-term tourist space, but the two cities' difficulties in the 1980s underscore the risks and sacrifices that accompanied wholesale reliance on tourism to transform urban fortunes.[8]

Nonetheless, a new breed of New Orleans leaders proceeded with the force of their convictions to spend their way to success. On the surface it appeared just another headlong plunge. In the years since Mayor Chep Morrison's determined campaign for international trade had temporarily made the city's port into one of the world's most successful, New Orleans leaders had exhibited complacency punctuated by periodic scrambles to find a panacea for a city in crisis. The old elite had taken comfort in their belief that the city's location on one of the world's greatest rivers and amid some of the world's richest plantations and oilfields guaranteed its prosperity. In the decade after the onset of the oil bust, however, newer Crescent City municipal and business leaders focused their energies as never before on fashioning a tourism-dominated economy.

Even as a new generation of municipal and business leaders supplanted the power establishment in the years after the 1960s, they held axiomatically to the notion that New Orleans's oil-port-tourism trinity made it "recession-proof." A closer look reveals otherwise. While newspaper articles touted the city's Sunbelt prosperity as late as 1984, New Orleans never matched the fortunes of regional rivals. In the ten years after 1975, the city managed only a 21 percent growth in employment, compared to 36 percent in Miami and a robust 71 percent in Atlanta and Dallas.[9] As a result of labor-saving changes in the shipping industry and local failure to invest in new technology, the port hemorrhaged jobs, putting thousands of longshoremen and stevedores out of work between the mid-1960s and the mid-1980s. For all its promise, industry failed to replace lost port jobs. The NASA lunar project that had injected more than ten thousand manufacturing jobs into the city's economy in the mid-1960s, prompting hopeful chamber of commerce lead-

ers to christen New Orleans "The Heart of the Space Crescent," dwindled by the
1970s. Likewise, Morial's Almonaster-Michoud Industrial District development
fell woefully short of its promised infusion of fifty thousand industrial jobs. During
the oil boom the petrochemical industry and oil and gas exploration injected billions of dollars into the state but added few employment opportunities. Although
Louisiana ranked second in industrial investment in the South after North Carolina in 1984, it created few new jobs. The petrochemical industry accounted for
much of the state's $2.07 billion industrial investment, yet it created only 4,359
jobs. By contrast, North Carolina's $2.67 billion bought 46,821 positions, and even
Mississippi, whose investment stood at a trim $441 million, produced 11,223 new
jobs.[10]

Not only did the oil boom produce few jobs, it masked stultifying problems.
Along with the decline in manufacturing and port employment came a severe
loss of tax base, a disturbing rise in crime and racial polarization, and the further
decay of the city's infrastructure. Only Mayor Landrieu's ability to persuade officials to bail out the city with funds drawn from flush federal urban programs and
the oil-enriched state treasury staved off a crisis in the 1970s. Landrieu's embrace
of tourism-oriented development doubtless cushioned the city by absorbing the
unemployed into low-paying service jobs, paving the way for eventual efforts to
unionize the local hospitality industry. But by the mid-1980s everything unrav-
eled. In the four years after 1984, federal and state grants to New Orleans plunged
from about $49 million to about $6 million, greatly shrinking the city's funds for
maintaining municipal services.[11] As New Orleans slid into the worst depression
since the 1930s, one local university economist remarked that the city "has hitched
its fortune to a falling star."[12]

The economic collapse of the mid-1980s prompted a civic push for new tourist
attractions to create service jobs and to draw outside investment and new sources
of tax revenues. The crisis also pointed to the need for greater commitment to
tourism marketing. Although Mayors Morrison and Landrieu had actively supported efforts to create and expand the Greater New Orleans Tourist and Convention Commission (GNOTCC) in 1960 and 1970, respectively, by the 1980s the
tourist commission again lagged far behind its counterparts in a number of other
cities. As late as 1986, when Barthelemy entered office, New Orleans spent only
$900,000 annually, just $200,000 more than in 1971. Much of this money went
to efforts to attract conventions—not to advertising the city to individuals and
families. When adjusted for inflation, the GNOTCC actually spent less than it had

fifteen years earlier. By contrast, Orlando devoted $25 million to tourism marketing, and Miami some $15 million.[13]

Unable to secure additional funding from a city government struggling to stay solvent, the GNOTCC had to turn to the longtime practice of collaborative forms of marketing that incurred no financial burden. Richard Freeman's Louisiana Coca-Cola Bottling Company featured the Big Easy in free trip offers printed on millions of soda cans. The GNOTCC worked with New York–based Bloomingdale's, London-based Harrod's, and Miami-based Burdine's department stores to present scenes of New Orleans as backdrops for fashion catalogs. The commission also contracted with several popular televised game shows to award New Orleans vacation prizes. In 1986 the commission even persuaded WWL-TV to contribute public service announcements urging city residents to "Invite a Friend to New Orleans."[14]

Even before the ill-fated world's fair had concluded, New Orleans leaders were already searching for answers to why tourism seemed to have stagnated. *Times-Picayune* columnist Allan Katz suggested in August 1984 that the French Quarter alone was no longer sufficient to support the tourism industry. Louisiana World Exposition marketing director George Williams concurred, observing that, by building up a massive tourism infrastructure in anticipation of the fair, developers had catapulted the city fully into tourism's big league. Now the city needed to change the way it marketed itself, shedding an attitude that bore striking similarity to the days when a small cabal of hoteliers filled their rooms with scant inducement. According to Williams, "The days when New Orleans could attract enough visitors to fill the French Quarter and 10,000 hotel rooms just by being New Orleans are over." Vieux Carré hotelier Mike Valentino summed up the growing consensus: "It's a little shameful to admit, but many of us in the tourism industry have thought of a marketing plan as assigning someone to sit by the telephone and take the reservations. Those of us who own or manage hotels . . . never worried about making a living—until now."[15]

The failure of the world's fair and the dilemma over how to fill thousands of new hotel rooms in the midst of a depression jarred tourism leaders out of their complacency. Rather than call into question the wisdom of placing so much faith in the economic trinity of tourism, shipping, and oil (none of which had reversed the city's continued decay), the crisis channeled local energies not into diversification but toward savvier tourism marketing. Gary Esolen, a former college dean, civil rights activist, and journalist who had moved to New Orleans from upstate

New York in 1978, sketched his vision of the future of tourism marketing in an in-fluential 1984 article in the leading local alternative newspaper *Gambit*. Like Mary Morrison, Lester Kabacoff, Allan Jaffe, and so many other transplants to the city, he sensed a neglected potential in New Orleans. Esolen, it turned out, was the only journalist who had publicly questioned the world's fair planning process and predicted failure before the fair even opened. Roundly dismissed until prophecy became reality, Esolen suddenly commanded attention. He argued that New Or-leans must promote itself to discretionary travelers, not just convention planners. Esolen outlined several problems the city faced and suggested ways of overcoming them. He called for detailed studies of how tourists perceived the city before and after their visit, the creation of a task force to implement a more effective market-ing strategy, and greater emphasis on more accurate depictions of New Orleans history and culture to offset the tendency to view the city primarily as a place to drink, carouse, and indulge carnal longings. This and a second Esolen article in 1985 prompted Swiss-born Royal Sonesta Hotel's general manager Hans Wandfluh to telephone the author and ask, "Do you ever do anything or just pontificate?"[16]

In 1986 Esolen and Wandfluh collaborated to form the Greater New Orleans Marketing Committee (GNOMC), a branch of the tourist commission specifically formed to promote the city to discretionary travelers. Wandfluh introduced the concept of pooling hotel rooms as a means of trade-out advertising. Every major hotel agreed to contribute a specified number of rooms for a specified number of nights into a pool. The GNOMC then hired a local company specializing in trade-out advertising to barter rooms for promotional advertisements. The hotels viewed these rooms as loss leaders that would stimulate repeat visits. Trade-out advertising was less than ideal in that it usually appeared in less prominent peri-odicals and smaller television markets. Nonetheless, trade-out well suited a city in financial straits.[17]

The success of the experiment, revealed in the gradual rebound in occupancy rates, helped convince a number of local organizations to contribute some $2 mil-lion to facilitate the kind of targeted study of tourist expectations that Esolen had championed. The Downtown Development District (a self-taxing agency created in 1974 to facilitate downtown improvements), the French Market Corporation, the Audubon Institute (a nonprofit that administered the Audubon Zoo and a growing catalog of nature-oriented attractions), the New Orleans Aviation Board, the City of New Orleans, and the local hotel and restaurant associations were among the leading contributors. With this seed money in hand, the GNOMC un-

dertook a campaign to demonstrate to the city the importance of tourism marketing. Initially targeting Dallas and Birmingham, the agency surveyed tourists
to determine their expectations prior to visiting the city and their impressions
following the trip. The tremendous response enabled the GNOMC to persuade
the city council to endorse a property-tax increase and a surcharge on the city's
hotel-room tax, with both revenues earmarked for tourism promotion.[18]

Introduced in March 1990 as Proposition One, the measure was defeated by
New Orleans voters. The GNOMC's bid nonetheless helped raise local awareness
of the importance of tourism now that the city's other economic pillars had crumbled. The estimated economic impact of tourism on New Orleans had soared more
than 1,000 percent from $223 million to $2.7 billion in the two decades after 1970.
Still, tourism leaders argued, given that Dallas, Atlanta, San Antonio, and Orlando
each spent between $7 and $10 million on tourism marketing, New Orleans could
not continue to compete successfully for the tourist dollar with its comparatively
meager $2.8 million allocation. Impressed with the necessity of shepherding tour-
ism, Mayor Barthelemy persuaded the city council to vote six to one in favor of
reorganizing the GNOMC as the New Orleans Tourism Marketing Corporation
(NOTMC), which would be politically tied to the municipal government through
appointments by the mayor and council.[19]

Indicative of the rising power of tourism interests and their close relationship
with city hall, less than seven months after voters rejected Proposition One, municipal and tourism interests agreed to a deal that promised to give NOTMC a $6.2
million marketing budget. Hotel operators approved an increase in the hotel tax
to produce an estimated $4.2 million in its initial year, while public and private
contributions were to fulfill the remainder of the budget. In the decade after its
inception in 1986 as the GNOMC, the marketing corporation increased its budget
from $1.6 million to $8.7 million, or 444 percent. Not only did the Barthelemy
administration and its successor (headed by Dutch Morial's son Marc) increase
its appropriation in the years following the oil bust, so did the state government,
which became more astute in promoting statewide tourism. Accordingly, the proportion of tourism funding derived from the public sector soared from 38 percent
in 1986 to 73 percent in 1996, reflecting the growing sense of alarm accompanying the city's economic crisis.[20] The increased municipal appropriation finally returned financially imperiled New Orleans to enjoying levels of public sponsorship
of tourism not seen since the Landrieu administration, when the city could rely on
flush, oil-generated state subsidies. Like many other American cities in the 1980s,

then, New Orleans staked its future in no small measure on catering to outsiders' desires as a way of fulfilling local citizens' needs.

In addition to stepping up the marketing of New Orleans to discretionary travelers, tourism interests continued to build infrastructure, including hotels, nightclubs, convention facilities, public transit lines, and downtown improvements, as well as new attractions calculated to appeal to families rather than the traditional mix of single men and couples. In the Barthelemy years, those business leaders who had begun to make tourism a priority in the 1960s and 1970s now coalesced into a more active, coordinated force for economic revival. In earlier years major business and civic projects often revolved around the leadership of Carnival captains such as Darwin Fenner and Richard Freeman. While Carnival, which was practically synonymous with the city's tourist image, had bound together the city's power establishment, an emerging tourism establishment showcased the talents of those who stood outside the Carnival social circle. In contrast to the largely native-born scions, these new leaders hailed from working-class, ethnic, or other nonelite New Orleans backgrounds, other American cities, and even other countries. By the time of the oil bust, the *Times-Picayune* was more likely to report on the actions of men like Esolen, Kabacoff, French Quarter restaurateurs Pip and Ralph Brennan, Audubon Zoo executive Ronald J. (Ron) Forman, and float builder Blaine Kern.

Many old-line whites still urged trade expansion and downtown construction as a means of modernization and snubbed sentimental efforts to save the French Quarter, while the new leaders usually recognized the importance of the New Orleans image. These newer leaders were divided between preservationists who sought to freeze any changes to the Quarter and those who supported developments they believed might enhance the district's tourist appeal. In the midst of economic crisis, development-minded leaders found common cause with a black mayor whose beleaguered city needed a determined plan of action. In the late 1960s Moon Landrieu saw a city with a dearth of leadership in a time of social ferment and economic malaise, but in the 1980s Sidney Barthelemy found a wealth of leaders ready to use tourism to solve the city's latest crisis.

In his effort to deliver New Orleans's majority-black population from financial straits, Mayor Barthelemy built his agenda around tourism. Barthelemy's tenure marked the maturation of the emerging alliance between black politicians and white tourism backers. In fact, unlike Moon Landrieu and Dutch Morial, Barthelemy won election in 1986 with massive white support and only scant black support. Hoping to offset the decline of oil and the port, he planned to double the economic impact of tourism, double the size of the new convention center, upgrade the city's airport, build a $40 million riverfront aquarium, and even attract a theme park to the riverfront.[21]

Of all Barthelemy's endeavors, the riverfront aquarium perhaps best illustrates the growing confluence of public and private interests in developing tourist attractions in New Orleans. The city had controlled many of the tourism-oriented development projects near the French Quarter riverfront in the 1970s, but the public-private partnership to build the Aquarium of the Americas in the oil-bust years reflected the growing power of private interests. The old elite previously had dominated municipal government by controlling the boards of numerous agencies and commissions not answerable to the mayor. Despite Dutch Morial's effort in the 1980s to gain control over these boards, considerable political clout and financial power remained out of reach for an increasingly cash-starved municipal government. Probably Morial's most bitter defeat came in 1983 when the Audubon Park Commission, which operated Audubon Park and the Audubon Zoo, eluded his attempts to divert its revenues into the city's general fund by reorganizing the zoo under the auspices of the Audubon Institute (later renamed Audubon Nature Institute) with private funding derived from the Friends of the Audubon Zoo. Ron Forman, the son of an uptown sheet-metal worker and a bookkeeper, had worked as an analyst for the Moon Landrieu administration in the early 1970s. Assigned to evaluate the beleaguered Audubon Zoo, Forman soon spearheaded a massive revitalization of the venue and later emerged as the leader of the Audubon Institute. Like the French Market Corporation, whose staff of forty-four managed the city-run public-market-turned-festival-marketplace and tripled its budget in the 1980s thanks to tourist spending, the Audubon Institute generated impressive revenues that never found their way to city hall. In the decade after 1980 the Audubon Institute doubled its staff and quadrupled its annual budget as it planned and built a new aquarium on the fringe of the Vieux Carré.[22]

Early in the planning process, after observing Baltimore's National Aquarium, city councilman James Singleton suggested that Forman consider building a new facility outside the Audubon Zoo rather than renovating the zoo's aging Odenheimer Aquarium.[23] Like Landrieu's Jackson Square Mall, Barthelemy's support of Forman's riverfront aquarium proved a lightning rod for preservationist outcry and illustrated the extent to which the French Quarter had become the center of a struggle between tradition and modernization. Mary Louise Christovich, president of the Louisiana Council for the Vieux Carré, complained to the mayor that the city had conveniently neglected to inform voters of its intention to build the venue atop the Bienville Street Wharf because doing so risked defeat. "We taxed ourselves to build an aquarium as an educational facility for our children," Christovich noted, not "to subsidize a tourist industry, that may well be choking the historical center that created it."[24]

Under the leadership of Mary Morrison, the Vieux Carré Property Owners, Residents and Associates (VCPORA, formerly VCPOA) filed a lawsuit in January 1987 to block construction of the aquarium because the city council had not approved the necessary bond issue before voters agreed to a special tax.[25] As the lawsuit crawled through the courts, the aquarium project pushed forward. In the summer of 1987 the city reached an agreement with the Dock Board which paved the way for the aquarium to be built atop the Bienville Street Wharf. Meanwhile, several corporations provided funding for the project, including the Amoco, Chevron, and Shell oil companies, New Orleans–based mineral mining giant Freeport-McMoRan, and tourism interests such as Jax Brewery, New Orleans Steamboat Company, and the James Rouse Company. Less than two years later, with funding substantially in place, a federal judge ruled against the VCPORA's injunction to stop the aquarium, removing all obstacles to its completion.[26]

Although preservationists proved powerless to stop it, the aquarium project rekindled an always smoldering public debate over how many tourist venues could be introduced in such a limited area without exerting undue pressure on the historic French Quarter. For much of the twentieth century, and especially since the 1940s, local leaders had increasingly funneled tourism development into the Vieux Carré and its immediate surroundings, clinging to the long-held notion that the district was a relict village surrounded by a modernizing metropolis. While the centralization of tourist services in these decades bolstered the city's popularity with convention planners as a "walking city" (at least from a tourist's perspective), it also placed enormous pressure on the French Quarter as a living neighborhood. In 1988, 1989, and 1990, with the aquarium project underway, the National Trust for Historic Preservation named the Vieux Carré as one of the eleven most endangered historic places in the United States, along with Virginia's Manassas National Battlefield Park, which at the same time faced plans to build a theme park called Disney's America.[27]

While the aquarium, which opened in September 1990, served as a catalyst for riverfront development, building on the earlier momentum generated by the 1984

Louisiana World Exposition, a number of other riverfront projects helped stitch together the city's tourist and convention districts. Tourism interests, headed by Pres Kabacoff and William Borah, formed the Riverfront Transit Coalition in 1984 to leverage federal urban transit funds to add a new streetcar line connecting riverfront areas on both sides of Canal Street. New Orleans, like other cities, had removed all of its streetcar lines by the 1960s, with the exception of the St. Charles Avenue line, whose olive and drab cars were nationally recognized tourist attractions. Like other cities seeking to stimulate excitement about visiting downtown areas in the wake of urban decay, New Orleans seized upon light-rail transit as a way of tying together points of interest. The riverfront streetcar line, with its "ladies in red" (red-painted streetcars), opened in time for the 1988 Republican National Convention and provided an important contribution to tourists' sense of the riverfront as a single attraction. Now tourists and conventioneers could move freely between the aquarium and other attractions such as the French Market, Jax Brewery, Riverwalk, and the convention center.[28]

The aquarium worried preservationists chiefly because it seemed to represent only the first in a series of tourism-oriented development plans by the Audubon Institute. Since the late 1940s, when Martha Gilmore Robinson had led the effort to create an open park along the riverfront at Jackson Square, preservationists had tried repeatedly to get the city to fashion a greenbelt along the entire French Quarter riverfront. Indeed, two months before the aquarium opened to the public, Ron Forman and Mayor Barthelemy jointly announced "Riverfront 2000," a comprehensive plan for developing the riverfront, unfortunately conceived behind closed doors. Just as planners chose the aquarium site before voters got a chance to approve, the city's riverfront master plan also eluded public scrutiny. The plan, which incorporated a third phase of the city's convention center, expansions of the aquarium and surrounding Woldenberg Park, a natural history museum, and an arboretum, would, according to a leading local economist, create at least 17,000 jobs and "lend New Orleans a progressive and even intellectual image." Echoing this assertion, the mayor went so far as to claim that the development might "truly rival the Smithsonian." New Orleanians who had followed earlier pronouncements about economic panaceas likely remembered the fifty thousand jobs promised but never delivered in the Almonaster-Michoud Industrial District and the Superdome's perennial financial trouble.[29]

Using the same rhetoric that had marked the local preservation movement since the 1960s, preservationists fumed that Forman's and Barthelemy's plans would turn the French Quarter into "a giant amusement park." Unlike Baltimore, whose Inner Harbor influenced New Orleanians interested in riverfront redevelopment, New Orleans had no master plan or coordinating agency for waterfront projects, only behind-the-scenes maneuvering by public and private interests. Forman, whose brilliant leadership turned around a once-decrepit Audubon Zoo and even managed to get taxpayers to allocate $5 million a year to support an aquarium in a city with collapsing tax funds for fire, police, and schools, had little patience for detractors: "We don't have time for people who say no. We just ask them to get out of the way." Indeed, Forman and other leading tourism interests constituted the city's new class of power brokers as old-line names faded from public view. Ultimately the plan foundered not because of preservationist opposition but because Riverfront 2000 had not involved the Dock Board, leading the port authority's directors to put the brakes on Forman's plan by citing the need to keep river wharves serviceable indefinitely.[30] Notwithstanding the demise of Riverfront 2000, the tourist transformation of the riverfront illustrates city hall's growing commitment to creating a highly concentrated zone of urban entertainment catering to the lucrative convention and tourist trade. The combined effect of heightened tourism development and savvy marketing accelerated the pace of change toward a tourism-dominated New Orleans, forever altering the city's architectural fabric, its jazz traditions, and its Carnival festivities.

As New Orleans's public and private partnership continued to advance tourism in the oil-bust years, the city experienced a tourism boom that began to dominate the city's course. Long in transition toward tourism, only in the 1980s did New Orleans finally regard the hospitality industry as its one economic bright spot. In the years that followed, the French Quarter reflected decades of public policies that favored commercial over residential interests. Preservationists, of course, had always found it necessary to make economic rather than simply aesthetic arguments for safeguarding the Vieux Carré. Although Mayor Dutch Morial had hoped to steer the New Orleans economy away from its dependence on tourism by cultivating industrialization and social welfare programs for the city's disadvantaged, he, like previous mayors, could not ignore the French Quarter, which remained in essence the city's number-one "factory."

In the wake of the world's fair, Morial appointed a committee on "The Future of the Quarter." Its chair, University of New Orleans professor Jerah Johnson, warned the VCC that in spite of the important improvements made in conjunction with preparations for the exposition, the French Quarter was in danger of losing

its appeal if the city did not "carefully guard against a drift towards homogeniza-
tion and prettification. The French Quarter's 'quaintness' comes, and should come,
not from artificial adornment—trees and shrubs lining every street, red brick and
fake stone sidewalks, and San Francisco–Key West paint jobs on its buildings—but
from its simple, solid nature as an urban neighborhood in a large, old port city in
the South."[31] Johnson's report, which also urged tighter control over souvenir and
trinket shops, demonstrated the distance the municipal government had traversed
in its involvement in French Quarter tourism and preservation in the postwar era,
for in previous years such a statement would have originated in the preservationist
community, not in city hall.

As it had so many times in the past two decades, once again the city government took up the issue of municipal engineering of the tourist experience in the
French Quarter. As tourism rapidly changed the face of the French Quarter in the
1980s, perhaps the most damning development, in the eyes of preservationists,
was the proliferation of shops selling souvenirs, T-shirts, and sexually oriented
items, as well as massage parlors, peep shows, and other adult services. According
to a Loyola University study, the most commercialized part of the French Quarter
(bounded by St. Ann, Iberville, Decatur, and Dauphine Streets) lost 17 percent of
its residents while increasing the number of gift and T-shirt shops by 229 percent
between 1961 and 1981. Uncertain how to stop the spread of such establishments,
the city council voted in August 1981 to place a moratorium on additional tourist
businesses until the city's planning commission could devise a workable zoning
restriction. Unfortunately, the legality of such restrictions proved dubious, and
the moratorium went unheeded during the impasse. Tellingly, the captain of the
NOPD's First District had asserted that one could hardly expect anything else in
a neighborhood that "has always been where pirates and seamen and all came,"
adding, "What do they think Jean Lafitte was? A Rotarian?"[32]

The public debate over the future of the French Quarter intensified as tourism
moved toward the center of the New Orleans economy in the second half of the
decade. In 1987 a tourist from Missouri expressed her revulsion upon seeing the
"downright filthy" Bourbon Street and questioned why a city of New Orleans's
stature could not attract a street full of "good music, good entertainment and good
food."[33] She was not alone. Preservationist and tourist outcry prompted Councilman Mike Early to propose a pair of *tout ensemble* ordinances designed to define
further the vague sense of purpose that had guided French Quarter preservation
since the inception of the VCC five decades earlier. Detractors had complained for
years that the commission, restricted by its charter to regulating only the exterior

of buildings and weakened by mayoral appointments of commissioners who often sided with developers, was powerless to protect the district from the proliferation of tacky souvenir shops.

Hoping to do what the VCC could not, Early introduced two ordinances, Nos. 14317 and 14321, to amend the city code to establish a system of licenses for all existing and future French Quarter businesses and to amend the Comprehensive Zoning Ordinance to prohibit or require city council approval for a variety of business establishments. Ordinance No. 14321 prohibited all tattoo parlors, massage parlors, adult establishments, and souvenir, novelty, and T-shirt shops opened after the enactment of the poorly enforced 1981 moratorium on such businesses. City council approval would be required annually for any business in the French Quarter to remain open. The law also specified that even pre-1981 tourist shops must have "high quality or unique merchandise," "enhance or embellish the French Quarter," be "compatible with the Tout Ensemble," and refrain from selling mass-produced, low-quality goods.[34]

On the night of October 5, 1987, most of Bourbon Street lay shrouded in darkness. More than fifty tourist businesses on the famed strip, as well as nearby streets, led by T-shirt shop owner and leader of Vieux Carré Merchants for Free Enterprise Frank Fortunato, staged a blackout in protest of Early's plan.[35] Much as their 1960s counterparts had viewed District Attorney Jim Garrison's vice raids as a travesty, business owners now argued that the French Quarter laws constituted an onerous government intrusion that punished hundreds of legitimate businesses, excused several years of municipal failure to enforce existing ordinances, and left too much room for public corruption. One businessman, in an open letter to city officials, wrote, "The French Quarter is our only hope left after the Oil Crisis . . . so now you want to legislate arbitrarily about what the tourists can buy? Tell me, what do you propose merchants offer the tourists with the high rent in the Quarter?" He also questioned whether T-shirt sellers were not preferable to the "door after door of Strip Tease joints" which characterized the French Quarter of the 1950s.[36] Insinuations of municipal corruption were rife. Harry Greenberger, who owned an antique store in the historic district, argued that the real problems confounding tourists were not undesirable stores but rather litter, filth, and crime, and suggested that the city's existing ordinances should be more faithfully enforced before resorting to draconian measures.[37] Another New Orleanian contended that "with the city's reputation for handicapping business with its long application processes and 'under the table' approvals, I feel this ordinance is a very improper move."[38]

Failing to garner city council approval, Early's ordinances finally passed in watered-down form in 1989, but they applied only to eight blocks of Bourbon Street. The tourist transformation continued in the years of indecision about stemming the tide of souvenir and gift shops. On the eve of World War II the French Quarter's thirty-nine gift shops had been largely confined to Royal Street and the immediate perimeter of Jackson Square. By 1986 some 177 gift shops lined several blocks of Bourbon, Royal, Chartres, Decatur, Toulouse, St. Peter, and St. Ann Streets. Between 1980 and 1988, the Quarter experienced a corresponding outflow of population as rising rents and commercialization prompted many residents to move elsewhere. Having lost about 15 percent of its residents in the twenty years before 1980, in the next eight years the Vieux Carré lost another one-third of its 1980 population of 3,804.[39]

By the mid-1990s the French Quarter faced a level of commercial encroachment not seen since the height of the 1960s hotel building boom. While a number of other tourism-oriented cities—notably Annapolis, Charleston, and San Antonio—had adopted tourism management plans, New Orleans continued to grapple with such issues on an ad hoc basis. With their city utterly dependent on tourism, many city leaders felt disinclined to place any controls on the industry's expansion. Although preservationists and developers had for more than two decades agreed that the French Quarter's appearance was important, the tourism boom placed them increasingly at odds over how much change was too much for the neighborhood to handle and still retain its charm. Street vendors, jazz musicians, pantomime artists, caricature painters, and fortune tellers clashed with residents, who resented the noise and crowds they drew. Haunted tours clogged streets and blocked sidewalks late at night as black-caped storytellers recounted and invented lurid tales of ghosts, voodoo queens, and paranormal phenomena in between stops at Quarter taverns. Illegal guest houses and time-share condominiums quietly edged out renters and resident property owners. Tourist-oriented businesses continued to fill more and more buildings. By 2000, fearful of the Quarter's capacity to keep absorbing commercial expansion, Gary Esolen warned that opening too many such establishments begged the question whether tourism "preserves or devours the things it celebrates."[40]

French Quarter preservationists also endured the intrusion of tourism-oriented development projects on the edges of their beloved historic preserve. These encroachments followed the example of Landrieu's riverfront and Jackson Square alterations in the 1970s and the construction of Canal Place, the Jax Brewery, and the Aquarium of the Americas in the 1980s. In the decade following the world's fair, a glut of hotel rooms and a stagnant economy stymied new downtown hotel construction. As the tourism boom lifted New Orleans out of the oil bust by the mid-1990s, however, developers began clamoring to meet growing demand following the 1991 expansion of the convention center. The new hotel boom highlighted the dramatic transformation of downtown New Orleans from a place where locals went to work and shop into one where tourists and conventioneers hung their hats after late nights on the town. If, as historian Robert M. Fogelson argues, suburbanization changed the American downtown from "the business district" to "the central business district" to "just another business district," the Vieux Carré progressed in two decades from "the tourist district" to "the central tourist district," one of several nodes of tourist activity. Canal Street had historically separated New Orleans past from New Orleans future, but the tourist transformation dissolved that distinction as the hospitality industry made both the engine of a new urban economy. The transformation also reflected decades of shifting local priorities away from the needs of residents and toward those of outsiders. New Orleans was becoming a city that existed to entertain and pamper visitors even as it became increasingly unlivable for large numbers of its own impoverished populace. From preservationists' perspective, however, the hotel boom was not so much a symbol of the city's failure to play the modernization game by the rules of other cities as a threat to the historic ambience that the shift toward tourism had helped preserve.[41]

Preservationists raised their vigilance as developers announced a spate of new hotel projects, many of them just outside the purview of the VCC on Canal Street. In 1996 a developer revealed plans to tear down the Sanlin and Friedberg buildings, a block of eleven mid-nineteenth-century commercial buildings, to erect a twenty-eight-story Marriott hotel across Canal Street from the original Marriott that the Landrieu administration had courted. Although later alterations such as a 1950s metal screen had obscured the architectural details, the complex retained a hidden Greek Revival design. Just as Martha Robinson, Mary Morrison, and other preservationists had warned of the negative consequences of architectural demolition for the city's tourism industry in the 1960s, freeway revolt veteran and French Quarter preservationist William Borah inveighed against the proposed demolitions in a letter to the Times-Picayune, noting that it would "chip away at the physical fabric of our city," which "draws increasing numbers of tourists."[42] Preservationists' opposition forced the developer to agree to save part of the nine-

teenth-century façade. Initially supportive of the revised plan despite preservationist outcry, Councilman Oliver Thomas changed his mind when he learned
that free people of color had owned the block in the 1840s. Unlike in the Bourbon
Orleans Hotel controversy three decades earlier, by the 1990s African Americans
held positions in city hall and were beginning to see black heritage preservation
as a goal to place alongside economic development, even if the African Americans
involved were Afro-Creoles who had occupied an often privileged middle tier in
the city's Caribbeanlike nineteenth-century racial hierarchy. With city councilmen
traditionally voting on the side of the councilmember whose district was affected,
Thomas's reversal killed the hotel plan, illustrating the complexity of the struggle
between preservation and profit in a tourist New Orleans.[43]

In 2000 another controversy erupted when local hotel developers Mickey
Palmer and Patrick Quinn announced plans for a four-hundred-room hotel to replace the closed Woolworth's store at the corner of Canal and Bourbon Streets.
The Woolworth's had been the site of one of the city's civil rights sit-ins almost
four decades earlier. The developers argued that the hotel, with its lacy façade of
iron galleries and large windows, would replace the dark, lifeless, and unsafe 100
block of Bourbon with a tourist-friendly gateway to the French Quarter. It would
also lure tourists away from where they increasingly concentrated along the riverfront and revitalize the upper downtown blocks of Canal Street. Preservationists,
however, chafed at the dimensions of the hotel, whose proposed 175-foot height
far exceeded the 85-foot limit imposed by local zoning law. The extent of local
concern for the integrity of the French Quarter revealed itself when preservationists won support from unlikely groups. Several hotel developers spoke out against
the proposed Canal Street hotel, arguing that making such a substantial exception
to zoning law was unfair to those developers who had worked within the bounds
and an unsettling precedent that could ultimately destroy the charm that made
people want to visit New Orleans. Even the AFL-CIO's Hospitality, Hotels and
Restaurants Organizing Council, a union that had been struggling unsuccessfully
for several years to win fairer working conditions for local tourism workers, sided
with preservationists in an attempt to exert pressure on the hotel industry.[44] In
the end, however, city officials' and developers' desires to do anything necessary
to expand the city's capacity for tourism proved too powerful for preservationists,
and the Astor Crowne Plaza, with its replica iron galleries, rose high above the
corner of Canal and Bourbon.

The Astor was just one of many new hotels that contributed to the transformation of the central business district into part of a "central tourist district." As oil-related business relocated to Houston and other cities in the 1990s, large blocks of office space fell empty. With tourism soaring, hotel developers set their sights on these buildings. By the early 2000s, Canal Street, once the hub of downtown shopping, was fast becoming a hotel row. In addition to the demolition of Woolworth's to build the Astor, two of the city's leading downtown department stores became hotels. Maison Blanche's twelve-story Beaux Arts–style building, constructed in the early 1900s, saw new life as a Ritz-Carlton, while D. H. Holmes, a department store whose famed clock remained etched in local lore, became the Chateau Sonesta Hotel. Many of the skyscrapers on Poydras Street, once home to corporate headquarters and regional offices of major oil- and port-related firms, now sported curtained windows as downtown New Orleans became a bedroom community of the French Quarter. The Lykes Steamship Company's office tower reopened as Loew's Hotel. BellSouth's building became the Drury Inn and Suites, while the Whitney National Bank's Morgan Branch gave way to the Wyndham Whitney Hotel. Even the New Orleans Cotton Exchange and International House, long symbols of the city's agricultural and commercial wealth, reopened as posh hotels. International House, once a clearinghouse for foreign trade services that used the city's hospitality as a hook for economic development, now simply provided expensive rooms for tourists and conventioneers. Tourism was no longer a means to a larger developmental goal but rather an end in itself.[45]

If the "central tourist district" accounted for the greatest level of investment, however, the tourist transformation extended well beyond it, indicative of a broader trend resulting from the maturation of the modern tourism industry. Around the region, the nation, and the world, historic city centers have become, literally, points of departure for tourists seeking distinctive personal discoveries in the interstices of an industry that renders an ever-growing catalog of attractions well known. Venice's Piazza San Marco, once the one must-see attraction in that city, has in recent years lost its firm hold on tourists who seek original experiences throughout the archipelago of islands that dot the lagoon surrounding the watery city. In New York, savvy tourists increasingly venture beyond Manhattan attractions such as Times Square, Broadway, SoHo, Fifth Avenue, South Street Seaport, and Central Park, trekking to emerging ethnic neighborhoods and locally popular entertainment districts in Brooklyn and the Bronx. In Charleston, South Carolina, the Old and Historic Charleston District became the center of an increasingly recognizable tourist region known as the Low Country, with tourists filtering outward to other renovated neighborhoods and outlying plantations, gardens, and beach resorts. Likewise, the New Orleans French Quarter lost some of its hold on those tourists who, more and more, spent several days in the city and wanted to see more than just the most famous attraction.

While nineteenth-century tourists had circulated widely throughout New Orleans, by the second half of the twentieth century tourism promoters had succeeded in concentrating tourism chiefly in the central city. With the exception of the Garden District, whose antebellum homes generated the opening of restaurants, hotels, and bed-and-breakfast inns, few other parts of New Orleans benefited directly from tourism. To be sure, the famed "cities of the dead" (the above-ground cemeteries clustered on the opposite end of Canal Street from the Quarter) and, during Carnival, the city's uptown parade routes occasionally enticed tourists out of the Vieux Carré. In addition, a few establishments such as the Camellia Grill, a diner housed in a white-columned mansion, flourished because of their location along the St. Charles Avenue streetcar line, which also served the Garden District. Nonetheless, a tourist was more likely to hop aboard a bus to go participate in a swamp or plantation tour outside the city than to spend time seeing New Orleans beyond the Quarter. While the French Quarter remained the engine of the city's tourism industry, by the post-oil-boom years the power generated by that engine enabled a spread of New Orleans's geography of tourism.

The 1984 world's fair, for all its troubles, catalyzed the development of a locally oriented scene of condominiums and loft apartments and an array of tourist attractions, eventually including a much-expanded Ernest N. Morial Convention Center, hotels, art galleries, restaurants, and museums, notably the National D-Day Museum, the Louisiana Children's Museum, and the Ogden Museum of Southern Art. The fair's short-lived aerial tramway across the Mississippi River also stimulated the development of Blaine Kern's Mardi Gras World museum and the restoration of historic Algiers Point, both still accessible by ferry.

The French Quarter continued to draw tourism development, spurring the erection of the garish Harrah's New Orleans Casino on the site of the former Rivergate convention hall at the foot of Canal Street and the emergence of entertainment and dining establishments just beyond its boundaries. Yet tourists traversed new paths across the city. The opening of the riverfront aquarium prompted the introduction of the *John James Audubon,* a small cruise vessel that ferried riders past the massive Mississippi River port terminals to the Audubon Institute's revitalized Audubon Zoo, creating, along with the St. Charles streetcar, a transportation loop for tourists. Similarly, the opening of the new Canal Street and North

Carrollton Avenue streetcars in 2003 provided a more tourist-friendly link to the cemeteries, City Park, and, for two weeks each year, Jazz Fest. A third tourist path followed Magazine Street to Audubon Park in response to the opening of scores of antique shops, art galleries, and restaurants on the once-decaying street in the past two decades.

Despite the exodus of population to suburbia, the fringes of New Orleans never sapped the city's hold on tourism. The many small tourist courts and motels that appeared in the mid-twentieth century had all but disappeared by the 1980s. A couple of Jefferson Parish communities tried unsuccessfully to woo tourists in the 1970s and 1980s. Metairie's Fat City and Kenner's Rivertown each attempted to appropriate the ambience of the French Quarter, but their distance from the tourist center sent both into steep decline. It remains to be seen whether the Six Flags New Orleans theme park, opened in 1999 as Jazzland on the swampy eastern edge of the city, will prove a lasting draw.[46]

The tourist transformation also contributed positively to the citywide spread of historic preservation in the three decades following the defeat of the riverfront expressway and particularly since the 1990s. The Friends of the Cabildo, a group formed to support the conservation of the historic Jackson Square building in which American and French statesmen signed the Louisiana Purchase in 1803, inaugurated the first sustained spread of preservation beyond the confines of the French Quarter and the Garden District. In the early 1970s it commissioned an architectural survey and held guided tours of the Coliseum Square neighborhood, which lay between the Garden District and downtown. Renaming the neighborhood the Lower Garden District in 1972, the organization built interest among locals and tourists in revitalizing the area's substantial nineteenth-century dwellings. The Junior League of New Orleans followed suit in 1974 by chartering the Preservation Resource Center, which offered advice and financial incentives to renovators and gradually extended its focus throughout the older districts of New Orleans. As more and more locals began to understand that the city's vast catalogue of architecturally significant structures lay close to the heart of New Orleans's lucrative tourist image, they pushed for the creation of local historic landmark districts like the one established on Canal Street. By the early 2000s, more than a dozen such districts covered most of the city's older neighborhoods and guarded against demolition of houses that, taken together, contributed immeasurably to the city's unique tourist image and enticed small entrepreneurs to open restaurants, jazz clubs, and bed-and-breakfast inns.[47]

In addition to its role in stimulating local interest in historic preservation throughout the city, the tourist boom also began to open locals' eyes to the need to preserve and promote the city's African American heritage. In this endeavor, New Orleans simply mirrored developments elsewhere in the United States, notably in Boston and Charleston, where African American culture has found its way into growing efforts to broaden the role of what historian and architect Dolores Hayden calls "place memory" in urban preservation and, by extension, cultural tourism.[48] The emergence of black tourism as a niche market in the city's tourist economy coincided with a national trend in the closing decades of the twentieth century. In the 1960s integration had diminished the need for a separate leisure and entertainment infrastructure for African Americans, pulling black tourists more fully into preexisting strategies of mass tourism marketing. In the 1970s and into the 1980s, New Orleans, like many other American cities, presented itself primarily to a single middle-class population of travelers, using historic architecture, jazz, Carnival, and sensory pleasures as enticements. By the second half of the 1980s, however, tourism promoters began to look at the growing black middle class as an ideal growth sector and worked to tailor a distinctive black tourist experience through the formation of the Greater New Orleans Black Tourism Network (GNOBTN) as an arm of the GNOTCC in 1990. The GNOBTN courted black conventions, family reunions, and cultural events to New Orleans and, notably, worked with Jazz Fest producer George Wein and other tourism interests to bring in the annual Essence Music Festival, sponsored by *Essence* magazine, beginning in 1995. But diverging from the path of mass tourism also necessitated highlighting black contributions to the primary aspects of the city's tourist image, none more so than jazz.[49]

Tourist interest in jazz, combined with the efforts of older musicians to revive the music and the willingness of younger generations of blacks to embrace it, played a critical role in making the art form something that one could readily find throughout the "Birthplace of Jazz." Tourist demand reawakened locals to the musical legacy, provided work for musicians, and supported events such as the New Orleans Jazz and Heritage Festival, whose proceeds made possible public performances and radio broadcasts as well as grants to nurture budding musical talent in the Crescent City. If the resurgence of interest in jazz had its downside, notably the blatant disregard of those tourists and enthusiasts who rudely barged into community churches and cemeteries to photograph and film jazz funerals or who sought to profit from the image of the city's Mardi Gras Indian tribes, it also produced a growing determination in the white and black communities that sites important to the development of jazz be preserved.

By the 1990s, as the *Washington Post* reported, more than 37,000 housing units in New Orleans lay empty. Many more that were occupied languished in various states of decay under the sweltering heat and humidity that mark the city's semitropical climate. To the burgeoning architectural salvage business, which daily stripped these structures of adornments and building materials to resell to eager homeowners around the South and beyond, they represented a gold mine more than living history. Yet hundreds of these houses and buildings held tremendous significance as the places where internationally known jazzmen were born, grew up, or played music. The preservation community, long dominated by whites who looked more to the city's French Creole and Old South traditions, seldom showed any interest in saving structures in African American parts of the city. Further, their successes had always owed in large part to their ability to persuade city officials, developers, and other civic leaders that preservation made sense from an economic standpoint as well as an aesthetic and historical one. It was easier to make such an argument for the French Quarter, of course, than for the impoverished, decaying, and often crime-ridden parts of the city that lay in back of the Quarter, downtown, and the Garden District, away from the river.[50]

For decades city leaders had given their blessing to projects that destroyed neighborhoods whites viewed as blighted even as they had more or less oiled the preservation machine in the French Quarter. The opening in the 1930s of the Municipal Auditorium and Beauregard Square, named for a Confederate general, had expropriated for white enjoyment Congo Square, the symbolic heart of the black community which had served as an antebellum recreational meeting place. The construction of the Iberville and Lafitte housing projects in the early 1940s wiped out large swaths of the famed Storyville red-light district that had nurtured jazz music, much to the dismay of jazz seeker Sterling Brown, who found no trace of the Basin Street he had imagined prior to his visit. By the late 1950s, city leaders okayed the razing of several blocks of the city's Black Storyville and Chinatown areas near South Rampart Street and Loyola Avenue to construct a new civic center, city hall, post office, and public library. The 1960s saw the redevelopment of a large part of the Tremé neighborhood into a cultural center and the destruction of North Claiborne Avenue to make way for the elevated Interstate Highway 10. The 1970s brought the renaming of Beauregard Square as Louis Armstrong Park, ostensibly a nod to black heritage, yet in the ensuing years city leaders attempted to lure a theme park to draw mostly white tourists into what would have become a privatized venue.

By the 1990s, a growing biracial effort began to save sites of black culture and memory in New Orleans. Much of the impetus for the change came from the African American community itself, particularly in Tremé, the city's best-known incubator of the living jazz tradition, where schemes to whiten a black neighborhood on the edge of the French Quarter had produced growing indignation among blacks. In 1989, Chicago jazz percussionist Luther Gray won a grant from the New Orleans Jazz and Heritage Foundation to teach percussion classes in Armstrong Park, which he found in such poor shape that he chose to take action. Gray and others formed the Congo Square Foundation and began working to get Congo Square listed on the National Register of Historic Places. Following the opposite path of jazzmen earlier in the century, Gray moved from Chicago to New Orleans in 1992. Only in 1997 did the city of New Orleans finally officially recognize the old slave grounds' historical significance by renaming it Congo Square, but the change reflected a variety of grassroots efforts to infuse new life into the long-neglected neighborhood in the shadow of the more famous Vieux Carré.[51]

Of perhaps greater importance to restoring Tremé were efforts to reassert black control over black culture. Long exploited by white profiteers and studied by white enthusiasts, New Orleans's black culture now became a focus for neighborhood revitalization. Among these initiatives was the formation in 1994 of the Black Men of Labor (BMOL), an organization to preserve and reacquaint locals with fragile traditions. Following the jazz funeral for local jazz legend Danny Barker, a group of men with ties to local Mardi Gras Indian tribes and social aid and pleasure clubs created the BMOL to renew community interest in earlier jazz traditions. In particular, the group hoped to revive a tradition in which the city's black longshoremen, long since forced into retirement or service-sector work by the shrinkage of the port's labor needs, staged an annual second-line parade on Labor Day. They envisioned this event as a beacon of hope in a community ravaged by crime, poverty, social pathologies, unemployment, and negative stereotypes. They also wanted to preserve traditional brass band music in the place where it had started as a response to years of white exhibiting of the art form in Preservation Hall and other French Quarter nightspots. Unlike the leading Carnival parades, which wended their way through the leafy, lily-white uptown neighborhoods into the heart of the city, the Black Men of Labor's parade meandered through Tremé, making stops at black clubs like Lorraine's Dugout and Little People's Place.[52]

Similarly, Sylvester Francis, an African American New Orleans native, began filming traditional jazz funerals in 1979, before the fruits of the tourism-oriented jazz revival began fully to tap black interest at the grassroots. With economic hardship, youth disinterest, and changing attitudes about funerary rites taking a toll, mock funerals for tourists and conventioneers increasingly outnumbered the dwindling number of real ones. Although Francis found it difficult to overcome general black apathy toward traditions now seen as entertainment for whites, he continued to document black street culture and encouraged the formation of brass band parades to fill the narrow streets with song once more. Between 1990 and 1997 alone, the number of second-line parades tripled. In 1999, hoping to enshrine black cultural contributions outside the city's tourist heart, Francis opened the Backstreet Cultural Museum in the old Blandin funeral parlor on St. Claude Street, where jazz funerals once assembled for processions to various aboveground "cities of the dead." The new museum gave Francis a place to display his impressive collection of donated Mardi Gras Indian tribal costumes and assorted memorabilia of black street culture. More importantly, however, it gave Tremé a symbolic cultural center that embraced rather than denied black agency in the making of New Orleans.[53]

Black efforts increasingly won the attention of white New Orleanians as well, producing alliances across the color line that would scarcely have been thinkable only two decades earlier, when the city's mass tourism focus stood at its peak. These alliances converged with the concurrent push to focus tourist attention on significant black heritage sites and customs. In 1999 the Preservation Resource Center partnered with Dillard University to form the African American Heritage Preservation Council as a vehicle for saving decaying jazz musicians' homes. The council began working to identify the most significant properties and concentrate on finding individuals willing to embrace renovations, ultimately forming a basis for jazz tours.[54] By 2001 the group's efforts prompted the municipal government to allocate $50,000 to save jazzmen's homes, but the Louisiana Department of Culture, Recreation and Tourism opted to earmark $1 million to support director Ken Burns' PBS documentary *Jazz* while giving nothing to the preservation effort itself.[55] Nevertheless, even the heightened attention accorded to the necessity of saving physical markers of black accomplishment in a majority-black city was an accomplishment, given the long history of exploitation, trivialization, or outright neglect of the African American contribution to New Orleans's distinctive and highly lucrative image.

Just as jazz moved closer to the core of New Orleans's tourist image in the late twentieth century, the Mardi Gras celebration expanded dramatically during and after the 1980s oil bust. Unlike French Quarter preservation and the jazz revival, however, Carnival continued to reflect the involvement of the city's old-line white community, which perennially infused its parades with literary and mythological allusions. Indeed, long after Mid-City, Bacchus, Endymion, and other socially inclusive parading krewes formed, old-line organizations such as Comus, Momus, and Proteus continued to reign over the city's parade route during the height of Carnival. The balance of the celebration, nonetheless, was rapidly tipping toward a tourist focus as the newer parades captivated the public much more effectively than the staid old-line processions.[56] A combination of glitzy "superkrewes" and the first direct challenge to the racially discriminatory practices of old-line Carnival krewes finally toppled the highly visible elite presence in New Orleans's most famous cultural event by the 1990s. In a city that had become largely African American, the use of city streets by racially discriminatory old-line parading krewes provoked a strident public debate over the future of Carnival.

In a city that began to measure its economic health by the tons of trash collected from the streets during the official twelve-day public celebration of Carnival, city leaders and some tourism promoters also toyed with ideas for increasing the commercial potential of Mardi Gras. While such efforts touched a raw nerve with Carnival traditionalists, who hoped to safeguard the perceived distinctiveness of the celebration, the commercialization of Carnival proceeded unchallenged in other ways, notably the emergence of a year-round industry dedicated to preparing for the annual event. Meanwhile, the Quarter celebration devolved more and more into an adult bacchanal in which traditional Carnival "throws" became the currency that bought sexual displays from strangers. Mardi Gras had long resonated in the American consciousness as a time when moral strictures might be relaxed. It had enticed countless millions who took advantage of the anonymity of the crowd and often the mask that granted license to behavior they dared not exhibit at home. As U.S. society and popular culture became more sexually permissive, New Orleans could no longer take its distinction as a libertine city for granted. The city had to become bawdier in order to retain its allure. By the closing years of the century, New Orleans's risqué image, which had matured in the Storyville red-light district a century before, had placed city leaders in the precarious position of balancing the lucrative image of saturnalia with the need to enforce the law.[57] Clearly, Mardi Gras played an integral role in the tourist transformation of New Orleans.

In the quarter century after the Voting Rights Act of 1965 began to undermine the ability of old-line white leaders to dominate New Orleans and many other cities, black politicians had taken their place among the nation's mayors and city councilmen everywhere the African American population lived in sufficient concentration to enjoy representation. While this phenomenon regrettably occurred in the context of declining federal and state support of cities, white flight, loss of tax base, and deindustrialization, it still gave African American leaders a clear voice in decisions that affected their increasingly black constituencies. As early as the 1970s, New Orleans's city limits contained a black majority, and by 1990 African Americans comprised 62 percent of the city proper. While the financially straitened municipal government had little capacity to rescue New Orleans from crumbling streets and decaying schools, it could strike a blow to the last vestiges of institutionalized racism. Carnival, according to its old-line patrons, had always existed as a civic gesture that the city's upper class bestowed on the citizenry at great cost to themselves. In their eyes, as Pie Dufour had argued in his *Southern Living* article in 1967, Mardi Gras required no public money and was truly "the greatest free show on earth."[58] As demonstrated in chapter five, however, the struggling city treasury not only devoted substantial subsidies to facilitate Carnival, it did so to support organizations that often excluded blacks, Jews, and other minorities. By 1990, rumblings of discontent stood poised to purge old-line participation from public Carnival, a move that some New Orleanians felt would sink the tourist trade as surely as any riverfront expressway could have done.

In 1991, more than two decades after the then-white city hall had granted Zulu the right to occupy the same parade route as the venerable Rex parade, Councilwoman Dorothy Mae Taylor introduced an ordinance that would prohibit Carnival organizations that refused to admit African American members from obtaining parade permits. Reacting to the proposed ordinance, sixty-five krewe captains and members released a statement calling the bill a "tragic mistake." Understanding well the economic boost that Mardi Gras brought to New Orleans in the form of tourism, city leaders scrambled to avert the loss of old-line parades. A mayor-appointed blue-ribbon committee studied alternatives and proposed that krewes simply be asked to pledge nondiscrimination. In a vitriolic December city council meeting with Carnival captains, which Peggy Wilson, the lone voice of the old elite on the city council, derided as an "inquisition," the council passed the anti-discrimination measure but thereafter promised krewes one year to comply before risking forfeiture of their parade permits, thus shifting the burden of proof away from Carnival krewes.[59] One by one, defiant old-line krewes opted out of public Carnival, beginning with the Knights of Momus in January 1992. In a collectively issued proclamation by Proteus, Momus, and Comus during the 1993 Carnival season, the old-line krewemen revealed their impotence in the city's changed power structure: "So, let the celebration that we sired proceed apace. Go forward, New Orleanians, with carefree abandon and Carnival gladness unabated." Nowhere did they acknowledge that their world of Carnival had already fallen into eclipse, thanks to the advent of superkrewes like Bacchus and Endymion.[60]

Much to the chagrin of elite krewe members who predicted that Carnival could not survive without them, a claim seemingly borne out when the 1993 celebration apparently prompted a drop in visitor spending, Mardi Gras continued. In 1993 Orleans Parish district attorney Harry Connick and his son, popular jazz pianist Harry Connick Jr., started Orpheus, the city's newest superkrewe, and obtained a Lundi Gras parade permit. Like Bacchus and Endymion, the Connicks' organization was open to anyone who could afford its $750-a-year dues regardless of race or gender.[61] Named for the Greek god of music, Orpheus built its parade themes around the city's rich musical traditions even as it turned its back on the exclusivity that characterized the castigated old-line krewes. When Orpheus first rolled in 1994, it seemed to erase the doubts of many tourism leaders and Carnival traditionalists that the antidiscrimination ordinance might undermine the popularity of Mardi Gras, for Carnival spending estimates soared 16 percent to $660 million between 1993 and 1994.[62]

Orpheus, like earlier superkrewes, simply underscored the growing popularity of New Orleans's Mardi Gras. Retailers and media companies alike set out to capitalize on the city's irrepressible Carnival celebration. As early as 1987 the cable television channel MTV broadcast continuously from Bourbon Street during the height of Carnival, while Iowa-based men's entertainment media giant Playboy Enterprises filmed Mardi Gras from the balcony of a Bourbon Street strip club. In 1990 Dallas-based Neiman-Marcus's holiday wish book featured a four-night Mardi Gras trip as its "His and Hers" gift.[63] The effort to commercialize Mardi Gras also involved the municipal government.

Echoing its devotion to stimulating tourism as the foundation for economic recovery in New Orleans, the Barthelemy administration hoped to license official Mardi Gras merchandise to raise funds for the city. For many years an unwritten rule had forbidden commercial sponsorship of Mardi Gras parades, culminating in the adoption of a city ordinance in 1985 banning all advertising in parades, but the city's fiscal crisis finally forced some public officials to reconsider.[64] As early as 1991 Mayor Barthelemy made a secretive arrangement with New Orleans Event

Marketing, Inc., whereby the company would develop a Carnival marketing strategy for the city and then split all resulting profits from merchandise sales evenly with city hall. The company, headed by one of Barthelemy's political appointees, was bought out by Atlanta-based Primedia two years later, having made little progress on its plan. Despite outcry from Carnival traditionalists and stern rebukes from the Mayor's Mardi Gras Coordinating Committee, Barthelemy's political ally Councilman Lambert Boissiere then drafted a set of measures to allow commercial sponsors to underwrite the city's expenses in providing services to support the annual event. Specifically, Boissiere hoped to enable the municipal licensing of an array of "official" Carnival products, such as T-shirts, hats, beer, and camera film. He contended that krewes in Jefferson Parish, including Argus, already utilized corporate largesse and noted that New Orleans desperately needed the money.[65] Like Moon Landrieu's *son-et-lumière* plan, Barthelemy's licensing plan proceeded without public knowledge until the final proposal emerged. With Barthelemy finishing his second term, the commercialization issue became a major point of contention in the 1994 mayoral race as some candidates sought to distance themselves from this particularly controversial example of city hall's connection to tourism.[66]

Purists judged Taylor's antidiscrimination ordinance and Barthelemy's licensing scheme as nothing less than the last nails in the coffin of a celebration that had already lost much of what distinguished it from other cities' parades. To one Carnival captain, commercialization threatened Mardi Gras as a "folk festival," albeit one that privileged those with money and standing. Likewise, *Times-Picayune* columnist James Gill complained that city hall, having made "Comus, Momus and Proteus the official pariahs of Carnival," now wanted "to replace them with advertising executives."[67] Illustrative of the extent to which tourism-oriented profits drove local discourse on public issues by the 1990s, opponents of the Barthelemy administration's Carnival licensing scheme included not only traditionalists but also thirty-five French Quarter merchants who feared that officially licensed Mardi Gras merchandise would chip away at profits in their more than one hundred shops.[68] Eventually the city council, with some of its members incensed by Barthelemy's failure to keep them apprised of his actions, killed the plan to license official Mardi Gras merchandise.[69]

The animus directed toward municipal efforts to regulate Carnival suggests the degree to which the myth of its uniqueness remained an article of faith in New Orleans. Far from being a true grassroots celebration, Mardi Gras created the illusion of distinctiveness not so much because it was fundamentally different from other cities' parades and festivals but because it cultivated a unique façade. If commercial interests could not actually "own" Mardi Gras, they could still capitalize on it. Indeed, in the 1980s and 1990s the celebration became more and more wedded to a tourism industry whose practices standardized experiences around the globe. Just as cruise lines and all-inclusive tropical resorts created package deals calculated to sell tourism as part of an attractive lifestyle rather than a series of travel services, New Orleans Mardi Gras became increasingly packaged in the years after various hotels began to offer tickets for stadium seating along parade routes or to attend Carnival ball reenactments and dinner-dances. With Endymion and Bacchus having filled gaps on Saturday and Sunday evenings, in 1987 public and private interests revived Lundi Gras, the day before Fat Tuesday, for many years a lull in the party. Prior to 1917 Rex, the King of Carnival, arrived by boat the eve of Mardi Gras, but, with the exception of the 1972 Rex centennial, the tradition lapsed until 1987, when Rex docked at the new Riverwalk festival marketplace. With four days now filled with festivities, tourists could purchase a $370 tour package that afforded accommodations in a first-class hotel, reserved seats in city-operated reviewing stands, tickets to a postparade dinner-dance, and a city tour, river cruise, and French Quarter buggy ride.[70]

Tourists went to New Orleans to observe Mardi Gras, but they also went to participate. To be sure, outsiders had always participated in Carnival in small numbers as guests of krewe members, but with the advent of newer parades many more made journeys of hundreds or even thousands of miles to ride in a parade. Reacting to a slump in Carnival krewe memberships in the wake of the oil bust, the Bards of Bohemia began selling tickets to tourists entitling them to ride in its annual parade in 1994. In the following year, the Krewe of Tucks attracted more than one hundred tourists to ride in its parade by advertising in *Condé Nast Traveler*. Then, in 1998, the Krewe of America, organized by a suburban New Orleans banker, appeared in the parade slot once held by old-line Comus, promising the first New Orleans parade comprised primarily of tourists. The prospect of a tourist parade did not sit well with traditionalists, including one local Carnival historian who lamented that Mardi Gras had degenerated into "a theme park to amuse visitors," adding that "now we have double-decker buses carrying Wayne Newton and Steven Seagal." Ignoring the fact that Mardi Gras had become closely attuned to tourist expectations well before the arrival of this organization, one editorial complained that "a parading horde of tourists who have no sense of Carnival traditions strikes us as antithetical to the season's history and spirit. It seems, literally, like the ultimate 'Americanization' of New Orleans."[71] New Orleans's Carnival had, of course, been moving toward greater inclusion of tourists for many years, notably with Owen Brennan's reenactment of the Alla ball for tourists in 1950. Only in the 1990s, however, after another half-century of tourism's impact on their city, did locals express outrage at the loss they felt. Although the Krewe of America proved short-lived, failing to attract nearly as many high-paying tourists as its planners anticipated, the controversy it generated underscored the extent to which local discourse now revolved around issues of commercial profit versus cultural authenticity.

In addition to filling the city's hotels for two weeks and shaping an inescapable year-round Carnival atmosphere, Mardi Gras gradually evolved into an important industry. In the late nineteenth and early twentieth centuries, dozens of American cities—including Atlanta, Cincinnati, Kansas City, Louisville, Memphis, and St. Louis—had copied New Orleans by creating their own Carnival parades, but most of these celebrations had long since vanished as these cities directed civic efforts in other directions.[72] By the 1980s and 1990s, however, an upsurge of interest in heritage and urban culture melded with cities' efforts to claim a share of the rapidly growing market for entertainment-based tourism. As a result, many cities looked not only to New Orleans's French Quarter but also to its Mardi Gras celebration as a model. After decades of modernizing forces that lessened the distinctions between urban centers, promoters were anxious to add local color, even if they borrowed their ideas from elsewhere. Underground Atlanta, Memphis's Beale Street, and Tampa's Ybor City mimicked French Quarter–style nightlife attractions. Likewise, Seattle, Austin, and a host of other cities initiated Mardi Gras celebrations, and Tampa followed up its century-old Gasparilla, itself a derivation of Carnival, with Guavaween, a Halloween festival with Mardi Gras influences.[73]

Such attractions looked to New Orleans not only for inspiration but also for props. Coupled with the increasing demand for equipment and merchandise to support New Orleans's own Carnival, the spread of similar festivals fueled the growth of a year-round industry in the Big Easy. Blaine Kern was among the beneficiaries of this trend. His Mardi Gras World, a museum built around his massive float-building facility in Algiers, across the Mississippi River from the French Quarter, called tourists' attention to the year-round, behind-the-scenes preparation that manufactured the spectacle they enjoyed each winter. It also elaborated the Bacchus cofounder's efforts to help tourists see behind the mask that had long kept them out of the old-line krewes' float-building dens. Kern, who got his start in the service of the old-line Krewe of Rex, now exemplified the standardization of Carnival. His facility leased floats often modified between parades to reflect each krewe's theme. In addition to float construction, Carnival required millions of dollars' worth of beaded necklaces, doubloons, and other trinkets and souvenirs for riders to toss to the crowds lining the streets. New Orleans–based companies, notably Accent Annex, began reselling Carnival throws imported from Hong Kong and elsewhere in the Far East for Carnival celebrations in Galveston and Port Arthur, Texas; Gulfport, Mississippi; and Mobile, Alabama. Gambino's, a leading New Orleans bakery, was by the late 1990s producing daily up to 5,000 king cakes—circular green, yellow, and purple iced pastries traditionally served at the Feast of the Epiphany but increasingly provided at any Carnival party. Gambino's shipped about half of its king cakes out of town in a kit that included beads, cups, and even a compact disc of Carnival music. In 1995 the emergence of "Virtual Bourbon Street," an online Carnival shopping center on the World Wide Web started by a Mandeville, Louisiana, entrepreneur, added to the long tradition of building public interest in New Orleans through exporting the city's culture. Thus, New Orleans businesses satisfied a growing national appetite for food and other products, reflecting the extent of the tourist transformation of Mardi Gras.[74]

In the 1960s and 1970s the GNOTCC had touted Mardi Gras as the "greatest free show on earth" to entice tourists to experience the wild and colorful Carnival celebration each winter. As tourism promoters discovered, the event hardly needed promotion, for the festivities became more freewheeling with each passing year. By the 1980s and 1990s, Carnival revelers on Bourbon Street, particularly those from out of town, were creating their own version of the flesh shows that lined the neon strip. One journalist noted, with a touch of irony, "How strange. On a street lined with porno arcades, and every conceivable visual combination of naked vertebrate life, people will stand under balconies for hours beseeching women with shouts, Mardi Gras beads and doubloons." The incidence of public nudity and even public sex acts led CBS to air a special episode of *48 Hours* called "Bedlam on Bourbon Street" in 1993. New Orleans police, for their part, selectively and sporadically enforced city ordinances, perpetually torn between encouraging and preventing the very forms of behavior that added to the city's unique allure and arguably contributed to the image that led MTV to cast one season of its popular "reality television" series *The Real World* in the city during Carnival. Following a feature in the February 2000 issue of *Playboy,* New Orleans mayor Marc

Morial warned of stern action against anyone who exhibited "lewd conduct." His threatened crackdown made national news headlines, prompting Morial to back away from his stance under pressure from some in the tourism establishment. The city's quandary over how to balance its carefully tended image of moral laxity with the need to ensure law and order underlined the deep imprint of tourism in a city that saw few alternatives to image maintenance. Tourists, not surprisingly, simply responded to the image created from many years of promoters' and tourists' acting on cues taken from each other.[75]

Tourism had been an important facet of New Orleans society and culture even in the nineteenth century. It had grown in the middle decades of the twentieth century as merchants, hoteliers, restaurateurs, nightclub operators, tourism promoters, and even city officials responded to Americans' growing interest in and ability to travel. New Orleans's tourism industry built upon the careful cultivation of the French Quarter and local cultural traditions such as Carnival and jazz, as well as on the growing effort to create a physical and promotional infrastructure of tourism that could translate national interest in New Orleans into a sustained, year-round industry. It managed to maintain the illusion of distinctiveness while becoming in some ways like other cities in the modern South. It even managed to conserve the racial underpinnings of the city's tourist appeal while ending decades of racial segregation. The city's leaders had increasingly cultivated the tourism industry by subscribing to public policies that assured that New Orleans met outsiders' expectations. Only in the crucible of the city's economic depression of the mid to late 1980s, however, did New Orleans leaders, like their counterparts in many American cities reeling from deindustrialization, finally embrace tourism as the focal point in their economic plans. The shift reflected not only the crisis in which the city found itself but also the growing political and economic strength of a biracial city hall working more closely than ever with business leaders who had invested heavily in tourism in the postwar years, particularly since the 1960s.

Long a city personified in literature and tourism promotion as a naughty, irresistible seductress, the Big Easy now had to prostitute its seductive appeal merely to survive. More and more, the preservation-minded New Orleanians who had embraced the city's culture and so effectively impressed upon civic and business leaders the economic value of its tourist image faced an industry that wanted no limits on its growth. Preservationists surely winced when, in one newspaper interview, a tour operator snapped, "If you don't like Mickey Mouse, you shouldn't live in Disney World."[76] In its effort to recoup economic stature by clinging to its past, New Orleans became a place that existed to satisfy the nostalgic and sensory desires of outsiders, a place obsessed with maintaining a façade that mirrored what tourists expected to find. Even as its schools, streets, and other public services decayed and crumbled, New Orleans lavished attention on its tourist image. By the beginning of the twenty-first century, it had become, in effect, a city on parade.

EPILOGUE

In an interview by *Times-Picayune* journalist Chris Rose in 2001, New York film and literary critic Rex Reed reminisced about his forays into decadent New Orleans as a youth growing up in 1950s Texas and Louisiana. Reed described the city's French Quarter as "Sodom and Gomorrah at my back door." He remembered nights spent watching "people doing conga lines in Chanel dresses with sailors and drag queens" at La Casa de los Marinos on Decatur Street, where the French Quarter's tattered edge flirted with a netherworld of warehouses, seamen's bars, and wharves along the Mississippi riverfront. Reed's recollection was of a city still in the process of myth making, a place that still brought together one of the most diverse assortments of humanity, resident and transient, on the continent. The New Orleans of Reed's memory was, for "a little Methodist kid from Texas who didn't know what a crawfish was, . . . an eye-opening experience." The French Quarter, like the city itself, was a place in transition from a unique locale where outsiders marveled at a distinctive culture that seemingly diverged from the mainstream of post-1930s modernization, to a place that consciously cultivated and packaged this image as part of a multibillion-dollar hospitality industry. Like many who visited the city at an earlier stage in the tourist transformation, Reed lamented that while he had "always wanted New Orleans to maintain that sense of laissez-faire decadence that I experienced at La Casa de los Marinos," the city had become something far different. For all the efforts New Orleanians made to capitalize on tourists' expectations of their city by safeguarding, enhancing, and institutionalizing its distinctive attributes, New Orleans morphed, in Reed's words, into "millions of tourists walking around with Hurricanes in the street."[1]

Indeed, a tourist visiting New Orleans today would be far more likely to forge memories of navigating a sea of drunken T-shirt-clad tourists on Bourbon Street, sipping fruity, red Pat O'Brien's drinks from souvenir "go-cups," and shouting for other tourists perched on iron balconies to toss beaded Mardi Gras necklaces purchased from gaudy souvenir shops that blared Cajun music through open doorways. Like so many Americans who knew New Orleans before the height of its tourist transformation, Reed captured the same sense of loss that gripped tradition-minded locals. Tourism, in their eyes, had turned the Crescent City into an ersatz caricature of itself, a "Creole Disneyland." Columnist and civil rights activist Lolis Eric Elie lamented that soon locals' "main job will be to lend an air of authenticity to a city that once had it in spades."[2]

Clearly, tourism has transformed New Orleans, plugging it into a global marketplace in which the tourism industry "manufactures" and "sells" experiences from San Francisco to Venice, Rio de Janeiro to Cairo, Honolulu to Hong Kong. Promising the possibility of discovering and experiencing the unique, tourism instead exerts a standardizing force on cities that cultivate it. Although the sights are different, everywhere one can count on recognized hotels, souvenir stands, shopping malls, and locals eager to extend their hospitality through service and entertainment. In New Orleans one can experience Carnival on demand by visiting the Mardi Gras exhibition at the Louisiana State Museum or purchasing and wearing purple, gold, and green baubles from French Quarter retailers even though actual Carnival parades no longer wend their way through the narrow Vieux Carré streets because the enormous crowds they now draw would severely compromise public safety. One can visit Preservation Hall, the jazz museum in the Old Mint, or any of several jazz clubs throughout the city, but on famed Bourbon Street one is more likely to hear country, pop, or dance music than anything indigenous to New Orleans. Noting the impact of tourism, Jack Mahen, a clarinetist in the Original Dukes of Dixieland from the 1950s to 1990s, said of Bourbon Street: "I don't go down there much anymore. There's very little jazz, and now there's very little of what made the street famous." In fact, in the opening years of the twenty-first century, out-of-town investors are firmly entrenched as nightclub operators, helping drive up rents on Bourbon Street between 50 and 100 percent as they mimic the types of entertainment one may easily find in other cities frequented by conventioneers.[3]

If New Orleans has in some respects adopted many of the characteristics of other American cities in its effort to remain a leading tourist and convention destination, it continues to beguile visitors with a culture that retains its distinctiveness. Ironically, as suggested elsewhere in this book, New Orleans's cultivation of a tourist image has safeguarded against deleterious spatial and cultural changes even as it has propelled the local economy and changed citizens' sense of their city. Christine Boyer has commented that the controversy in the twentieth century over the future of the French Quarter demonstrates "that other than aesthetic values were at the heart of preservation activity, that the spirit of place enhanced tourism, protected property values, and supported the urban economy."[4]

Indeed, southern cities have been among the most successful in their ability to fuse cultural preservation and economic development, doing so in ways that allow the illusion of tradition to mask modernization. New Orleanians' experience with tourism tells much about its impact on urban places and the trajectory of modern southern urban history. As David Goldfield and other historians have demonstrated, southern cities not only lagged behind other U.S. cities in their post–Civil War development, they also continued to maintain a degree of cultural distinctiveness throughout the twentieth century. While some cities realized the commercial and industrial development that Atlanta journalist Henry W. Grady anticipated in his "New South Creed," others—notably, New Orleans, Charleston, Key West, Savannah, and Wilmington, North Carolina—lay on the periphery of the twentieth-century economic boom, either in coastal or mountain areas. Well before the appearance of a "Rust Belt" in the urban North, such southern cities learned to capitalize on their cultural heritage, either to attract business investment or as an end in itself.

Just as New Orleans cultivated an image mixing Carnival traditions, Creole culture, and Dixieland music, cities around the region beckoned tourists by branding themselves with various forms of heritage. Charleston, Savannah, and Williamsburg relied on their colonial legacy, while Miami, San Antonio and Tampa promoted their Latin American roots. Memphis promoted blues music, and Nashville, Lexington, and Austin became country and bluegrass centers. Chattanooga, Richmond, and Vicksburg touted their role in the Civil War. Whereas the "civic-commercial elite" that historian Blaine Brownell examined in the South of the 1920s and 1930s engaged in urban rivalries by trumpeting signs that their cities were assuming an air of modernity, the effect of tourism in the modern South, and elsewhere, may be measured by looking at the lengths to which city leaders go to emphasize their communities' distinctive cultural attributes (or to manufacture them if they do not exist).[5]

Perhaps nowhere was the use of culture more central than in the exploitation of African American history and heritage. The modern tourism industry became highly adept at marketing the black experience across the South, although it did so differently in different places. Many southern cities focused tourist attention on the mythology of the Old South, only rarely incorporating black perspectives that shattered the myth. For many years Atlanta's biggest attractions included the homes of *Gone With The Wind* author Margaret Mitchell and of Joel Chandler Harris, who popularized African trickster tales in *The Tales of Uncle Remus*. Similarly, Natchez, Mississippi, constructed its tourist image around annual tours of its gracious antebellum homes. In the past thirty years, a few southern cities began to emphasize a different strand of African American history—the civil rights movement. Atlanta, Birmingham, and Greensboro opened museums that depict various aspects of the struggle to win racial equality, providing a long-missing counterpoint to white-centered uses of race in the tourist trade. New Orleans reinforced and diverged from these regional patterns of race-based tourism. While it certainly cultivated the Old South myth in the several decades after the Civil War, New Orleans never developed the story of black freedom struggles to the extent that other regional cities did. Typical of the city's failure to address fully the conundrums of its uneasy race relations during the height of the civil rights movement, New Orleans packaged black culture through a focus on jazz. Doing so reinforced the city's penchant for accentuating its carefree, "laissez les bon temps rouler" mentality while masking its legacies of slavery and Jim Crow. Thus, New Orleans could obscure any connection a visitor might conjure between the racial inequities of the past and those written into a present-day social and physical landscape fractured along racial lines.

The New Orleans experience also sheds light on the impact of tourism on the local urban culture on which it depends. Everywhere the reliance on tourism, as Hal Rothman suggests in *Devil's Bargains,* has forced communities to undergo cultural change. Perhaps nowhere is this truer than in the South, where reverence for an imagined past runs especially deep. The ambivalence with which many New Orleanians and tourists greeted the changes wrought by tourism in the Crescent City helps contextualize similar developments elsewhere. For example, several years after New Orleans boosters created the New Orleans Jazz and Heritage Festival as a hook to beckon cultural tourists, in 1977 Charleston began hosting Spoleto Festival USA, a state-sponsored two-week visual and performing arts celebration modeled on a similar celebration in Spoleto, Italy. Much like New Orleans, Charleston had seen extensive, elite-led architectural preservation campaigns even in the 1920s but remained, in the words of one local journalist, "a sleepy Southern town caught in the quagmire of poverty" until the Spoleto Festival began, energizing the city's tourist image, which in turn exerted increasing pressures on Charleston's ability to absorb the impact of tourism. Just as Rex Reed lamented New Orleans's diminished ambience, the *Charleston Post and Courier* writer commented that Charleston had lost its character: "Now she's all tarted up, but she's lost her charm, because her charm was her people who held on to those houses generation after generation because there was no place else to go. Land became real estate. Who knew?"[6]

If tourism recast New Orleans's culture, it arguably saved the French Quarter from vanishing, just as it bolstered jazz, Carnival, and many other signifiers of the city's cultural legacy. It also reshaped the larger city spatially even as it grew more concentrated in the "central tourist district." It was the tourist transformation that enabled locals to cast aside hopes that their city would become more like the prosperous commercial and industrial rivals that dotted the Sunbelt in the second half of the twentieth century and instead embrace New Orleans's distinctiveness, just as newcomers to the city had done for more than two centuries. If the spatial reorientation of New Orleans's social and cultural landscape in some ways produced a city that previous generations would scarcely recognize, tourism also conserved a physical cityscape of historic structures that provided an evocative stage on which new generations could improvise and reenact elements of New Orleans culture that, because they enjoyed such widespread attention, resonated all the more profoundly among locals, natives and transplants alike. New Orleans was, in effect, an urban palimpsest—a preserved city on which heritage seekers inscribed new meanings over time.[7]

Tourism, however, has not saved New Orleans from the urban problems that afflict many American cities and has in some respects prompted local leaders to ignore problems or remedy them in superficial ways calculated to suffice as window dressing for visitors. To be sure, the tourism industry lifted the fortunes of some cities. While Las Vegas, another of the nation's most popular tourist cities, built a booming entertainment-oriented economy and well-paid workforce around the expansion of its gaming industry, Charleston used its historic homes as the foundation for an economic development strategy that made it the fastest growing metropolis in the Carolinas by the beginning of the twenty-first century. Likewise, New York, San Francisco, Boston, Chicago, and Washington, D.C., have benefited from tourism while remaining viable in myriad other economic realms. In stark contrast, New Orleans's turn to tourism produced considerably less economic prosperity, more closely approximating the unhappy results of Atlantic City, New Jersey's experiment with casino gambling as a panacea for economic malaise. Why was this so? How could New Orleans, a city that perennially rates among travelers' favorite destinations, find itself so hampered by misfortune? In large part, the answer lies in larger structural problems such as the dearth of dry, developable land, economic changes that diminished the city's oil and port industries, outside perceptions of local corruption and dissipation, a conservative tax structure that impedes municipal budgets, and the presence of a large disadvantaged population without access to decent education, housing, medical care, job skills training, and city services. Probably more importantly, however, is that tourism exerted the most positive influence in those cities that did not suffer the intractable problems of Atlantic City—or New Orleans. For the Big Easy, tourism simply offered an easy alternative to tackling such problems, encouraging local leaders to address problems only as they pertained to the maintenance of a good national image. Just as Miami leaders sought to sequester their city's slums out of sight of downtown, New Orleans leaders hoped to purge their city's "central tourist district" of any signs of poverty and crime, leading to the increasing spatial differentiation of the city into privileged and disadvantaged districts.

As architectural historian Stewart Brand has commented, New Orleans's tourist image relies to some extent on fostering a "cult of decay," but walking the fine line between appearing "plastic" and moldering away has proved exceedingly difficult.[8] Maintaining a favorable tourist image has long been difficult for New Orleans, and by the 1970s it meant upholding this image while covering up a stark reality. The Big Easy was a declining metropolis on the brink of fiscal ruin, gripped by dire poverty and vicious crime, and falling apart under an unforgiving semitropical climate. Notwithstanding Mayor Dutch Morial's inducements to industry and efforts to create new social programs, federal funds to cities dried up, oil severance tax-sharing windfalls from the state trailed off, and the property-tax homestead exemption denied the city its due. Dilapidated schools and municipal layoffs became ubiquitous. Under such circumstances, promoting tourism became a stopgap measure, producing revenues from the city's hefty sales tax and hotel room tax. But it proved increasingly difficult to maintain the city's appearance as funding for landscaping and street paving fell short of nature's efficiency in deluging New Orleans, leaving its neutral grounds weed strewn and its streets pocked with craters and sinkholes. Officials continued, with the help of the self-taxing Downtown Development District, to allocate funds to maintain infrastructure in the city center and adjacent French Quarter but let other parts of the city go to seed.

Worse, street crime posed the biggest threat to the stability of the city's multibillion-dollar tourism industry. If New Orleans thrived on its reputation as a sin city, it did so through the careful cultivation of a freewheeling atmosphere in which personal risks were more apparent than real. The periodic shooting deaths of prominent conventioneers in and around the French Quarter produced a far worse public relations brouhaha than the occasional Mickey Finn poisonings of earlier years, leading some convention planners to reconsider holding meetings in New Orleans. By 1982, national newspapers reported that New Orleans ranked as the fourth deadliest metropolitan area in the nation, a dubious distinction later surpassed when the city became the nation's murder capital in the next decade. In this respect, New Orleans mirrored growing rates of violent crime in many southern cities, notably Houston, Miami, and Atlanta.[9] Dutch Morial appointed a French Quarter task force to develop strategies for safeguarding the city's leading tourist space, ultimately leading to the opening of a new police precinct, the appointment of a foot patrol, and the imposition of a juvenile curfew, as well as the publication of a tourist brochure entitled "For a Safer Visit." The task force even urged the Catholic Archdiocese of New Orleans to close St. Louis Cemetery No. 1 to tourists but ultimately settled for asking the tourist commission to strike the attraction from its brochures.[10]

Year after year the national news media latched onto the unfolding story of a city with an enchanting ambience juxtaposed with a crumbling economy and soaring crime. During Mardi Gras in 1989, the CBS Evening News depicted the city as a "Carnival of Crime," prompting the local CBS affiliate WWL to threaten to withhold assistance to the network the following year, and leading the city council to cobble together a resolution urging a local boycott of the news program.[11] But the bad news kept coming. Following a scandal in which New Orleans police officers arrested and detained hundreds of tourists on charges of minor traffic violations in 1992 and 1993, even harassing jazz saxophonist and Tonight Show bandleader Branford Marsalis, news reports told Americans in 1994 about the city's climbing murder count, which reached 389 in 1993 and 421 the following year. Mardi Gras publicity now vied with murder publicity, as 60 Minutes and the NBC Nightly News reported the grim story. Even though most of the murders occurred in the city's drug-infested housing projects and surrounding slums, the murders of two tourists in 1994 seized inordinate attention, echoing a sensational news story that had blackened Miami's reputation the previous year when two foreign tourists were killed. Perhaps no story caught fire nationally more than the shocking revelations of corruption and brutality in the New Orleans Police Department (NOPD) in the mid-1990s. When NOPD officers murdered several innocent citizens in 1995, international attention again fixated on a tourist city in turmoil. Mayor Marc Morial, who took office in 1994, undertook a massive purge and reform of the police department, making it clear that fears of lost tourist business figured prominently in public policy decisions once tourism had worked its transformation on the city.

Although local leaders often touted tourism as a panacea for economic troubles, these problems scarcely lessened as the industry became more thoroughly entrenched, calling into question the common assumption that tourism is simply a golden economic development strategy. To be sure, the city's ability to entice people to live in its many old neighborhoods, in large part a result of cultivating tourism, probably slowed the rate of population loss. New Orleans proper lost more than 130,000 residents in the thirty years after 1960, almost half of that number in the oil-bust 1980s alone, but only about 12,000 in the 1990s. Still, even cultivating heritage tourism failed to generate the population boost enjoyed in New York, Chicago, Boston, and San Francisco. While many parts of the Big Easy experienced a rise in per capita income in the 1990s, mirroring a national pattern, large swaths of the city became poorer. Tourism and the city's discovery of its own heritage clearly led to a growing chasm between favored and neglected neighborhoods and induced racial separation where residential integration had once prevailed. While the Lower Garden District became, according to the alternative magazine *Utne Reader*, "the hippest neighborhood north of the Rio Grande," the largely African American neighborhoods of Central City, Gert Town, Hollygrove, and Lower Ninth Ward continued to decay. Clearly, tourism fueled gentrification, producing at best a checkered effect on the city's social landscape.[12]

The story of New Orleans's tourist transformation is a bittersweet one. By most accounts, the city has proved highly successful in molding itself to tourist expectations while retaining the ability to cultivate more than a façade of distinctiveness. As cities throughout the nation grapple with the deleterious effects of postindustrial urban decline, their leaders look longingly at New Orleans, a city that created a truly remarkable tourism infrastructure without completely sacrificing the cultural legacy so beloved by New Orleanians and the visitors they host. To an extent, tourism has proven a good fit for the city. It has enabled New Orleans to attract substantial outside investment, reinvigorate local devotion to historic neighborhoods and cultural practices, and provide tens of thousands of jobs in a city that arguably could ill afford to focus all its efforts on tackling its many entrenched problems as inducement for other modes of economic development.

Yet the Big Easy should prompt caution among those who would place great faith in tourism, for even in a city widely viewed as the nation's most interesting and exotic, tourism has mainly aggrandized the developers, investors, and operators who saw its potential while denying a large proportion of the populace much hope of upward mobility. New Orleans wears a mask, flaunting its beautiful architecture, delicious food, frenetic revelry, and fascinating folkways while hiding its face—decadent slums, deprivation and crime, and apathy and despair. Those fortunate enough to spend a vacation or purchase a home sequestered amid iron-lace balconies, flickering gas lamps, horse-drawn carriages, and oak-canopied streets enjoy the New Orleans portrayed in film, television, literature, popular music, travel guides, and magazines. Those unfortunate ones who live amid dilapidated shotgun houses, broken windows, graffiti, and treeless, pot-holed streets suffer a New Orleans untouched by the colorful paint, bright signs, festive umbrellas, and bronze plaques that connote tourism. They are unseen by tour bus passengers and unheard by local officialdom. New Orleans, like all cities that came to depend on any industry, whether steelmaking, automobile assembly, textile production, or tourism, ultimately subordinated all other concerns to the bottom line. The city long known for its colorful Carnival parades found that its best bet lay in putting itself on parade.

POSTSCRIPT

> The temptation will be strong to transform New Orleans into "New Orleans," a
> smaller, prettified version of itself, all packaged quaintness and garish fun.
>
> —JUSTIN DAVIDSON (2005)

As this book goes to press, New Orleans is a city forever altered, a city with an uncertain future. On the morning of August 29, 2005, Katrina bore down on the Big
Easy as a powerful Category 4 hurricane. Long accustomed to hurricanes, those
New Orleanians who could flee by car or plane did so, as did most tourists. On the
day before the projected landfall, Mayor Ray Nagin announced the city's first-ever
mandatory evacuation. The National Weather Service, usually matter-of-fact in its
forecasting, warned that Katrina would likely destroy half of all homes and that
skyscrapers would sway, "some to the point of total collapse."[1] On the night before
the storm crashed upon the city, one could sense a somber tone on televised news-
casts, whose anchors seemed to realize that the city so beloved for its rich culture
might be swept off the map. Tourists who could not leave prepared to ride out the
hurricane in several of the larger hotels in and around downtown New Orleans,
while those locals without the means to leave filed into shelters, most of them
into the saucerlike Superdome. Initial reports following the hurricane suggested
that coastal Mississippi endured the brunt of the storm and that New Orleans apparently weathered Katrina without the apocalyptic scenario that had dominated
news reports in previous days.

On the morning of August 30, the morning shows brought the horrific news
that a twenty-foot storm surge on Lake Pontchartrain had forced water down the
several fingerlike canals that extend deep into city, breaching the levee system
and sending torrents of floodwater into New Orleans. In the days that followed,
Americans learned that untold thousands of people, mostly poor and working-
class African Americans, were trapped in a flood that had consumed 80 percent of
New Orleans. Some parts of the city lay under more than ten feet of water. Each
day the situation grew more desperate as streams of evacuees fled the fetid wa-
ters, which became a muddy, toxic gumbo of corpses, human waste, gasoline, and

chemicals. News cameras rolled, capturing the plight of the underclass and a few unfortunate tourists as conditions grew dire. By midweek, thousands of desperate people huddled under the baking sun on raft-like sections of interstate ramps, on the concrete tarmac surrounding the Superdome (now an island), and in and around the Ernest N. Morial Convention Center, where many reportedly lay dead or dying. Looters ransacked stores, mostly searching for food and water, while a few armed individuals terrorized the city and seemed to confirm in the public's mind the idea of New Orleans as a lawless city now descended into hellish chaos. Hundreds of police officers turned in their badges in despair; at least two committed suicide. More than one thousand New Orleanians perished.

Although most media attention rightly focused on the human disaster and why the relief effort reached the sodden city only after it appeared too late to save many, attention at times also turned to the fate of one of the nation's most treasured yet troubled cities. With hundreds of thousands of its former residents parsed out across the United States, including more than ten thousand in Houston's Astrodome alone, the prospect of a permanent New Orleans diaspora seemed at hand amid reports that it could take months, if not years, to rebuild the almost completely depopulated city. Literally overnight, Baton Rouge ballooned into Louisiana's largest city, while Houston swelled with the influx of some 125,000 New Orleanians. Countless evacuees contemplated starting new lives in cities and towns throughout the country.[2]

Adam Nossiter of the Associated Press, a fifteen-year New Orleans transplant, deftly captured the paradox of New Orleans. "You could live in a kind of dream-state in New Orleans," he observed, "lulled into ignoring the crumbling houses you drove past, and their destitute inhabitants. In a city so beautifully green, so full of beguiling architecture, so appealingly laid-back, how easy it was." Nossiter recalled his ability to partake in the city's mythic, ritualized lifestyle, sensing the presence of great deprivation and yet able to lose himself in the "douceur de vivre" that New Orleans afforded. He noted with mixed disgust and amusement the callous and paranoid attitude of those uptowners then gathered for shelter in a downtown hotel, whose "fantasies of insurrection echoed those found in the literature on antebellum New Orleans." For them, as for the nation, Katrina had laid bare the persisting racial chasms that under ordinary circumstances one might choose to ignore. Katrina shattered mythic New Orleans as nothing else could.[3]

Where does New Orleans go from here? Some reports suggest that perhaps more than 50 percent of the city's 485,000 residents will not return, presenting

New Orleans with the prospect of becoming a much smaller, poorer city.[4] Yet the most celebrated parts of the city—the French Quarter, Garden District, and Uptown—dodged the brunt of the storm's punishment. A bowl of architectural confections will again entice those with a taste for New Orleans heritage. Drab streetcars and Mardi Gras floats will surely creak and groan down St. Charles Avenue again. Bourbon Street will again fill with hurricane-sipping tourists sampling either karaoke or striptease. As one former Louisiana tourism official pointed out, "The core of the historic district . . . is intact, so you can rebuild around that."[5] Indeed, the infrastructure of tourism, so deliberately concentrated in a central tourist district on the relatively high ground along the Mississippi River, remains intact. The state of post-Katrina New Orleans suggests that the city will become less a Pompeii than a Venice—not a forgotten ruin but a bustling tourist city that struggles to accommodate a flood of pleasure seekers while fighting back the relentless sea.

In a city that for decades constructed an economy increasingly reliant on tourism, the pressure for a quick fix will be powerful and influential. Tellingly, the optimistic voices of some local tourism leaders already rise above the chorus of despair, including one hopeful prediction that "the convention business will rebound stronger than ever" as a result of renovations that will accompany the rebuilding. Even the notorious Morial Convention Center, once cleansed of its visible record of human suffering, may again become New Orleans's biggest "factory," producing consumers for the city's service economy.[6]

In the wake of Katrina, it is quite possible that, as *Times-Picayune* columnist Lolis Eric Elie put it in 2001, locals' "main job will be to lend an air of authenticity to a city that once had it in spades."[7] Like many observers, Elie believed that tourism had damaged New Orleans by turning its fragile culture into an outwardly directed one and that much of the city's authenticity had long since disappeared. Yet from the vantage point of 2005, it becomes clear that New Orleans's mythic quality, so appealing to tourists, was always more than a façade. The city's celebrated culture was, despite the many cheap plastic baubles and trinkets that adorned French Quarter shop windows, as much a product of its people as its historic architecture and contrived tourism industry. New Orleans existed not only in the dreams of tourists but in the daily lives of its own people. For every musician who played strains of jazz in Jackson Square or at Jazz Fest, thousands more were each day honing their skills on trumpets or sousaphones in middle and high school bands or on front stoops in neighborhoods whose contributions to jazz were legion. For every chef who experimented with Nouvelle Creole cuisine to the delight of French Quarter diners, how many thousands of lifelong New Orleanians continued to cook traditional Creole food for their families? For every fabled mansion featured on Garden District walking tours, thousands of graceful if careworn architectural gems lined the streets of the *other* New Orleans that tourists rarely saw. The situation of a set of tourist attractions in a city where, as Nossiter mused, "the vine growing out of the wall, and the crack in the ceiling, might be considered ornamental rather than blemishing," always provided something far more powerfully alluring than the atomized attractions of countless other more modernized American cities.

Katrina spared New Orleans's vital French Quarter, all but emptying it of people and commerce. Should the city rebuild in smaller form, it seems likely that the Vieux Carré will face even greater battles over its future. Just as hotel operators, tourism-oriented store owners, developers, street performers, tourism workers, preservationists, and tourists shaped what the French Quarter became, they will in their interactions define what the French Quarter becomes. If events following the hurricane are any indication, one may expect the Vieux Carré and the city itself to undergo many of the same struggles over the definition and disposition of place that they did prior to Katrina's devastation. Tourism is unlikely to render New Orleans nothing more than a ersatz "Creole Disneyland," for residents will continue to contest such a clear-cut outcome. One week after Katrina plowed inland, it was not affluent vacationers and tourism operators who clung to life in the French Quarter, but instead "the working poor, the residents of the cramped space above the restaurants and shops."[8] It is entirely possible that they will form the core of an ongoing Bohemian flavor that has long lent truth to the city's image, but theirs will likely prove an uphill battle.

The conundrum facing New Orleans is not whether tourism will continue to play a major role in the city. Undoubtedly, it will. It is whether the returning New Orleanians will include those who love the city's traditional architecture and whether they will prove as influential in restoring or rebuilding neighborhoods as they did in preserving them before Katrina. It is whether the people, many of them poor and African American and—until recently—invisible, will return in sufficient numbers and with sufficient fond memories of traditional ways to reconstitute the substance behind the façade of New Orleans. And, perhaps more importantly, it is whether New Orleans leaders can create a new tourism industry with more than the empty promises of economic revitalization of years past for a city that decayed even as it lavished attention on its image. It seems likely that New Orleans will again become a "city on parade." One may hope it becomes a place worth not only visiting but calling home.

NOTES

ARC Amistad Research Center, Tulane University, New Orleans
CCC Chamber of Commerce Collection
CORE Congress of Racial Equality
GNOTCC Greater New Orleans Tourist and Convention Commission
HJA William Ransom Hogan Jazz Archive, Tulane University
HRC Human Relations Committee General Office Files
NAACP National Association for the Advancement of Colored People
NOMCVB New Orleans Metropolitan Convention and Visitors Bureau
NOPL New Orleans Public Library
TU Department of Special Collections, Tulane University
UNO Department of Special Collections, University of New Orleans

NOTES TO INTRODUCTION

1. Robert R. Weyeneth, *Historic Preservation for a Living City: Historic Charleston Foundation, 1947–1997* (Columbia: University of South Carolina Press, 2000); Char Miller, "Tourist Trap: Visitors and the Modern San Antonio Economy," in Hal K. Rothman, ed., *The Culture of Tourism, the Tourism of Culture* (Albuquerque: University of New Mexico Press, 2003); Robert Hodder, "Savannah's Changing Past: Historic Preservation Planning and the Social Construction of a Historic Landscape, 1955–1985," in Mary Corbin Sies and Christopher Silver, eds., *Planning the Twentieth-Century American City* (Baltimore: Johns Hopkins University Press, 1996); Don Doyle, *New Men, New Cities, New South: Atlanta, Nashville, Charleston, Mobile, 1860–1910* (Chapel Hill: University of North Carolina Press, 1990).

2. Oakley Hall, *The Manhattaner in New Orleans* (New York, 1857), quoted in Joseph G. Tregle Jr., "Creoles and Americans," in Arnold R. Hirsch and Joseph Logsdon, eds., *Creole New Orleans: Race and Americanization* (Baton Rouge: Louisiana State University Press, 1992), 158.

3. Tregle, "Creoles and Americans," 132; M. Christine Boyer, *The City of Collective Memory: Its Historical Imagery and Architectural Entertainments* (Cambridge: MIT Press, 1994), 323.

4. Nina Silber, *The Romance of Reunion: Northerners and the South, 1865–1900* (Chapel Hill: University of North Carolina Press, 1993), esp. chap. 3, "Sick Yankees in Paradise"; Reid Mitchell, *All on a Mardi Gras Day: Episodes in the History of New Orleans Carnival* (Cambridge: Harvard University Press, 1995), esp. chap. 6, "Northerners."

5. Alecia P. Long, *The Great Southern Babylon: Sex, Race, and Respectability in New Orleans, 1865–1920* (Baton Rouge: Louisiana State University Press, 2004).

6. "Old and New Louisiana," *Scribner's Monthly* 7 (Nov. 1873): 11; "Old and New Louisiana—II," *Scribner's Monthly* 7 (Dec. 1873): 129–60, vertical file "Descriptions: New Orleans, 1860–1979," Louisiana Collection, Department of Special Collections, Tulane University (hereafter TU); Boyer, *City of Collective Memory*, 323.

7. Quoted in Bernard Lemann, *The Vieux Carré—A General Statement* (New Orleans: Tulane University, School of Architecture, 1966), 21; Michael Serino, "In the Italian Quarter," *Primo* (Mar.–Apr. 2002): 35–37; Henri Gandolfo, interview by Dorothy Schlesinger, Oct. 3, 1974, Friends of the Cabildo Oral History Project, transcript, TU; Young Men's Business League, *New Orleans of 1894: Its Conditions, Its Prospects* (New Orleans: L. Graham and Son, 1894), vertical file "Descriptions: New Orleans, 1880–1899," TU; "A White City," *Get Busy* (New Orleans Progressive Union), Sept. 17, 1906, vertical file "Organizations: New Orleans Progressive Union, 'Get Busy,'" TU.

8. Boyer, *The City of Collective Memory*, 325–29.

9. Lemann, *The Vieux Carré*, 26; Jeannette Raffray, "Origins of the Vieux Carré Commission, 1920–1941," *Louisiana History* 40, no. 3 (Summer 1999): 286–87.

10. George Brown Tindall, *The Emergence of the New South, 1913–1945* (Baton Rouge: Louisiana State University Press and the Littleton Fund for Southern History of the University of Texas, 1967), 694.

11. David R. Goldfield, "The City as Southern History: The Past and the Promise of Tomorrow," in Joe P. Dunn and Howard L. Preston, eds., *The Future South: A Historical Perspective for the Twenty-First Century* (Urbana: University of Illinois Press, 1991), 32.

12. Hal K. Rothman, *Neon Metropolis: How Las Vegas Started the Twenty-First Century* (New York: Free Press, 2002); Doyle, *New Men*; Numan V. Bartley, *The New South, 1945–1980* (Baton Rouge: Louisiana State University Press, 1995); Arnold R. Hirsch, "New Orleans: Sunbelt in the Swamp," in Richard M. Bernard and Bradley R. Rice, eds., *Sunbelt Cities: Politics and Growth Since World War II* (Austin: University of Texas Press, 1983).

13. On tourism in the West, see Hal K. Rothman, *Devil's Bargains: Tourism in the Twentieth-Century American West* (Lawrence: University Press of Kansas, 1998); David M. Wrobel and Patrick T. Long, eds., *The Culture of Tourism, the Tourism of Culture; Seeing and Being Seen: Tourism in the American West* (Lawrence: University Press of Kansas, 2001); Leah Dilworth, *Imagining Indians in the Southwest: Persistent Visions of a Primitive Past* (Washington, D.C.: Smithsonian Institution Press, 1996); Phoebe S. Kropp, "'All Our Yesterdays': The Spanish Fantasy Past and the Politics of Public Memory in Southern California, 1884–1939" (Ph.D. diss., University of California, San Diego, 1999); Scott C. Zeman, "Traveling the Southwest: Creation, Imagination, and Invention" (Ph.D. diss., Arizona State University, 1998); and Chris Wilson, *The Myth of Santa Fe: Creating a Modern Regional Tradition* (Albuquerque: University of New Mexico Press, 1997). On tourism in the South, see Richard D. Starnes, ed., *Southern Journeys: Tourism, History, and Culture in the Modern South* (Tuscaloosa: University of Alabama Press, 2003); Jack E. Davis, *Race against Time: Culture and Separation in Natchez since 1930* (Baton Rouge: Louisiana State University Press, 2001). On the rise of urban tourism, see Catherine Cocks, *Doing the Town: The Rise of Urban Tourism in the United States, 1850–1915* (Berkeley: University of California Press, 2001). On Las Vegas, see Eugene P. Moehring, *Resort City in the Sunbelt: Las Vegas, 1930–2000*, 2d ed. (Reno: University of Nevada Press, 2000); and Rothman, *Devil's Bargains*, and *Neon Metropolis*.

14. Jon Sterngass, *First Resorts: Pursuing Pleasure at Coney Island, Newport, and Saratoga Springs* (Baltimore: Johns Hopkins University Press, 2001); Robert W. Rydell, *All the World's a Fair: Visions of*

Empire at American International Expositions, 1876–1916 (Chicago: University of Chicago Press, 1984); Jim Weeks, *Gettysburg: Memory, Market, and an American Shrine* (Princeton: Princeton University Press, 2003); Marguerite S. Shaffer, *See America First: Tourism and National Identity, 1880–1940* (Washington, D.C.: Smithsonian Institution Press, 2001); Patsy West, *The Enduring Seminoles: From Alligator Wrestling to Ecotourism* (Gainesville: University Press of Florida, 2002); Cocks, *Doing the Town*.

15. Scoop Kennedy, *Dining in New Orleans* (New Orleans: Borman House, 1945), 51, 79.

16. Lizabeth Cohen, *A Consumers' Republic: The Politics of Mass Consumption in Postwar America* (New York: Alfred A. Knopf, 2003).

17. Rothman, *Devil's Bargains;* Calvin Trillin, "U.S. Journal: New Orleans: On the Possibility of Houstonization," *New Yorker* 50 (Feb. 17, 1975): 95.

NOTES TO CHAPTER ONE

Epigraph: William A. Emerson Jr., "The *New* New Orleans," *Collier's* 130, no. 22 (Nov. 29, 1952): 42.

1. Virginius Dabney, "What's Happened to Old New Orleans?" *Saturday Evening Post* 226, no. 15 (Oct. 10, 1953): 41. See illustration.

2. Don Doyle, *New Men, New Cities, New South: Atlanta, Nashville, Charleston, Mobile, 1860–1910* (Chapel Hill: University of North Carolina Press, 1990).

3. Edward F. Haas, *DeLesseps S. Morrison and the Image of Reform: New Orleans Politics, 1946–1961* (Baton Rouge: Louisiana State University Press, 1974), 16–17.

4. Ibid., 19, 22–23.

5. Hamilton Basso, "Can New Orleans Come Back?" *Forum* 103, no. 3 (Mar. 1940): 124–27.

6. Eli N. Evans, *The Provincials: A Personal History of Jews in the South* (New York: Free Press, 1997), 200–202; Rabbi Julian B. Feibelman, "The History of the Jewish Community in New Orleans," Speech Commemorating the 250th Anniversary of the Founding of New Orleans, Dixon Hall, Tulane University, Apr. 22, 1968, vertical file "Jews in New Orleans," Louisiana Collection, TU.

7. Arthur E. Carpenter, "Gateway to the Americas: New Orleans's Quest for Latin American Trade, 1900–1970" (Ph.D. diss., Tulane University, 1987), 154–57.

8. John M. Barry, *Rising Tide: The Great Mississippi Flood of 1927 and How It Changed America* (New York: Simon and Schuster, 1997), 219–21. Hereafter I refer to this rather amorphous group using Barry's "power establishment" interchangeably with *bluebloods, old elite, old-line whites, Carnival elite,* and *Carnival establishment.* While such terms run the risk of giving an impression of unbroken class-based solidarity, the reader should not infer that these people were of a piece. Rather, they tended to hold firmly to an ethos that privileged the cultural, social, economic, and at times political preeminence of those prominent Anglo-Saxons with deep family roots in New Orleans.

9. Map in *Eureka News Bulletin* (Higgins Industries) 1, no. 2 (Feb. 1942): 8, folder 65-1, Higgins Industries Collection, Department of Special Collections, UNO.

10. "Journey in America: III," *New Republic* 111 (Nov. 27, 1944): 684; map in *Eureka News Bulletin.*

11. Raymond Moley, "Louisiana Renaissance," *Newsweek* 29, no. 7 (Feb. 17, 1947): 108.

12. Ken Hulsizer, "New Orleans in Wartime," in Max Jones and Albert McCarthy, eds., *Jazz Review* (London: Jazz Music Books, 1945), 3–4.

13. "Journey in America: III," 684.

14. Numan V. Bartley, *The New South, 1945–1980* (Baton Rouge: Louisiana State University Press, 1995).

15. Dabney, "What's Happened," 41; "The Great New Orleans 'Steal,'" *Fortune* 38 (Nov. 1948): 102.

16. "The Great New Orleans 'Steal,'" 102.

17. David Goldfield, *Cotton Fields and Skyscrapers: Southern City and Region, 1607–1980* (Baton Rouge: Louisiana State University Press, 1982); James C. Cobb, *The Selling of the South: The Southern Crusade for Industrial Development, 1936–1990* (Urbana: University of Illinois Press, 1993). See also David Goldfield, "Writing the Sunbelt," *OAH Magazine of History* 18, no. 1 (Oct. 2003): 5–10.

18. "The Great New Orleans 'Steal,'" 102.

19. Dabney, "What's Happened," 122.

20. Carpenter, "Gateway to the Americas," 164–66; Stanley Meisler, "New Orleans: Future Hub of the Americas," *American Mercury* 88, no. 421 (Feb. 1959): 19–20.

21. Meisler, "New Orleans," 19.

22. Haas, *DeLesseps S. Morrison and the Image of Reform*, 51. Although Moses' plan languished for more than a decade, it laid the groundwork for a heated controversy over the proper use of the land along the banks of the Mississippi River as it passed the French Quarter below Canal Street, one which, as I argue in chapter 2, proved crucial to the future of the tourism industry in New Orleans.

23. "Welcome, Chep," *Trade Winds* (May 1, 1946): 2, cited in Carpenter, "Gateway to the Americas," 92.

24. "The Great New Orleans 'Steal,'" 102–3; Carpenter, "Gateway to the Americas," 200; Meisler, "New Orleans," 21.

25. Dabney, "What's Happened," 122.

26. Carpenter, "Gateway to the Americas," 126.

27. Ibid., 139–42, 147–48.

28. Ibid., 106–8, 181; Meisler, "New Orleans," 21.

29. Carpenter, "Gateway to the Americas," 169, 171, 321.

30. Ibid., 312–15, 324–25.

31. "The Great New Orleans 'Steal,'" 103.

32. DeLesseps S. Morrison, Inaugural Address, May 6, 1946, folder 1, box 37, deLesseps S. Morrison Papers, TU.

33. Ethelyn Orso, "Sicilian Immigration into Louisiana," in Carl A. Brasseaux, ed., *A Refuge for All Ages: Immigration in Louisiana History,* Louisiana Purchase Bicentennial Series in Louisiana History, vol. 10 (Lafayette: Center for Louisiana Studies, University of Southwestern Louisiana, 1996), 603–7.

34. William Langkopp, executive vice president, Greater New Orleans Hotel-Motel Association, interview by author, New Orleans, July 5, 2001; John DeMers, *French Quarter Royalty: The Tumultuous Life and Times of the Omni Royal Orleans Hotel* (New Orleans: Omni Royal Orleans Hotel, 1993), 71–72; Minutes, Executive Committee, Chamber of Commerce of New Orleans Area, Nov. 15, 1954, Minutes, Chamber of Commerce, 1954, vol. 2, Chamber of Commerce Collection (hereafter CCC), UNO.

35. *Association of Commerce News Bulletin,* Dec. 26, 1949, TU.

36. See, e.g., deLesseps S. Morrison to C. E. Woolman, President, Delta Airlines, May 20, 1948; Morrison to Samuel Zemurray, President, United Fruit Company, Aug. 11, 1948, folder 1, box 46, Morrison Papers, TU.

37. James N. Harsh to Honorable deLesseps S. Morrison, Mayor, and Honorable Members of the

City Council, Mar. 28, 1956, folder "Hotel, Proposed at Royal & Conti, 1959," box S59-11, deLesseps S. Morrison Papers, New Orleans Public Library (hereafter NOPL).

38. Michael Johns, *Moment of Grace: The American City in the 1950s* (Berkeley: University of California Press, 2002).

39. J. Parham Werlein to Honorable deLesseps S. Morrison, Mayor, and Honorable Members of the City Council, Apr. 4, 1956; Rose Brener to Honorable deLesseps S. Morrison, Mayor, and Honorable Members of the City Council, Apr. 9, 1956; and Sam Friedberg to Honorable deLesseps S. Morrison, Mayor, and Honorable Members of the City Council, Apr. 5, 1956, folder "Hotel, Proposed at Royal & Conti, 1959," box S59-11, Morrison Papers, NOPL.

40. Owen P. Brennan to Honorable deLesseps S. Morrison, Mayor, and Honorable Members of the City Council, Apr. 26, 1956, folder "Hotel, Proposed at Royal & Conti, 1959," box S59-11, Morrison Papers, NOPL.

41. C. C. Cantrell to deLesseps S. Morrison, Apr. 28, 1956, folder "Hotel, Proposed at Royal & Conti, 1959," box S59-11, Morrison Papers, NOPL.

42. Holland-America Line to Morrison, Apr. 20, 1956; Nathan Hale Snider to Morrison, Apr. 23, 1956, folder "Hotel, Proposed at Royal & Conti, 1959," box S59-11, Morrison Papers, NOPL.

43. David R. McGuire Jr., to James Wilkinson III, May 3, 1956, folder "Hotel, Proposed at Royal & Conti, 1959," box S59-11, Morrison Papers, NOPL.

44. Lloyd S. Cobb, President, International House, Address to Young Men's Business Club, May 23, 1951, folder 26, box 37, Morrison Papers, TU.

45. Minutes, Association of Commerce, Dec. 14, 1939, CCC; Minutes, Association of Commerce, Oct. 9, 1940, CCC; Editorial, "Play and Profit," *New Orleans Item*, Feb. 26, 1941; Minutes, Executive Committee, CVB, Association of Commerce, Jan. 18, 1946, CCC; *Association of Commerce News Bulletin*, Feb. 16, 1948, TU.

46. Minutes, Chamber of Commerce, Oct. 4, 1954, CCC; *Social Register, New Orleans* (New York: Social Register Association, 1952), 126.

47. Scott Wilson to Morrison, Mar. 30, 1959, Morrison Correspondence, B4 (Feb. 6, 1959–June 1963), Scott Wilson Papers, TU; Minutes, Chamber of Commerce, Nov. 15, 1954, CCC.

48. Minutes, Chamber of Commerce, Mar. 18, 1959, CCC.

49. Minutes, Chamber of Commerce, Mar. 16, 1959, CCC.

50. Minutes, Chamber of Commerce, Mar. 18, 1959, CCC.

51. Minutes, Chamber of Commerce, Mar. 21, 1960, CCC; New Orleans Tourism Planning Committee Report, Mar. 1960, UNO.

52. "Tourist Group Set Up for N.O.," *New Orleans Times-Picayune*, Apr. 5, 1960; GNOTCC letterhead, folder "Tourist Commission—1961," box S61-13, Victor H. Schiro Papers, NOPL.

53. Harry M. England to Dennis Lacey, Executive Assistant to the Mayor, Dec. 11, 1963, folder "Tourist Commission—1963," box S63-29, Schiro Papers.

54. Editorial: "A $25,000 Joke," *New Orleans States-Item*, Aug. 25, 1969.

55. "City Government Support of Tourist & Convention Bureaus As of September 1967," folder "New Orleans Tourist & Convention Commission—1968," box S68-10, Schiro Papers.

56. *New Orleans, Strategic City of the South: A Pictorial-Statistical Presentation to the National Football League* (New Orleans: David Kleck and Associates; New Orleans Pro Football Club, Inc., 1965). On deindustrialization and the urban crisis, see esp. Thomas J. Sugrue, *The Origins of the Urban Crisis: Race*

and Inequality in Postwar Detroit (Princeton: Princeton University Press, 1996).

57. Peirce F. Lewis, *New Orleans: The Making of an Urban Landscape*, 2d ed. (Santa Fe: Center for American Places, 2003), 71–72; Carpenter, "Gateway to the Americas," 318, 326–37.

58. Sid Moody, AP news article, Apr. 2, 1972, quoted in Bill Rushton, "What the One Big Paper Doesn't Want You to Know about Mardi Gras," *Vieux Carré Courier*, Apr. 23–27, 1972.

NOTES TO CHAPTER TWO

Epigraph: Charles Suhor, "The 'French Quarters,'" *New Orleans* (Feb. 1970): 60; Charles Suhor, "The Unique, Syncopated Non-Jet Set Rhythm of New Orleans," *Gentlemen's Quarterly* [Apr. 1970], vertical file "New Orleans Jazz," Willam Ransom Hogan Jazz Archive (hereafter HJA).

1. Mrs. Jacob H. Morrison, interview by Jacob Geiser III, New Orleans, Aug. 2, 1977, Friends of the Cabildo Oral History Project, tape in NOPL; Joe Bacon, "Preservation: The Morrison Message," *New Orleans* (Aug. 1982): 54–55.

2. *Social Register, New Orleans* (New York: Social Register Association, 1952); Lou Wylie to Hon. Joseph Di Rosa, Councilman-at-Large, July 30, 1970, folder "Steering Committee for the Vieux Carré," box 4, Moon Landrieu Papers, NOPL; James Aswell, "New Orleans Takes the Cure," *Saturday Evening Post* 219 (Jan. 25, 1947): 54.

3. Morrison interview.

4. Jeannette Raffray, "Origins of the Vieux Carré Commission, 1920–1941," *Louisiana History* 40, no. 3 (Summer 1999): 288–89, 291. As Raffray notes, preservationists' effort to create a bulwark against commercial encroachment in the French Quarter predated the 1940s or even the 1930s. In September 1926 the VCC successfully blocked an effort to open a cabaret called the Little Club on Royal Street. Nonetheless, the increasing impact of tourism-oriented establishments came in the war years.

5. Alecia P. Long, *The Great Southern Babylon: Sex, Race, and Respectability in New Orleans, 1865–1920* (Baton Rouge: Louisiana State University Press, 2004).

6. "Quarter Sights & Sounds," *Old French Quarter News*, June 11, 1943, Louisiana Division, NOPL.

7. "Gypsies, Marooned By War, Settle in Quarter, Tell Fortunes as Mates Toil in Shipyards," *Old French Quarter News*, Aug. 20, 1943.

8. "175 Shelby Guests Tour Vieux Carre," *Old French Quarter News*, May 4, 1945.

9. "Army Movie Features N.O.," *Old French Quarter News*, Mar. 30, 1945.

10. "'Voodooism' Once Held Orleanians In Grip," *Old French Quarter News*, Mar. 31, 1944.

11. New Orleans Association of Commerce advertisement, *Arts and Decoration* 55 (Mar. 1942): 37.

12. *New Orleans for the Tourist: The Southern Metropolis* (Illinois Central Passenger Department, 1902–03); *New Orleans: An Outline of the Points of Interest in the City and How to Reach Them* (Passenger Department, Southern Pacific Sunset Route, 1905), vertical File "Descriptions—New Orleans, 1903–1918," Louisiana Collection, TU; Josiah Gross, *Guide to Old French Quarter*, [1905], vertical file, "Neighborhoods—Vieux Carré," Louisiana Collection, TU; "Old Absinthe House is Sold: Famed Spot is Purchased by Brennan," *Old French Quarter News*, Oct. 15, 1943.

13. "Niteries Reel under Tax Punch: Business Shows Drop; Bite on Service Men," *Old French Quarter News*, May 5, 1944.

14. Ken Hulsizer, "New Orleans in Wartime," in Max Jones and Albert McCarthy, eds., *Jazz Review* (London: Jazz Music Books, 1945), 3–4.

15. "Quarter Sights and Sounds," *Old French Quarter News*, Sept. 3, 1943.

16. "Serviceman Praises French Quarter to Popular New York Newspaper 'PM,'" *Old French Quarter News*, Mar. 24, 1944.

17. W. H. Russell, "I Ain't Gonna Study War No More," *Jazz* (Aug. 1942): 22.

18. "Quarter Sights Thrill Visitors: Crowds Flock to Orleans for Holiday," *Old French Quarter News*, Sept. 6, 1946.

19. Morrison interview.

20. Lee Davis, "Vieux Carre Group Asks Strict Laws," *New Orleans Times-Picayune*, Apr. 11, 1950.

21. "Senator Hotel in Quarter to House Seamen," *Old French Quarter News*, May 19, 1944; "Abandon Plans to House Negro Seamen in Area: Proposal is Called Off After Groups Protest," *Old French Quarter News*, June 16, 1944.

22. "French Quarter Group Seeking Ruling on Ban," *Old French Quarter News*, Mar. 9, 1945.

23. Anthony Stanonis, "'A Woman of Boundless Energy': Elizebeth Werlein and Her Times," *Louisiana History* 46, no. 1 (Winter 2005): 6, 8, 15–16; R. L. Polk's *New Orleans City Directory* (Dallas: R. L. Polk, 1945, 1971).

24. Hulsizer, "New Orleans in Wartime," 3.

25. "The Great New Orleans 'Steal,'" *Fortune* 38 (Nov. 1948): 103.

26. Thomas Griffin, "The French Quarter," *Holiday* 15, no. 3 (Mar. 1954): 56; David Cuthbert, "A Smoother Bourbon," *New Orleans Times-Picayune*, May 25, 1996; Rick Delaup, *Eccentric New Orleans*, www.eccentricneworleans.com (accessed Nov. 23, 2001).

27. DeLesseps S. Morrison to Lloyd E. Hoye, May 5, 1948, folder 1, box 46, Morrison Papers, TU; "Ban on Obscene Shows is Passed," *New Orleans Times-Picayune*, Apr. 9, 1949.

28. Flannery Lewis, "'Girlie' Signs on Bar Are Protested," *New Orleans Item*, Aug. 14, 1948; "Night Club Signs Ordered Removed," *New Orleans Times-Picayune*, Dec. 16, 1948.

29. "Tighter Quarter Controls Urged," *New Orleans Times-Picayune*, Jan. 27, 1949.

30. Editorial, "A Resident Complains about the Quarter," *New Orleans States*, Mar. 25, 1950; John Chase editorial cartoons, *New Orleans States*, Mar. 28 and Apr. 5, 1950.

31. Griffin, "The French Quarter," 56; Alex S. Waller Jr., "Joy Still Reigns on Bourbon Street," *Chicago Tribune*, Apr. 24, 1960; L. J. Dumestre to John J. Grosch Sr., New Orleans District Attorney's Office, July 6, 1958, folder "Vieux Carré Property Owners and Associates—1958," box S58-39, Morrison Papers, NOPL.

32. J. Mark Souther, "Making 'America's Most Interesting City': Tourism and the Construction of Cultural Image in New Orleans, 1940–1984," in Richard D. Starnes, ed., *Southern Journeys: Tourism, History, and Culture in the Modern South* (Tuscaloosa: University of Alabama Press, 2003), 121; Christine Wiltz, *The Last Madam: A Life in the New Orleans Underworld* (New York: Faber and Faber, 2000), 147, 149.

33. "Club Owners Criticize DA On Crackdown," *New Orleans States-Item*, Sept. 6, 1962; "Bourbon Street Losing Its Lures," *New York Times*, Sept. 5, 1965; Jason Berry, Jonathan Foose, and Tad Jones, *Up from the Cradle of Jazz: New Orleans Music since World War II* (Athens: University of Georgia Press, 1986); John F. Henahan, "Bourbon St.: Nobody Here but Us Lemmings," *Village Voice*, May 7, 1964; *New Orleans States-Item*, Apr. 20, 1966.

34. Howard Jacobs, "Bourbon Street Held 'Eden of Epidermis,'" *New Orleans Times-Picayune*, Aug. 21, 1973.

35. Gunther Barth, *City People: The Rise of Modern City Culture in Nineteenth-Century America* (New York: Oxford University Press, 1980); Catherine Cocks, *Doing the Town: The Rise of Urban Tourism in the United States, 1850–1915* (Berkeley: University of California Press, 2001).

36. Sarah Deutsch, *Women and the City: Gender, Space, and Power in Boston, 1870–1940* (New York: Oxford University Press, 2000); Long, *Great Southern Babylon;* Stephanie E. Yuhl, *A Golden Haze of Memory: The Making of Historic Charleston* (Chapel Hill: University of North Carolina Press, 2005).

37. Arrest Books, New Orleans Police Department, Third Precinct, 1945, and First District, 1952, 1955, 1960, NOPL. An examination of arrest records for the middle years of the twentieth century reveals that, consistently, men comprised approximately four-fifths of those arrested in the French Quarter, suggesting the prevalence of male-centered spaces in the district.

38. Cuthbert, "A Smoother Bourbon"; Maurice Kowalewski, "Flies in the Bourbon: A Walking Tour of Bourbon Street without the Benefit of Rose Colored Hurricane Glasses," *New Orleans* (Mar. 1973): 74–77, 89–93.

39. "Crash Stirs Vieux Carré; Heavy Traffic, Old Walls Blamed," *New Orleans Item,* Apr. 28, 1948.

40. Lee Davis, "Vieux Carré Group Asks Strict Laws," *New Orleans Times-Picayune,* Apr. 11, 1950.

41. Marjorie Roehl, "Dr. Bernhard Head: Quarter Trucks Face Curb," *New Orleans Item,* Apr. 29, 1948.

42. "History of the Vieux Carré Commission," undated manuscript, folder "Vieux Carré Commission—1958," box S58-7, Schiro Papers.

43. Walter W. Gallas, "Neighborhood Preservation and Politics in New Orleans: Vieux Carré Property Owners, Residents and Associates, Inc. and City Government, 1938–1983" (M.A. thesis, University of New Orleans, 1996), 31.

44. David A. Bensman (Sheboygan, Wis.) to Mayor Morrison, Dec. 6, 1960, folder "Vieux Carré Commission—1960," box S60-33, Morrison Papers, NOPL.

45. Real Estate Research Corporation, *Economic Survey of the Central Area of New Orleans* (New Orleans: Chamber of Commerce of the New Orleans Area, 1959).

46. Mark P. Lowrey, "Our Past and Future," *Vieux Carré Courier,* Nov. 24, 1967.

47. Victor H. Schiro to Harnett T. Kane, President, Louisiana Council for the Vieux Carré, Sept. 21, 1961, folder "Vieux Carré Commission—1961," box S61-14, Schiro Papers.

48. William J. Long to Hon. Victor H. Schiro, Nov. 21, 1962, folder "Vieux Carré Commission—1962," box S62-29, Schiro Papers.

49. Gallas, "Neighborhood Preservation and Politics," 41, 43.

50. Robert R. Weyeneth, *Historic Preservation for a Living City: Historic Charleston Foundation, 1947–1997* (Columbia: University of South Carolina Press, 2000), 80.

51. Jon C. Teaford, "Urban Renewal and Its Aftermath," *Housing Policy Debate* 11, no. 2 (2000): 447.

52. John DeMers, *French Quarter Royalty: The Tumultuous Life and Times of the Omni Royal Orleans Hotel* (New Orleans: Omni Royal Orleans Hotel, 1993), 41, 45, 47–48.

53. Ibid., 49–50.

54. Ibid., 51–52.

55. Gallas, "Neighborhood Preservation and Politics," 47.

56. E. V. Benjamin Jr., Darwin S. Fenner, Richard W. Freeman, William G. Helis Jr., Edgar B. Stern Jr., and Laurence M. Williams to Hon. deLesseps S. Morrison, Jan. 23, 1957, folder "Hotel, Proposed at Royal & Conti, 1959," box S59-11, Morrison Papers, NOPL.

57. Michael Peter Smith and Marlene Keller, "'Managed Growth' and the Politics of Uneven Development in New Orleans," in Susan S. Fainstein, Norman I. Fainstein, Richard Child Hill, Dennis Judd, and Michael P. Smith, *Restructuring the City: The Political Economy of Urban Redevelopment* (New York and London: Longman, 1983), 135; "Ground Broken for $3 Million Quarter Motel," *New Orleans States-Item*, Aug. 1, 1964.

58. Marcel Vaudreuil to Martha G. Robinson, Mar. 6, 1963, folder 3, box 6, Martha Gilmore Robinson Papers, TU.

59. Gallas, "Neighborhood Preservation and Politics," 51, 54.

60. Editorial, "Baffling 'Issue' re[garding] Ballroom," *New Orleans Times-Picayune*, Mar. 24, 1963.

61. Brief biographical manuscript, folder 2, box 1, Robinson Papers; Walda Katz and Faith Fogle, "An Active Woman Citizen," *Pioneer* (Isidore Newman School, New Orleans) (Dec. 1962), 24–26, folder 6, box 1, Robinson Papers.

62. Martha G. Robinson, interview by [unknown], June 11, 1971, folder 10, box 1, Robinson Papers. Robinson's inherited "memory" of the Old South resembles that of Alice Ravenel Huger Smith, a preservation-minded elite Charlestonian, described in Yuhl, *Golden Haze of Memory*, 60–63.

63. "Block Holy Family Sisters Again in Selling Property," *Louisiana Weekly*, Mar. 23, 1963.

64. Mrs. Falvey J. Fox, President, Founders Chapter, Louisiana Colonials, Resolution, Jan. 9, 1963, folder 1, box 6, Robinson Papers.

65. Mrs. John A. Sutherlin, President, Christian Woman's Exchange, to Robinson, Jan. 12, 1963, folder 1, box 6, Robinson Papers.

66. Edith Gilmore Huguley to Victor Schiro, Jan. 23, 1963, folder 1, box 6, Robinson Papers.

67. Robinson to James J. Coleman, Feb. 14, 1963; Robinson to A. Perez Jr., Feb. 14, 1963, folder 2, box 6, Robinson Papers.

68. Editorial, "Preserve Quadroon Ballroom for Whom?" *Louisiana Weekly*, Mar. 23, 1963.

69. Martha Ann Samuel, "What's Ahead for Vieux Carre? Individuals Have Ideas, Predictions for Future," *New Orleans Times-Picayune*, Mar. 31, 1963.

70. Robinson to Major Gen. Edward S. Bres (Washington, D.C.), Mar. 25, 1963, folder 3, box 6, Robinson Papers.

71. Mary M. Morrison to Robinson, June 7, 1963, folder 6, box 6, Robinson Papers.

72. "Rezone Motion Due for Quarter Hotel," *New Orleans States-Item*, Jan. 27, 1966; "Council Okays Rezoning for Quarter Hotel," *New Orleans States-Item*, Apr. 21, 1966.

73. Mrs. J. H. Campbell, "Louisiana Colonials Meet Held in Carroll Buck Home," *Daily Star* (Hammond, La.), Jan. 16, 1964, folder 6, box 1, Robinson Papers.

74. Kathy Bell to Martha G. Robinson, June 23, 1966, folder 19, box 7, Robinson Papers; John R. Howell to Schiro, n.d., folder "VCPOA—1966," box S66-31, Schiro Papers; M. J. Davidson to Clarence O. Dupuy Jr., n.d., folder "Dupuy, Clarence O.—1962," box S62-8, Schiro Papers; Margaret Ayres to New Orleans Chamber of Commerce, [received Mar. 19, 1959], folder "Vieux Carré Commission—1959," box S59-2, Morrison Papers, NOPL.

75. John Lang, "Exotic French Quarter Fights for Its Mere Existence," *Press-Enterprise* (Riverside, Calif.), Apr. 3, 1966, folder "Vieux Carré Commission—1966," box S66-30, Schiro Papers.

76. Bill Rushton, "Cityscape: Disneyland's 'New Orleans Square,'" *Vieux Carré Courier*, Sept. 15–21, 1972; Max Jacobson, "Magical Milestones," *Los Angeles Times*, Feb. 1, 1998; William E. Borah and Richard O. Baumbach Jr., *The Second Battle of New Orleans: A History of the Vieux Carré Riverfront Expressway Controversy* (University: University of Alabama Press, 1981).

77. *Vieux Carré Courier,* Apr. 28, 1967.

78. Larry E. Choppin to Schiro, Aug. 8, 1968, folder "French Quarter Hotel-Motel Association—1968," box 68-5, Schiro Papers.

79. *Vieux Carré Courier,* Jan. 31, 1969.

80. Alexander J. Reichl, "Historic Preservation and Progrowth Politics in U.S. Cities," *Urban Affairs Review* 32, no. 4 (Mar. 1997): 530.

81. Bernard J. Frieden and Lynne B. Sagalyn, *Downtown, Inc.: How America Rebuilds Cities* (Cambridge, Mass.: MIT Press, 1989), 45–46.

82. Michael L. Kurtz, "DeLesseps S. Morrison: Political Reformer," *Louisiana History* 17, no. 1 (Winter 1976): 36.

83. Editorial, "Good Will on the River," *Vieux Carré Courier,* Jan. 27–Feb. 2, 1962.

84. "Background: Secrecy," *Vieux Carré Courier,* Jan. 22, 1965; editorial, "Preparing for Battle," *Vieux Carré Courier,* Mar. 19, 1965; "Tulane Study Replaces Road," *Vieux Carré Courier,* Oct. 29, 1965.

85. Leon Pradel, President, Place Pontalba Committee, to Martha Robinson, Jan. 10, 1956, and W. J. Amoss, Director, New Orleans Dock Board, to Pradel, Apr. 26, 1956, folder 21, box 4, Robinson Papers.

86. "Residents Group Dark on 'Sound and Light,'" *Vieux Carré Courier,* Feb. 5, 1965; "Thousands Sign Petition," *Vieux Carré Courier,* Mar. 5, 1965; Robinson to editor, *New Orleans Times-Picayune,* Aug. 23, 1966, folder 22, box 7, Robinson Papers.

87. "Named Sorted in Road Fight," *Vieux Carré Courier,* Mar. 5, 1965.

88. George W. Healy Jr., to Martha Robinson, Apr. 13, 1966, folder 17; Robinson to William King Self (Memphis, Tenn.), Aug. 31, 1966, folder 22, box 7, Robinson Papers.

89. "Suppressed Column," *Vieux Carré Courier,* Dec. 9, 1966.

90. "Schiro, You've Got Our Vote," *Vieux Carré Courier,* Apr. 2, 1965; Richard Baumbach and William Borah, "The Second Battle of New Orleans," *Vieux Carré Courier,* Mar. 17, 1967.

91. Baumbach and Borah, "Second Battle"; "U.S. to Consider Other Routes," *Vieux Carré Courier,* Apr. 28, 1967.

92. Raymond A. Mohl, "Saving the Vieux Carré: Inside the New Orleans Freeway Revolt," unpublished manuscript, used with author's permission. Mohl argues that Udall was a well-known supporter of national historic sites.

93. Martha Robinson to F. Edward Hebert, U.S. Representative, Jan. 16, 1967; Robinson to Sen. Russell P. Long, Jan. 20, 1967; and Robinson to Claude F. Deemer, President, Elfreth's Alley Association (Philadelphia, Penn.), Jan. 20, 1967, folder 1, box 8, Robinson Papers.

94. "Road Delay Two Years?" *Vieux Carré Courier,* Dec. 9, 1966.

95. Martha Robinson to Mel Leavitt, Program Director, WDSU-TV, Sept. 1, 1966; and Robinson to Mrs. Dallas Read (Chevy Chase, Md.), Sept. 3, 1966, folder 23, box 7, Robinson Papers.

96. Mohl argues that although the preservationist campaign against the riverfront expressway was critical, changes in federal administration must not be overlooked as factors leading to the plan's ultimate demise. He cites the 1966 formation of the new U.S. Department of Transportation, which brought the former Bureau of Public Roads under the control of political appointees who often had other concerns besides highway construction. Mohl notes that the first DOT secretary, Alan S. Boyd, expressed concern over the impact that interstate highways would have in urban areas, while his

successor John A. Volpe parted company with his highway-building colleagues, assuming firm stands against highways that sliced through inner-city neighborhoods and even advocating "multi-modal" transportation systems to lessen the deep impact of automobiles on cities.

97. Martha Robinson to Clarisse Johns (Regent, Monroe, La., Chapter, Colonial Dames of America), July 11, 1966; Robinson to Mrs. Riley (Regent, Alexandria, La., Chapter, Colonial Dames of America), July 11, 1966; Robinson to Mrs. James A. Thom III (President, Baton Rouge Foundation for Historical Louisiana), July 12, 1966; and Josephine Stewart, Oak Alley Plantation (Vacherie, La.) to Robinson, July 12, 1966, folder 20, box 7, Robinson Papers.

98. Bernard Trappey to Gov. John J. McKeithen Jr., July 6, 1966; and A. Wylie McDougall to McKeithen, July 6, 1966, folder 20, box 7, Robinson Papers.

99. Martha Robinson to Mrs. Don F. Tobin (San Antonio, Tex., Conservation Society), Sept. 1, 1966; Robinson to A. G. Keuttner (Atlanta, Ga.), Sept. 1, 1966; Robinson to Kimberly B. Cheney (Chairman, Save the Park Committee, New Haven, Conn.), n.d.; and Robinson to Gerhardt Kramer (President, Landmarks Association of St. Louis, Mo.), Sept. 7, 1966, folder 23, box 7; Margaret R. Ingate (Vice President, Mobile, Ala., Preservation Society) to Robinson, Sept. 28, 1966, folder 24, box 7; Arlo I. Smith (Chairman, Citizens to Preserve Overton Park, Memphis, Tenn.) to Robinson, Nov. 30, 1966, folder 27, box 7; List of Organizations in Various States Sympathetic to Joining a National Committee of Protest Against Improper Routing of Federal Highways, Jan. 1968, folder 10, box 8, Robinson Papers.

100. Robinson to Mrs. Simons Vanderhorst Waring, Aug. 26, 1966, folder 22, box 7, Robinson Papers. It is unknown whether Waring cooperated.

101. Elizabeth La Branche to Louisiana Council for the Vieux Carré, Apr. 3, 1967, folder 4, box 8, Robinson Papers.

102. Mohl, "Saving the Vieux Carré." Borah and Baumbach, *The Second Battle of New Orleans,* as the only book-length treatment of the riverfront expressway controversy, remains an indispensable source, although the authors strangely deemphasize their own very important role in defeating the road.

103. Tom Bethell, "Road Foes Borah and Baumbach: A Tale of Two Citizens," *Vieux Carré Courier,* Mar. 23–29, 1973.

104. "Ready to File Road Suit," *Vieux Carré Courier,* Feb. 3, 1967.

105. "'Ground-level OK: Council Vote is 4 to 3," *Vieux Carré Courier,* Jan. 17, 1969; "Roadway: Reroute or Depress," *Vieux Carré Courier,* Mar. 16, 1969.

106. Harnett Kane, "Another's Opinion," *Vieux Carré Courier,* Apr. 4, 1969; "PR Firm Plugs Expressway: Hired by Chamber for $1,000 Per Month," *Vieux Carré Courier,* May 30, 1969; Bill Bryan, "No Road: Volpe Transfers U.S. Funds to Outer Beltway," *Vieux Carré Courier,* July 4, 1969.

107. Suhor, "The 'French Quarters,'" 54.

108. Mary Morrison to Scott Wilson, Dec. 30, 1964, folder "Vieux Carré Property Owners and Associates—1964," box S64-31, Schiro Papers.

NOTES TO CHAPTER THREE

This chapter appears in earlier form in J. Mark Souther, "Into the Big League: Conventions, Football, and the Color Line in New Orleans," *Journal of Urban History* 29 (Sept. 2003): 694–725.

Epigraph: Victor H. Schiro to Executive Committee, American Chemical Society (Washington, D.C.), Feb. 17, 1965, folder "Conventions—1965," box S65-7, Schiro Papers. Glen Douthit, executive director of the Greater New Orleans Tourist and Convention Commission, wrote this letter for Schiro to send under his own name.

1. "Protest By Negro Gridders Cancels N.O. All-Star Game," *New Orleans Times-Picayune*, Jan. 11, 1965.

2. Ibid.

3. Lizabeth Cohen, *A Consumers' Republic: The Politics of Mass Consumption in Postwar America* (New York: Alfred A. Knopf, 2003), 186–87, 190.

4. On the civil rights struggle in New Orleans, see esp. Adam Fairclough, *Race and Democracy: The Civil Rights Struggle in Louisiana, 1915–1972* (Athens: University of Georgia Press, 1995); Arnold R. Hirsch, "Simply a Matter of Black and White: The Transformation of Race and Politics in Twentieth-Century New Orleans," in Arnold R. Hirsch and Joseph Logsdon, eds., *Creole New Orleans: Race and Americanization* (Baton Rouge: Louisiana State University Press, 1992), 262–319.

5. Edward F. Haas, "The Southern Metropolis, 1940–1976," in Blaine A. Brownell and David R. Goldfield, eds., *The City in Southern History: The Growth of Urban Civilization in the South* (Port Washington, N.Y.: Kennikat Press, 1977), 168–72. Haas points the way for my treatment of tourism and civil rights in observing that New Orleans's tourist trade suffered from the negative publicity surrounding the city's inability to adopt swiftly a moderate plan for desegregation.

6. On black migration to southern cities, see Numan V. Bartley, *The New South, 1945–1980* (Baton Rouge: Louisiana State University Press, 1995), 8–14.

7. DeLesseps S. Morrison to Bernadine Cline (Jamestown, N.D.), Dec. 28, 1948, folder 13, box 3, deLesseps S. Morrison Papers, TU.

8. Danny Barker, *A Life in Jazz*, ed. Alyn Shipton (London: Oxford University Press, 1986), 71, quoted in Helen A. Regis, "'Keeping Jazz Funerals Alive': Blackness and the Politics of Memory in New Orleans," in Celeste Ray, ed., *Southern Heritage on Display: Public Ritual and Ethnic Diversity within Southern Regionalism* (Tuscaloosa: University of Alabama Press, 2003), 46. In contrast to the leading white hotels, each of which had an average of about five hundred guest rooms, the largest black hostelry in the mid-1950s had only fifty units. See *Crescent City Sepia Host Buyers and Tourist Guide to New Orleans*, 1956–57, Louisiana Division, NOPL.

9. *Crescent City Sepia Host.*

10. Edward F. Haas, *DeLesseps S. Morrison and the Image of Reform: New Orleans Politics, 1946–1961* (Baton Rouge: Louisiana State University Press, 1974), 250–51; Arthur E. Carpenter, "Gateway to the Americas: New Orleans's Quest for Latin American Trade, 1900–1970" (Ph.D. diss., Tulane University, 1987), 202; Glen Douthit, Mayor's Office Public Relations Director, to Morrison, May 27, 1954, folder "Mayoralty—Reading File, May 27, 1954," box 52, Morrison Papers, TU; Douthit to Morrison, Sept. 8, 1954, folder "Mayoralty—Reading File, September 8, 1954," box 53, Morrison Papers, TU.

11. Numan V. Bartley, *The Rise of Massive Resistance: Race and Politics in the South during the 1950s* (Baton Rouge: Louisiana State University Press, 1999).

12. "Measures Added to Constitution: 23 New Amendments Are Now Official," *New Orleans Times-Picayune*, Dec. 11, 1954; "Senate Passes Louisiana Bill on Segregation," *Daily Oklahoman* (Oklahoma City), July 6, 1956, *Facts on Film*, 1954–58, J14, 3985, Amistad Research Center (hereafter ARC).

13. Vernon Winslow, interview notes by Jane D. Julian, Apr. 13, 1972, vertical file "Racism and Jazz," HJA.

14. "Tavern Owners File Test Suit," *Pittsburgh Courier*, Feb. 22, 1964, *Facts on Film*, 1963–64, J4, 335, ARC.

15. Tad Jones, "'Separate but Equal': The Laws of Segregation and Their Effect on New Orleans Black Musicians, 1950–1964," *Living Blues Magazine* (Dec. 1987): 27.

16. "Why Louis Armstrong Can't Go Home Again: 'Unconstitutional' La. Law Nixes Satchmo's Mixed Band," *Jet* (Nov. 26, 1959): 57–58, vertical file "Racism and Jazz," HJA.

17. "Georgia Regents Back Bowl Game," *Nashville Tennessean*, Dec. 6, 1955, folder "Multimedia Newspaper Clippings, 1955," Preston and Bonita Valien Collection (in process), ARC.

18. "Bowl Group Urges 'Serious Consideration' of Race Bar," *New Orleans Times-Picayune*, July 14, 1956.

19. Minutes of Meeting, Executive Committee, Chamber of Commerce of the New Orleans Area, July 16, 1956, Minutes, Chamber of Commerce, 1956, vol. 2, CCC.

20. Quoted in Elizabeth Jacoway and David R. Colburn, eds., *Southern Businessmen and Desegregation* (Baton Rouge: Louisiana State University Press, 1982), 9. For more on the city's old elite, see Phyllis Hutton Raabe, "Status and Its Impact: New Orleans' Carnival, the Social Upper Class and Upper-Class Power" (Ph.D. diss., Pennsylvania State University, 1973); Rosary Hartel O'Brien, "The New Orleans Carnival Organizations: Theatre of Prestige" (Ph.D. diss., University of California, Los Angeles, 1973); Charles Y. W. Chai, "Who Rules New Orleans: A Study of Community Power Structure," *Louisiana Business Survey* 16, no. 5 (Oct. 1971): 2–11.

21. Bartley, *The Rise of Massive Resistance*, 313.

22. For more on the Citizens' Council movement, see Neil R. McMillen, *The Citizens' Council: Organized Resistance to the Second Reconstruction, 1954–64* (Urbana: University of Illinois Press, 1971), 64–72, 231–34, 286–97.

23. Kent B. Germany, "Making a New Louisiana: American Liberalism and the Search for the Great Society in New Orleans, 1964–1974" (Ph.D. diss., Tulane University, 2000), 63, 74. Economic concerns brought white moderates into the debate over civil rights at varying rates in different southern cities. On Atlanta, see Harvey K. Newman, *Southern Hospitality: Tourism and the Growth of Atlanta* (Tuscaloosa: University of Alabama Press, 1999), chap. 6; and David Andrew Harmon, *Beneath the Image of the Civil Rights Movement and Race Relations: Atlanta, Georgia, 1946–1981* (New York: Garland, 1996), chap. 4. On Dallas, see Dulaney, "Whatever Happened in Dallas?" 78–85. On Houston, see Thomas R. Cole, *No Color Is My Kind: The Life of Eldrewey Stearns and the Integration of Houston* (Austin: University of Texas Press, 1997), chap. 3. On Birmingham, see Bartley, *The New South*, 332.

24. Liva Baker, *The Second Battle of New Orleans: The Hundred-Year Struggle to Integrate the Schools* (New York: HarperCollins, 1996), 398–400.

25. Ibid., 336, 339.

26. Ibid., 414–16; McMillen, *The Citizens' Council*, 65–66. On Thanksgiving Day, Perez announced he would open the St. Bernard Parish public schools to "displaced" white children. By January 1961 about 60 percent of the students in the two affected Orleans Parish schools had accepted the offer, and another 10 percent made other arrangements.

27. Baker, *Second Battle*, 416, 434; Statement by Glen Douthit, Executive Director, Greater New

Orleans Tourist and Convention Commission, Dec. 21, 1960, folder "Tourist Commission—1960," box SPR60-10, Morrison Papers, NOPL.

28. Baker, *Second Battle*, 410.

29. Morrison to Claude Sitton, Dec. 2, 1960, folder "Integration School Crisis (6)," box SPR60-3, Morrison Papers, NOPL.

30. William J. P. McVay, M.D. (St. Louis, Mo.), to Morrison, Dec. 8, 1960, folder "Integration School Crisis (6)," box SPR60-3, Morrison Papers, NOPL.

31. See folders "Integration—1960 (1–2)," box SPR60-2, and "Integration School Crisis—1960 (4–8)," box SPR60-3, Morrison Papers, NOPL, esp. John Eggleston (Omaha, Neb.) to Morrison, Nov. 29, 1960, folder "Integration School Crisis (5)," and Jack Howard (Silver Spring, Md.) to Morrison, Jan. 3, 1961, folder "Integration School Crisis (8)."

32. See esp. Robert B. Tufts (Hastings-on-Hudson, N.Y.) to Morrison, Nov. 28, 1960, folder "Integration—1960 (1)," box SPR60-2, Morrison Papers, NOPL.

33. For example, Morrison to Robert B. Tufts, Dec. 12, 1960, folder "Integration—1960 (2)," box SPR60-2, Morrison Papers, NOPL.

34. Baker, *Second Battle*, 434.

35. Albert P. Blancher, General Manager, Bayou Tours, Inc., to James A. Noe Jr., General Manager, WNOE, n.d. [Dec. 1960?], folder "Integration School Crisis (8)," box SPR60-3, Morrison Papers, NOPL.

36. Morrison, letter to the editor, *New York Herald Tribune*, Feb. 1, 1961, folder "Integration School Crisis (8)," box SPR60-3, Morrison Papers, NOPL.

37. E. Lysle Aschaffenburg, President and Managing Director, Pontchartrain Hotel, to Victor H. Schiro, Aug. 31, 1961, folder "Integration—1961," box S61-5, Schiro Papers.

38. George W. Healy Jr. to James J. Coleman, Feb. 13, 1963, Minutes, Chamber of Commerce, 1963, vol. 1, CCC.

39. Statement of James J. Coleman, Feb. 14, 1963, Minutes, Chamber of Commerce, 1963, vol. 1, CCC.

40. Minutes of Meeting, Executive Committee, Chamber of Commerce of the New Orleans Area, Jan. 16, 1963, Minutes, Chamber of Commerce, 1963, vol. 1, CCC.

41. Minutes of Meeting, Executive Committee, Chamber of Commerce of the New Orleans Area, Feb. 18, 1963, Minutes, Chamber of Commerce, 1963, vol. 1, CCC; John B. Furey to Hugh Downs, Feb. 25, 1963, folder "Correspondence, February 7–28, 1963," box 73, NAACP (New Orleans Branch) Collection (hereafter NAACP Papers), UNO.

42. "First Organized Lunch Sit-in Staged in N.O.," *New Orleans States-Item*, Sept. 9, 1960; "Seven in Sit-in Here Arrested: Group Disrupts Business Nearly Five Hours," *New Orleans Times-Picayune*, Sept. 10, 1960; "Pickets Defy Sit-in Arrests," *New York Daily News*, Sept. 11, 1960, Series V, no. 44, Papers of the Congress of Racial Equality (hereafter CORE Papers), ARC.

43. CORE Subcommittee on Priorities, Summary of Activities, New Orleans, 1961, CORE Papers; Oretha Castle, Chairman, New Orleans CORE, to [recipient unknown], Dec. 28, 1961, folder "Correspondence—December 8–29, 1961," box 72, NAACP Papers; Joyce Bernadette Taylor, Ruthie Wells, George Raymond Jr., open letters, Jan. 7, 1962, folder "Correspondence—January 1–29, 1962," box 72, NAACP Papers.

44. "Citizens Council Lashes Report, Vows Fight against Any Lunch Counter Mixing," *New Orleans Times-Picayune*, June 26, 1962.

45. George L. Singelmann, Citizens' Council of Greater New Orleans, to New Orleans Branch NAACP, Apr. 17, 1962, folder "Correspondence—April 13–30, 1962," box 73, NAACP Papers; McMillen, *The Citizens' Council,* 66–67, 230–31. McMillen suggests that, although its claims of having more than fifty thousand members seem exaggerated, the Council in New Orleans was a formidable voice that, in the absence of vocal moderate leadership, exerted influence beyond its numbers.

46. Editorial, WDSU-TV, Apr. 24, 1962, transcript, folder "Correspondence—April 13–30, 1962," box 73, NAACP Papers.

47. "Citizens Councils Hit Any Plans for Restaurant Mixing," *Baton Rouge State Times,* June 27, 1962, *Facts on Film,* 1961–62, J5, 1741, ARC.

48. Minutes of Meeting, Executive Committee, Chamber of Commerce of the New Orleans Area, June 20, 1961, Minutes, Chamber of Commerce, 1961, vol. 2, CCC.

49. Castle to [City Hall?], June 11, 1963, folder "Correspondence—June 1–11, 1963," box 74, NAACP Papers. Unlike other southern cities, in the antebellum period New Orleans had a large, distinguished community of free people of color, one with rich ties to Roman Catholicism and the city's affluent Seventh Ward and bonds of kinship in the white and black communities. This "Afro-Creole" legacy continued to manifest itself socially, culturally, and politically throughout the twentieth century. On the role of Afro-Creoles in the New Orleans civil rights movement, see Arnold R. Hirsch, "Simply a Matter of Black and White: The Transformation of Race and Politics in Twentieth-Century New Orleans," in Arnold R. Hirsch and Joseph Logsdon, eds., *Creole New Orleans: Race and Americaniza-tion* (Baton Rouge: Louisiana State University Press, 1992). For background on earlier Afro-Creole leadership, see esp. Caryn Cossé Bell, *Revolution, Romanticism, and the Afro-Creole Protest Tradition in Louisiana, 1718–1868* (Baton Rouge: Louisiana State University Press, 1997).

50. Raphael Cassimere Jr., President, New Orleans Branch NAACP Youth Council, to Roy Wilkins, Executive Secretary, NAACP, Nov. 7, 1962, folder "Correspondence—November 1–15, 1962," box 73, NAACP Papers; "Lunch Counters in N.O. Stores Desegregated," *Baton Rouge State Times,* Sept. 12, 1962, and Hedrick Smith, "New Orleans Surprised as Stores Integrate," *New York Times,* Sept. 13, 1962, *Facts on Film,* 1962–63, J8, 2600, ARC.

51. Minutes of Meeting, Executive Committee, Chamber of Commerce of the New Orleans Area, Mar. 16, 1959, Minutes, Chamber of Commerce, 1959, vol. 1, CCC; "N.O. Held Losing on Conventions: State Segregation Law Effect Cited by Weiss," *New Orleans Times-Picayune,* Jan. 31, 1962.

52. Thomas G. Smith, "Outside the Pale: The Exclusion of Blacks from the National Football League, 1934–1946," *Journal of Sport History* 15, no. 3 (Winter 1988): 255–81.

53. Cole, *No Color Is My Kind,* 76–79.

54. Ray A. Liuzza, interview by author, New Orleans, June 20, 2001.

55. Scott Wilson to Morrison, Mar. 30, 1959, Morrison Correspondence, B4 (Feb. 6, 1959–June 1963), Scott Wilson Papers.

56. Allan Katz, "How Football Saved a City," *New Orleans* (Jan. 1990): 85.

57. David F. Dixon, telephone interview by author, Jan. 11, 2001; Katz, "How Football Saved a City," 85.

58. Dixon interview; Katz, "How Football Saved a City," 85–86. Although the Tulane board of administrators agreed to integrate the stadium for the NFL exhibition game, all other football games, including the Sugar Bowl, remained segregated for one more season.

59. Dr. Leonard L. Burns, telephone interview by author, June 14, 2001; Burns, interview by Kim Lacy Rogers, May 14, 1979, Oral History Project, ARC.

60. Dr. Raphael Cassimere Jr., interview by author, New Orleans, June 11, 2001.

61. "Daisy Bates Sues Louisiana Hotels," *Baltimore Afro-American*, Nov. 10, 1962, and "Suit Seeks to Integrate La. Hotels," *Baton Rouge State Times*, Dec. 8, 1962, Facts on Film, 1962–63, J8, 2428, ARC.

62. *McCain v. Davis*, 217 F. Supp. 661 (1963 U.S. Dist.); "Hotel Segregation Law Held Invalid: Action May End Long-Standing Custom," *New Orleans Times-Picayune*, May 19, 1963.

63. "Legion Stands Pat on N.O. Site: Threatened Transfer of Convention Averted," *New Orleans Times-Picayune*, May 2, 1963.

64. Arthur J. Chapital Sr., Chairman, Legal Redress Committee, New Orleans Branch, NAACP, to Bernard J. Bagert, Chairman, American Legion Host Committee, Apr. 19, 1963, folder "Correspondence—April 15–30, 1963," box 74, NAACP Papers.

65. Minutes of Meeting, Executive Committee, Chamber of Commerce of the New Orleans Area, Apr. 23, 1963, Minutes, Chamber of Commerce, 1963, vol. 1, CCC.

66. "N.O. Gathering of Legion Off: Lack of Desegregated Housing is Reason," *New Orleans Times-Picayune*, May 21, 1963.

67. Castle to [City Hall?], June 11, 1963, folder "Correspondence—June 1–11, 1963," box 74, NAACP Papers.

68. Ernest N. Morial to Lolis E. Elie, Chairman, Citizens Committee of Greater New Orleans, Sept. 4, 1963, folder "Correspondence—September 1–14, 1963," box 74, NAACP Papers. Remarkably, Mayor Schiro remained largely unmoved in his support of segregation despite clear signs that federal mandates and local activism would soon make his position untenable. In the summer of 1963, Dutch Morial warned Schiro that blacks would not tolerate the "spoon feeding" of their rights much longer. Schiro refused Morial's call for a biracial committee on human rights, which might have helped city hall at least symbolically bridge the divide between the races, and also reneged on an earlier promise to integrate the city's swimming pools, closing them instead. (See Hirsch, "Simply a Matter of Black and White," 287–88.) Civil rights leader Nils R. Douglas recalled, "As it turned out, all we received [from Schiro] were empty promises." Perhaps worst of all, the city administration stood by as the black Rev. Avery C. Alexander was brutally dragged by his heels up a flight of stairs in City Hall after being denied service in the basement cafeteria. (See Nils R. Douglas, [untitled manuscript], n.d., box 1, Nils R. Douglas Collection, ARC.

69. "Four Orleans Hotels Accept Negro Guests," *Baton Rouge State Times*, Sept. 10, 1963, *Facts on Film*, 1963–64, J3, 160, ARC.

70. "U.S. Officers Told to Shun Meeting: Pentagon Acts as Hotel in New Orleans Bars Negro," *New York Times*, Apr. 28, 1964, Facts on Film, 1963–64, J3, 159, ARC; Edward J. Cocke, "CORE Requests Officials Skip N.O. Meeting," *Baton Rouge State Times*, May 12, 1964, Facts on Film, 1963–64, J3, 159, ARC; Paul Atkinson, "Trade Group to Move Last Two Sessions," *New Orleans Times-Picayune*, May 13, 1964.

71. "Negroes Served in La. Cafeterias," *New Orleans States-Item*, July 4, 1964.

72. William Murphy, "Bourbon Street Apparently Unchanged by 'Rights' Act," *Meridian Star*, July 14, 1964, Facts on Film, 1964–65, J2, 227, ARC. This article originated with the UPI wire service. Like many other AP and UPI stories on efforts to assure equal access to public accommodations, this news failed to appear in the leading New Orleans dailies.

73. Raphael Cassimere Jr., President, New Orleans Youth Council, NAACP, to Herbert Hill, Labor Director, NAACP, New York, July 26, 1965, folder "Youth Council Correspondence—July 1965," box

301–7, NAACP Papers; Cassimere to Lee's Hamburger, June 15, 1965, folder "Youth Council Correspondence—January–June, 1965," box 301-7, NAACP Papers.

74. "CORE Test Team Closes Schwegmann Cafeteria," *Louisiana Weekly*, July 25, 1964; "Sue Schwegmann Bros.," *Louisiana Weekly*, Aug. 8, 1964; Advertisement: "Now is the Time for All White Persons to Come to the Aid of Schwegmann Bros. Giant Super Markets," *New Orleans States-Item*, Aug. 14, 1964. The grocery tycoon finally caved under the weight of lawsuits and promised to integrate his cafeterias and hire African Americans for more than the most menial jobs.

75. David F. Dixon to Joseph W. Simon Jr., Jan. 19, 196[5], folder "Football Club, Inc.—1966," box S66-8, Schiro Papers. (This letter was misdated 1966 and thus appears in the 1966 folder.)

76. Statement of Mayor Victor H. Schiro, Jan. 11, 1965, folder "Race Relations (1)," box SPR-32, Public Relations Office, Schiro Papers.

77. Schiro to F. Winter Trapolin, Jan. 21, 1965, folder "Race Relations (1)," box SPR-32, Public Relations Office, Schiro Papers. Schiro's lack of public courage, even in the wake of federal civil rights protections, seriously undermined compliance in New Orleans.

78. Hap Glaudi sports editorial transcript, Jan. 11, 1965, WWL-TV, Channel 4, folder "All Star Game—1965," box S65-1, Schiro Papers.

79. Mayor Hartsfield coined the slogan "The City Too Busy To Hate" to promote Atlanta in the midst of the growing civil rights struggle.

80. Girard T. Bryant to Schiro, Jan. 12, 1965, folder "Race Relations (1)," box SPR-32, Public Relations Office, Schiro Papers.

81. "Dr. E. E. Fields Reports on Racial Progress in Miami and New Orleans," *The Call* (Kansas City, Mo.), Jan. 29, 1965, folder "Race Relations (1)," box SPR-32, Public Relations Office, Schiro Papers.

82. Ernest W. Bostick to Schiro, received Jan. 18, 1965, folder "All Star Game—1965," box S65-1, Schiro Papers. See also Mark S. Shapiro (Chicago) to Schiro, Jan. 11, 1965, folder "Race Relations (1)," box SPR-32, Public Relations Office, Schiro Papers.

83. Schiro to Executive Committee, American Chemical Society (Washington, D.C.), Feb. 17, 1965, folder "Conventions—1965," box S65-7, Schiro Papers.

84. Victor O. Jones, "Mr. Dixon's Imagination Probably Correct, and That's Okay," *Boston Globe*, Jan. 18, 1965, folder "Race Relations (1)," box SPR-32, Schiro Papers.

85. Lloyd Angeron (Morgan City, La.) to Schiro, n.d. [Jan. 1965], and Luther L. Elfer (New Orleans) to Schiro, Jan. 11, 1965, folder "All Star Game—1965," box S65-1, Schiro Papers.

86. Chester A. Gauslin to Schiro, Jan. 12, 1965, folder "All Star Game—1965," box S65-1, Schiro Papers.

87. H. to Schiro, Jan. 29, 1965, folder "Integration—1965," box S65-13, Schiro Papers. Although the return address on the attached envelope reads 824 Canal Street, the address of the old-guard Boston Club, the writer's failure to sign his full name makes it impossible to ascertain whether he was, in fact, a member of that organization.

88. Jackson G. Ricau to Schiro, Aug. 4, 1965, folder "Integration—1965," box S65-13, Schiro Papers. While it seems unlikely that white voters remained oblivious to the realities of the racial situation by 1965, the persistence of vacillation among city leaders when confronted with these new realities, I argue, prevented a more concerted effort to promote integration and safeguard a lucrative tourist image.

89. Paul Coates, "Southern Hospitality's Wonderful—Then You Drop over the Cliff," *Los Angeles Times*, Jan. 22, 1965, folder "Race Relations (1)," box SPR-32, Public Relations Office, Schiro Papers.

90. Martha L. Barkoff to Schiro, Jan. 13, 1965, folder "Race Relations (1)," box SPR-32, Public Relations Office, Schiro Papers. Situated along South Claiborne Avenue, approximately midway between the Central Business District and the University Section, Broadmoor is a predominantly middle- to upper-middle-class white neighborhood with a significant Jewish population.

91. Willis Stoesz to Schiro, Jan. 11, 1965, folder "All Star Game–1965," box S65-1, Schiro Papers.

92. Katz, "How Football Saved a City," 86. The New Orleans Pro Football Club, however, took no chances, commissioning public relations consultant David Kleck to produce a glossy book that touted New Orleans's many signs of economic and social progress. In reference to the role of the city's NASA facility in producing rockets for the lunar mission, the book optimistically dubbed New Orleans the "Heart of the Space Crescent." On the opening page appeared a statement from a leading black leader which extolled the city's racial progress, clearly in an effort to convince the NFL that New Orleans had turned the corner in its racial struggle. See *New Orleans, Strategic City of the South: A Pictorial-Statistical Presentation to the National Football League* (New Orleans: David Kleck and Associates; New Orleans Pro Football Club, Inc., 1965).

93. Nils R. Douglas, "AFL Incident Shows City's Lack," *Clarion Herald* (New Orleans), Feb. 4, 1965, in box 1, Douglas Collection.

94. Statement by Rev. John Baringer to New Orleans City Council, Jan. 14, 1965, folder "Race Relations—1965," box 10, John J. Petre Records, NOPL.

95. Trapolin to Schiro, Sept. 6, 1963, and Jan. 12, 1965, folder "Race Relations (1)," box SPR-32, Public Relations Office, Schiro Papers.

96. "3 File Charge Against Vieux Carre Eatery," *Louisiana Weekly*, Jan. 30, 1965; John E. Rousseau, "NAACP Youth Council Officers to Fight Jazz Corner 'Trespass' Rap," *Louisiana Weekly*, Jan. 30, 1965.

97. Edward D. Shanklin Sr., Field Representative, AFL-CIO, to Hubert H. Humphrey, Vice President of the United States, Nov. 23, 1965, folder "Integration—1965," box S65-13, Schiro Papers.

98. Seymour Weiss to Schiro, Feb. 15, 1965, folder "The Roosevelt—1965," box S65-25, Schiro Papers.

99. A. W. Dent, President, Dillard University, to Glen Douthit, June 14, 1965, folder "New Orleans Tourist and Convention Commission—1965," box S65-20, Schiro Papers.

100. My statement in this chapter is supported by numerous letters in the folder "Complaints: Discrimination," box 57, NAACP Papers.

101. Walter M. Goodwin, Complaint to New Orleans Branch NAACP, June 27, 1967, and Mervin Williams, Complaint to New Orleans Branch NAACP, Aug. 9, 1967, folder "Complaints: Discrimination, May–August 1967," box 57, NAACP Papers; Human Relations Committee pamphlet [untitled], folder "Public Accommodations Ordinance," box 3, Human Relations Committee General Office Files (hereafter HRC), NOPL.

102. Zinetta A. Burney, Complaint to New Orleans Branch NAACP, Oct. 24, 1967, folder "Complaints: Discrimination, September–December 1967," box 58, NAACP Papers.

103. Patrick E. Sinclair, Complaint to New Orleans Branch NAACP, Apr. 17, 1968, folder "Complaints: Discrimination, April 15–30, 1968," box 58, NAACP Papers; Samuel White, Complaint to New Orleans Branch NAACP, July 8, 1968, folder "Complaints: Discrimination, June–July 1968," box 58, NAACP Papers; Lawrence Ellis Jr., Complaint to Human Relations Committee, July 28, 1969, folder "Complaints—Public Accommodations," box 1, HRC.

104. "Visitors Complain about Service," *Louisiana Weekly*, Aug. 2, 1969; Marcus Neustadter Jr., Local Convention Chairman, Frontiers International, to Human Relations Committee, July 30, 1969, folder "Human Relations—1969," box S69-5, Schiro Papers.

105. Resolution, 1969 Head Start and Child Development Conference, [1969], folder "Complaints—Public Accommodations," box 1, HRC; "Convention Puts Heat On for Equal Accommodations," *Louisiana Weekly*, Nov. 29, 1969.

106. Wallace L. Young Jr., President, New Orleans Branch NAACP, to Dr. Kenneth O. Johnson, Executive Secretary, American Speech and Hearing Association, Washington, D.C., Oct. 20, 1969, and Joseph W. Simon Jr. to Johnson, Oct. 29, 1969, folder 13, box 395, CCC.

107. "AFT Confab Pickets Biased Bar Near Convention Site," *Louisiana Weekly*, Aug. 30, 1969; "AFT Files Million $ Suit Against 2 Downtown Bars," *Louisiana Weekly*, Sept. 27, 1969.

108. Anthony Gagliano, President, New Orleans Coalition, to James A. Nassikas, President, Greater New Orleans Hotel and Motel Association, Nov. 4, 1969, folder "Public Accommodations (Correspondence)," box 3; Herman J. Penn, Manager, the Rivergate, letter to the editor, *Progress* (HRC Monthly Report), Dec. 1969, folder "Progress—1969–1970," box 3; HRC pamphlet, folder "Public Accommodations Ordinance," box 3, HRC.

109. Charlie Wicks, Chase Bag Co., to Joseph W. Simon Jr., June 17, 1969, folder 16, box 47, CCC; Charles Keller Jr. to Schiro, Dec. 4, 1969, folder "Correspondence—December 1–8, 1969," box 93, NAACP Papers.

110. John A. Pecoul Jr., Executive Director, HRC, Memo, Nov. 6, 1969, folder "Complaints—Public Accommodations," box 1, HRC.

111. Landrieu had been the lone dissenting voice against maintaining school segregation as a freshman state representative in the Louisiana legislature in 1960–61. As a city councilman (1965–69), Landrieu pushed through the ordinance that created the Human Relations Committee and succeeded in removing the Confederate flag from city council chambers (Hirsch, "Simply a Matter of Black and White," 293).

112. Hirsch, "Simply a Matter of Black and White," 288–90.

113. Randolph G. Dodd to Schiro, Dec. 19, 1969, folder "Complaints—1969," box S69-3, Schiro Papers.

114. HRC Memorandum to Groups and Individuals Supporting the Public Accommodations Ordinance, Dec. 17, 1969, folder "Complaints—Public Accommodations," box 1, HRC.

115. Charles L. deLay, Secretary, Studs Club, to Schiro, Dec. 23, 1969, folder "Complaints—1969," box S69-3, Schiro Papers; Allan Katz, "Full Access Law Pushed by Civic, Tourist Leaders," *New Orleans States-Item*, Dec. 19, 1969.

116. Quoted in "Free Access Law," *Progress* (Jan.–Feb. 1970), folder "Progress—1969–1970," box 3, HRC.

NOTES TO CHAPTER FOUR

Portions of this chapter appear in earlier form in J. Mark Souther, "Making the 'Birthplace of Jazz': Tourism and Musical Heritage Marketing in New Orleans," *Louisiana History* 44, no. 1 (Winter 2003): 39–73; and Souther, "Making 'America's Most Interesting City': Tourism and the Construction of Cultural Image in New Orleans, 1940–1984," in Richard D. Starnes, ed., *Southern Journeys: Tourism, History, and Culture in the Modern South* (Tuscaloosa: University of Alabama Press, 2003), 114–37.

Epigraphs: Ken Hulsizer, "New Orleans in Wartime," *Jazz Review* (London: Jazz Music Books, 1945), 6; Paula Crouch, "New Orleans: Where Jazz Is King," *Atlanta Journal and Constitution Magazine*, Mar. 12, 1978.

1. Sterling A. Brown, "Farewell to Basin Street," *Record Changer* (Fairfax, Va.) (Dec. 1944), 7–9, 51, vertical file "World War II and Jazz," HJA.

2. Social scientists and historians alike have tended to malign tourism as a damaging agent. See, e.g., V. L. Smith, ed., *Hosts and Guests: The Anthropology of Tourism* (Philadelphia: University of Pennsylvania Press, 1977); Hal K. Rothman, *Devil's Bargains: Tourism in the Twentieth-Century American West* (Lawrence: University Press of Kansas, 1998).

3. Art Anderson, cover notes, *Paul Barbarin's Bourbon Street Beat*, Southland LP 237, Phonograph Collection, HJA; Owen P. White, "Meet and Drink," *Collier's* 84, no. 7 (Aug. 17, 1929): 8–9; Ronald L. Morris, *Wait until Dark: Jazz and the Underworld, 1880–1940* (Bowling Green, Ohio: Bowling Green University Popular Press, 1980), 101.

4. John S. Wilson, "A Real New Orleans Sound: The Story of Preservation Hall and Its Ancient Jazzmen," *High Fidelity* 13 (Sept. 1963): 59–60.

5. Charles Edward Smith, "Land of Dreams," in Frederick Ramsey Jr. and Charles Edward Smith, eds., *Jazzmen* (London: Sidgwick and Jackson, 1957), 268; Allan P. Merriam and Raymond W. Mack, "The Jazz Community," *Social Forces* 38 (Mar. 1960): 213; Bruce Boyd Raeburn, "New Orleans Style: The Awakening of American Jazz Scholarship and Its Cultural Implications" (Ph.D. diss., Tulane University, 1991), 268–70. Several noted jazz critics traveled to New Orleans and other cities in the late 1930s and early 1940s to report on the state of jazz music. Their essays appeared in the first edition of *Jazzmen*, published in the United States near the end of World War II.

6. Hulsizer, "New Orleans in Wartime," 6; Morroe Berger to Paula Wainer, Jan. 23, 1943, in Morroe Berger, "Letters from New Orleans," *Annual Review of Jazz Studies* 7 (1994–95): 64; Harry Lim, "Way Down Yonder . . . " *Metronome* (Oct. 1943): 36; Eugene Williams, "New Orleans Today: A Wealth of Talent Is Concealed," unidentified periodical, 63, vertical file "World War II and Jazz," HJA.

7. *New Orleans Item*, Mar. 26, 1916; George Hartman, "New Orleans Today," *Jazz Record* (Jan. 1945): 4, HJA; Williams, 65; Orin Blackstone, "Down in New Orleans," *H.R.S. Society Rag* (Dec. 1940): 8, vertical file "History, Legend, Myth," HJA; Blackstone, "From the Birthplace of Jazz," *Pickup* (Birmingham, Eng.) (Jan. 1946): 4, vertical file "History, Legend, Myth," HJA; Smith, "Land of Dreams," 268.

8. Berger to Wainer, Jan. 20, 1943, in Berger, "Letters from New Orleans," 52.

9. Heyward Hale Broun, "Down in New Orleans," *H.R.S. Society Rag* (Sept. 1940), 13–17, vertical file "History, Legend, Myth," HJA.

10. Wilson, "Real New Orleans Sound," 60.

11. Reebee Garofalo, "Crossing Over, 1939–1989," in Jannette L. Dates and William Barlow, eds., *Split Image: African Americans in the Mass Media* (Washington, D.C.: Howard University Press, 1990), 60.

12. August W. Staub and Kaye de Metz, "Jazz: First as Dance?" *Second Line* (New Orleans Jazz Club) (Summer 1976): 18.

13. Jennifer Quale, "'Brass Band' Notes from the 'Curator of Jazz,'" *New Orleans Times-Picayune*, July 11, 1977.

14. "Jazz Museum to Be Established in Orleans," *Old French Quarter News*, Apr. 14, 1944, Louisiana Division, NOPL.

15. Raeburn, "New Orleans Style," 295–99; Michael Edmonds, "Around New Orleans," *Jazz Music* (London) 4, no. 1 (1949): 6.

16. Johnny Wiggs, "Wiggs—Self-Explained," *Second Line* (Spring 1977): 8.

17. Raeburn, "New Orleans Style," 300–1.

18. *David Brinkley's Journal*, Jan. 10, 1962, NBC-TV Film, 16-mm composite print, HJA; Harold Dejan, *Everything Is Lovely!* (Pijnacker, the Netherlands: Holland Olympia Publishers, Ltd., 1989), 255.

19. *David Brinkley's Journal*; Mardi Gras Lounge photographs, box 3, Ralston Crawford Collection, HJA.

20. Jack V. Buerkle and Danny Barker, *Bourbon Street Black: The New Orleans Black Jazzman* (New York: Oxford University Press, 1973), 91, 108, 116.

21. On white responses to black popular music, see Brian Ward, *Just My Soul Responding: Rhythm and Blues, Black Consciousness, and Race Relations* (Berkeley: University of California Press, 1998).

22. Johnny DeDroit, interview by Richard B. Allen and Dexter Thompson, Mar. 16, 1973, taped interview digest, 15, HJA; Raeburn, "New Orleans Style," 315–16.

23. Two-minute tape recording for Mayor Morrison, First Anniversary Celebration of Dixieland Jambake Broadcast, folder 25, box 37, Morrison Papers, TU.

24. Joe Mares Jr., interview by William Russell, Apr. 8, 1960, Oral History Collection, HJA; Bruce Boyd Raeburn, conversation with author, New Orleans, Jan. 3, 2001.

25. John Larkins, cover designs for *New Orleans Creole Jazz Band*, Southland LP 234; *Dreaming Down the River to New Orleans*, Southland LP 238; *Paul Barbarin's Bourbon Street Beat*, Southland LP 237, Phonograph Collection, HJA.

26. Art Anderson, cover notes, *Dixieland Down South*, Southland LP 220; *Mardi Gras Parade Music from New Orleans*, Southland LP 207; *Echoes of New Orleans*, Southland LP 239; *New Orleans Creole Jazz Band*, Southland LP 234, Phonograph Collection, HJA.

27. Robert W. Rydell, *All the World's a Fair: Visions of Empire at American International Expositions, 1876–1916* (Chicago: University of Chicago Press, 1984); Marguerite S. Shaffer, *See America First: Tourism and National Identity, 1880–1940* (Washington, D.C.: Smithsonian Institution Press, 2001); Mares interview, Apr. 8, 1960, 9; Joe Mares Jr., interview by Walt Richter, Sept. 1966, Oral History Collection, HJA; *Second Line* (Nov.–Dec. 1954): 29–30.

28. "Johnny St. Cyr Back at Top," *Second Line* (Sept.–Oct. 1961): 18; "Mares Sends All-Stars to Disneyland," *Second Line* (Jan.–Feb. 1963): 7.

29. Paul Crawford, notes on "Dixieland at Disneyland," Sept. 1964, vertical file "Disneyland Jazz," HJA.

30. Program, "5th Annual Dixieland at Disneyland, September 25–26, 1964," vertical file "Disneyland Jazz," HJA.

31. Newsletter of the New Orleans Jazz Club of California (Orange, Calif.), Sept. 21, 1964, vertical file "Disneyland Jazz," HJA.

32. "Who Said Dixieland Was Dying?" *Second Line* (Sept.–Oct. 1967): 101.

33. Jill Jackson, "N.O. Bands at Disneyland," *New Orleans Times-Picayune*, Sept. 30, 1965.

34. William Carter, *Preservation Hall: Music from the Heart* (New York: W. W. Norton, 1991), 110–12, 114–15, 132.

35. Wilson, "A Real New Orleans Sound," 63.

36. Carter, *Preservation Hall,* 116, 204. Quote is from Preservation Hall handbill [1961], vertical file "Bars, Buildings, Etc., Local: Preservation Hall, 1961–1962," HJA.

37. Butch Thompson with Charlie DeVore, "Keeping the Faith: Allan Jaffe (1935–1987)," *Mississippi Rag* (Minneapolis, Minn.) (Apr. 1987): 1–2. Quote is from Allan Jaffe, interview by Tony Luckenbach and Walt Richter, Sept. [n.d.], 1966, Oral History Collection, HJA.

38. "Parlor and Patio," *Vieux Carré Courier,* May 5–11, 1962; David Zinman, "New Orleans Jazzmen Staging Last Stand," *St. Louis Globe-Democrat,* Aug. 22, 1961, vertical file "Bars, Buildings, Etc., Local: Preservation Hall, 1961–1962," HJA; Wilson, "A Real New Orleans Sound," 63.

39. Carter, *Preservation Hall,* 188, 199–202. French Quarter horse-and-buggy tour drivers sometimes contributed to the misconception by telling tourists that Preservation Hall was the birthplace of New Orleans jazz. See Don Marquis, "Preservation Hall: A Brief History," *Second Line* (Summer 1987): 17.

40. Carter, *Preservation Hall,* 184–87, 233–34, 245.

41. John Norris, "Way Down Yonder in New Orleans," *Coda* (Toronto) 4 (Dec. 1961): 28, vertical file "History, Legend, Myth," HJA.

42. Thompson and DeVore, "Keeping the Faith," 3.

43. Carter, *Preservation Hall,* 216, 218–19.

44. "Youths Find Jazz Alive," *Vieux Carré Courier,* Aug. 6, 1965.

45. Wilson, "A Real New Orleans Sound," 63.

46. Carter, *Preservation Hall,* 263. For a discussion of growing American nostalgia in the second half of the twentieth century, see Michael Kammen, *Mystic Chords of Memory: The Transformation of Tradition in American Culture* (New York: Alfred A. Knopf, 1991), esp. chap. 16. On the growing public interest in historical and cultural authenticity, see Jim Weeks, *Gettysburg: Memory, Market, and an American Shrine* (Princeton: Princeton University Press, 2003); Steven D. Hoelscher, *Heritage on Stage: The Invention of Ethnic Place in America's Little Switzerland* (Madison: University of Wisconsin Press, 1998); and Anders Greenspan, *Creating Colonial Williamsburg* (Washington, D.C.: Smithsonian Institution Press, 2002).

47. Wilson, "A Real New Orleans Sound," 133.

48. Barbara Pyle, "More a Reunion Than a Funeral, Barbarin Rites Reveal N.O. Culture," *Hullabaloo* (Tulane University), Apr. 18, 1969, vertical file "Olympia Brass Band, 1969," HJA.

49. Charles Klaveness, "Hot Jazz Goes Cool," *Houston Post,* Apr. 27, 1969, vertical file "Olympia Brass Band, 1969," HJA.

50. Bob Byler, "Dancing in the Aisles," *Mississippi Rag* (Aug. 1977): 2.

51. "Now It Will Be Told (Why There Was No 1953 Festival)," *Second Line* (Mar.–Apr. 1954): 14; "1954 Jazz Festival," *Second Line* (Nov.–Dec. 1954): 7; "Tarnished Slipper," *Second Line* (Nov.–Dec. 1954): 23; "Report on the 1955 Jazz Festival," *Second Line* (Nov.–Dec. 1955): 30.

52. Sim Myers, "About Jazz," *New Orleans Times-Picayune,* Sept. 4, 1958; Editorial: "Why Always 'Greener Pastures'?" *Second Line* (Mar.–Apr. 1959): 11.

53. Spring Fiesta advertisement, *Vieux Carré Courier,* May 5–11, 1962.

54. Olaf C. Lambert, President, New Orleans International Jazz Festival, to Victor H. Schiro, Jan. 21, 1965, folder "International Jazz Festival–1965," box S65-13, Schiro Papers; Virginia Burguieres to Schiro, Jan. 20, 1965, folder "Jazz Festival–1965," box S65-14, Schiro Papers.

55. Pie Dufour, "A la Mode: Variety of Music Promises Busy Time for Summer Listening," *New*

Orleans States-Item, June 23, 1965; "4-Day Jazz Festival Set At New Orleans," *Mobile (Ala.) Press Register*, June 27, 1965. Both in vertical file "Festivals—Local: International Jazz Festival, 1965–67, HJA.

56. Monifa Ife Johnson, "The Coming of Jazzfest: Jazz Festivals, Desegregation and Tourism in New Orleans, 1940–1970" (master's thesis, Tulane University, 2000), 15, 24; "Extension of Remarks of Hon. Edwin W. Edwards of La. in the Hse. of Reps., February 21, 1966," *Congressional Record*, Feb. 21, 1966, A861.

57. Minutes of Preliminary Planning Committee, Mar. 24, 1967; Minutes of Talent Committee, Dec. 1, 1967; Minutes of Joint Meeting of Jazz Planning and Talent Committees, Dec. 15, 1967; Frank Gagnard to Durel Black, Mar. 6, 1967; 250th Anniversary of the Founding of New Orleans, Dec. 1967 bulletin, vertical file "International Jazz Festival, 1968," HJA; Peter Finney, "Opening Won't Be the Same Without Walker," *New Orleans Times-Picayune*, July 14, 1996.

58. "Jazzfest '68: The Last Word," *Second Line* (July–Aug. 1968): 87; New Orleans International Jazz Festival, Inc., Balance Sheet, June 30, 1969, vertical file "International Jazz Festival 1969," HJA; Talent Budget for Jazz Fest '69, Feb. 28, 1969, vertical file "International Jazz Festival, 1969," HJA; "Jazz Buff Criticizes Lack of Interest in Old-Timers," *Louisiana Weekly*, June 22, 1968; "N.O. Jazzmen Slighted," *Vieux Carré Courier*, May 24, 1968; Charles Suhor, "Jazz and the New Orleans Press," *Down Beat* (Elmhurst, Ill.) (June 12, 1969): 19; Johnson, "The Coming of Jazzfest," 70.

59. "Brass Bands: Founders Wouldn't Recognize Their Funky Descendants," *New Orleans Times-Picayune*, Oct. 12, 1993.

60. Helen A. Regis, "'Keeping Jazz Funerals Alive': Blackness and the Politics of Memory in New Orleans," in Celeste Ray, ed., *Southern Heritage on Display: Public Ritual and Ethnic Diversity within Southern Regionalism* (Tuscaloosa: University of Alabama Press, 2003), 39–40, 43.

61. Jason Berry, "Echoes of the Beat of the Streets," *New Orleans Times-Picayune*, Dec. 19, 1989.

62. Charles Chamberlain, conversation with author, New Orleans, Jan. 10, 2001.

63. Richard H. Knowles, *Fallen Heroes: A History of New Orleans Brass Bands* (New Orleans: Jazzology Press, 1996), 244–46.

64. Joachim E. Berendt, text on cover of *Harold Dejan's Olympia Brass Band* album, vertical file "Olympia Brass Band, 1972–1973," HJA.

65. Notes on Paul Crawford [n.d.], vertical file "Olympia Brass Band, 1970–1971"; Richard B. Allen, notes on Avery "Kid" Howard Funeral, Apr. 2, 1966, vertical file "Olympia Brass Band to 1966," HJA. A helicon is a type of coiled marching tuba carried over the shoulder and first made in Vienna in the mid-nineteenth century. Most tuba players in New Orleans brass bands used a sousaphone instead because it better projected the sound forward.

66. Paul R. Crawford, notes on Olympia Brass Band [n.d.]; Lillian DePass, notes on Olympia Brass Band, June 20, 1960; vertical file "Olympia Brass Band to 1966," HJA.

67. Smithsonian Institution, invitation to "Music Making—American Style," Aug. 3–31, 1966, vertical file "Olympia Brass Band to 1966," HJA; "New Orleans Jazz Brought to Washington," *New Orleans States-Item*, July 2, 1967.

68. Louisiana Tourist Development Commission press release, 1969, vertical file "Tourism," HJA; *New Orleans States-Item*, July 14, 1970.

69. "Groundbreaking Planned for West Berlin Volksfest," *New Orleans Times-Picayune*, Mar. 13, 1968.

70. David Cuthbert, "All That Jazz," *New Orleans Times-Picayune*, Aug. 12, 1968.

71. Art Napoleon, "Sound of Sudden Magic," *Jazz Journal* (London): Dec. 1968, vertical file "Olympia Brass Band, 1967," HJA.

72. Jim Manning, "Saints Debut Full of Orleans Flavor," *New Orleans States-Item*, Sept. 18, 1967; Betty B. Rankin, notes on Olympia Brass Band, Jolly Bunch Social Aid and Pleasure Club Parade, Sept. 17, 1967, vertical file "Olympia Brass Band, 1967," HJA.

73. James A. Perry, "Orleans Given Video Boost," *New Orleans States-Item*, Jan. 12, 1970.

74. Klaveness, "Hot Jazz Goes Cool."

75. Knowles, *Fallen Heroes*, 214.

76. Richard B. Allen, notes on Avery "Kid" Howard funeral, Apr. 2, 1966, vertical file "Olympia Brass Band to 1966," HJA.

77. Eleanor D. Ellis, notes on Olympia Brass Band at Wilbert Tillman funeral, Feb. 16, 1967, vertical file "Olympia Brass Band, 1967," HJA.

78. Eleanor D. Ellis, notes on Olympia Brass Band funeral, Feb. 24, 1968, vertical file "Olympia Brass Band, 1968," HJA.

79. Quale, "'Brass Band' Notes."

80. Regis, "'Keeping Jazz Funerals Alive,'" 47.

81. "N.O. Jazz Concert Scheduled Sunday," *New Orleans States-Item*, July 21, 1967; Richard B. Allen, notes on Olympia Brass Band, Tremé Sports Annual Parade, July 30, 1967, vertical file "Olympia Brass Band to 1966," HJA.

82. Richard B. Allen, notes on Caldonia Club, Olympia Brass Band, Jan. 24, 1971, vertical file "Olympia Brass Band, 1970–1971," HJA.

83. John Beecher, "Walking into Trouble: Terror in the Streets of the South," *San Francisco Chronicle*, Sept. 6, 1964.

84. Belle Street, notes on Olympia Brass Band, Tremé Sports Social Aid and Pleasure Club Annual Parade, July 28, 1968, vertical file "Olympia Brass Band, 1968," HJA.

85. Program from "Back-a-Town," Spring 1980, vertical file "Olympia Brass Band, 1974–1985," HJA.

86. Peirce F. Lewis, *New Orleans: The Making of an Urban Landscape* (Cambridge, Mass.: Ballinger Publishing, 1976), 44–45.

87. Program from "Back-a-Town."

88. Mick Burns, *The Great Olympia Band* (New Orleans: Jazzology Press, 2001), 153; Dejan, *Everything Is Lovely*, 65; Scott Aiges and John McCusker, "Keeping the Sound Alive," *New Orleans Times-Picayune*, Oct. 12, 1993.

89. Regis, "'Keeping Jazz Funerals Alive,'" 42–43.

NOTES TO CHAPTER FIVE

Epigraph: Sid Moody, AP news article, Apr. 2, 1972, quoted in Bill Rushton, "What the One Big Paper Doesn't Want You to Know about Mardi Gras," *Vieux Carré Courier*, Apr. 23–27, 1972.

1. Charles L. Dufour, "Mardi Gras Is More Fun If You Are Dressed For It. Here Is the Greatest Free Show on Earth," *Southern Living* (Feb. 1967): 14, 19.

2. David Glassberg, *Sense of History: The Place of the Past in American Life* (Amherst: University of Massachusetts Press, 2001), 62, 72–73.

3. Munro S. Edmonson, "Carnival in New Orleans," *Caribbean Quarterly* 4, no. 3–4 (Mar.–June 1956 double issue): 240–41.

4. Clarence A. Becknell, Thomas Price, and Don Short, "History of the Zulu Social Aid & Pleasure Club, Inc.," *Welcome to Zulu,* www.mardigrasneworleans.com/zulu (accessed May 7, 2001).

5. See, e.g., Jon Sterngass, *First Resorts: Pursuing Pleasure at Saratoga Springs, Newport, and Coney Island* (Baltimore: Johns Hopkins University Press, 2001).

6. Harnett T. Kane, "Zulu Coming Here to Weave Spell of African Splendor," *Sunday Item-Tribune* (New Orleans), Feb. 4, 1940; program, "Zulu Social Aid & Pleasure Club, 1941," vertical file "Carnival—Organizations—Zulu," HJA, cited in Reid Mitchell, *All on a Mardi Gras Day: Episodes in the History of New Orleans Carnival* (Cambridge: Harvard University Press, 1995), 183.

7. Mitchell, *All on a Mardi Gras Day.* My analysis of Zulu's role in tourism builds on Mitchell's work.

8. Ibid., 175–76; "Flambeau Carriers Struck for Pay Hike," *Louisiana Weekly,* Mar. 9, 1946; Abe J. Schulman, "Postwar Mardi Gras," *Jazz Record* (Apr. 1946): 4, HJA.

9. Mitchell, *All on a Mardi Gras Day,* 176–77; "Flambeau Carriers Struck for Pay Hike"; "1st Parade On Tonight," *New Orleans Item,* Feb. 11, 1947; "God of Mirth, Momus, Rules City Tonight," *New Orleans Item,* Feb. 24, 1949.

10. John A. Provenzano, "Mardi Gras, Chic la Pai," *Jazz Record* (Apr. 1946): 11.

11. Calvin Trillin, "A Reporter at Large: The Zulus," *New Yorker* 40 (June 20, 1964): 105.

12. Trillin, "The Zulus," 53, 103; Howard Jacobs, "Head-Hunters on the Loose," *New Orleans Times-Picayune/New Orleans States Magazine* (Feb. 27, 1949): 46–47.

13. Mitchell, *All on a Mardi Gras Day,* 182–83.

14. Tad Jones, "'Separate But Equal': The Laws of Segregation and Their Effect on New Orleans Black Musicians, 1950–1964," *Living Blues Magazine* 77 (Dec. 1987): 28; "Negro Groups Start Mardi Gras Boycott," *New York Times,* Mar. 1, 1957.

15. Advertisement, "A Fight For Dignity—Zulu Does Not Represent the Negro!" *Louisiana Weekly,* Feb. 11, 1961, and *New Orleans States-Item,* Feb. 13, 1961. Tellingly, the *States-Item* version of the petition omitted the portion accusing white merchants of paying blacks to act like savages.

16. Mitchell, *All on a Mardi Gras Day,* 179; "The King Resigns," *Newsweek,* Feb. 13, 1961; Kim Lacy Rogers, *Righteous Lives: Narratives of the New Orleans Civil Rights Movement* (New York: New York University Press, 1993), 46.

17. Mitchell, *All on a Mardi Gras Day,* 190; Flyer, Zulu Social Aid and Pleasure Club Honorary Organization, Feb. 1967, vertical file "Clubs & Societies: SAPCs: Zulu SAPC (1966–1968)," HJA; Hermann Deutsch, "Icy Zulu Drama Has Racy Finale," *New Orleans States-Item,* Feb. 11, 1967; "Anyone for Shriving? (Two Radical Views)," *Vieux Carré Courier,* Feb. 16, 1968.

18. Belle Street, notes on Zulu Social Aid and Pleasure Club, Dec. 13, 1968, vertical file "Clubs & Societies: SAPCs: Zulu SAPC (1966–1968)," HJA.

19. Ed Cocke, "A Requiem for Zulu," *New Orleans* (Feb. 1970): 43; Martin Waldron, "It's Fat Tuesday in New Orleans, and 500,000 Enjoy, Enjoy," *New York Times,* Feb. 19, 1969; Don Lee Keith, "King Zulu the Great Rules Calmly Over Zany Parade," *New Orleans Times-Picayune,* Feb. 19, 1969; Emile Lafourcade, "From Tramps to Big-Time Carnival Club," *New Orleans Times-Picayune,* Feb. 3, 1978.

20. Waldron, "It's Fat Tuesday in New Orleans"; Charlotte Hays, "Inside the Zulu Ball!" *Vieux Carré Courier,* Mar. 9–15, 1973.

21. Pie Dufour, "Some Carnival After-Thoughts," *New Orleans States-Item*, Feb. 12, 1970.

22. "Pullman Building 6 'Towns' for Carnival; Expect High Number of Rail Guests," *New Orleans Item*, Feb. 22, 1949; Gerald W. Taitt, "Carnival Has Town Straining at Seams," *New Orleans Item*, Feb. 10, 1947; Glen Douthit to Mrs. Wallace Kudick (Kewaunee, Wis.), Jan. 5, 1953, folder 4, box 36, Morrison Papers, TU.

23. Glen Douthit to deLesseps S. Morrison, Feb. 9, 1961, folder "Mardi Gras—1961," box 15, New Orleans Office of the Mayor, Chief Administrative Office Records, NOPL.

24. Minutes, Meeting of Parade Captains, Mar. 3, 1961, and Minutes, Meeting of the Mayor's Advisory Committee on Mardi Gras Parades, Apr. 25, 1961, folder "Mayor's Advisory Committee on Carnival Parades," box 1, New Orleans Office of the Mayor, Boards and Commissions Records, NOPL; Ordinance No. 2431, Aug. 3, 1961, folder "Mardi Gras—1961," box 1, John J. Petre Collection, NOPL.

25. "Mardi Gras Parades to Be Telecast," *New Orleans Item*, Feb. 22, 1949.

26. Dennis J. Lacey Jr., Executive Assistant to Mayor, to Lloyd F. Gaubert, Mar. 5, 1965, and Lacey to Emmett J. Bieger, President, New Orleans Hotel Association, Jan. 14, 1965, folder "Carnival (#5)—1965," box S65-3, Schiro Papers.

27. Ted Liuzza, "U.S. Sees Mardi Gras on 'Comedy Hour,'" *New Orleans Item*, Feb. 21, 1955.

28. News of New Orleans, Public Relations Section, City of New Orleans, "History and Background of Mardi Gras," 1949, vertical file "Carnival History," TU; Faye Sherman, "Bacchus to Hold Ball for Tourists," *Item*, Jan. 2, 1950; Owen Brennan, "All Out for Visitors' Ball," *New Orleans Item*, Feb. 17, 1950; deLesseps S. Morrison to Mrs. Frank F. Celino, Jan. 9, 1953, folder 4, box 36, Morrison Papers, TU. The Krewe of Alla took its name from Algiers, Louisiana, a one-time suburb on the west bank of the Mississippi River that had since been annexed into the city of New Orleans.

29. *R. L. Polk's New Orleans City Directory* (Dallas: R. L. Polk, 1968); Myron Tassin, *Bacchus* (Gretna, La.: Pelican, 1975), 21; Hoke May, "A Bright Spot in the City's Tourism Troubles," *New Orleans* (Sept. 1968): 11; Samuel Kinser, *Carnival, American Style: Mardi Gras at New Orleans and Mobile* (Chicago: University of Chicago Press, 1990), 102–3.

30. Shirley Harrison, "Mardi Gras Mambo: Carnival Culture Teams with Counter Culture," *New Orleans* (Mar. 1984): 48.

31. James Gill, *Lords of Misrule: Mardi Gras and the Politics of Race in New Orleans* (Jackson: University Press of Mississippi, 1997), 212; anonymous interview by author, New Orleans, July 12, 2001.

32. Ronnie Virgets, "Bacchus Lets Us Down," *New Orleans Times-Picayune*, Dec. 4, 1987.

33. Gill, *Lords of Misrule*, 212; Richard Bordelon, "Krewes-ing in the Suburbs," *New Orleans* (Feb. 1979): 41.

34. Calvin Trillin, "U.S. Journal: New Orleans: Mardi Gras," *New Yorker* 44 (Mar. 9, 1968): 138–44; Eli N. Evans, *The Provincials: A Personal History of Jews in the South* (New York: Free Press, 1997), 212; Bordelon, "Krewes-ing," 29, 35.

35. Kim Chatelain, "Founder of Endymion Once Went Door-to-Door," *New Orleans Times-Picayune/States-Item*, Feb. 16, 1985.

36. Christine Manalla, "Past Master," *New Orleans* (Jan.–Feb. 1999): 48–49; Gill, *Lords of Misrule*, 211.

37. Here I appropriate the term *spatial practices* with gratitude to Catherine Cocks, whose *Doing the Town: The Rise of Urban Tourism in the United States, 1850–1915* (Berkeley: University of California Press, 2001) discusses the "spatial practices of tourism."

38. John Newlin, "The Case against Carnival," *Wavelength* (New Orleans) 41 (Mar. 1984): 21.

39. "531 Tons of Trash Picked Up," *New Orleans States-Item*, Feb. 18, 1966; "Trash Tonnage Good Success Index," *New Orleans States-Item*, Feb. 14, 1969; "Season's Trash Equals 1,287 Tons," *New Orleans States-Item*, Feb. 6, 1970; "Mardi Gras Garbage New Record," *New Orleans States-Item*, Feb. 24, 1971.

40. Ross Yockey, "Mardi Gras Safety Needs Eyed By N.O. Leaders," *New Orleans States-Item*, Feb. 11, 1967; Dale Curry, "Civic Clubs, Council Join Push For More Maskers," *New Orleans States-Item*, Feb. 4, 1970; "1970 Carnival Perhaps Best, Giarrusso Says," *New Orleans States-Item*, Feb. 11, 1970.

41. "9 Reasons to Avoid New Orleans' Mardi Gras," *Focus* (Feb. 1951): 53, reprinted in Newlin, "The Case against Carnival," 21; Wesley Jackson, "Good News from the Middle of Hell," *New Orleans Times-Picayune*, Feb. 6, 1975.

42. "1969 Mardi Gras Scored by Critics," *New York Times*, Feb. 23, 1969; Larry LaMarca to Victor H. Schiro, Feb. 13, 1967, folder "Proposed Ordinance Re: Sale of Beverages in Glass & Cans—1967," box S67-18, Schiro Papers; Tom Bethell, "The Street People: Why They Come to Mardi Gras," *Vieux Carré Courier*, Mar. 2–8, 1973; Joseph Giarrusso to Maurice E. (Moon) Landrieu, Feb. 20, 1969, folder "Police #2—1969," box S69-10, Schiro Papers.

43. Bethell, "The Street People."

44. "Most Trying Mardi Gras: Police Warn Loiterers after 88 Youths Booked," *New Orleans States-Item*, Feb. 9, 1970; "103 Arrested in Crackdown on Hippie Herd," *New Orleans States-Item*, Feb. 9, 1970; Carol Flake, *New Orleans: Behind the Masks of America's Most Exotic City* (New York: Grove, 1994), 82; "Al Hirt's Famous Lip Cut By Brick Hurled at Float," *New Orleans States-Item*, Feb. 9, 1970; Timothy D. Kelly (Minneapolis, Minn.) to Moon Landrieu, Aug. 28, 1970, folder 4, box 21, Moon Landrieu Collection, Department of Special Collections and Archives, Loyola University, New Orleans.

45. "Keep Mardi Gras Family Style," *New Orleans Times-Picayune*, Apr. 16, 1972.

46. Jerry Cohen, "Hippies Find Good Home in New Orleans," *Los Angeles Times*, Feb. 28, 1971; "Carnival Problems; Possible Solutions," *New Orleans Times-Picayune*, Feb. 22, 1972.

47. "Push Preservation of Mardi Gras," *New Orleans Times-Picayune*, June 27, 1972; GNOTCC brochure, quoted in Wentworth Brewster, "An Introduction to Carnival: Its History, Idiosyncracies, Etc.," *Figaro*, Feb. 5, 1975.

48. Stephen Green, "The Young Claim a Bit of Mardi Gras' Action: Swinging New Orleans Squares Fret About Unwanted Hordes," *National Observer* (London), n.d. (1971), vertical file "Carnival (New Orleans), 1970–1979," HJA.

49. Cohen, "Hippies Find Good Home."

50. Green, "The Young Claim a Bit of Mardi Gras' Action."

51. John A. Pecoul, Staff Report to Mr. Richard Kernion, n.d. (1971), folder "Mardi Gras," box 2, HRC; "Celebrating Mardi Gras on the Tulane Campus: Carnival Visitors Accommodated on Campus Without Major Incident," *Hullabaloo* (Tulane University), Mar. 5, 1971.

52. Cohen, "Hippies Find Good Home"; Terry H. Anderson, *The Movement and the Sixties: Protest in America from Greensboro to Wounded Knee* (New York: Oxford University Press, 1995), 174.

53. J. Douglas Murphy, "Mardi Gras Coalition's Final Year?" *New Orleans Times-Picayune*, Feb. 7, 1975; "Transients Warned," *New Orleans Times-Picayune*, Feb. 12, 1977; "Coalition Offers Mardi Gras Help," *New Orleans Times-Picayune*, Feb. 16, 1980.

54. Bruce Eggler, "'Big Easy' Mothballed By Tourism Marketers," *New Orleans Times-Picayune*, July 12, 1991. In 1991, New Orleans tourism promoters considered abandoning the nickname "The Big

Easy" out of fear that it detracted from their growing efforts to appeal to touring families. Much like the 1970s controversy over "The Greatest Free Show on Earth," the later debate over the use of a name popularized by the 1987 film *The Big Easy* reflected the fine line officials walked between indulging and restraining the city's naughty reputation.

55. Don W. Gettings to Harry England, Mar. 22, 1962, folder "Tourist Commission—1962," box S62-28, Schiro Papers.

56. A. L. Jung Jr., President, Jung Hotel, to Richard B. Montgomery Jr., President, Chamber of Commerce of the New Orleans Area, Dec. 19, 1966, Minutes, CCC.

57. David F. Dixon to Darwin S. Fenner, Jan. 9, 1967, folder "Domed Stadium—1967," box S67-5, Schiro Papers.

58. Darwin S. Fenner to David F. Dixon, Feb. 3, 1967, folder "Domed Stadium—1967," box S67-6, Schiro Papers.

59. David Lowenthal, *The Past Is a Foreign Country* (Cambridge, Eng.: Cambridge University Press, 1985), 293; "A New Orleans Theme Park," folder "Domed Stadium (2)—1967," box S67-5, Schiro Papers.

60. Rushton, "What the One Big Paper Doesn't Want You to Know about Mardi Gras."

61. "Bacchus Puts Dome on the Map—Parade Map, That Is," *New Orleans Times-Picayune*, Jan. 24, 1976; "Carnival: People, Beads and Booze," *New Orleans Times-Picayune*, Feb. 28, 1976.

62. Joyce Davis Robinson, "Superdome Is Pushed for Mardi Gras," *New Orleans Times-Picayune*, Sept. 16, 1976; "2 Carnival Specials Scheduled at Dome," *New Orleans Times-Picayune*, Feb. 3, 1978; "Carnival Concert to Roll," *New Orleans Times-Picayune*, Feb. 16, 1980; "Popeye's Ready with 100,000 Purple Throws," *New Orleans Times-Picayune*, Feb. 11, 1982; Roy Furchgott, "For New Orleans, Mardi Gras Is Becoming an All-Year Cash Cow," *New York Times*, Feb. 7, 1999.

63. Renee Peck, "Tourists Book a Ball," *New Orleans Times-Picayune*, Mar. 5, 1984.

64. Mark Baker, "Mardi Gras: Everybody's Laughing," *U.S. News & World Report* (Feb. 10, 1986): 78; "Mardi Gras Cheers the Float Makers," *New York Times*, Mar. 3, 1981; Bridget O'Brian, "The Business of Making of Carnival So Glamorous," *New Orleans Times-Picayune*, Feb. 22, 1987.

NOTES TO CHAPTER SIX

Epigraph: Mary M. Morrison to Editor, *New Orleans Times-Picayune*, July 24, 1989.

1. "New Hotel as Old as Vieux Carré," *New Orleans Times-Picayune*, Jan. 12, 1975. This article appeared in a hotel advertisement designed as a fictitious newspaper called *LeMoyne Lagniappe*.

2. Peirce Lewis, "To Revive Urban Downtowns, Show Respect for the Spirit of the Place," *Smithsonian* 6 (Sept. 1975): 38, 40. Donald Deskins, then a professor at Pennsylvania State University, spoke of the Quarter as a "Creole Disneyland."

3. Paul A. Fabry, "Economic Growth in N.O. Is Expected to Continue," *New Orleans Times-Picayune*, Jan. 23, 1972.

4. Arnold R. Hirsch, "New Orleans: Sunbelt in the Swamp," in Richard M. Bernard and Bradley R. Rice, eds., *Sunbelt Cities: Politics and Growth Since World War II* (Austin: University of Texas Press, 1983), 122–23.

5. Calvin Trillin, "New Orleans Unmasked," *New Yorker* 73 (Feb. 2, 1998): 40.

6. Allan Katz, "Are We Overtaking Atlanta?" *New Orleans Times-Picayune*, Jan. 10, 1982.

7. James R. Bobo, *The New Orleans Economy: Pro Bono Publico?* (New Orleans: Division of Business and Economic Research, College of Business Administration, University of New Orleans, 1975), 61.

8. Bernard J. Frieden and Lynne B. Sagalyn, *Downtown, Inc.: How America Rebuilds Cities* (Cambridge, Mass.: MIT Press, 1989), 268.

9. Allan Katz, "New Industries on Board," *New Orleans Times-Picayune*, Nov. 1, 1981; Katz, "The Tourist Explosion," *New Orleans Times-Picayune*, Mar. 4, 1984; Bill Rushton, "Cityscape," *Vieux Carré Courier*, Aug. 4–10, 1972. Dupepe's grandfather, Frank Clancy, was an Irish-born rancher and longtime Jefferson Parish sheriff. See Christine Lacoste Bordelon, "Family Ties: Kenner's Growth Attributed to Clancy Kin," *New Orleans Times-Picayune* (Kenner edition), July 16, 2000.

10. Rushton, "Cityscape."

11. Charlotte Hays, "Inside the Zulu Ball!" *Vieux Carré Courier*, Mar. 9–15, 1973.

12. James K. Glassman, "The Whitney Breaks the Billion Mark," *Figaro*, Jan. 22, 1975; Robert E. Norton, "Shark Repellant for the Whitney," *New Orleans* (Apr. 1984): 50.

13. Phyllis Hutton Raabe, "Status and Its Impact: New Orleans' Carnival, the Social Upper Class and Upper-Class Power" (Ph.D. diss., Pennsylvania State University, 1973), 119–21; John Pope, "James H. Jones, Financer of Dome," *New Orleans Times-Picayune*, Aug. 11, 1998. Jones was among the most outspoken critics of the Carnival elite-dominated New Orleans banking establishment's conservatism.

14. "A Sunbelt City Plays Catch-up," *Business Week*, Mar. 6, 1978; Clancy DuBos, "Between a Rock and Canal Place: The Education of Joseph Canizaro," *New Orleans* (Oct. 1978): 61–62.

15. Peter Eisinger, "The Politics of Bread and Circuses: Building the City for the Visitor Class," *Urban Affairs Review* 35, no. 3 (Jan. 2000): 320–21.

16. Michael Peter Smith and Marlene Keller, "'Managed Growth' and the Politics of Uneven Development in New Orleans," in Susan Fainstein, Norman I. Fainstein, Richard Child Hill, Dennis Judd, and Michael P. Smith, *Restructuring the City: The Political Economy of Urban Redevelopment* (New York: Longman, 1983), 134–36.

17. Calvin Trillin, "U.S. Journal: New Orleans: On the Possibility of Houstonization," *New Yorker* 50 (Feb. 17, 1975): 94–98.

18. Hirsch, "New Orleans: Sunbelt in the Swamp," 118; Charles Y. W. Chai, "Who Rules New Orleans? A Study of Community Power Structure," *Louisiana Business Survey* 16, no. 5 (Oct. 1971): 10; Rosary Hartel O'Brien, "The New Orleans Carnival Organizations: Theater of Prestige" (Ph.D. diss., University of California, Los Angeles, 1973), 179–83; Nick Lemann, "What Does Mardi Gras Mean? 21 Theories to Help You Get the Big Picture," *New Orleans* (Feb. 1974): 51, 54.

19. Phil Johnson, *A WWL-TV Editorial* (transcript), Jan. 2, 1970, folder "WWL-TV Editorials," box SPR-53, Mayor Victor H. Schiro Public Relations Office Records, Schiro Papers, NOPL.

20. Stella Pitts, "Dirty, Dreary, Depressing: That's Bourbon Street by Day," *New Orleans Times-Picayune*, Feb. 10, 1974; Mrs. Charles E. Egan (Metairie, La.), letter to Editor, *New Orleans Times-Picayune*, Feb. 7, 1977; Joe Massa, "Quarter Task Force Is Formed," *New Orleans Times-Picayune*, Jan. 26, 1977; Editorial: "Walk on the Wild Side," *New Orleans Times-Picayune*, Jan. 29, 1977.

21. "Bourbon, Royal Streets to Close," *Vieux Carré Courier*, July 16–22, 1971.

22. Martha Robinson to Advisory Council on Historic Preservation, Jan. 31, 1974, folder 5, box 21, Robinson Papers.

23. Mary M. Morrison, "Square Improvements?" *Vieux Carré Courier*, Dec. 20–26, 1973.

24. Mrs. August W. Mysing to Editor, *New Orleans States-Item*, Nov. 16, 1973, folder 12, box 1, Robinson Papers.

25. "Pedestrian Mall Reactions," *Vieux Carré Courier*, Sept. 25, 1970.

26. James H. Gillis, "Son et Lumiere Show in Square," *New Orleans Times-Picayune*, Apr. 26, 1973; Frank Gagnard, "Casting a Pall on Sound, Light," *New Orleans Times-Picayune*, Apr. 29, 1973; Philip D. Carter, "Does Gen. Jackson Need Show Biz?" *Vieux Carré Courier*, June 1–7, 1973; Mary Morrison, "What's Happening at the Vieux Carre Commission?" *Vieux Carré Courier*, May 25–31, 1973.

27. "Suit Attacks Son et Lumiere," *New Orleans Times-Picayune*, Aug. 18, 1973; "Judge Stops Sound-Light Until Plan Satisfies Laws," *New Orleans Times-Picayune*, Oct. 25, 1973; "VCC Okays Sound-Light Idea," *New Orleans Times-Picayune*, Jan. 23, 1974; James H. Gillis, "Politics, Power and the People," *New Orleans Times-Picayune*, June 19, 1975; Millie Ball, "1,000 Citizens Boo 'Sound and Light,'" *New Orleans Times-Picayune*, July 20, 1975; "Lights Out," *Vieux Carré Courier*, Aug. 14–20, 1975.

28. F. Monroe Labouisse Jr., "The Death of the Old French Market," *New Orleans* (June 1975): 72–73, 76–78; *R. L. Polk's New Orleans City Directory* (Dallas: R. L. Polk, 1945, 1965); John Edw. Fazzio, Secretary, French Market Corporation, to Victor H. Schiro, May 25, 1966, folder "French Market Corporation—1966," box S66-8, Schiro Papers.

29. "Market Revamp Told," *Vieux Carré Courier*, Mar. 12, 1971; Labouisse, "Death of the Old French Market," 72.

30. Lanny Thomas, "Vieux Carré Memories," *New Orleans States-Item*, June 10, 1977.

31. Martha Robinson to Editor, *New Orleans Times-Picayune*, Apr. 5, 1975.

32. French Market Corporation Subject Files, folders 382, 392, 399, 401, NOPL; Paul Atkinson, "French Market Project to Spark Tourism Bonus," *New Orleans Times-Picayune*, Nov. 24, 1972; "Jackson Square Meets the Mississippi," *Southern Living* (June 1977): 82–83.

33. Robert R. Weyeneth, *Historic Preservation for a Living City: Historic Charleston Foundation, 1947–1997* (Columbia: University of South Carolina Press, 2000), 102.

34. Laurance Eustis, President, Metropolitan Area Committee, to Moon Landrieu, June 12, 1970, folder "Tourism (MAC)," box 51, Moon Landrieu Collection, NOPL.

35. Henry Asher, "Man of Vision: Kabacoff Reorganized Tourist Commission," *New Orleans Times-Picayune*, Aug. 15, 1982; Report of the MAC Tourism Committee, May 27, 1970, folder "Tourism (MAC)," box 51, Landrieu Collection, NOPL.

36. Albert Aschaffenburg, President, Pontchartrain Hotel, to Landrieu, May 27, 1970, folder "Tourist Promotion," box 51, Landrieu Collection, NOPL.

37. MAC Press Release, June 12, 1970, folder "Tourist Promotion"; GNOCC Press Release, Dec. 15, 1970, folder "Tourism (MAC)," box 51, Landrieu Collection, NOPL.

38. GNOTCC, *Annual Report, 1971–72* (New Orleans: New Orleans Metropolitan Convention and Visitors Bureau [hereafter NOMCVB]).

39. Clarence Doucet, "Texan to Take Top Tourism Post," *New Orleans Times-Picayune*, Oct. 16, 1970; GNOTCC, *Annual Report, 1971–72, 1972–73* (New Orleans: NOMCVB).

40. GNOTCC, *Annual Report, 1973–74, 1978–79* (New Orleans: NOMCVB).

41. Rosemary James, "Mason's Strip . . . The New Basin Street," *New Orleans* (Mar. 1977): 38–41;

Ronnie Virgets, "Weeds Take Over as Hard Times Hit N.O. Version of Vegas Strip," *New Orleans Times-Picayune*, Jan. 11, 1987.

42. Charlotte Hays, "Who Owns the French Quarter?" *Vieux Carré Courier*, Feb. 9–15, 1973; *Vieux Carré Demonstration Study* (New Orleans: Marcou, O'Leary and Associates, 1968), 60–62.

43. Charlotte Hays, "The Quarter's Black Exodus," *Vieux Carré Courier*, June 18–24, 1971; J. E. Bourgoyne, "Vieux Carré Commission: Too Strong or Too Weak?" *New Orleans Times-Picayune*, Dec. 30, 1973.

44. George C. [illegible] to Honorable Ernest N. Morial, Aug. 30, 1978, folder "French Quarter, 1978–1986," box B23, Ernest N. Morial Papers, NOPL.

45. "Remove Quarter Buses, City Planners Suggest," *New Orleans Times-Picayune*, July 6, 1972; James H. Gillis, "Council Okays Mini-Buses for French Quarter Routes," *New Orleans Times-Picayune*, Mar. 16, 1973; "'Gee, Dad, It's a Whatzit: Mini-Buses Ride Quarter," *New Orleans Times-Picayune*, Nov. 14, 1973.

46. Joe Massa, "Quarter Bus Limits Fail," *New Orleans Times-Picayune*, Jan. 18, 1980.

47. "Tourism and the Quarter: Weighing Pros and Cons," *New Orleans Times-Picayune*, Aug. 17, 1978.

48. Joe Massa, "Bill Would End Bus Sightseeing in Vieux Carré," *New Orleans Times-Picayune*, Dec. 7, 1979.

49. Joe Massa, "Quarter Bus Limits Fail"; Editorial: "Quarter Bus Ban Defeated," *New Orleans Times-Picayune*, Jan. 21, 1980.

50. Joe Massa, "City Council Settles Tour Bus Problem," *New Orleans Times-Picayune*, Mar. 14, 1980; Joe Massa, "Council May Ban Trucks on Some Quarter Streets," *New Orleans Times-Picayune*, Oct. 2, 1981; Joan Treadway, "Early to Propose Truck Ban on Two Quarter Streets," *New Orleans Times-Picayune*, Mar. 3, 1983; Joan Treadway, "Decatur Truck Ban Approved," *New Orleans Times-Picayune*, Mar. 4, 1983.

51. Mark Lowrey to Editor, *New Orleans Times-Picayune*, Jan. 14, 1976.

52. "Groups Oppose Parade Routing," *New Orleans Times-Picayune*, Aug. 14, 1972; "73 Parades Will Bypass Quarter," *New Orleans Times-Picayune*, Aug. 25, 1972; "Deputy Brands Parade Route Change Hasty," *New Orleans Times-Picayune*, Sept. 13, 1972; Mrs. Jacob H. Morrison to Editor, *New Orleans Times-Picayune*, Jan. 14, 1976.

53. Roy Reed, "New Orleans Seeks to Mute the Sound of Street Music," *New York Times*, Dec. 29, 1974; Earl G. Duffy, Key Biscayne, Fla. (Past President, New Orleans Jazz and Heritage Foundation), to Editor, *New Orleans Times-Picayune*, Jan. 19, 1975.

54. M. Marv Dupree, to Editor, *New Orleans Times-Picayune*, Feb. 1, 1975, in response to James Walsh, Athol, Mass., to Editor, *New Orleans Times-Picayune*, Jan. 19, 1975.

55. Paul Atkinson, "Jazzmen Told: Keep Movin,'" *New Orleans Times-Picayune*, Feb. 21, 1975.

56. Pierre V. Degruy, "Tap Dancers Make Club Bosses See Red," *New Orleans Times-Picayune*, Sept. 3, 1979; Degruy, "Ordinance Would Govern Quarter Street Showmen," *New Orleans Times-Picayune*, Sept. 12, 1979.

57. Christopher Drew, "The Troubled Port: Flagship of Area's Economy Losing Out to Hustling Rivals," *New Orleans Times-Picayune*, June 13, 1982.

58. Ray A. Liuzza, interview by author, New Orleans, June 20, 2001.

59. Christopher M. Law, *Urban Tourism: Attracting Visitors to Large Cities* (London: Mansell Publishing, 1993), 49; Dennis R. Judd and Susan S. Fainstein, "Global Forces, Local Strategies, and Urban Tourism," in Judd and Fainstein, eds., *The Tourist City* (New Haven: Yale University Press, 1999), 40.

60. John M. Findlay, *Magic Lands: Western Cityscapes and American Culture after 1940* (Berkeley: University of California Press, 1992), 214–16; Allan Katz, "San Antonio's Fair Was a Disaster, But They Say It Turned City Around," *New Orleans Times-Picayune*, Aug. 4, 1981; Rebecca Mowbray and Greg Thomas, "Time-Release Renewal," *New Orleans Times-Picayune*, May 9, 2004.

61. Frieden and Sagalyn, *Downtown, Inc.*, 274–75.

62. Bridget O'Brian and Dean Baquet, "Going Broke: Troubled Story of a World's Fair," *New Orleans Times-Picayune*, Nov. 11, 1984.

63. Frieden and Sagalyn, *Downtown, Inc.*, 269–70; Paul Atkinson, "N.O. Losing Out on Conventions," *New Orleans Times-Picayune*, Oct. 26, 1978; Larry R. Ford, *America's New Downtowns: Revitalization or Reinvention?* (Baltimore: Johns Hopkins University Press, 2003); Heywood T. Sanders, "Building the Convention City: Politics, Finance, and Public Investment in Urban America," *Journal of Urban Affairs* 14, no. 2 (1992): 136.

64. Liz Galtney, "Downtown Development Struggle," *New Orleans Gambit*, Jan. 29, 1983; Allan Katz, "Exhibition Hall Already Attracting Customers," *New Orleans Times-Picayune*, Jan. 25, 1981; Nan Perales, "History: Selling Idea Was the First Step," *New Orleans Times-Picayune*, Jan. 13, 1985. Forstall began working at the Monteleone Hotel in 1955, became its general manager six years later, served on the board of the GNOTCC, and was among the early members of the Krewe of Bacchus. Mervin Trail, a medical specialist, professor, and later chancellor of Louisiana State University's medical school, arrived in New Orleans from Maryland in 1968, becoming a leader in the GNOTCC as well as a charter member of Bacchus. Forstall and Trail, like Brennan, represented the "new blood" that characterized tourism leadership by the 1980s. See "Frederick Forstall, N.O. Hotel Manager," *New Orleans Times-Picayune*, June 25, 2003, and John Pope, "LSU Med School Chancellor Trail Is Dead at 67," *New Orleans Times-Picayune*, Jan. 4, 2001.

65. Editorial, "World's Fair," *New Orleans Times-Picayune*, Sept. 12, 1978.

66. Ed Anderson, "Fair Official Hopes Crawfish and Jazz Will Sell the State," *New Orleans Times-Picayune*, Apr. 13, 1981; George Hager, "World's Fair Is Approved by President," *New Orleans Times-Picayune*, Apr. 18, 1981; O'Brian and Baquet, "Going Broke"; Wayne King, "Failed Fair Gives New Orleans a Painful Hangover," *New York Times*, Nov. 12, 1984.

67. Monte Piliawsky, "The Impact of Black Mayors on the Black Community: The Case of New Orleans' Ernest Morial," in Charles Vincent, ed., *The African American Experience in Louisiana*, part C, *From Jim Crow to Civil Rights*, Louisiana Purchase Bicentennial Series in Louisiana History, vol. 11 (Lafayette: Center for Louisiana Studies, University of Louisiana at Lafayette, 2002), 533; Vincent Lee, "Tourism No Cure for N.O.—Morial," *New Orleans Times-Picayune*, Jan. 18, 1978.

68. Editorial, "World's Fair," *New Orleans Times-Picayune*, Sept. 12, 1978; Allan Katz, "Fair's Black Hiring Unfair," *New Orleans Times-Picayune*, Sept. 12, 1982.

69. "Street Repairs in Fr. Qtr.," *Vieux Carré Commission Advisory*, No. 1 (1983), vertical file "Neighborhood Associations—Vieux Carré Commission," Louisiana Collection, TU; "Work on Quarter Streets to Begin within Two Weeks," *New Orleans Times-Picayune*, May 5, 1983.

70. Frieden and Sagalyn, *Downtown, Inc.*, 239–40.

71. Jeannette Hardy, "Wet, Wild Fantasyland Envisioned by Architects," *New Orleans Times-Picayune*, May 3, 1981.

72. GNOTCC, *Annual Report*, 1970–71 (New Orleans: NOMCVB); Laurence Alexander, "Massage Parlor Is Raided Again, 2 Workers Jailed," *New Orleans Times-Picayune*, Feb. 5, 1983; Jason DeParle, "DA Raid in French Quarter Nets 33 Street Crime Suspects," *New Orleans Times-Picayune*, Apr. 27, 1984; "Bourbon Becomes a Mall," *New Orleans Times-Picayune*, Apr. 6, 1984; Joan Treadway, "Follow Up: Revamped Lafayette Mall Should Charm Pedestrians," *New Orleans Times-Picayune*, May 6, 1984.

73. Pete Axthelm, "A Midsummer's Mardi Gras," *Newsweek*, July 16, 1984; Gayle Ashton and Paul Atkinson, "Gondola, Monorail Balance High-Price Complaints," *New Orleans Times-Picayune*, May 14, 1984.

NOTES TO CHAPTER SEVEN

Epigraphs: James Gill, "Gradually Sacrificing a Heritage," *New Orleans Times-Picayune*, Nov. 17, 1986; Rick Bragg, "Merrymaking Is Clashing With Tradition in Mardi Gras Tableaux," *New York Times*, Feb. 23, 1998. Henri Schindler is a leading New Orleans Mardi Gras historian and cultural critic known for his passionate defense of Carnival traditions.

1. Sidney J. Barthelemy to Bud Dare, Director, Disney Development (Lake Buena Vista, Fla.), Apr. 30, 1986, folder "Disneyworld (1986–1987)," box 39, Sidney J. Barthelemy Papers, NOPL.

2. Allan Katz, "Boom Isn't Coming to N.O.—It's Here," *New Orleans Times-Picayune*, Jan. 25, 1981; "Are We Overtaking Atlanta?" *New Orleans Times-Picayune*, Jan. 10, 1982.

3. Bridget O'Brian and Dean Baquet, "Going Broke: Troubled Story of a World's Fair," *New Orleans Times-Picayune*, Nov. 11, 1984.

4. Ibid.

5. Ibid.; Nan Perales and Dean Baquet, "For Spurney, Dream Never Panned Out," *New Orleans Times-Picayune*, Nov. 13, 1984.

6. On the relationship between the world's fair and Warehouse District revitalization, see Ann Breen and Dick Rigby, *Intown Living: A Different American Dream* (Westport, Conn.: Praeger, 2004), 162–64.

7. Angela Mequet Carll, "Fair Brought End to Hotel Boom," *New Orleans Times-Picayune*, Jan. 27, 1985; William Langkopp, interview by author, July 5, 2001; Allan Katz, "Overseas Marketing Gives Boost to N.O. Tourism," *New Orleans Times-Picayune*, July 22, 1986; Frank Donze, "Financial Problems Leave Their Mark on Area Business," *New Orleans Times-Picayune*, Nov. 12, 1984; Nan Perales, "Hotels Trying to Ride Out Slump," *New Orleans Times-Picayune*, June 9, 1985.

8. James Conaway, "The Millionaire and the Fair," *Washington Post*, Apr. 11, 1982; Richard Locker, "Knoxville Regains Its Fair-city Feel," *Memphis Commercial Appeal*, Aug. 16, 1992.

9. Editorial, "After the Golden Age," *New Orleans Times-Picayune*, June 2, 1988.

10. Editorial, "Big Money, Few Jobs," *New Orleans Times-Picayune*, Apr. 17, 1985.

11. Allan Katz, "City Falling Apart," *New Orleans Times-Picayune*, Oct. 23, 1988.

12. John Hall, "Economic Hurricane Batters N.O. Area Economy," *New Orleans Times-Picayune*, Dec. 29, 1985.

13. Frank Donze, "City to Launch Major Tourist Marketing Drive," *New Orleans Times-Picayune*, June 18, 1987.

14. GNOTCC, *Annual Report*, 1985–86, 1986–87 (New Orleans: NOMCVB).

15. Allan Katz, "How to Market the Fair and City," *New Orleans Times-Picayune*, Aug. 5, 1984; "Long-term Marketing Program," *New Orleans Times-Picayune*, June 2, 1985.

16. Gary Esolen, "Developing Tourism in New Orleans," *New Orleans Gambit*, Oct. 20, 1984; Bruce Eggler, "Marketing N.O.: Anti-establishment Career Leads to Top Job in Tourism, *New Orleans Times-Picayune*, Feb. 22, 1991.

17. Gary Esolen, interview by author, New Orleans, Feb. 21, 2000.

18. Ibid.

19. Robert Foster, Warren Reuther, Pat Quinn, and Tom Peterson to Sidney Barthelemy, Oct. 13, 1989, and Ralph O. Brennan, Warren L. Reuther, Sid Siddiqi, and Wiley D. McCormick to Barthelemy, Mar. 9, 1990, folder "Greater New Orleans Tourist and Convention Commission (1989–1993) folder 1," box 52, Barthelemy Papers; Bruce Eggler, "Tourism Plan Takes Rocky Road to Council OK," *New Orleans Times-Picayune*, Jan. 19, 1990; Bruce Eggler, "Tourism Leaders Want New Ideas after Tax Defeat," *New Orleans Times-Picayune*, Mar. 7, 1990.

20. Bruce Eggler, "Tourism Plan Has $2 Million Nut to Crack," *New Orleans Times-Picayune*, Sept. 24, 1990; GNOTCC, *Annual Report*, 1986–87 (New Orleans: NOMCVB); NOMCVB, *Annual Report*, 1996–97 (New Orleans: NOMCVB).

21. Beverly Hendrix Wright, "New Orleans: A City That Care Forgot," in Charles Vincent, ed., *The African American Experience in Louisiana*, part C, *From Jim Crow to Civil Rights*, Louisiana Purchase Bicentennial Series in Louisiana History, vol. 11 (Lafayette: Center for Louisiana Studies, University of Louisiana at Lafayette, 2002), 499; Allan Katz, "Airport Goals," *New Orleans Times-Picayune*, Oct. 12, 1986.

22. Coleman Warner, "Budget Handcuffs Agencies," *New Orleans Times-Picayune*, May 5, 1991; Chris Rose, "Ron Forman: The 60-Second Interview," *New Orleans Times-Picayune*, Oct. 17, 2002.

23. Susan Feeney, "Aquarium Project Resuscitated by City Council," *New Orleans Times-Picayune*, June 9, 1984.

24. Mary Louise Christovich to Sidney J. Barthelemy, June 4, 1987, folder "Aquarium (folder 1)—1987–1990," box 4, Barthelemy Papers.

25. Susan Finch, "Quarter Group Sues to Stop Aquarium," *New Orleans Times-Picayune*, Jan. 10, 1987.

26. Nan Powers and Frank Donze, "Dock Board and City Reach Deal on Aquarium Site," *New Orleans Times-Picayune*, July 15, 1987; Gayle Ashton, "Big Oil Gives $1.6 Million to Aquarium," *New Orleans Times-Picayune*, Oct. 29, 1987; Bruce Eggler, "Aquarium Foes Lose Round as Court Denies Injunction," *New Orleans Times-Picayune*, June 15, 1989.

27. Bruce Eggler, "Quarter in Peril, Congress Told," *New Orleans Times-Picayune*, June 25, 1988; Keith Weldon Medley, "Big Gamble in the Big Easy," *Historic Preservation* 46 (July–Aug. 1994): 30.

28. Errol Laborde, "The Drive for a Riverfront Streetcar," *New Orleans Gambit*, Sept. 1, 1984; Bruce Eggler, "On First Birthday, Route's Future Looks Bright," *New Orleans Times-Picayune*, Aug. 13, 1989.

29. For additional information on riverfront development, see documents in folder 21, box 4, Robinson Papers; Raymond J. Boudreaux to Editor, *New Orleans Times-Picayune*, June 11, 1984; Steve Brooks, "City's Future at Stake; Consensus Ends There," *New Orleans Times-Picayune*, July 15, 1990.

30. *Historic Riverfront as the Front Yard of the Vieux Carré*, prepared for VCPORA by Lowrey-Hess-Boudreaux, Architects, Oct. 10, 1990, copy in author's possession; Steve Brooks, "No Lack of Ideas, But

Only Forman Offers Blueprints," *New Orleans Times-Picayune*, July 15, 1990; "Like It or Not, Forman Factor Is Driving Force," *Time-Picayune*, July 17, 1990; "Not So Fast: Docks Needed, Port Says," *New Orleans Times-Picayune*, July 17, 1990.

31. Jerah Johnson, Chairman, The Future of the Quarter Committee, "The Future of the Quarter: A Report Rendered to the V.C.C.," Feb. 26, 1985, folder "Vieux Carré Commission," box J71, Morial Papers.

32. Rick Raber, "Paradise Lost? City Tries To Clean Up Quarter's Act," *New Orleans Times-Picayune*, Sept. 19, 1983; Editorial, "Zoning vs. Quarter Blight," *New Orleans Times-Picayune*, Aug. 3, 1981.

33. Yvonne S. Bohrer (Springfield, Missouri) to Mayor and City Council, City of New Orleans, Oct. 7, 1987, folder "French Quarter Ordinances (1987–1988)," box 49, Barthelemy Papers.

34. PAW [?] to MRS [?], Memorandum: Proposed Fr. Qtr. "Tout Ensemble" Ordinances, Oct. 29, 1987, folder "French Quarter Ordinances (1987–1988)," box 49, Barthelemy Papers.

35. Coleman Warner, "Permit Protest Darkens Bourbon," *New Orleans Times-Picayune*, Oct. 6, 1987.

36. Charles E. Clark (River Ridge, La.) to Editor, *New Orleans Times-Picayune*, Oct. 9, 1987, folder "French Quarter Ordinances (1987–1988)," box 49, Barthelemy Papers. This letter was copied to Mayor Barthelemy and seven city council members.

37. Harry Greenberger to Editor, *New Orleans Times-Picayune*, Oct. 15, 1987, folder "French Quarter Ordinances (1987–1988)," box 49, Barthelemy Papers.

38. Sylvia Roy, President, Louisiana C.C.I.M. Chapter, to Mike Early, Nov. 4, 1987, folder "French Quarter Ordinances (1987–1988)," box 49, Barthelemy Papers.

39. Steve Brooks, "Residents Flee Quarter While Tourists Stream In," *New Orleans Times-Picayune*, July 16, 1990.

40. Coleman Warner, "Tourist Trap," *New Orleans Times-Picayune*, Nov. 5, 1997; Lill LeGardeur, "These Tours Rattle Quarter Residents," *New Orleans Times-Picayune*, Oct. 17, 2000; Bruce Eggler, "UNO Outlines Ways To Keep the Quarter a Neighborhood," *New Orleans Times-Picayune*, Dec. 3, 1992; "Tourism Promoter Upbeat on N.O.," *New Orleans Times-Picayune*, Jan. 30, 2000.

41. Robert M. Fogelson, *Downtown: Its Rise and Fall, 1880–1950* (New Haven: Yale University Press, 2003).

42. William E. Borah, letter to the editor, *New Orleans Times-Picayune*, May 1, 1996.

43. Coleman Warner, "Preservationists Fight Demolitions on Canal St.," *New Orleans Times-Picayune*, Apr. 5, 1996; "Thomas Wants to Save Facades," *New Orleans Times-Picayune*, May 14, 1996; James Gill, "Old Buildings, Black Merchants," *New Orleans Times-Picayune*, May 5, 1996.

44. Bruce Eggler, "Panel Urges Rejection of Tall Hotel," *New Orleans Times-Picayune*, Apr. 19, 2000; Bruce Eggler and Stewart Yerton, "Towers of Trouble? Hotels Vie with History," *New Orleans Times-Picayune*, May 7, 2000; Stewart Yerton, "Union Takes Advantage of Zoning Squabble," *New Orleans Times-Picayune*, May 7, 2000.

45. Greg Thomas, "International House Taking On a New Mission," *New Orleans Times-Picayune*, Apr. 18, 1997.

46. Bruce Eggler, "Coming Attractions," *New Orleans Times-Picayune*, Sept. 19, 1999.

47. Friends of the Cabildo, *New Orleans Architecture*, vol. 1, *The Lower Garden District* (Gretna, La.: Pelican Publishing, 1971), xv–xvi; Keith Weldon Medley, "Big Gamble in the Big Easy," *Historic Preservation* 46 (July–Aug. 1994): 29.

48. Dolores Hayden, *The Power of Place: Urban Landscapes as Public History* (Cambridge, Mass.: MIT Press, 1995), esp. chap. 3; Robert R. Weyeneth, *Historic Preservation for a Living City: Historic Charleston Foundation, 1947–1997* (Columbia: University of South Carolina Press, 2000).

49. Stewart Yerton, "Celebration of Heritage, Music Will Aid Tourism," *New Orleans Times-Picayune,* June 25, 1995; Jaquetta White, "Multicultural Welcome," *New Orleans Times-Picayune,* July 7, 2002.

50. Coleman Warner, "Two Come to the Defense of City's Housing Image," *New Orleans Times-Picayune,* Aug. 31, 1995; Carlos Monje Jr., "Dismantling History: Historic Homes Easier to Tear Down Than Fix Up," *New Orleans Times-Picayune,* July 27, 1997.

51. Lolis Eric Elie, "Slave Square Wins Respect," *New Orleans Times-Picayune,* Jan. 28, 1998.

52. Lolis Eric Elie, "Traditions Resurrected," *New Orleans Times-Picayune,* Aug. 29, 1997; "Music Makers to Be Saluted," *New Orleans Times-Picayune,* Aug. 21, 1998.

53. Jerry Brock, "The Culture Collector," *New Orleans Gambit,* Aug. 7, 2001; Jesse Katz, "New Orleans Parade Tradition Advances Black Men's Image," *Los Angeles Times,* Sept. 4, 1997; Jay Mazza, "All Saints Day Tribute to Jazz Funerals," *Louisiana Weekly,* Oct. 1999.

54. Lolis Eric Elie, "City May Yet Embrace Its Jazz Heritage," *New Orleans Times-Picayune,* Nov. 19, 1998; Bruce Eggler, "Home Treated with 'Kid' Gloves," *New Orleans Times-Picayune,* Mar. 7, 2002; Lynne Jensen, "Students Add Life to Jazz Landmark," *New Orleans Times-Picayune,* July 6, 2002.

55. Lolis Eric Elie, "If You Show 'Jazz,' Fans Will Come," *New Orleans Times-Picayune,* Jan. 12, 2001; "Park Your Cynicism on Bourbon," *New Orleans Times-Picayune,* Aug. 3, 2001.

56. Allen Rosenzweig and Mickey Caplinger, "Rating the Passing Parades," *New Orleans Figaro,* Mar. 9, 1981.

57. J. Mark Souther, "City in Amber: Race, Culture, and the Tourist Transformation of New Orleans, 1945–1995" (Ph.D. diss., Tulane University, 2002). See chapter 6 for a more thoroughgoing analysis of the city's quandary concerning how to go about enforcing local laws while not killing the French Quarter's allure for tourists.

58. Charles L. Dufour, "Mardi Gras Is More Fun If You Are Dressed for It. Here Is the Greatest Free Show on Earth," *Southern Living* (Feb. 1967): 14.

59. James Gill, *Lords of Misrule: Mardi Gras and the Politics of Race in New Orleans* (Jackson: University Press of Mississippi, 1997), 224–25, 227, 239; "Council Debate Is Today," *New Orleans Times-Picayune,* Dec. 19, 1991; Rebecca Thiem, "Masks Came Off Emotions During Volatile Meeting," *New Orleans Times-Picayune,* Dec. 20, 1991; Dawn Ruth, "Carnival Groups Given One Year to Comply," *New Orleans Times-Picayune,* Dec. 20, 1991.

60. Bruce Eggler, "Momus Was Master of Satire," *New Orleans Times-Picayune,* Jan. 12, 1992; Gill, *Lords of Misrule,* 256.

61. Reni Haley-Davidson, "N.O. Krewe of Orpheus Plans Super Show," *New Orleans Times-Picayune,* May 8, 1993; Finch, "Connick's Krewe Recruiting Members," *New Orleans Times-Picayune,* Aug. 20, 1993.

62. Anne Rochell, "Strange Krewe at Mardi Gras," *Atlanta Constitution,* Feb. 22, 1998; Alfred Charles, "Revelers Made 1994 a Carnival to Bank On," *New Orleans Times-Picayune,* Jan. 27, 1995.

63. Press release, Patricia Gravino, "Tony Department Store Issues Annual Holiday Catalogue," *Associated Press,* Sept. 11, 1990; Press Release, "MTV Wreaks Havoc with 'Mardi Gras Madness,'" *PR Newswire,* Feb. 20, 1987.

64. Tyler Bridges, "Krewes Toss Around Idea of Parade Sponsors," *New Orleans Times-Picayune*, Feb. 26, 1995.

65. Clancy DuBos, "Marketing Mambo?" *New Orleans Gambit*, Mar. 16, 1993; James Gill, "Picking Apart a Patronage Plum," *New Orleans Times-Picayune*, Feb. 18, 1994.

66. Christina Cheakalos, "Did New Orleans Sell Soul By Marketing Mardi Gras? 'Official' Trademark Seen as Slap at Tradition," *Atlanta Constitution*, Feb. 2, 1994.

67. DuBos, "Marketing Mambo?"; James Gill, "Turning a Buck on Carnival," *New Orleans Times-Picayune*, Dec. 12, 1993.

68. Dawn Ruth, "Mardi Gras Licensing Attacked," *New Orleans Times-Picayune*, Dec. 17, 1993.

69. James Gill, "The Commercialization of Carnival," *New Orleans Times-Picayune*, Mar. 1, 1995.

70. Frank Donze, "Lundi Gras Revelry to Revive Tradition," *New Orleans Times-Picayune*, Nov. 19, 1986; Allan Katz, "City Experiences One of Its Most Successful Carnivals," *New Orleans Times-Picayune*, Mar. 8, 1987.

71. David Snyder, "Carnival Ride Lures World's Travelers," *New Orleans Times-Picayune*, Feb. 15, 1988; Susan Finch, "Grand Tour: Krewe to Sell Rides," *New Orleans Times-Picayune*, June 30, 1992; Calvin Baker, "Out-of-towners High on Tucks Parade," *New Orleans Times-Picayune*, Feb. 26, 1995; Errol Laborde, "They're Not Really Krewes; They're Korporations," *New Orleans Citybusiness*, Aug. 18, 1997; Rick Bragg, "Merrymaking Is Clashing with Tradition in Mardi Gras Tableaux," *New York Times*, Feb. 23, 1998; Editorial, "Americanization, Part 2," *New Orleans Gambit*, Sept. 2, 1997.

72. Arthur Hardy, "Our Carnival Cousins," *Arthur Hardy's Mardi Gras Guide*, vol. 26 (Metairie, La.: Arthur Hardy Enterprises, Inc., 2002), 37–38, 42, 88–90.

73. Ed Anderson, "Austin Not Giving Up Mardi Gras For Lent," *New Orleans Times-Picayune*, Mar. 7, 1987; Janet McConnaughey, "Mardi Gras Fever Spreads: Far-flung Cities in on the Action," *Chicago Sun-Times*, Feb. 10, 1997; Babita Persaud, "The Ghosts of Guavaween Past," *St. Petersburg Times*, Oct. 29, 1999.

74. "Mardi Gras Cheers the Float Makers," *New York Times*, Mar. 3, 1981; Bridget O'Brian, "The Business of Making Carnival So Glamorous," *New Orleans Times-Picayune*, Feb. 22, 1987; Judi Russell, "Cashing In on Carnival," *New Orleans Citybusiness* (Feb. 3–9, 1997), 1, 40; Roy Furchgott, "For New Orleans, Mardi Gras Is Becoming an All-Year Cash Cow," *New York Times*, Feb. 7, 1999; James Varney, "Internet Riders Joining Revelry: Mardi Gras Sent to World On-line," *New Orleans Times-Picayune*, Feb. 27, 1995.

75. Mary Foster, "New Orleans Finds Its Cultural Uplift Descending into Tawdry Self-Parody," *Buffalo News*, Feb. 23, 1998; "New Orleans Police Deliver Mardi Gras Nudity Warning," *St. Louis Post-Dispatch*, Feb. 28, 2000.

76. LeGardeur, "These Tours Rattle Quarter Residents."

1. Chris Rose, "Rex and Remembrance," *New Orleans Times-Picayune*, Apr. 3, 2001.

2. Lolis Eric Elie, "Our Town Is Being Invaded," *New Orleans Times-Picayune*, May 23, 2001.

3. Rebecca Mowbray, "The New Bourbon Kings," *New Orleans Times-Picayune*, Feb. 10, 2002.

4. M. Christine Boyer, *The City of Collective Memory: Its Historical Imagery and Architectural Entertainments* (Cambridge: MIT Press, 1994), 391.

5. While historians have yet to explore many of the manifestations of cultural tourism in the urban South, the essays in Richard D. Starnes, ed., *Southern Journeys: Tourism, History, and Culture in the Modern South* (Tuscaloosa: University of Alabama Press, 2003), suggest the ongoing importance of southern culture in southern economic development. On the southern "commercial-civic elite," see esp. Blaine A. Brownell, *The Urban Ethos in the South, 1920–1930* (Baton Rouge: Louisiana State University Press, 1975).

6. David Farrow, "Spoleto in '77, Hugo in '89 Changed Charleston Forever," *Charleston Post and Courier,* May 6, 2004.

7. My colleague Mary Wren Bivins may take credit for suggesting the palimpsest metaphor as an instructive way of viewing New Orleans.

8. Wendell Rawls Jr., "Poverty Underlies New Orleans Sheen of Prosperity," *New York Times,* Sept. 8, 1980; Stewart Brand, *How Buildings Learn: What Happens after They're Built* (New York: Penguin, 1994).

9. "Murder-robbery of Tourist Sets Off Alarm in New Orleans," *Houston Post,* Sept. 21, 1980; "Hyatt Held Liable in Slaying of Maine Visitor," *New Orleans Times-Picayune,* Jan. 10, 1984; Editorial, "Tourism and Crime," *New Orleans Times-Picayune,* Feb. 22, 1984; "N.O. Ranked 4th Most Lethal City in FBI Reports," *New Orleans Times-Picayune,* Sept. 1, 1983; Mike Christensen, "New Orleans's Mean Streets Echo Atlanta's Crime Crisis," *Atlanta Journal and Constitution,* Apr. 13, 1980.

10. James C. Parsons, Superintendent, NOPD, to Cindy Fromherz, French Quarter Task Force, Jan. 24, 1980, folder "French Quarter Task Force, 1980 (Jan.–Mar.)," box B3; pamphlet, "The Mayor's French Quarter Task Force Welcomes You to the Vieux Carré," n.d. [early 1980s], folder "French Quarter Task Force," box M9; French Quarter Task Force Minutes, Mar. 27, 1980, folder "French Quarter Task Force, 1980 (Jan.–Mar.)," box B3; Morial to Archbishop Philip M. Hannan, Sept. 29, 1980, folder "Tourism, 1979–1985," box B32, Morial Papers.

11. Mark Lorando, "CBS Not Apple of WWL's Eye," *New Orleans Times-Picayune,* Feb. 20, 1989; Lorando, "CBS Stands by Its Man," *New Orleans Times-Picayune,* Feb. 27, 1989.

12. Gordon Russell, "Drawn to New Orleans," *New Orleans Times-Picayune,* Aug. 26, 2001.

NOTES TO POSTSCRIPT

Epigraph: Justin Davidson, "The City Fabric Must Be Rewoven Block by Block," *Cleveland Plain Dealer,* Sept. 9, 2005.

1. Gordon Russell, "Surge Likely to Top N.O. Levee System," *New Orleans Times-Picayune,* Aug. 29, 2005.

2. Richard Morin and Lisa Rein, "Some of the Uprooted Won't Go Home Again," *Washington Post,* Sept. 16, 2005. On the racial dimensions of the New Orleans disaster, see, e.g., Nicholas Lemann, "Comment: In the Ruins," *New Yorker* 81 (Sept. 12, 2005): 33–36; David Remnick, "Letter from Louisiana: High Water," *New Yorker* 81 (Oct. 3, 2005): 48–57.

3. Adam Nossiter, Associated Press, "What New Orleans Was: Awakening from the City's Dream State, Facing a Nightmare," Sept. 6, 2005.

4. Susan Saulny, "Putting Down New Roots on More Solid Ground," *New York Times,* Sept. 7, 2005; Morin and Rein, "Some of the Uprooted Won't Go Home Again."

5. Rebecca Mowbray, "Conventions Put Off in New Orleans," *New Orleans Times-Picayune*, Sept. 6, 2005.

6. Ibid.

7. Lolis Eric Elie, "Our Town Is Being Invaded," *New Orleans Times-Picayune*, May 23, 2001.

8. Allen G. Breed, "French Quarter Holdouts Become Tribe of Survivors, Divvy Up Labor," *Cleveland Plain Dealer*, Sept. 5, 2005.

BIBLIOGRAPHY

Abbreviations

ARC   Amistad Research Center, Tulane University, New Orleans
HJA   William Ransom Hogan Jazz Archive, Tulane University
NOPL New Orleans Public Library
TU   Department of Special Collections, Tulane University
UNO Department of Special Collections, University of New Orleans

Manuscript Collections

Sidney J. Barthelemy Papers, City Archives, NOPL
Chamber of Commerce Collection, UNO
Congress of Racial Equality (CORE) Papers, ARC
Ralston Crawford Collection, HJA
Nils R. Douglas Collection, ARC
Human Relations Committee General Office Files, NOPL
Moon Landrieu Collection, Special Collections and Archives, Loyola University
Moon Landrieu Papers, City Archives, NOPL
Earnest N. Morial Papers, City Archives, NOPL
deLesseps S. Morrison Papers, TU
deLesseps S. Morrison Papers, City Archives, NOPL
NAACP (New Orleans Branch) Collection, UNO
John J. Petre Records, NOPL
Phonograph Collection, HJA
Martha Gilmore Robinson Papers, TU
Victor H. Schiro Papers, NOPL
Preston and Bonita Valien Collection (in process), ARC
Vertical Files, HJA
Vertical Files, Louisiana Collection, TU
Scott Wilson Papers, TU

Newspapers and Newsletters

Association of Commerce News Bulletin (Association of Commerce, New Orleans)
Atlanta Journal and Constitution
Eureka News Bulletin (Higgins Industries, New Orleans)
Louisiana Weekly
Meridian Star (Mississippi)
New Orleans CityBusiness
New Orleans Figaro
New Orleans Gambit
New Orleans Item
New Orleans States
New Orleans States-Item
New Orleans Times-Picayune
New York Times
Old French Quarter News
Second Line (New Orleans Jazz Club, New Orleans)
Vieux Carré Courier

Other Primary Sources

Arrest Books. New Orleans Police Department. NOPL.
Crescent City Sepia Host Buyers and Tourist Guide to New Orleans, 1956–57. Louisiana Division. NOPL.
David Brinkley's Journal, Jan. 10, 1962, NBC-TV film, 16 mm composite print. HJA.
Facts on Film. Nashville: Southern Education Reporting Service, 1954–65. ARC.
Historic Riverfront as the Front Yard of the Vieux Carré. Prepared for VCPORA by Lowrey-Hess-Boudreaux, Architects, Oct. 10, 1990.
McCain v. Davis, 217 F. Supp. 661 (1963 U.S. Dist.).
New Orleans, Strategic City of the South: A Pictorial-Statistical Presentation to the National Football League. New Orleans: David Kleck and Associates; New Orleans Pro Football Club, Inc., 1965. Howard-Tilton Memorial Library, Tulane University.
New Orleans Tourism Planning Committee Report. March 1960. UNO.

Interviews

Burns, Dr. Leonard L. Telephone interview by J. Mark Souther. June 14, 2001.
———. Interview by Kim Lacy Rogers. May 14, 1979. Oral History Project. ARC.
Cassimere, Dr. Raphael, Jr. Interview by J. Mark Souther. New Orleans. June 11, 2001.

DeDroit, Johnny. Interview by Richard B. Allen and Dexter Thompson. Mar. 16, 1973. HJA.

Dixon, David F. Telephone interview by J. Mark Souther. Jan. 11, 2001.

Esolen, Gary. Interview by J. Mark Souther. New Orleans. Feb. 21, 2000.

Gandolfo, Henri. Interview by Dorothy Schlesinger. Oct. 3, 1974. Friends of the Cabildo Oral History Project. TU.

Jaffe, Allan. Interview by Tony Luckenbach and Walt Richter. Sept. [n.d.], 1966. Oral History Collection. HJA.

Langkopp, William. Interview by J. Mark Souther. New Orleans. July 5, 2001.

Liuzza, Ray A. Interview by J. Mark Souther. New Orleans. June 20, 2001.

Mares, Joe, Jr. Interview by Walt Richter. Sept. 1966. Oral History Collection. HJA

———. Interview by William Russell. Apr. 8, 1960. Oral History Collection. HJA.

Morrison, Mrs. Jacob H. Interview by Jacob Geiser III. New Orleans. Aug. 2, 1977. Friends of the Cabildo Oral History Project. NOPL.

Secondary Sources

"The Great New Orleans 'Steal.'" *Fortune* 38 (Nov. 1948): 102–3.

"Jackson Square Meets the Mississippi." *Southern Living* (June 1977): 80–83.

"Journey in America: III." *New Republic* 111 (Nov. 27, 1944): 684+.

"The King Resigns." *Newsweek* (Feb. 13, 1961).

"A Sunbelt City Plays Catch-up." *Business Week* (Mar. 6, 1978): 69.

Anderson, Terry H. *The Movement and the Sixties: Protest in America from Greensboro to Wounded Knee.* New York: Oxford University Press, 1995.

Aswell, James. "New Orleans Takes the Cure." *Saturday Evening Post* 219 (Jan. 25, 1947): 30+.

Axthelm, Pete. "A Midsummer's Mardi Gras." *Newsweek* (July 16, 1984).

Bacon, Joe. "Preservation: The Morrison Message." *New Orleans* (Aug. 1982).

Baker, Liva. *The Second Battle of New Orleans: The Hundred-Year Struggle to Integrate the Schools.* New York: HarperCollins, 1996.

Baker, Mark. "Mardi Gras: Everybody's Laughing." *U.S. News & World Report* (Feb. 10, 1986): 78.

Barry, John M. *Rising Tide: The Great Mississippi Flood of 1927 and How It Changed America.* New York: Simon and Schuster, 1997.

Barth, Gunther. *City People: The Rise of Modern City Culture in Nineteenth-Century America.* New York: Oxford University Press, 1980.

Bartley, Numan V. *The New South, 1945–1980.* Baton Rouge: Louisiana State University Press, 1995.

———. *The Rise of Massive Resistance: Race and Politics in the South during the 1950s.* Baton

Rouge: Louisiana State University Press, 1999.

Basso, Hamilton. "Can New Orleans Come Back?" *Forum* 103, no. 3 (Mar. 1940): 124–28.

Becknell, Clarence A., Thomas Price, and Don Short. "History of the Zulu Social Aid & Pleasure Club, Inc." *Welcome to Zulu* (www.mardigrasneworleans.com/zulu).

Bell, Caryn Cossé. *Revolution, Romanticism, and the Afro-Creole Protest Tradition in Louisiana, 1718–1868.* Baton Rouge: Louisiana State University Press, 1997.

Berger, Morroe. "Letters from New Orleans." *Annual Review of Jazz Studies* 7 (1994–95): 47–73.

Bernard, Richard M., and Bradley R. Rice, eds. *Sunbelt Cities: Politics and Growth Since World War II.* Austin: University of Texas Press, 1983.

Berry, Jason, Jonathan Foose, and Tad Jones. *Up from the Cradle of Jazz: New Orleans Music since World War II.* Athens: University of Georgia Press, 1986.

Bobo, James R. *The New Orleans Economy: Pro Bono Publico?* New Orleans: Division of Business and Economic Research, College of Business Administration, University of New Orleans, 1975.

Borah, William E., and Richard O. Baumbach Jr. *The Second Battle of New Orleans: A History of the Vieux Carré Riverfront Expressway Controversy.* University: University of Alabama Press, 1981.

Bordelon, Richard. "Krewes-ing in the Suburbs." *New Orleans* (Feb. 1979): 41.

Boyer, M. Christine. *The City of Collective Memory: Its Historical Imagery and Architectural Entertainments.* Cambridge, Mass.: MIT Press, 1994.

Brand, Stewart. *How Buildings Learn: What Happens after They're Built.* New York: Penguin, 1994.

Brasseaux, Carl A., ed. *A Refuge for All Ages: Immigration in Louisiana History.* Louisiana Purchase Bicentennial Series in Louisiana History, vol. 10. Lafayette: Center for Louisiana Studies, University of Southwestern Louisiana, 1996.

Breen, Ann, and Dick Rigby. *Intown Living: A Different American Dream.* Westport, Conn.: Praeger, 2004.

Brownell, Blaine A., and David R. Goldfield, eds. *The City in Southern History: The Growth of Urban Civilization in the South.* Port Washington, N.Y.: Kennikat Press, 1977.

Buerkle, Jack V., and Danny Barker. *Bourbon Street Black: The New Orleans Black Jazzman.* New York: Oxford University Press, 1973.

Burns, Mick. *The Great Olympia Band.* New Orleans: Jazzology Press, 2001.

Byler, Bob. "Dancing in the Aisles." *Mississippi Rag* (Aug. 1977): 1–4.

Carpenter, Arthur E. "Gateway to the Americas: New Orleans's Quest for Latin American Trade, 1900–1970." Ph.D. dissertation, Tulane University, 1987.

Carter, William. *Preservation Hall: Music from the Heart.* New York: W. W. Norton, 1991.

Chai, Charles Y. W. "Who Rules New Orleans: A Study of Community Power Structure." *Louisiana Business Survey* 16, no. 5 (Oct. 1971): 2–11.

Cobb, James C. *The Selling of the South: The Southern Crusade for Industrial Development, 1936–1990.* Urbana: University of Illinois Press, 1993.

Cocke, Ed. "A Requiem for Zulu." *New Orleans* (Feb. 1970): 42–43+.

Cocks, Catherine. *Doing the Town: The Rise of Urban Tourism in the United States, 1850–1915.* Berkeley: University of California Press, 2001.

Cohen, Lizabeth. *A Consumers' Republic: The Politics of Mass Consumption in Postwar America.* New York: Alfred A. Knopf, 2003.

Cole, Thomas R. *No Color Is My Kind: The Life of Eldrewey Stearns and the Integration of Houston.* Austin: University of Texas Press, 1997.

Dabney, Virginius. "What's Happened to Old New Orleans?" *Saturday Evening Post* 226, no. 15 (Oct. 10, 1953): 40–41+.

Dates, Jannette L., and William Barlow, eds. *Split Image: African Americans in the Mass Media.* Washington, D.C.: Howard University Press, 1990.

Davis, Jack E. *Race against Time: Culture and Separation in Natchez since 1930.* Baton Rouge: Louisiana State University Press, 2001.

Dejan, Harold. *Everything Is Lovely!* Pijnacker, the Netherlands: Holland Olympia Publishers, Ltd., 1989.

Delaup, Rick. *Eccentric New Orleans* (www.eccentricneworleans.com).

DeMers, John. *French Quarter Royalty: The Tumultuous Life and Times of the Omni Royal Orleans Hotel.* New Orleans: Omni Royal Orleans Hotel, 1993.

Deutsch, Sarah. *Women and the City: Gender, Space, and Power in Boston, 1870–1940.* New York: Oxford University Press, 2000.

Dilworth, Leah. *Imagining Indians in the Southwest: Persistent Visions of a Primitive Past.* Washington, D.C.: Smithsonian Institution Press, 1996.

Doyle, Don. *New Men, New Cities, New South: Atlanta, Nashville, Charleston, Mobile, 1860–1910.* Chapel Hill: University of North Carolina Press, 1990.

DuBos, Clancy. "Between a Rock and Canal Place: The Education of Joseph Canizaro." *New Orleans* (Oct. 1978).

Dufour, Charles L. "Mardi Gras Is More Fun If You Are Dressed for It. Here Is the Greatest Free Show on Earth." *Southern Living* (Feb. 1967): 14+.

Dunn, Joe P., and Howard L. Preston, eds. *The Future South: A Historical Perspective for the Twenty-first Century.* Urbana: University of Illinois Press, 1991.

Edmonds, Michael. "Around New Orleans." *Jazz Music* (London) 4, no. 1 (1949).

Edmonson, Munro S. "Carnival in New Orleans." *Caribbean Quarterly* 4, no. 3–4 (Mar.–June 1956): 233–45.

Eisinger, Peter. "The Politics of Bread and Circuses: Building the City for the Visitor Class." *Urban Affairs Review* 35, no. 3 (Jan. 2000): 316–33.

Emerson, William A., Jr. "The New New Orleans." *Collier's* 130, no. 22 (Nov. 29, 1952): 42–45.

Evans, Eli N. *The Provincials: A Personal History of Jews in the South.* New York: Free Press, 1997.

Fainstein, Susan S., Norman I. Fainstein, Richard Child Hill, Dennis Judd, and Michael P. Smith. *Restructuring the City: The Political Economy of Urban Redevelopment.* New York: Longman, 1983.

Fairclough, Adam. *Race and Democracy: The Civil Rights Struggle in Louisiana, 1915–1972.* Athens: University of Georgia Press, 1995.

Findlay, John M. *Magic Lands: Western Cityscapes and American Culture after 1940.* Berkeley: University of California Press, 1992.

Flake, Carol. *New Orleans: Behind the Masks of America's Most Exotic City.* New York: Grove Press, 1994.

Fogelson, Robert M. *Downtown: Its Rise and Fall, 1880–1950.* New Haven: Yale University Press, 2003.

Ford, Larry R. *America's New Downtowns: Revitalization or Reinvention?* Baltimore: Johns Hopkins University Press, 2003.

Frieden, Bernard J., and Lynne B. Sagalyn. *Downtown, Inc.: How America Rebuilds Cities.* Cambridge, Mass.: MIT Press, 1989.

Friends of the Cabildo. *New Orleans Architecture.* Vol. 1, *The Lower Garden District.* Gretna, La.: Pelican Publishing, 1971.

Gallas, Walter W. "Neighborhood Preservation and Politics in New Orleans: Vieux Carré Property Owners, Residents and Associates, Inc. and City Government, 1938–1983." M.A. thesis, University of New Orleans, 1996.

Germany, Kent B. "Making a New Louisiana: American Liberalism and the Search for the Great Society in New Orleans, 1964–1974." Ph.D. diss., Tulane University, 2000.

Gill, James. *Lords of Misrule: Mardi Gras and the Politics of Race in New Orleans.* Jackson: University Press of Mississippi, 1997.

Glassberg, David. *Sense of History: The Place of the Past in American Life.* Amherst: University of Massachusetts Press, 2001.

Goldfield, David. *Cotton Fields and Skyscrapers: Southern City and Region, 1607–1980.* Baton Rouge: Louisiana State University Press, 1982.

———. "Writing the Sunbelt." *OAH Magazine of History* 18, no. 1 (Oct. 2003): 5–10.

Greater New Orleans Tourist and Convention Commission. *Annual Report.* 1971–79, 1986–87. New Orleans: GNOTCC.

Greenspan, Anders. *Creating Colonial Williamsburg.* Washington, D.C.: Smithsonian Institution Press, 2002.

Griffin, Thomas. "The French Quarter." *Holiday* 15, no. 3 (Mar. 1954): 52–56+.

Haas, Edward F. *DeLesseps S. Morrison and the Image of Reform: New Orleans Politics, 1946–1961.* Baton Rouge: Louisiana State University Press, 1974.

Hardy, Arthur. "Our Carnival Cousins." *Arthur Hardy's Mardi Gras Guide.* Vol. 26. Metairie, La.: Arthur Hardy Enterprises, Inc., 2002.

Harmon, David Andrew. *Beneath the Image of the Civil Rights Movement and Race Relations: Atlanta, Georgia, 1946–1981*. New York: Garland, 1996.

Harrison, Shirley. "Mardi Gras Mambo: Carnival Culture Teams with Counter Culture." *New Orleans* (Mar. 1984): 46–51.

Hartman, George. "New Orleans Today." *Jazz Record* (Jan. 1945): 4–6.

Hayden, Dolores. *The Power of Place: Urban Landscapes as Public History*. Cambridge, Mass.: MIT Press, 1995.

Hirsch, Arnold R., and Joseph Logsdon, eds. *Creole New Orleans: Race and Americanization*. Baton Rouge: Louisiana State University Press, 1992.

Hoelscher, Steven D. *Heritage on Stage: The Invention of Ethnic Place in America's Little Switzerland*. Madison: University of Wisconsin Press, 1998.

Hulsizer, Ken. "New Orleans in Wartime." In Max Jones and Albert McCarthy, eds., *Jazz Review*. London: Jazz Music Books, 1945.

Jacoway, Elizabeth, and David R. Colburn, eds. *Southern Businessmen and Desegregation*. Baton Rouge: Louisiana State University Press, 1982.

James, Rosemary. "Mason's Strip . . . The New Basin Street." *New Orleans* (Mar. 1977): 38–41.

Johns, Michael. *Moment of Grace: The American City in the 1950s*. Berkeley: University of California Press, 2002.

Johnson, Monifa Ife. "The Coming of Jazzfest: Jazz Festivals, Desegregation and Tourism in New Orleans, 1940–1970." Master's thesis, Tulane University, 2000.

Jones, Max, and Albert McCarthy, eds. *Jazz Review*. London: Jazz Music Books, 1945.

Jones, Tad. "'Separate but Equal' : The Laws of Segregation and Their Effect on New Orleans Black Musicians, 1950–1964." *Living Blues Magazine* 77 (Dec. 1987): 24–28.

Judd, Dennis R., and Susan S. Fainstein, eds. *The Tourist City*. New Haven: Yale University Press, 1999.

Kammen, Michael. *Mystic Chords of Memory: The Transformation of Tradition in American Culture*. New York: Alfred A. Knopf, 1991.

Katz, Allan. "How Football Saved a City," *New Orleans* (Jan. 1990): 85.

Kinser, Samuel. *Carnival, American Style Mardi Gras at New Orleans and Mobile*. Chicago: University of Chicago Press, 1990.

Knowles, Richard H. *Fallen Heroes: A History of New Orleans Brass Bands*. New Orleans: Jazzology Press, 1996.

Kowalewski, Maurice. "Flies in the Bourbon: A Walking Tour of Bourbon Street without the Benefit of Rose Colored Hurricane Glasses." *New Orleans* (Mar. 1973): 74–77+.

Kropp, Phoebe S. "'All Our Yesterdays' : The Spanish Fantasy Past and the Politics of Public Memory in Southern California, 1884–1939." Ph.D. diss., University of California, San Diego, 1999.

Kurtz, Michael L. "DeLesseps S. Morrison: Political Reformer." *Louisiana History* 17, no. 1 (Winter 1976): 19–39.

Labouisse, F. Monroe, Jr. "The Death of the Old French Market." *New Orleans* (June 1975): 72–73+.

Law, Christopher M. *Urban Tourism: Attracting Visitors to Large Cities.* London: Mansell, 1993.

Lemann, Bernard. *The Vieux Carré: A General Statement.* New Orleans: School of Architecture, Tulane University, 1966.

Lemann, Nicholas. "Comment: In the Ruins," *New Yorker* 81 (Sept. 12, 2005): 33–36.

Lemann, Nick. "What Does Mardi Gras Mean?" *New Orleans* (Feb. 1974): 43–56+.

Lewis, Peirce F. *New Orleans: The Making of an Urban Landscape.* Cambridge, Mass.: Ballinger, 1976.

———. *New Orleans: The Making of an Urban Landscape,* 2d ed. Santa Fe: Center for American Places, 2003.

———. "To Revive Urban Downtowns, Show Respect for the Spirit of the Place." *Smithsonian* 6 (Sept. 1975): 33–41.

Lim, Harry. "Way Down Yonder. . . ." *Metronome* (Oct. 1943): 36, 38.

Long, Alecia P. *The Great Southern Babylon: Sex, Race, and Respectability in New Orleans, 1865–1920.* Baton Rouge: Louisiana State University Press, 2004.

Lowenthal, David. *The Past Is a Foreign Country.* Cambridge, U.K.: Cambridge University Press, 1985.

Manalla, Christine. "Past Master." *New Orleans* (Jan.–Feb. 1999).

May, Hoke. "A Bright Spot in the City's Tourism Troubles." *New Orleans* (Sept. 1968): 10–13.

McMillen, Neil R. *The Citizens' Council: Organized Resistance to the Second Reconstruction, 1954–64.* Urbana: University of Illinois Press, 1971.

Medley, Keith Weldon. "Big Gamble in the Big Easy." *Historic Preservation* 46 (July–Aug. 1994): 26–31.

Meisler, Stanley. "New Orleans: Future Hub of the Americas." *American Mercury* 88, no. 421 (Feb. 1959): 19–22.

Merriam, Allan P., and Raymond W. Mack. "The Jazz Community," *Social Forces* 38 (Mar. 1960).

Mitchell, Reid. *All on a Mardi Gras Day: Episodes in the History of New Orleans Carnival.* Cambridge, Mass.: Harvard University Press, 1995.

Moehring, Eugene P. *Resort City in the Sunbelt: Las Vegas, 1930–2000,* 2d ed. Reno: University of Nevada Press, 2000.

Mohl, Raymond A. "Saving the Vieux Carré: Inside the New Orleans Freeway Revolt." Unpublished manuscript.

Moley, Raymond. "Louisiana Renaissance." *Newsweek* 29, no. 7 (Feb. 17, 1947): 108.

Morris, Ronald L. *Wait until Dark: Jazz and the Underworld, 1880–1940.* Bowling Green, Ohio: Bowling Green University Popular Press, 1980.

New Orleans Metropolitan Visitors and Convention Bureau. *Annual Report*. 1996–97. New Orleans: NOMVCB.

Newlin, John. "The Case against Carnival." *Wavelength* (New Orleans) 41 (Mar. 1984): 16–18.

Newman, Harvey K. *Southern Hospitality: Tourism and the Growth of Atlanta*. Tuscaloosa: University of Alabama Press, 1999.

O' Brien, Rosary Hartel. "The New Orleans Carnival Organizations: Theatre of Prestige." Ph.D. diss., University of California, Los Angeles, 1973.

Provenzano, John A. "Mardi Gras, Chic la Pai." *Jazz Record* (Apr. 1946): 11–12.

R. L. Polk's New Orleans City Directory. Dallas: R. L. Polk, 1945, 1965, 1968, 1971.

Raabe, Phyllis Hutton. "Status and Its Impact: New Orleans' Carnival, the Social Upper Class and Upper-Class Power." Ph.D. diss., Pennsylvania State University, 1973.

Raeburn, Bruce Boyd. "New Orleans Style: The Awakening of American Jazz Scholarship and Its Cultural Implications." Ph.D. diss., Tulane University, 1991.

Raffray, Jeannette. "Origins of the Vieux Carré Commission, 1920–1941." *Louisiana History* 40, no. 3 (Summer 1999): 283–98.

Ramsey, Frederick, Jr., and Charles Edward Smith, eds. *Jazzmen*. London: Sidgwick and Jackson, 1957.

Ray, Celeste, ed. *Southern Heritage on Display: Public Ritual and Ethnic Diversity within Southern Regionalism*. Tuscaloosa: University of Alabama Press, 2003.

Real Estate Research Corporation, *Economic Survey of the Central Area of New Orleans*. New Orleans: Chamber of Commerce of the New Orleans Area, 1959.

Reichl, Alexander J. "Historic Preservation and Progrowth Politics in U.S. Cities." *Urban Affairs Review* 32, no. 4 (Mar. 1997): 513–35.

Remnick, David. "Letter from Louisiana: High Water," *New Yorker* 81 (Oct. 3, 2005): 48–57.

Rogers, Kim Lacy. *Righteous Lives: Narratives of the New Orleans Civil Rights Movement*. New York: New York University Press, 1993.

Rothman, Hal K., ed. *The Culture of Tourism, the Tourism of Culture*. Albuquerque: University of New Mexico Press, 2003.

———. *Devil's Bargains: Tourism in the Twentieth-Century American West*. Lawrence: University Press of Kansas, 1998.

———. *Neon Metropolis: How Las Vegas Started the Twenty-First Century*. New York: Free Press, 2002.

Russell, W. H. "I Ain't Gonna Study War No More." *Jazz* (New York) (Aug. 1942): 22–23.

Rydell, Robert W. *All the World's a Fair: Visions of Empire at American International Expositions, 1876–1916*. Chicago: University of Chicago Press, 1984.

Sanders, Heywood T. "Building the Convention City: Politics, Finance, and Public Investment in Urban America." *Journal of Urban Affairs* 14, no. 2 (1992): 135–60.

Schulman, Abe J. "Postwar Mardi Gras." *Jazz Record* (Apr. 1946): 4–5.

Serino, Michael. "In the Italian Quarter." *Primo* (Carnegie, Penn.) (Mar.–Apr. 2002): 35–37.

Shaffer, Marguerite S. *See America First: Tourism and National Identity, 1880–1940.* Washington, D.C.: Smithsonian Institution Press, 2001.

Sies, Mary Corbin, and Christopher Silver, eds. *Planning the Twentieth-Century American City.* Baltimore: Johns Hopkins University Press, 1996.

Silber, Nina. *The Romance of Reunion: Northerners and the South, 1865–1900.* Chapel Hill: University of North Carolina Press, 1993.

Smith, Thomas G. "Outside the Pale: The Exclusion of Blacks from the National Football League, 1934–1946." *Journal of Sport History* 15, no. 3 (Winter 1988): 255–81.

Smith, V. L., ed. *Hosts and Guests: The Anthropology of Tourism.* Philadelphia: University of Pennsylvania Press, 1977.

Social Register, New Orleans. New York: Social Register Association, 1952.

Souther, J. Mark. "City in Amber: Race, Culture, and the Tourist Transformation of New Orleans, 1945–1995." Ph.D. diss., Tulane University, 2002.

———. "Into the Big League: Conventions, Football, and the Color Line in New Orleans." *Journal of Urban History* 29 (Sept. 2003): 694–725.

———. "Making the 'Birthplace of Jazz' : Tourism and Musical Heritage Marketing in New Orleans." *Louisiana History* 44, no. 1 (Winter 2003): 39–73.

Stanonis, Anthony. "'A Woman of Boundless Energy': Elizebeth Werlein and Her Times." *Louisiana History* 46, no. 1 (Winter 2005): 5–26.

Starnes, Richard D., ed. *Southern Journeys: Tourism, History, and Culture in the Modern South.* Tuscaloosa: University of Alabama Press, 2003.

Sterngass, Jon. *First Resorts: Pursuing Pleasure at Coney Island, Newport, and Saratoga Springs.* Baltimore: Johns Hopkins University Press, 2001.

Sugrue, Thomas J. *The Origins of the Urban Crisis: Race and Inequality in Postwar Detroit.* Princeton: Princeton University Press, 1996.

Suhor, Charles. "The 'French Quarters.'" *New Orleans* (Feb. 1970): 45+.

———. "Jazz and the New Orleans Press." *Down Beat* (Elmhurst, Ill.) (June 12, 1969).

———. "The Unique, Syncopated Non-Jet Set Rhythm of New Orleans." *Gentlemen's Quarterly* (Apr. 1970): 84+.

Tassin, Myron. *Bacchus.* Gretna, La.: Pelican, 1975.

Teaford, Jon C. "Urban Renewal and Its Aftermath." *Housing Policy Debate* 11, no. 2 (2000): 443–65.

Thompson, Butch, with Charlie DeVore. "Keeping the Faith: Allan Jaffe (1935–1987)." *Mississippi Rag* (Apr. 1987): 1–4.

Tindall, George Brown. *The Emergence of the New South, 1913–1945.* Baton Rouge: Louisiana State University Press and the Littleton Fund for Southern History of the University of Texas, 1967.

Trillin, Calvin. "New Orleans Unmasked." *New Yorker* 73 (Feb. 2, 1998): 38–43.

———. "A Reporter at Large: The Zulus." *New Yorker* 40 (June 20, 1964): 41–42+.

———. "U.S. Journal: New Orleans: On the Possibility of Houstonization." *New Yorker* 50 (Feb. 17, 1975): 94–98.

———. "U.S. Journal: New Orleans: Mardi Gras." *New Yorker* 44 (Mar. 9, 1968): 138–44.

Vieux Carré Demonstration Study. New Orleans: Marcou, O'Leary and Associates, 1968.

Vincent, Charles, ed. *The African American Experience in Louisiana.* Part C, *From Jim Crow to Civil Rights.* Louisiana Purchase Bicentennial Series in Louisiana History, vol. 11. Lafayette: Center for Louisiana Studies, University of Louisiana at Lafayette, 2002.

Ward, Brian. *Just My Soul Responding: Rhythm and Blues, Black Consciousness, and Race Relations.* Berkeley: University of California Press, 1998.

Weeks, Jim. *Gettysburg: Memory, Market, and an American Shrine.* Princeton: Princeton University Press, 2003.

West, Patsy. *The Enduring Seminoles: From Alligator Wrestling to Ecotourism.* Gainesville: University Press of Florida, 2002

Weyeneth, Robert R. *Historic Preservation for a Living City: Historic Charleston Foundation.* Columbia: University of South Carolina Press, 2000.

White, Owen P. "Meet and Drink." *Collier's* 84, no. 7 (Aug. 17, 1929): 8–9+.

Wilson, Chris. *The Myth of Santa Fe: Creating a Modern Regional Tradition.* Albuquerque: University of New Mexico Press, 1997.

Wilson, John S. "A Real New Orleans Sound: The Story of Preservation Hall and Its Ancient Jazzmen." *High Fidelity* 13 (Sept. 1963): 59–63+.

Wiltz, Christine. *The Last Madam: A Life in the New Orleans Underworld.* New York: Faber and Faber, 2000.

Wrobel, David M., and Patrick T. Long, eds. *Seeing and Being Seen: Tourism in the American West.* Lawrence: University Press of Kansas, 2001.

Yuhl, Stephanie E. *A Golden Haze of Memory: The Making of Historic Charleston.* Chapel Hill: University of North Carolina Press, 2005.

Zeman, Scott C. "Traveling the Southwest: Creation, Imagination, and Invention." Ph.D. diss., Arizona State University, 1998.

INDEX